TOM STRONG BOOK 1

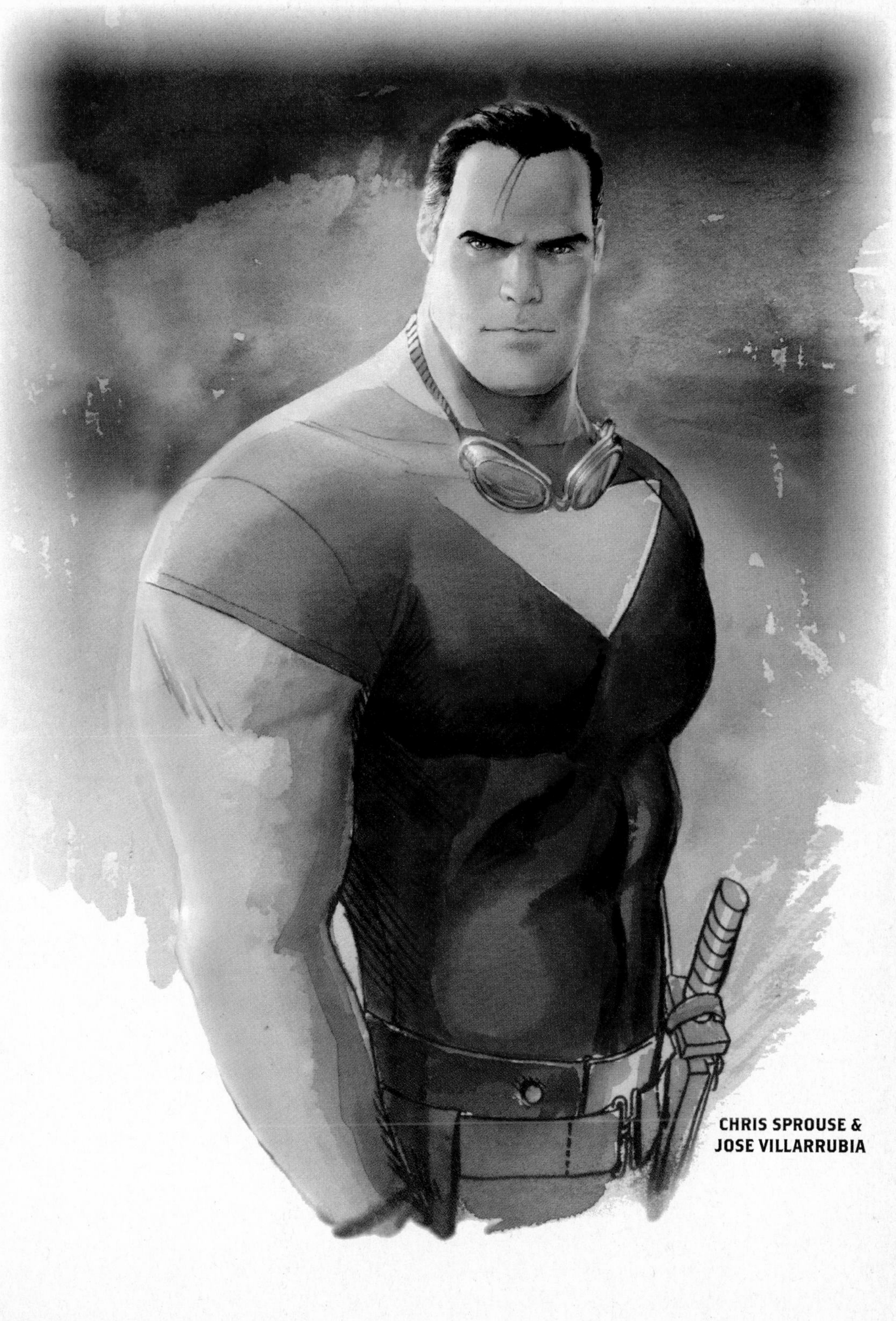

CHRIS SPROUSE &
JOSE VILLARRUBIA

JIM LEE
Editorial Director

JOHN NEE
VP and General Manager

SCOTT DUNBIER
Group Editor
Tom Strong Editor

ERIC DESANTIS
Assistant Editor

Special thanks to
Cully Hamner and Zander Cannon
for layout assistance

Front and Back cover art by
CHRIS SPROUSE and ALAN GORDON

Title Page art by
CHRIS SPROUSE and JOSE VILLARUBIA

TOM STRONG: BOOK ONE. Published by America's Best Comics, LLC. Cover, design pages
and compilation © 2000 America's Best Comics, LLC. TOM STRONG and all related
characters and elements are trademarks of America's Best Comics. All Rights Reserved.
Originally published in single magazine form as TOM STRONG, #1-7. Copyright © 1999,
2000 America's Best Comics. Editorial Offices: 888 Prospect, #240, La Jolla, CA 92037.
Any similarities to persons living or dead are purely coincidental. America's Best Comics
does not read or accept unsolicited submissions of ideas, stories or artwork.
PRINTED IN CANADA.
SECOND PRINTING. ISBN 1-56389-664-8

TOM STRONG

ALAN MOORE
writer

CHRIS SPROUSE
penciller

ALAN GORDON
inker

ADDITIONAL ART BY

ARTHUR ADAMS

GARY FRANK & CAM SMITH

DAVE GIBBONS

JERRY ORDWAY

TAD EHRLICH
MIKE GARCIA
WILDSTORM FX
coloring

TODD KLEIN
lettering,
logos and
design

TOM STRONG
created by
Alan Moore and
Chris Sprouse

AMERICA'S
BEST COMICS

BORN WITH THE CENTURY: TOM STRONG AND HIS CITY

It was in the "Mauve Nineties" at the end of the last century that an employee of the U.S. Patents Office, allegedly, tendered his resignation with the simple explanation that his job was obsolete because by 1899 everything had already been discovered or invented. This was by no means an unusual view. Victorian science believed that every natural phenomenon could be explained by the existence of a phantom, almost transcendental substance known as "Ether." There were some loose ends that still remained to be tied up, admittedly, but by and large the late Victorians were confident that they knew absolutely everything. They were the perfect pinnacle of human history, and, with perfection thus achieved, the science and society that followed them would be unchanging and unchanged until the end of time. Put simply, there were no surprises left. Unfortunately, during 1881, two U.S. physicists named Albert Michelson and Edward Morley proved that "Ether" did not exist; never had existed. Shortly after that, the twentieth century occurred.

Millennium City, situated not far from New York upon the eastern seaboard of America, was one of several U.S. cities built around the turning of the century in a fulfillment of the social programs instigated by U.S. President David Goodman Croley fourteen years before, in 1886. President Croley (1829-1889), a former journalist and financial forecaster turned politician made, during his term in office, many farsighted decisions that would greatly alter and improve the landscape of America, preparing it for the turbulent and unprecedented century that Croley, seemingly alone amongst his many great political contemporaries, had predicted lay ahead. Astonishingly, Croley accurately foresaw photo-electronic printing processes, air travel, multinational corporations, motion pictures, the expansion of New York City to its present size and the female emancipation movement. His minor eccentricities, such as his strong conviction that books in the future would be printed in bright yellow ink on purple paper, we shall overlook, and concentrate instead on his triumphs, namely the passing of the New Cities Bill in 1886, which subsequently led to the construction of Millennium City, one of the twentieth century's greatest architectural wonders.

The most instantly arresting feature of the city is, of course, the sheer and staggering height of its main buildings. Necessitated by the relatively small land-area available on which to build the city, and made possible by breakthroughs in concrete technology, the greater number of the city's towering, almost dream-like structures were designed by the both youthful and renowned turn-of-the-century architect Winsor McCay (1871-1934). McCay, while still a youth in Spring Lake, Michigan, had been inspired by then-President Croley's vision of a twentieth-century America complete with motion-picture houses, the idea of which was something close to an obsession for the talented young draftsman, who at one point dabbled in experiments with cartoon animation before settling to the career he would become more famous for. It was McCay who, realizing that those tenants in the upper reaches of his new and lofty buildings might feel isolated, first proposed the high-altitude cable-car complex that links the city's many spires. This has, of course, since been immortalized in the Cole Porter standard *Nothing but the Best for You* with its memorable couplet,

"We'll go to Millennium City and honey,
we'll ride on a sky-car for two;
There won't be a girl there half as pretty.
It's nothing but the best for you."

Some commentators have suggested a connection between the immense scale of the city and the somewhat larger-than-life citizens it has produced across the decades. The world-famous operatic diva Quinta Desrault was born as plain Quinta Stevens in the Soupbone district north of Laundry Street, while noted modern "Reality Artist" Lazlo Camphor and heavy weight boxer Johnny Nectarine grew up within just two streets of each other, on Neon Street and Xenon Street respectively. Aside from the great contribution made to culture by Millennium City and its populace, however, it must also be said that the cloud-piercing metropolis has helped produce the greater portion of this century's most colorful and startling criminals. In the 1930s, the notorious deformed gangster boss Charles Costanza ("Charley Bones"), changed to a

...alking X-ray image by prolonged exposure
to a form of "Heavy Water," ruled the West
side of Millennium City for the better part of
ten years. Less powerful, though hardly less
noteworthy or spectacular, were rubber-
faced confidence trickster Denby Jilks,
known also as Charade, and the accom-
plished female contract murderer Vanilla
Tuesday. No list of Millennium City's criminal
fraternity would be complete, however, without mention of its most well-known and cel-
ebrated member, the complex and brilliant
psychopath named Paul Saveen.

Paul Dorian Saveen, born in 1899 in
neighboring New York, arrived in Millennium
City sometime during 1917, already wealthy
from the sale of several basic patents such
as a design for hover-buggies and sound-
sensitive paint (actually rather queasy-look-
ing in most real domestic applications) that
marred many fashion-conscious homes during its brief vogue in the 1950s. Not satisfied
with the accumulation of mere wealth,
Saveen saw in the infant city a great opportunity to build a power base from which he
could oversee and even possibly control the
twentieth century as it unfolded. His mete-
oric rise to criminal supremacy of the
American east coast, if not of the entire
United States itself, was only halted by the
unforeseen arrival on these shores, during
the 1920s, of the man whose name has since
become synonymous with that of Millennium
City. A man born on New Year's Day 1900 and
thus almost exactly as old as the town itself.

Tom Strong and Paul Saveen were enemies from the moment that they met, and
were destined to clash in battle many times
across the next few decades. The decent and
likable genius/muscleman from the unchart-
ed isle of Attabar Teru achieved an instant
popularity with Millennium City and its pop-
ulation that has lasted to this day, which
may indeed have been a factor in Saveen's
gradually mounting hatred and resentment
for the young adventurer across the years of
their first few encounters. During this time,
Saveen was reported dead on several occa-
sions, only to return to plague Tom Strong
anew. In 1992, however, a bleached skeleton
found in a jeep out in the deserts of West
Africa was conclusively identified from dental records as that of the eighty-four-year-
old criminal mastermind, which suggests
that upon this occasion, rumors of his death

are not exaggerated.

Millennium City's love affair with Tom
Strong, meanwhile, went from strength to
strength. Already popular for his defeat of
Saveen's huge and city-threatening
"Mechanthrope" in 1922, it was Strong's
return to the city in the 1930s with his bride
Dhalua that assured a place for him in the
public's hearts. Idolized by both men and
women, Dhalua Strong found herself used as
inspiration by a horde of dress designers
and hair stylists, culminating in the classic
"Dhalua Look" adopted by so many women,
especially black women, in the early 1940s.

This was also the decade in which the
newspapers first coined the blanket term
"Strongmania" to describe the vast amount
of licensed Tom Strong merchandise available to an apparently insatiable public .
Dhalua dolls, spark-spitting Tom Strong ray-
guns and, most sought-after of all, miniature clockwork replicas of the adventurer's
mechanical companion Pneuman filled the
nation's toy shops, while its magazine racks
bulged first with pulp magazines, then later
comic books, in which were detailed adventures of Strong and his friends, both gen-
uine and fictional. RKO Pictures produced
two adventure serials, *Tom Strong* and *The
New Adventures of Tom Strong,* both starring
Kirk Alyn as Tom, while in the middle sixties
Hanna-Barbera's *Tom Strong Cartoon Hour*
was massively popular amongst the under-
twelves.

Later additions to Strong's family, notably
daughter Tesla and the educated ape King
Solomon, have not diminished the now nine-
ty-nine-year-old adventurer's enduring popularity, nor have his exploits become less
spectacular. Recent encounters with the
technological monstrosity known as The
Modular Man, or with the massed parallel-
world might of the assembled Aztech Empire
serve only to demonstrate the long-lived
hero's great adaptability and knack for mov-
ing with the times. As both he and the city
that is his adopted home move inexorably
towards their hundredth birthdays on the
stroke of the millennium, let us be confident
that for Tom Strong, Millennium City, and the
world in general, all the most hair-raising
thrills and most spectacular surprises are
yet to come. Here's to the next hundred
years!

— Alan Moore

CHAPTER ONE

**In which an Origin is Revealed,
an Aerial Crime is Attempted,
and TOM gains a New Fan.**

**Cover art:
Alex Ross (A)
Chris Sprouse &
Al Gordon (B)**

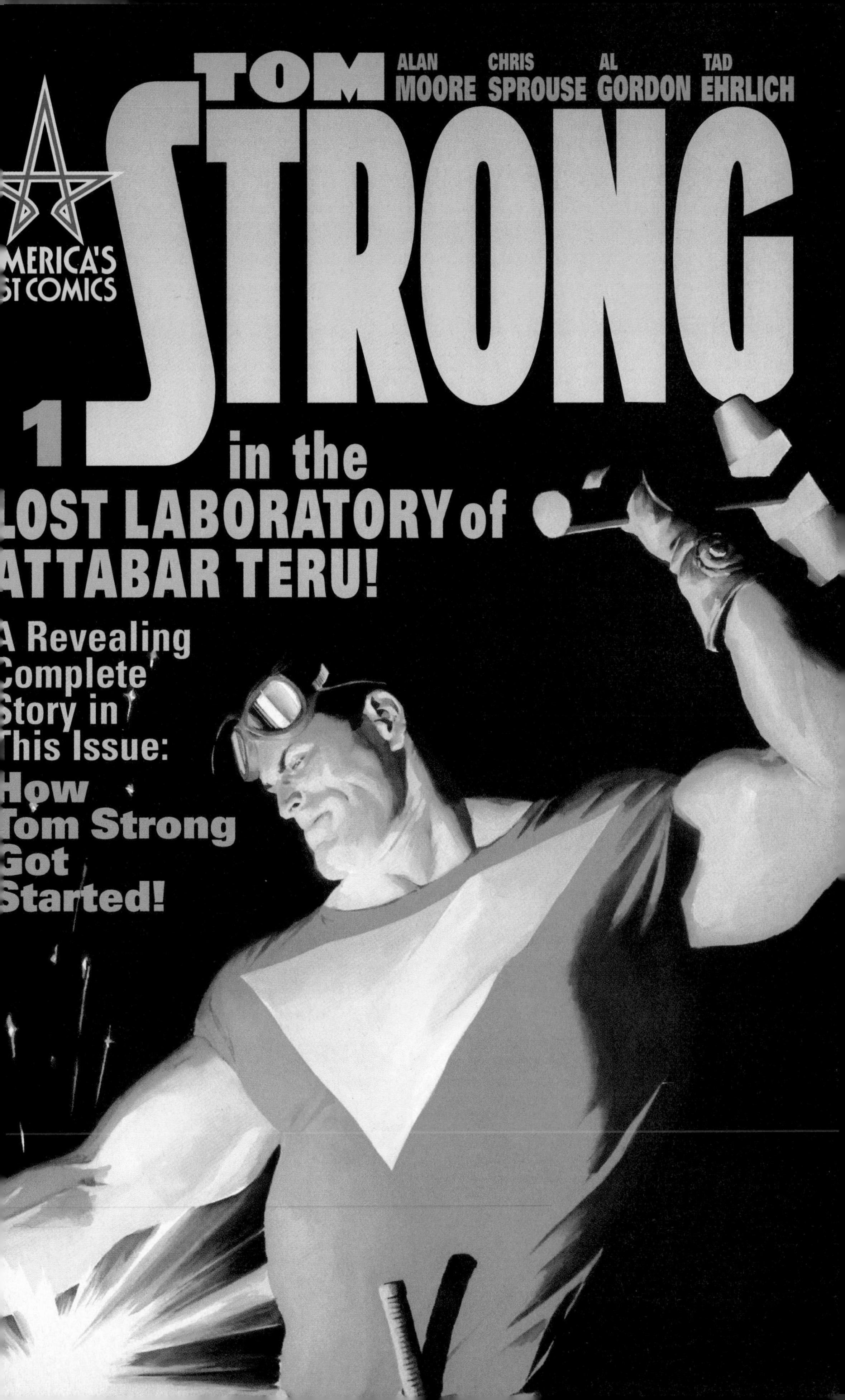
TOM
ALAN MOORE
CHRIS SPROUSE
AL GORDON
TAD EHRLICH
STRONG
MERICA'S
ST COMICS
1
in the
LOST LABORATORY of
ATTABAR TERU!
A Revealing
omplete
tory in
his Issue:
How
om Strong
Got
Started!

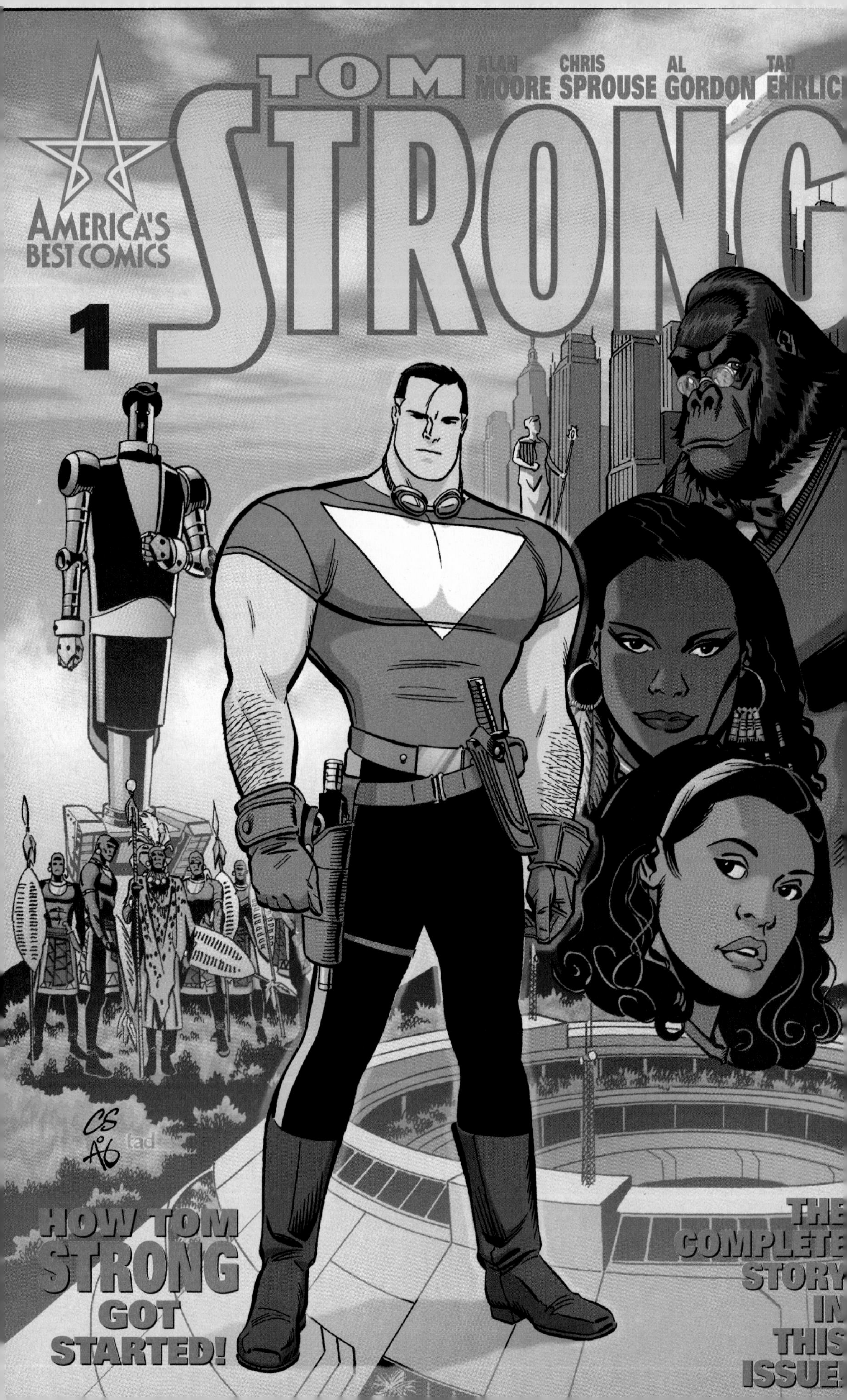
AMERICA'S BEST COMICS
TOM STRONG
ALAN MOORE
CHRIS SPROUSE
AL GORDON
TAD EHRLIC
1
HOW TOM STRONG GOT STARTED!
THE COMPLETE STORY IN THIS ISSUE!

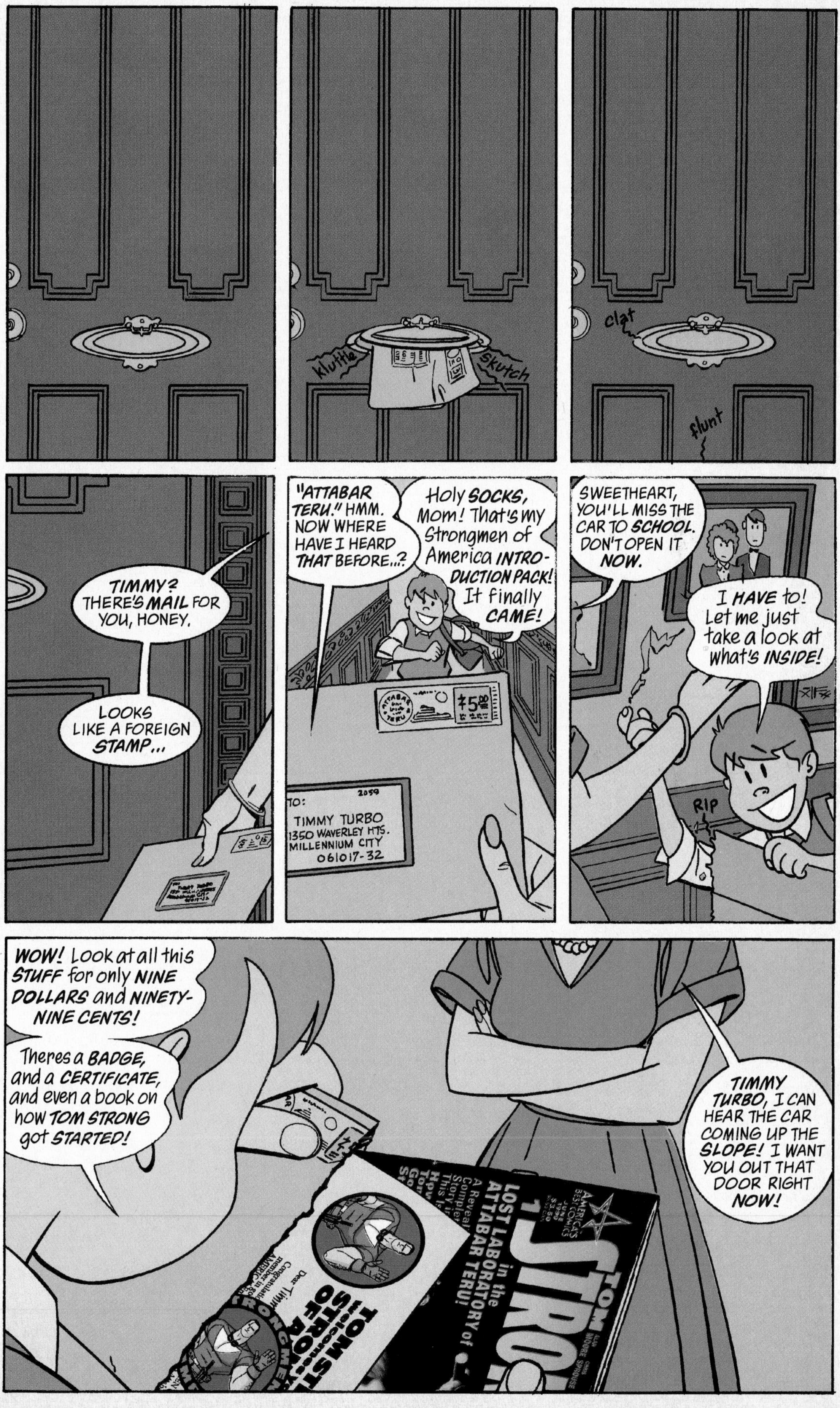
kluttle
skutch
clat
flunt
TIMMY? THERE'S MAIL FOR YOU, HONEY.
LOOKS LIKE A FOREIGN STAMP...
"ATTABAR TERU." HMM. NOW WHERE HAVE I HEARD THAT BEFORE...?
Holy SOCKS, Mom! That's my Strongmen of America INTRODUCTION PACK! It finally CAME!
TO:
2059
TIMMY TURBO
1350 WAVERLEY HTS.
MILLENNIUM CITY
061017-32
SWEETHEART, YOU'LL MISS THE CAR TO SCHOOL. DON'T OPEN IT NOW.
I HAVE to! Let me just take a look at what's INSIDE!
RIP
WOW! Look at all this STUFF for only NINE DOLLARS and NINETY-NINE CENTS!
Theres a BADGE, and a CERTIFICATE, and even a book on how TOM STRONG got STARTED!
TIMMY TURBO, I CAN HEAR THE CAR COMING UP THE SLOPE! I WANT YOU OUT THAT DOOR RIGHT NOW!
AMERICA'S BEST COMICS
TOM STRONG
LOST LABORATORY in the ATTABAR TERU!
TOM STRONG
STRONGMEN

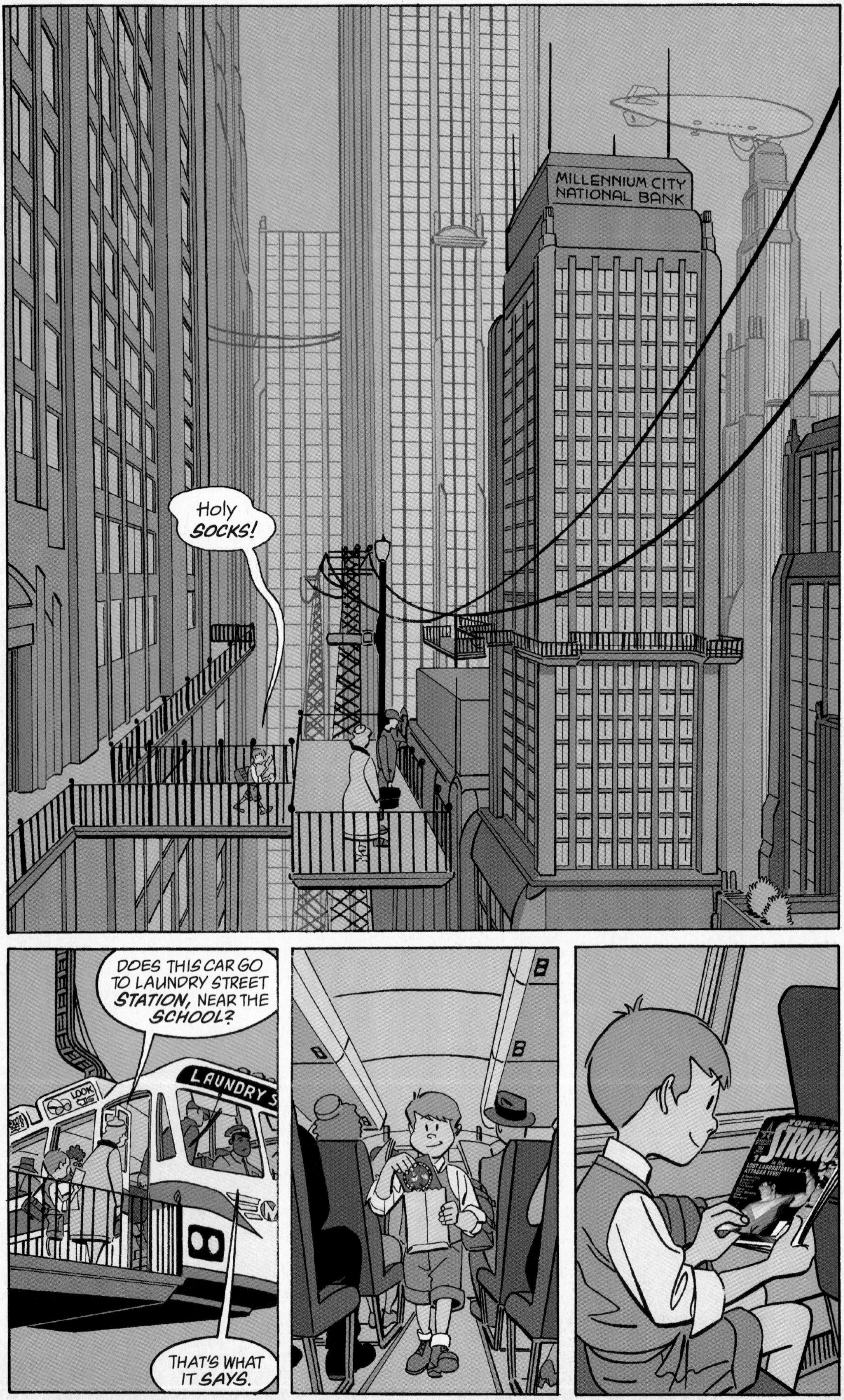

MILLENNIUM CITY NATIONAL BANK
Holy SOCKS!
DOES THIS CAR GO TO LAUNDRY STREET STATION, NEAR THE SCHOOL?
THAT'S WHAT IT SAYS.

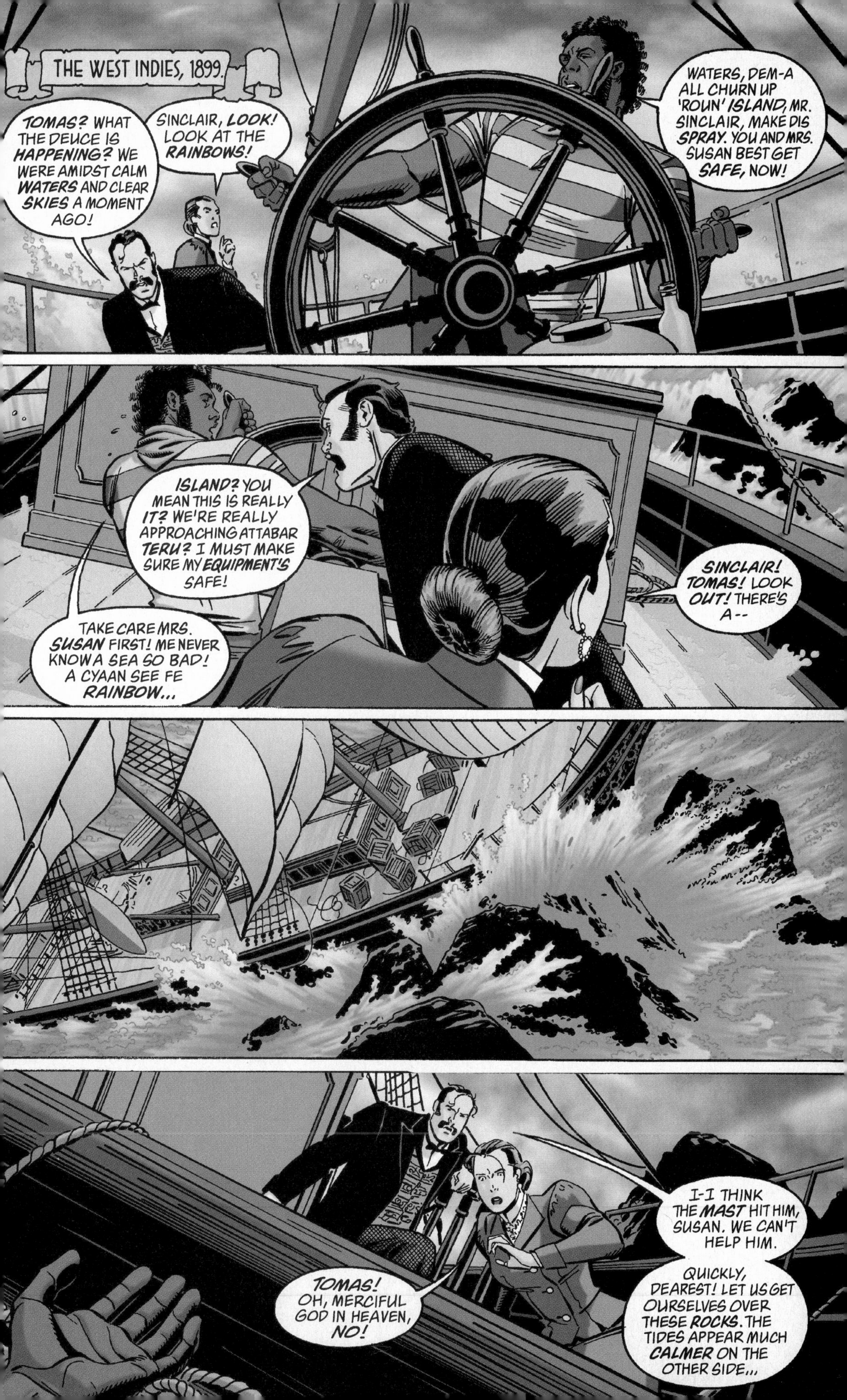
THE WEST INDIES, 1899.
TOMAS? WHAT THE DEUCE IS HAPPENING? WE WERE AMIDST CALM WATERS AND CLEAR SKIES A MOMENT AGO!
SINCLAIR, LOOK! LOOK AT THE RAINBOWS!
WATERS, DEM-A ALL CHURN UP 'ROUN' ISLAND, MR. SINCLAIR, MAKE DIS SPRAY. YOU AND MRS. SUSAN BEST GET SAFE, NOW!
ISLAND? YOU MEAN THIS IS REALLY IT? WE'RE REALLY APPROACHING ATTABAR TERU? I MUST MAKE SURE MY EQUIPMENT'S SAFE!
TAKE CARE MRS. SUSAN FIRST! ME NEVER KNOW A SEA SO BAD! A CYAAN SEE FE RAINBOW...
SINCLAIR! TOMAS! LOOK OUT! THERE'S A--
TOMAS! OH, MERCIFUL GOD IN HEAVEN, NO!
I-I THINK THE MAST HIT HIM, SUSAN. WE CAN'T HELP HIM.
QUICKLY, DEAREST! LET US GET OURSELVES OVER THESE ROCKS. THE TIDES APPEAR MUCH CALMER ON THE OTHER SIDE...

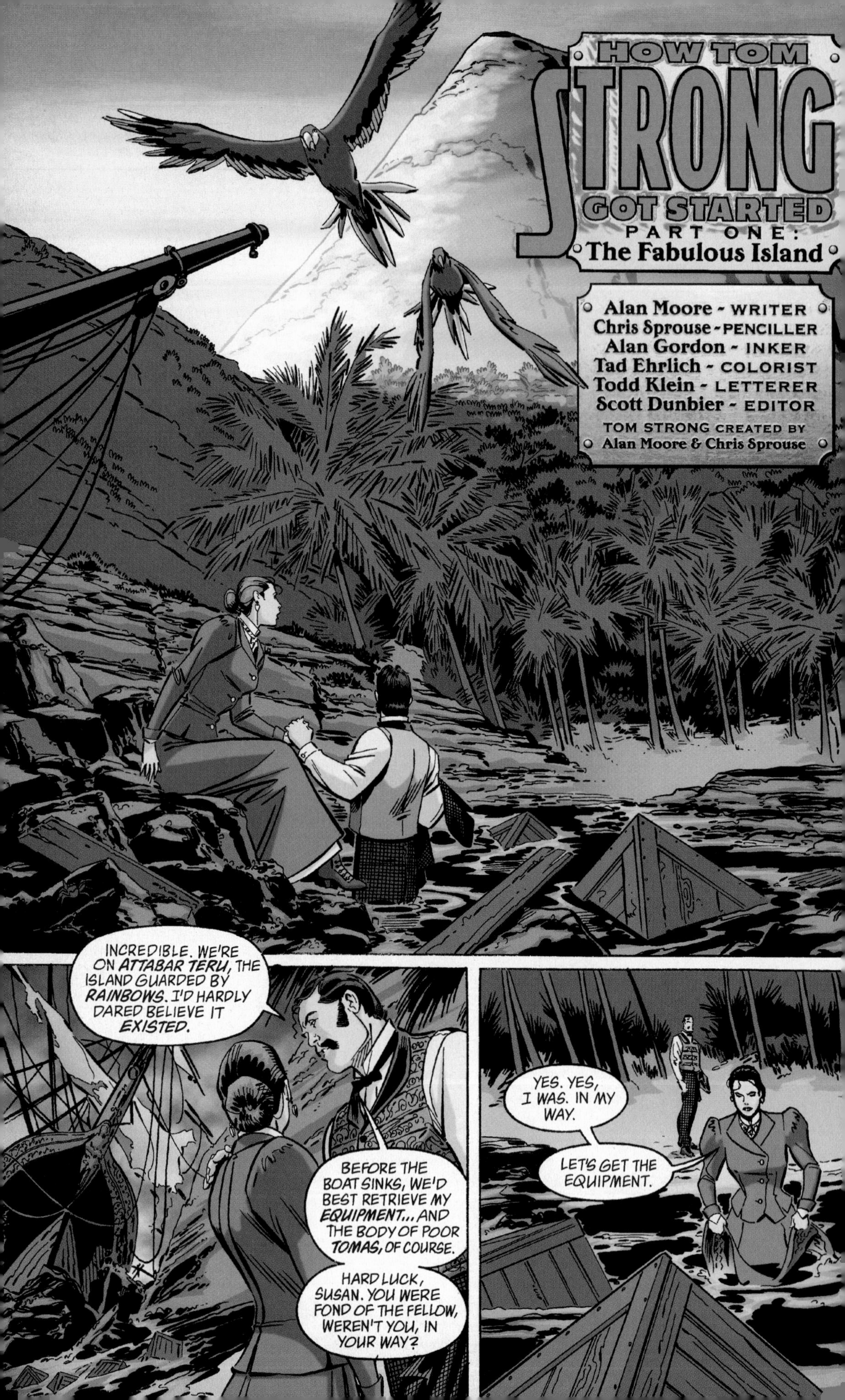
HOW TOM STRONG GOT STARTED
PART ONE: The Fabulous Island
Alan Moore - WRITER
Chris Sprouse - PENCILLER
Alan Gordon - INKER
Tad Ehrlich - COLORIST
Todd Klein - LETTERER
Scott Dunbier - EDITOR
TOM STRONG CREATED BY Alan Moore & Chris Sprouse
INCREDIBLE. WE'RE ON ATTABAR TERU, THE ISLAND GUARDED BY RAINBOWS. I'D HARDLY DARED BELIEVE IT EXISTED.
BEFORE THE BOAT SINKS, WE'D BEST RETRIEVE MY EQUIPMENT... AND THE BODY OF POOR TOMAS, OF COURSE.
HARD LUCK, SUSAN. YOU WERE FOND OF THE FELLOW, WEREN'T YOU, IN YOUR WAY?
YES. YES, I WAS. IN MY WAY.
LET'S GET THE EQUIPMENT.

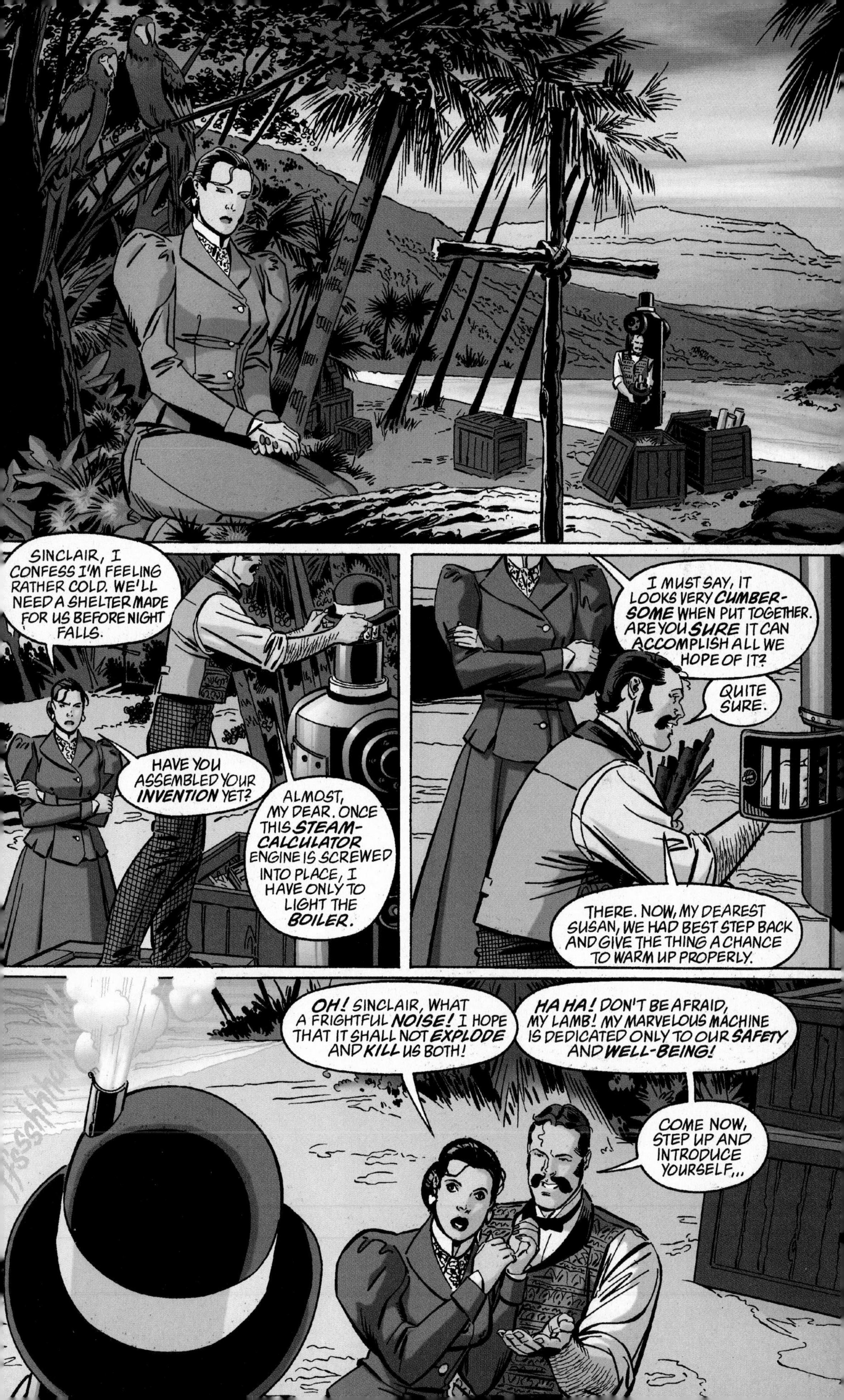
SINCLAIR, I CONFESS I'M FEELING RATHER COLD. WE'LL NEED A SHELTER MADE FOR US BEFORE NIGHT FALLS.
HAVE YOU ASSEMBLED YOUR INVENTION YET?
ALMOST, MY DEAR. ONCE THIS STEAM-CALCULATOR ENGINE IS SCREWED INTO PLACE, I HAVE ONLY TO LIGHT THE BOILER.
I MUST SAY, IT LOOKS VERY CUMBERSOME WHEN PUT TOGETHER. ARE YOU SURE IT CAN ACCOMPLISH ALL WE HOPE OF IT?
QUITE SURE.
THERE. NOW, MY DEAREST SUSAN, WE HAD BEST STEP BACK AND GIVE THE THING A CHANCE TO WARM UP PROPERLY.
OH! SINCLAIR, WHAT A FRIGHTFUL NOISE! I HOPE THAT IT SHALL NOT EXPLODE AND KILL US BOTH!
HA HA! DON'T BE AFRAID, MY LAMB! MY MARVELOUS MACHINE IS DEDICATED ONLY TO OUR SAFETY AND WELL-BEING!
COME NOW, STEP UP AND INTRODUCE YOURSELF...

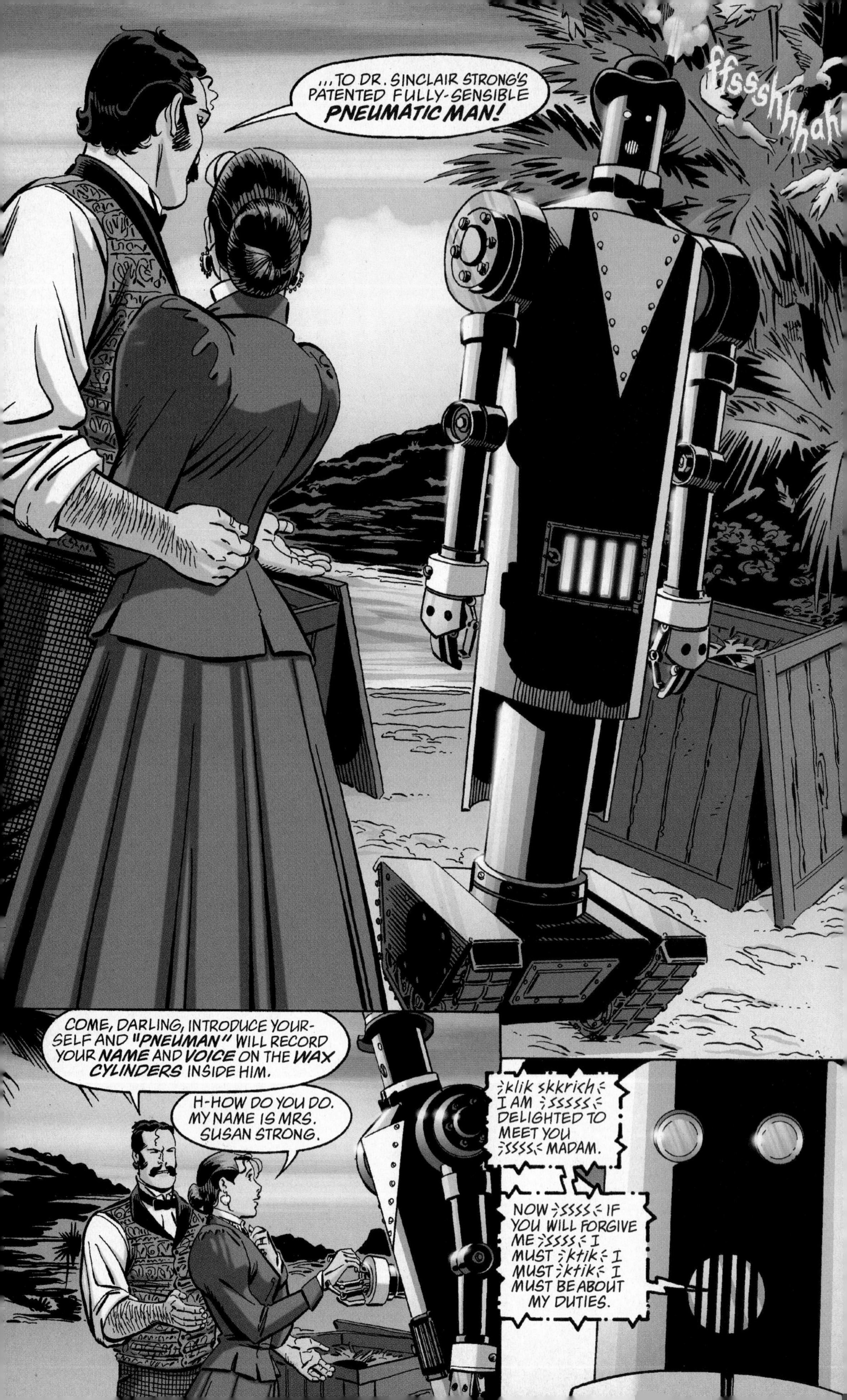
...TO DR. SINCLAIR STRONG'S PATENTED FULLY-SENSIBLE PNEUMATIC MAN!
ffssshhhah!
COME, DARLING, INTRODUCE YOURSELF AND "PNEUMAN" WILL RECORD YOUR NAME AND VOICE ON THE WAX CYLINDERS INSIDE HIM.
H-HOW DO YOU DO. MY NAME IS MRS. SUSAN STRONG.
klik skkrich I AM sssss DELIGHTED TO MEET YOU ssss MADAM.
NOW ssss IF YOU WILL FORGIVE ME ssss I MUST ktik I MUST ktik I MUST BE ABOUT MY DUTIES.

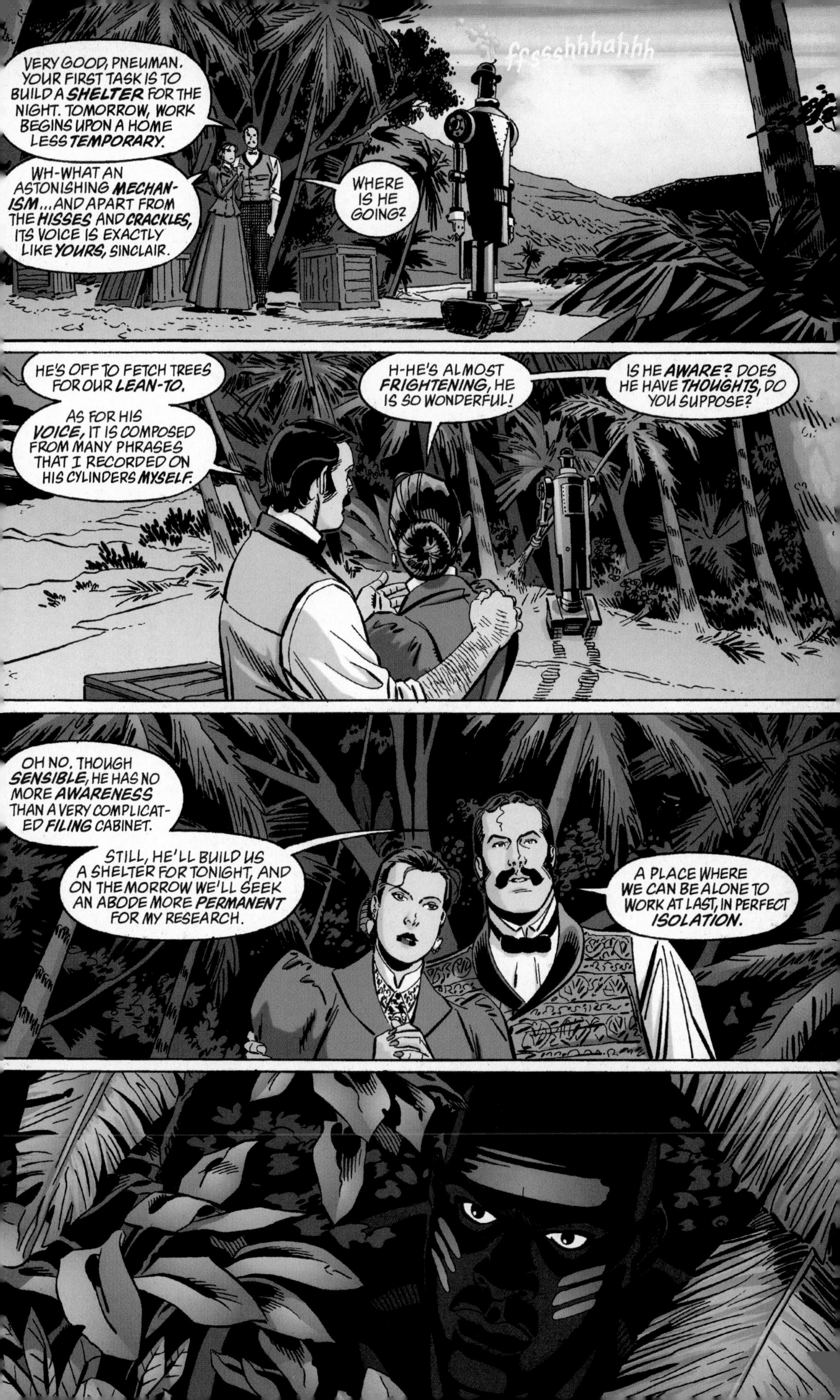
ffssshhhahhh
VERY GOOD, PNEUMAN. YOUR FIRST TASK IS TO BUILD A SHELTER FOR THE NIGHT. TOMORROW, WORK BEGINS UPON A HOME LESS TEMPORARY.
WH-WHAT AN ASTONISHING MECHANISM... AND APART FROM THE HISSES AND CRACKLES, ITS VOICE IS EXACTLY LIKE YOURS, SINCLAIR.
WHERE IS HE GOING?
HE'S OFF TO FETCH TREES FOR OUR LEAN-TO.
AS FOR HIS VOICE, IT IS COMPOSED FROM MANY PHRASES THAT I RECORDED ON HIS CYLINDERS MYSELF.
H-HE'S ALMOST FRIGHTENING, HE IS SO WONDERFUL!
IS HE AWARE? DOES HE HAVE THOUGHTS, DO YOU SUPPOSE?
OH NO. THOUGH SENSIBLE, HE HAS NO MORE AWARENESS THAN A VERY COMPLICATED FILING CABINET.
STILL, HE'LL BUILD US A SHELTER FOR TONIGHT, AND ON THE MORROW WE'LL SEEK AN ABODE MORE PERMANENT FOR MY RESEARCH.
A PLACE WHERE WE CAN BE ALONE TO WORK AT LAST, IN PERFECT ISOLATION.

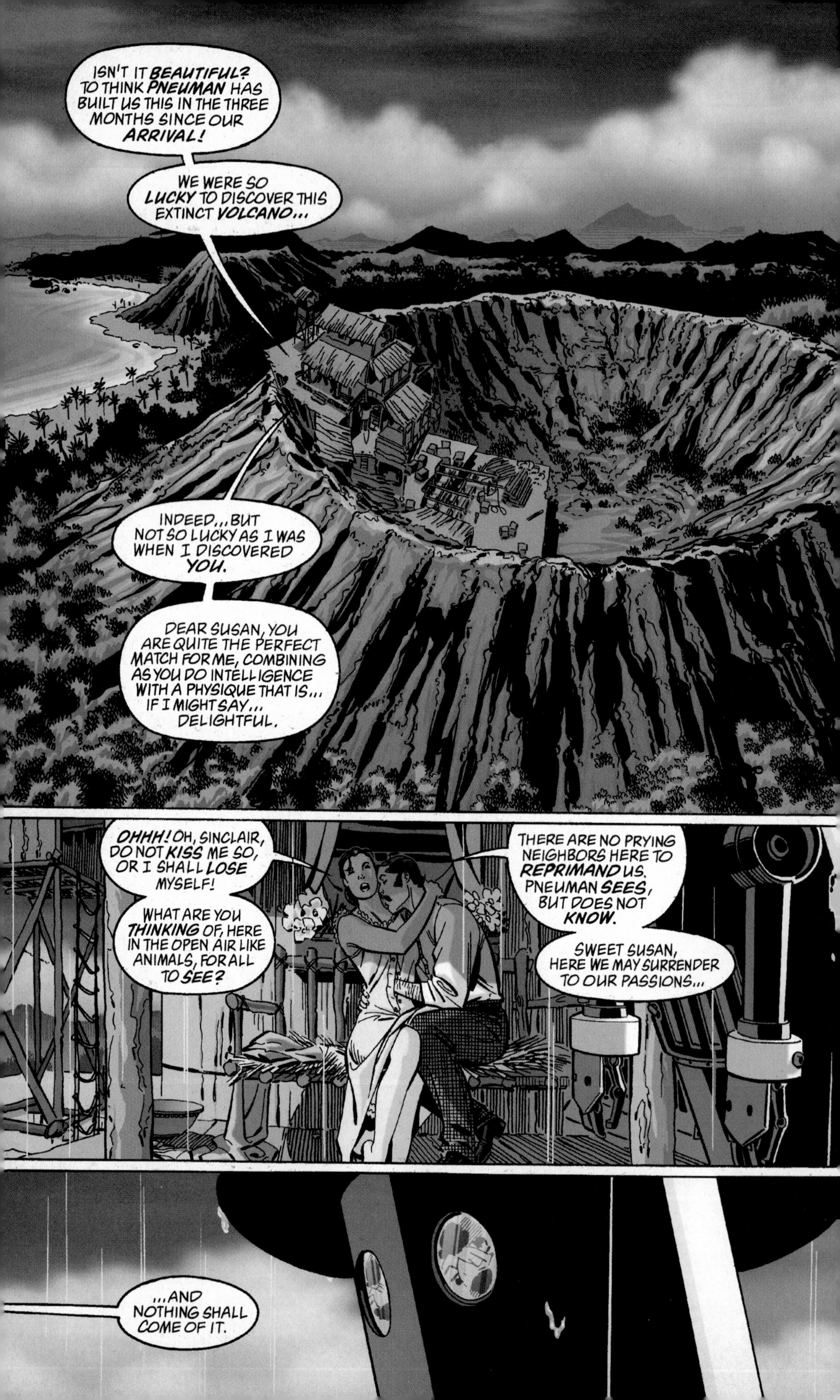
ISN'T IT BEAUTIFUL? TO THINK PNEUMAN HAS BUILT US THIS IN THE THREE MONTHS SINCE OUR ARRIVAL!
WE WERE SO LUCKY TO DISCOVER THIS EXTINCT VOLCANO...
INDEED... BUT NOT SO LUCKY AS I WAS WHEN I DISCOVERED YOU.
DEAR SUSAN, YOU ARE QUITE THE PERFECT MATCH FOR ME, COMBINING AS YOU DO INTELLIGENCE WITH A PHYSIQUE THAT IS... IF I MIGHT SAY... DELIGHTFUL.
OHHH! OH, SINCLAIR, DO NOT KISS ME SO, OR I SHALL LOSE MYSELF!
WHAT ARE YOU THINKING OF, HERE IN THE OPEN AIR LIKE ANIMALS, FOR ALL TO SEE?
THERE ARE NO PRYING NEIGHBORS HERE TO REPRIMAND US. PNEUMAN SEES, BUT DOES NOT KNOW.
SWEET SUSAN, HERE WE MAY SURRENDER TO OUR PASSIONS...
...AND NOTHING SHALL COME OF IT.

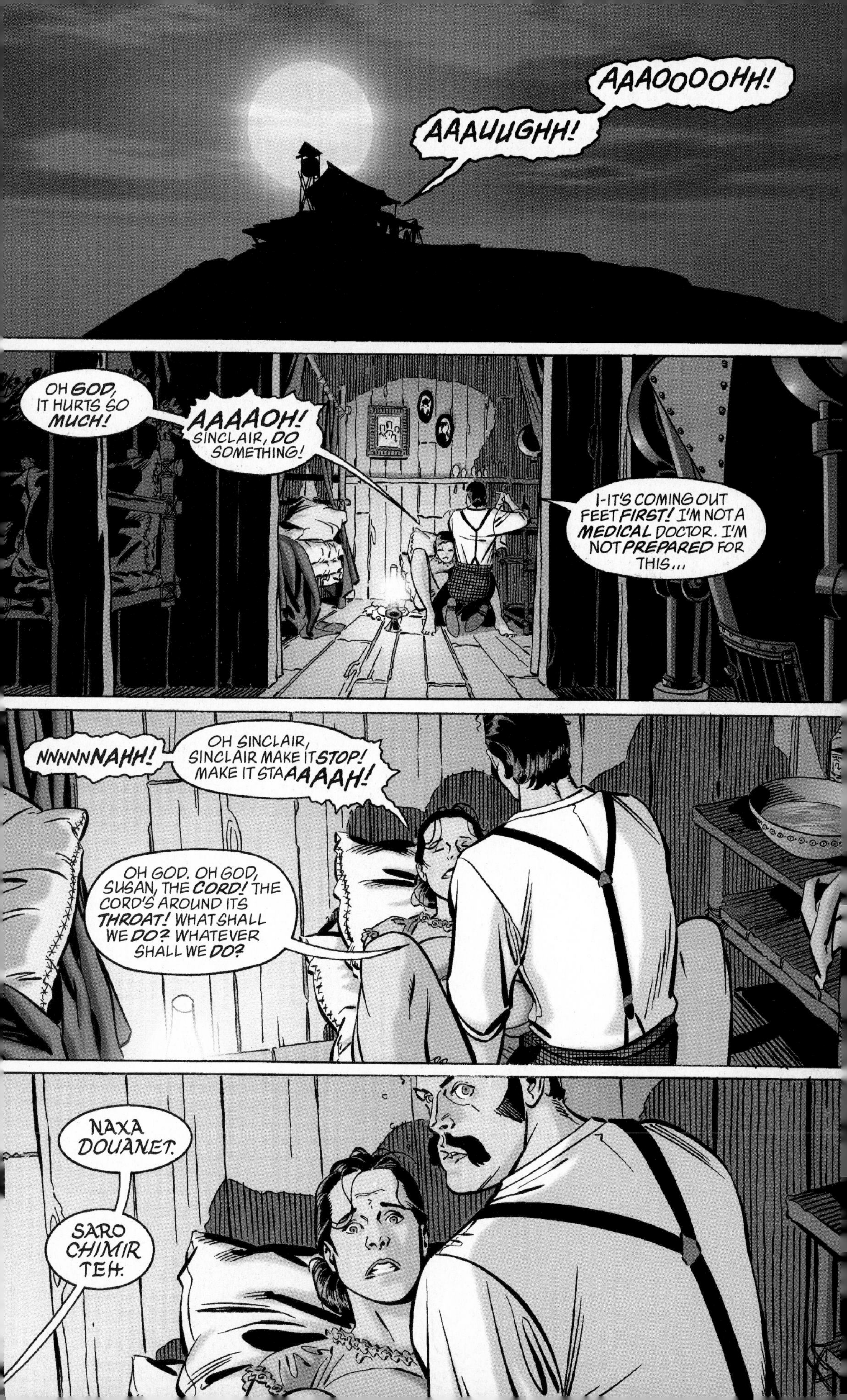
AAAOOOOHH!
AAAUUGHH!
OH GOD, IT HURTS SO MUCH!
AAAAOH! SINCLAIR, DO SOMETHING!
I-IT'S COMING OUT FEET FIRST! I'M NOT A MEDICAL DOCTOR. I'M NOT PREPARED FOR THIS...
NNNNNNAHH!
OH SINCLAIR, SINCLAIR MAKE IT STOP! MAKE IT STAAAAAH!
OH GOD. OH GOD, SUSAN, THE CORD! THE CORD'S AROUND ITS THROAT! WHAT SHALL WE DO? WHATEVER SHALL WE DO?
NAXA DOUANET.
SARO CHIMIR TEH.

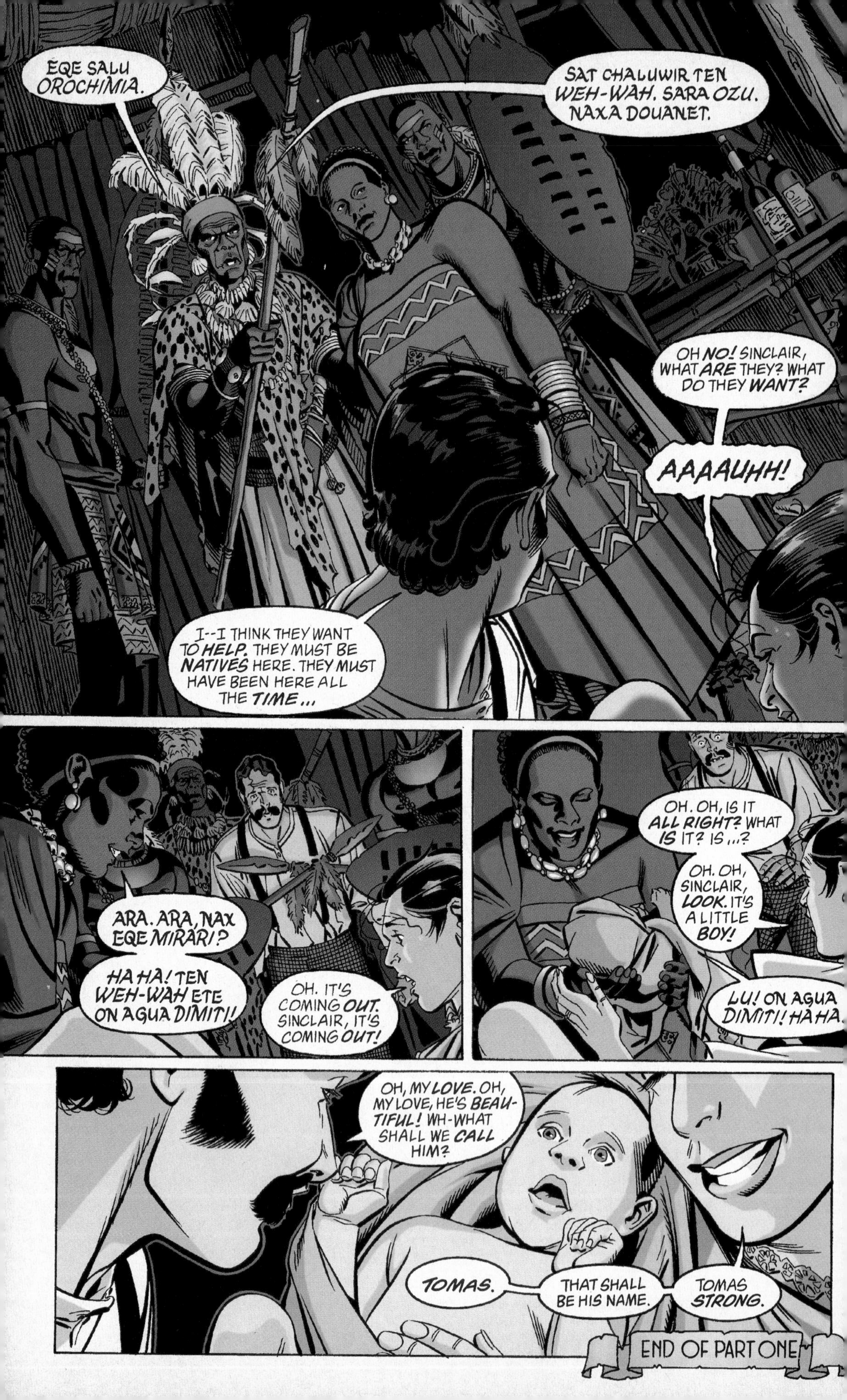
EQE SALU OROCHIMIA.
SAT CHALUWIR TEN WEH-WAH. SARA OZU. NAXA DOUANET.
OH NO! SINCLAIR, WHAT ARE THEY? WHAT DO THEY WANT?
AAAAUHH!
I--I THINK THEY WANT TO HELP. THEY MUST BE NATIVES HERE. THEY MUST HAVE BEEN HERE ALL THE TIME...
ARA. ARA, NAX EQE MIRARI?
HA HA! TEN WEH-WAH ETE ON AGUA DIMITI!
OH. IT'S COMING OUT. SINCLAIR, IT'S COMING OUT!
OH. OH, IS IT ALL RIGHT? WHAT IS IT? IS...?
OH. OH, SINCLAIR, LOOK. IT'S A LITTLE BOY!
LU! ON AGUA DIMITI! HA HA.
OH, MY LOVE. OH, MY LOVE, HE'S BEAU-TIFUL! WH-WHAT SHALL WE CALL HIM?
TOMAS.
THAT SHALL BE HIS NAME.
TOMAS STRONG.
END OF PART ONE

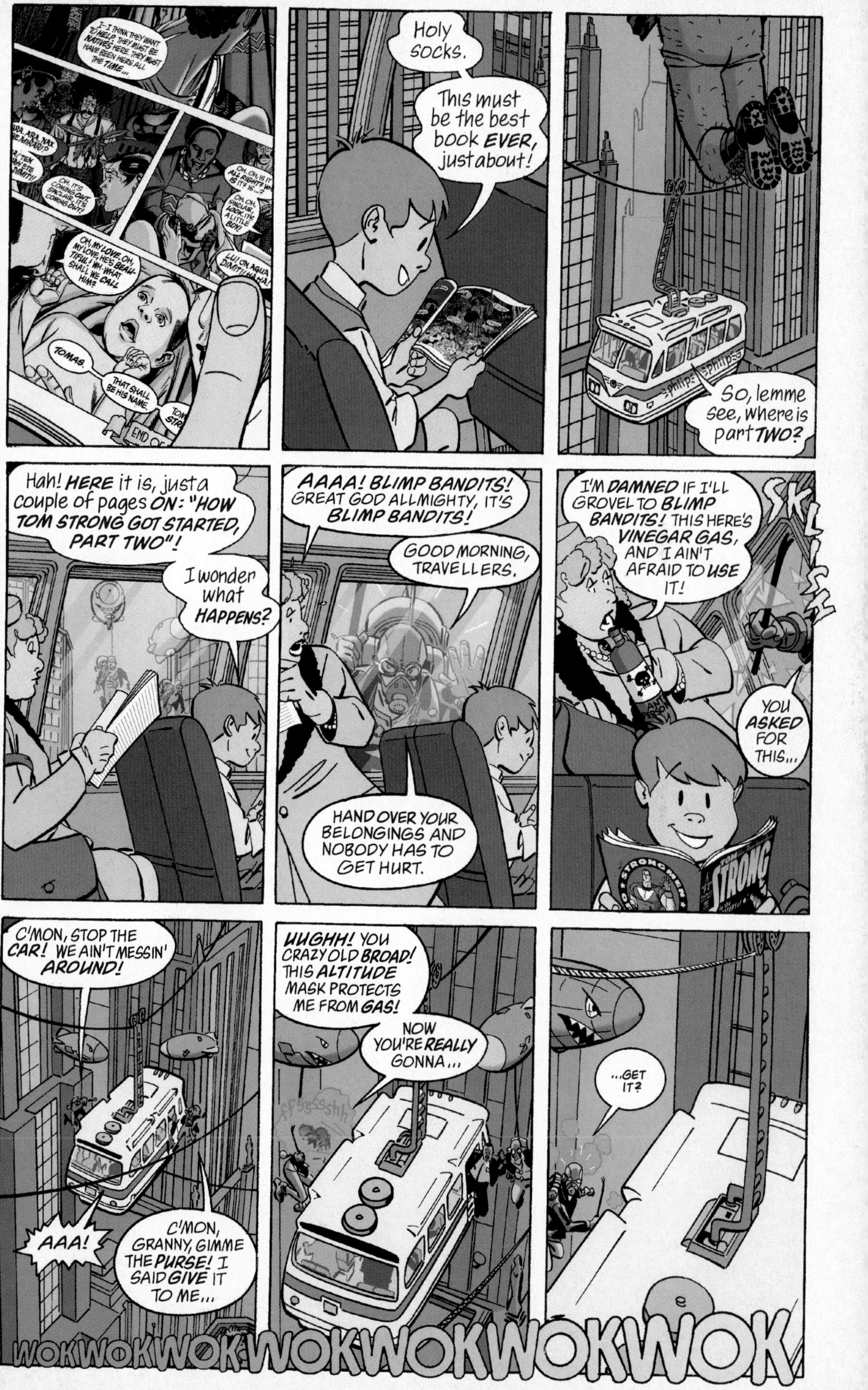
I--I THINK THEY WANT TO HELP. THEY MUST BE NATIVES HERE. THEY MUST HAVE BEEN HERE ALL THE TIME...
OH, IT'S COMING OUT. SINCLAIR, IT'S COMING OUT!
OH, OH, SINCLAIR, LOOK. IT'S A LITTLE BOY!
OH, MY LOVE. OH, MY LOVE, HE'S BEAUTIFUL! WH-WHAT SHALL WE CALL HIM?
TOMAS.
THAT SHALL BE HIS NAME.
Holy socks.
This must be the best book EVER, just about!
So, lemme see, where is part TWO?
Hah! HERE it is, just a couple of pages ON: "HOW TOM STRONG GOT STARTED, PART TWO"!
I wonder what HAPPENS?
AAAA! BLIMP BANDITS! GREAT GOD ALLMIGHTY, IT'S BLIMP BANDITS!
GOOD MORNING, TRAVELLERS.
HAND OVER YOUR BELONGINGS AND NOBODY HAS TO GET HURT.
I'M DAMNED IF I'LL GROVEL TO BLIMP BANDITS! THIS HERE'S VINEGAR GAS, AND I AIN'T AFRAID TO USE IT!
YOU ASKED FOR THIS...
C'MON, STOP THE CAR! WE AIN'T MESSIN' AROUND!
AAA!
C'MON, GRANNY, GIMME THE PURSE! I SAID GIVE IT TO ME...
UUGHH! YOU CRAZY OLD BROAD! THIS ALTITUDE MASK PROTECTS ME FROM GAS!
NOW YOU'RE REALLY GONNA...
...GET IT?
WOKWOKWOKWOKWOKWOKWOK

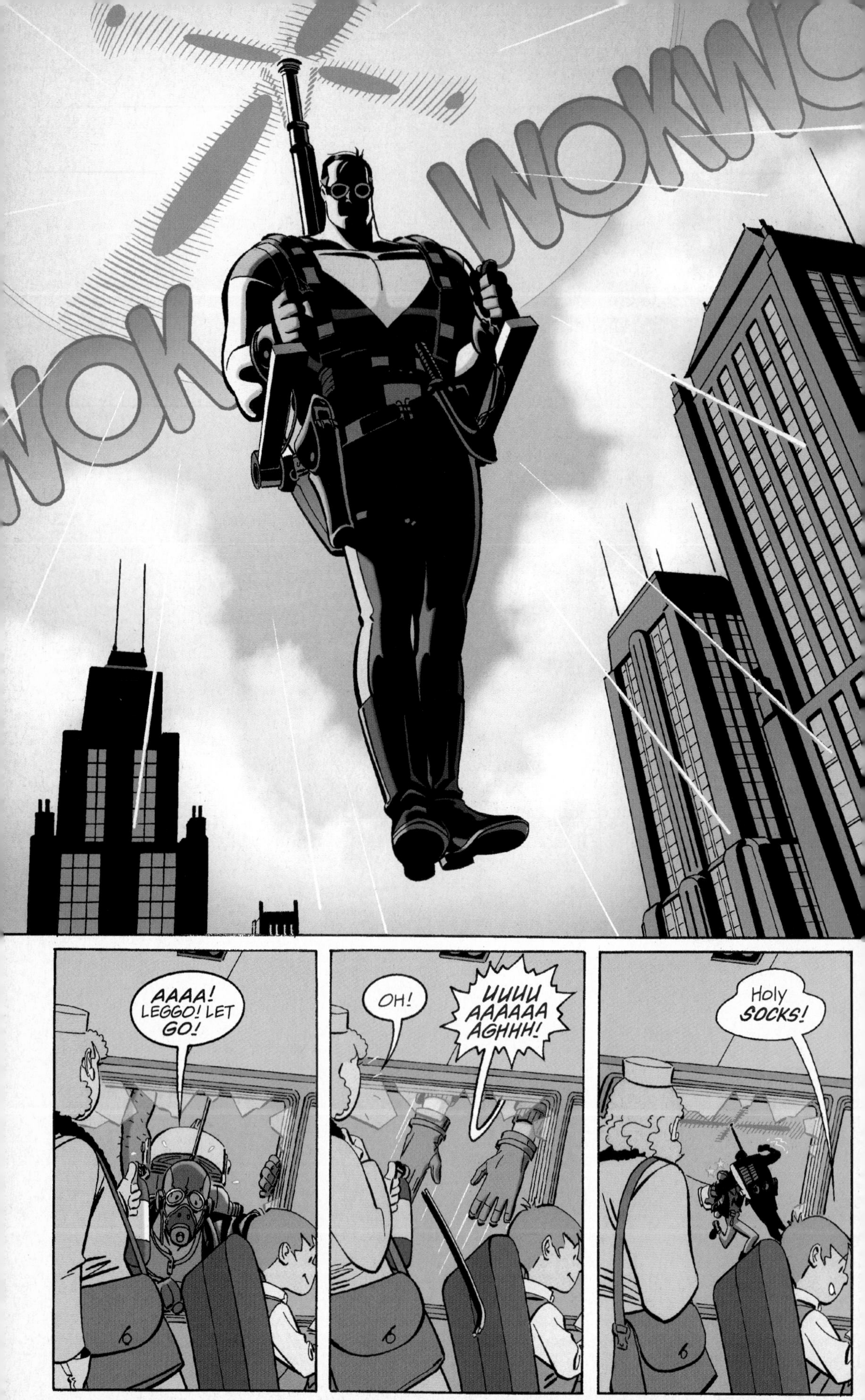
WOKWOKWOKWO
AAAA! LEGGO! LET GO!
OH!
UUUU AAAAAA AGHHH!
Holy SOCKS!

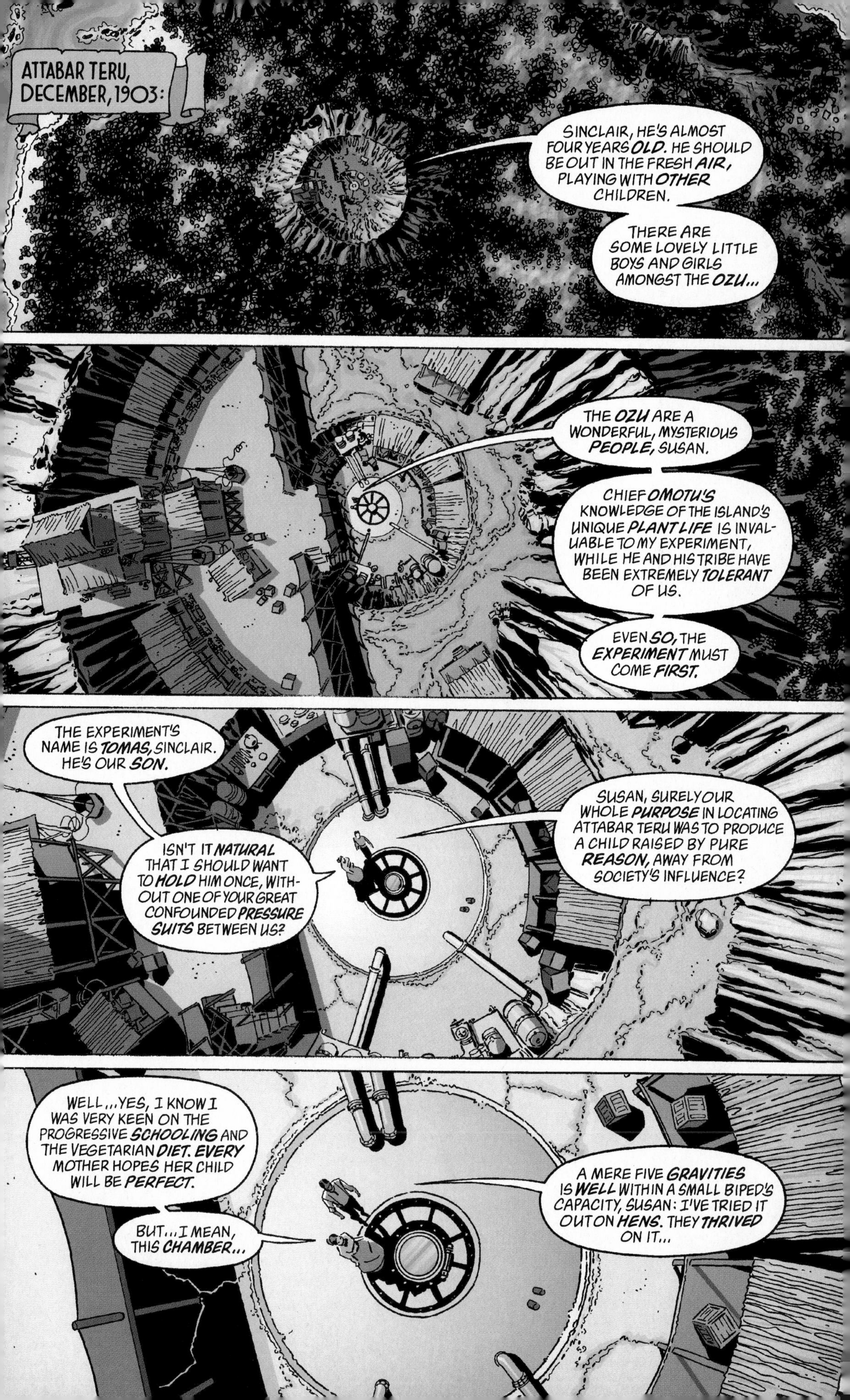
ATTABAR TERU, DECEMBER, 1903:
SINCLAIR, HE'S ALMOST FOUR YEARS OLD. HE SHOULD BE OUT IN THE FRESH AIR, PLAYING WITH OTHER CHILDREN.
THERE ARE SOME LOVELY LITTLE BOYS AND GIRLS AMONGST THE OZU...
THE OZU ARE A WONDERFUL, MYSTERIOUS PEOPLE, SUSAN.
CHIEF OMOTU'S KNOWLEDGE OF THE ISLAND'S UNIQUE PLANT LIFE IS INVALUABLE TO MY EXPERIMENT, WHILE HE AND HIS TRIBE HAVE BEEN EXTREMELY TOLERANT OF US.
EVEN SO, THE EXPERIMENT MUST COME FIRST.
THE EXPERIMENT'S NAME IS TOMAS, SINCLAIR. HE'S OUR SON.
ISN'T IT NATURAL THAT I SHOULD WANT TO HOLD HIM ONCE, WITHOUT ONE OF YOUR GREAT CONFOUNDED PRESSURE SUITS BETWEEN US?
SUSAN, SURELY OUR WHOLE PURPOSE IN LOCATING ATTABAR TERU WAS TO PRODUCE A CHILD RAISED BY PURE REASON, AWAY FROM SOCIETY'S INFLUENCE?
WELL... YES, I KNOW I WAS VERY KEEN ON THE PROGRESSIVE SCHOOLING AND THE VEGETARIAN DIET. EVERY MOTHER HOPES HER CHILD WILL BE PERFECT.
BUT... I MEAN, THIS CHAMBER...
A MERE FIVE GRAVITIES IS WELL WITHIN A SMALL BIPED'S CAPACITY, SUSAN: I'VE TRIED IT OUT ON HENS. THEY THRIVED ON IT...

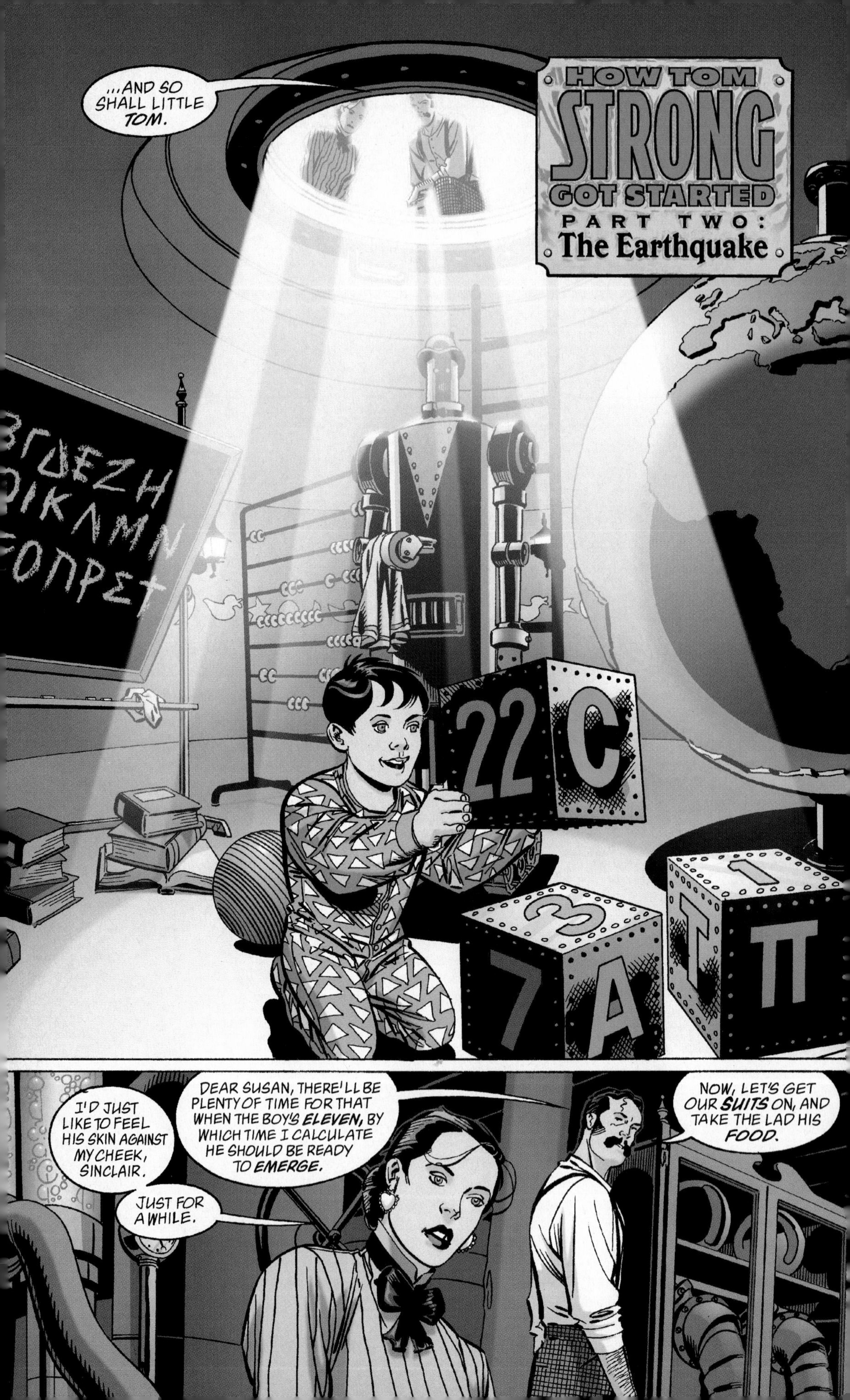
...AND SO SHALL LITTLE TOM.
HOW TOM STRONG GOT STARTED
PART TWO:
The Earthquake
I'D JUST LIKE TO FEEL HIS SKIN AGAINST MY CHEEK, SINCLAIR.
JUST FOR A WHILE.
DEAR SUSAN, THERE'LL BE PLENTY OF TIME FOR THAT WHEN THE BOY'S ELEVEN, BY WHICH TIME I CALCULATE HE SHOULD BE READY TO EMERGE.
NOW, LET'S GET OUR SUITS ON, AND TAKE THE LAD HIS FOOD.

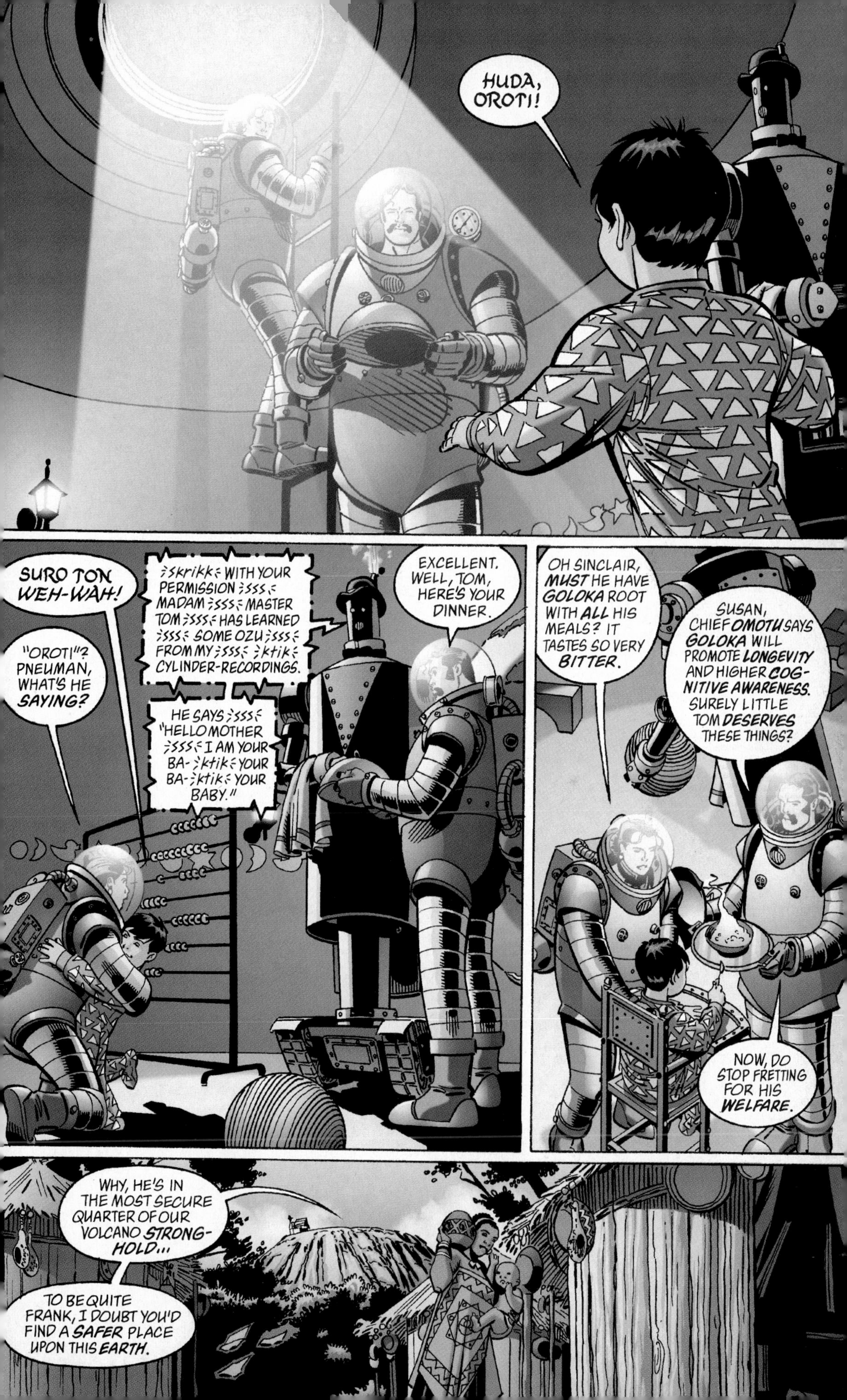

HUDA, OROTI!
SURO TON WEH-WAH!
"OROTI"? PNEUMAN, WHAT'S HE SAYING?
≈skrikk≈ WITH YOUR PERMISSION ≈sss≈ MADAM ≈sss≈ MASTER TOM ≈sss≈ HAS LEARNED ≈sss≈ SOME OZU ≈sss≈ FROM MY ≈sss≈ ≈ktik≈ CYLINDER-RECORDINGS.
HE SAYS ≈sss≈ "HELLO MOTHER ≈sss≈ I AM YOUR BA- ≈ktik≈ YOUR BA- ≈ktik≈ YOUR BABY."
EXCELLENT. WELL, TOM, HERE'S YOUR DINNER.
OH SINCLAIR, MUST HE HAVE GOLOKA ROOT WITH ALL HIS MEALS? IT TASTES SO VERY BITTER.
SUSAN, CHIEF OMOTU SAYS GOLOKA WILL PROMOTE LONGEVITY AND HIGHER COGNITIVE AWARENESS. SURELY LITTLE TOM DESERVES THESE THINGS?
NOW, DO STOP FRETTING FOR HIS WELFARE.
WHY, HE'S IN THE MOST SECURE QUARTER OF OUR VOLCANO STRONGHOLD...
TO BE QUITE FRANK, I DOUBT YOU'D FIND A SAFER PLACE UPON THIS EARTH.

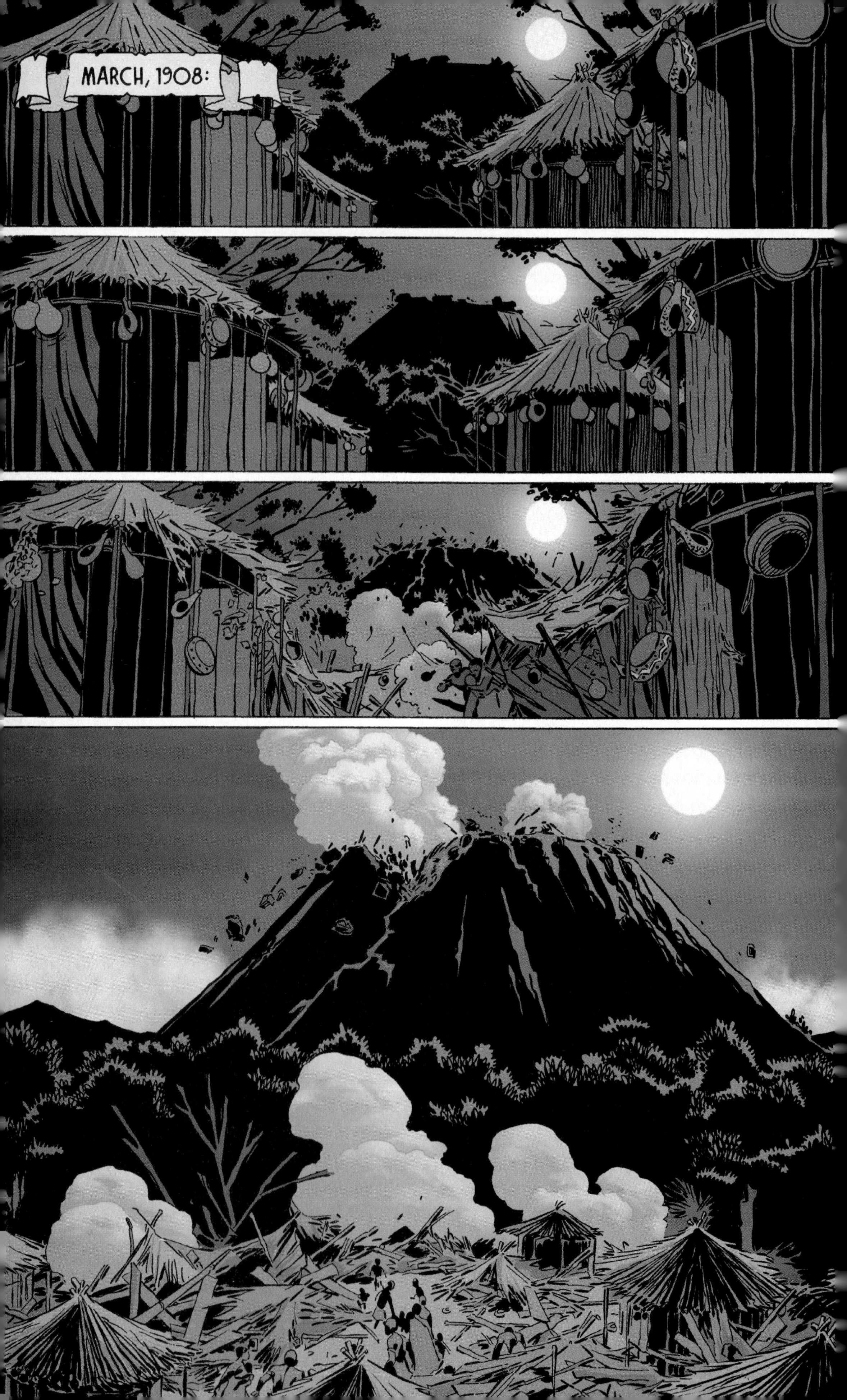
MARCH, 1908:

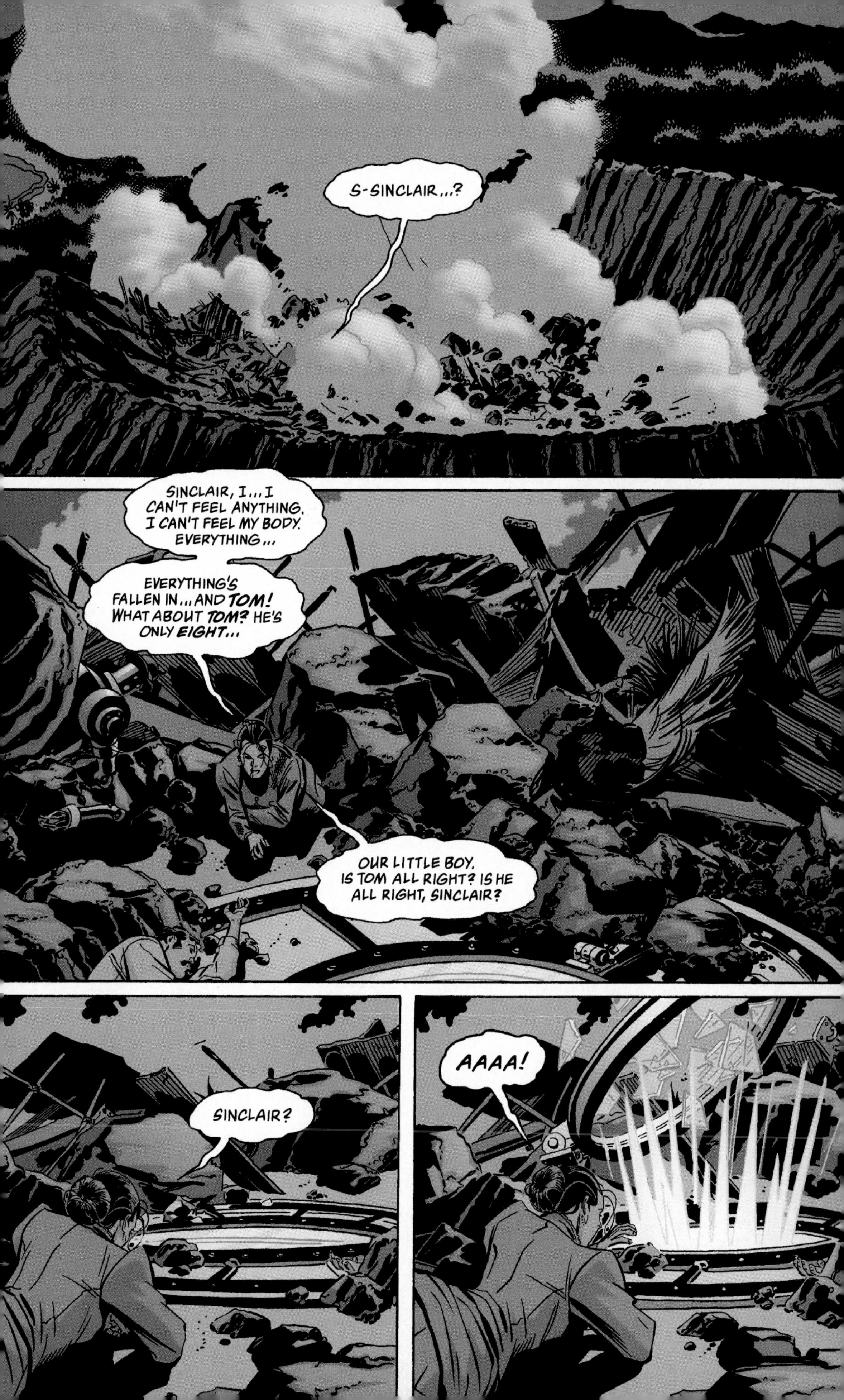
S-SINCLAIR...?
SINCLAIR, I... I CAN'T FEEL ANYTHING. I CAN'T FEEL MY BODY. EVERYTHING...
EVERYTHING'S FALLEN IN... AND TOM! WHAT ABOUT TOM? HE'S ONLY EIGHT...
OUR LITTLE BOY. IS TOM ALL RIGHT? IS HE ALL RIGHT, SINCLAIR?
SINCLAIR?
AAAA!

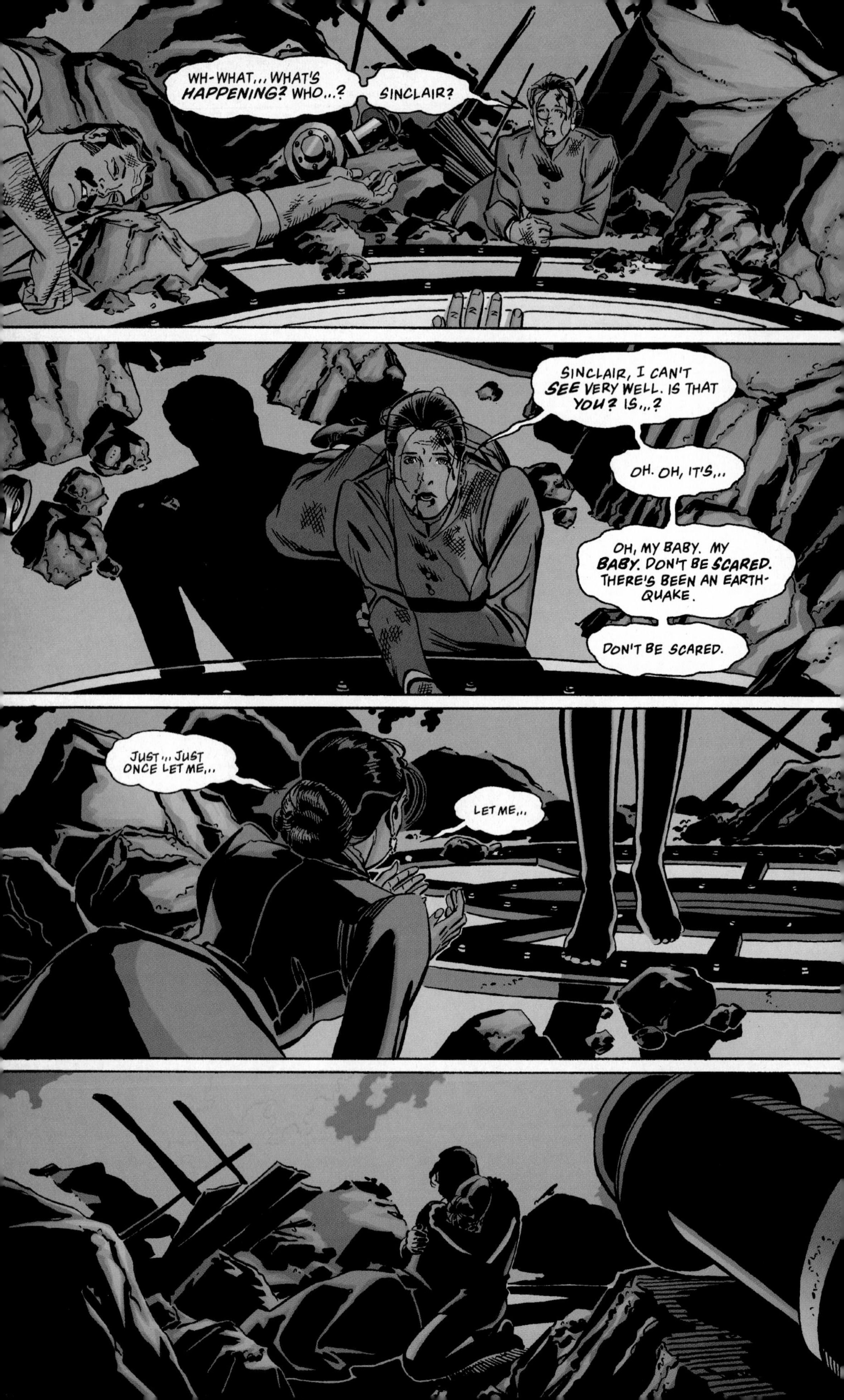
WH-WHAT... WHAT'S HAPPENING? WHO...?
SINCLAIR?
SINCLAIR, I CAN'T SEE VERY WELL. IS THAT YOU? IS...?
OH. OH, IT'S...
OH, MY BABY. MY BABY. DON'T BE SCARED. THERE'S BEEN AN EARTH-QUAKE.
DON'T BE SCARED.
JUST... JUST ONCE LET ME...
LET ME...

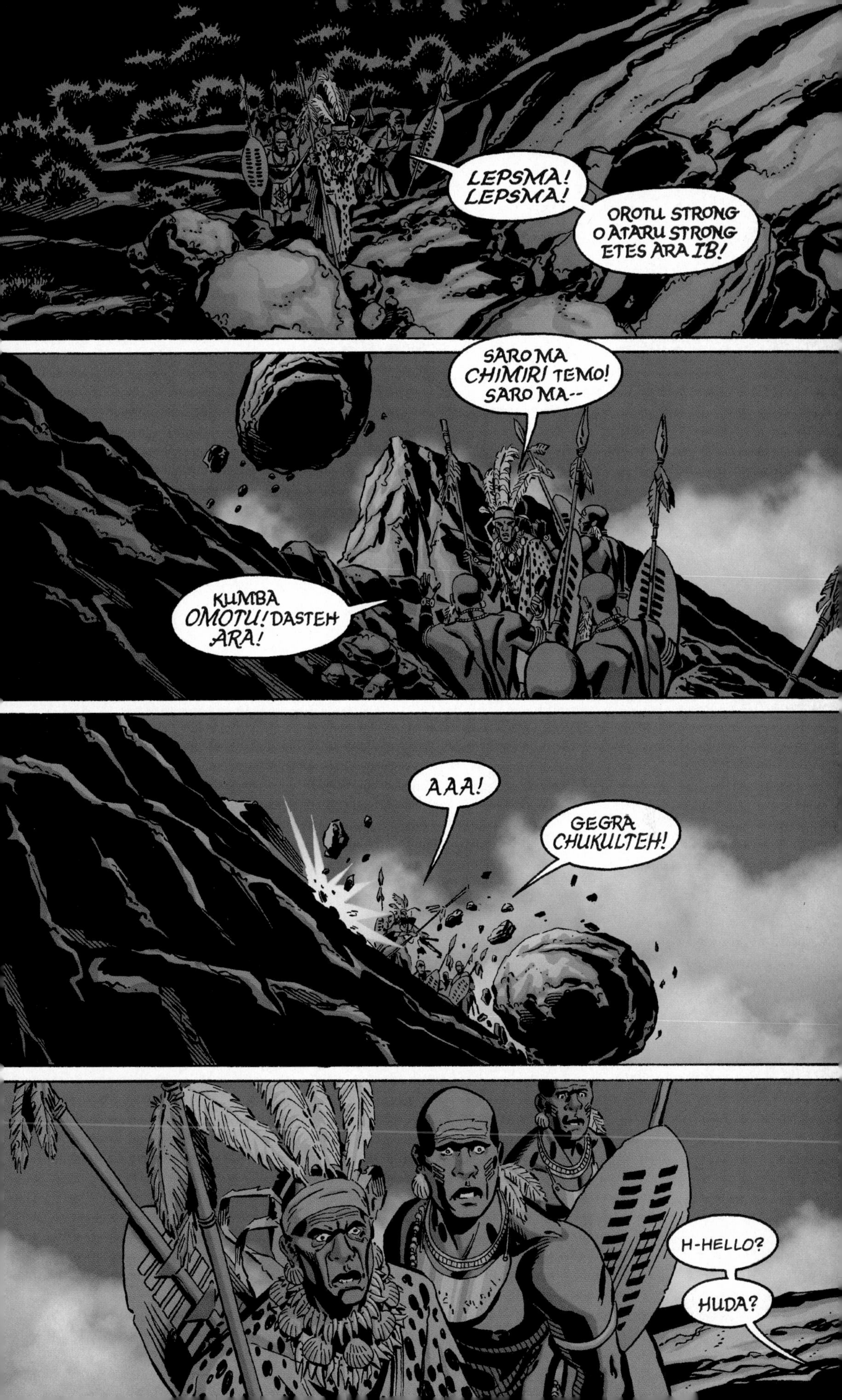
LEPSMA! LEPSMA!
OROTU STRONG O ATARU STRONG ETES ARA IB!
SARO MA CHIMIRI TEMO! SARO MA--
KUMBA OMOTU! DASTEH ARA!
AAA!
GEGRA CHUKULTEH!
H-HELLO?
HUDA?

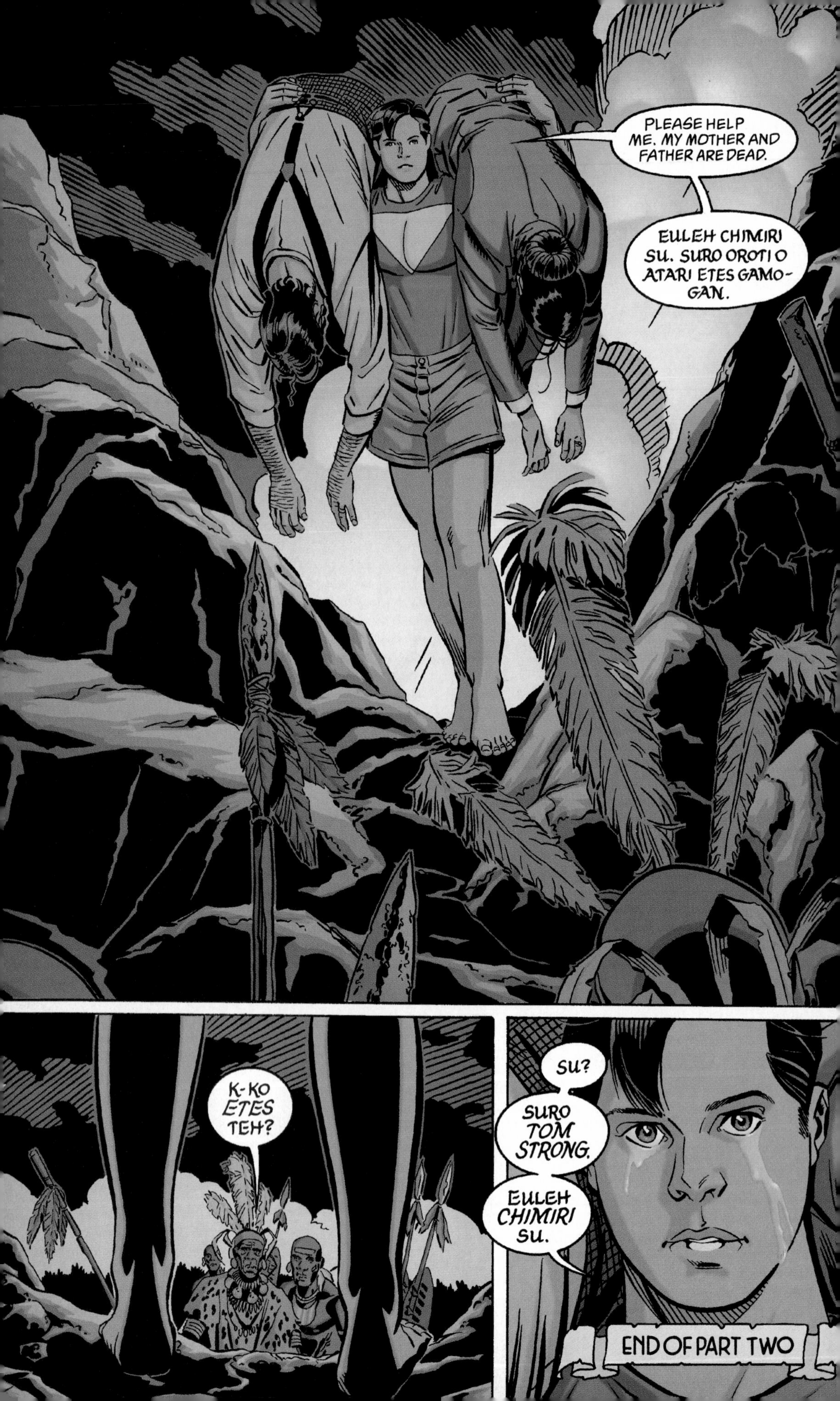
PLEASE HELP ME. MY MOTHER AND FATHER ARE DEAD.
EULEH CHIMIRI SU. SURO OROTI O ATARI ETES GAMO-GAN.
K-KO ETES TEH?
SU?
SURO TOM STRONG.
EULEH CHIMIRI SU.
END OF PART TWO

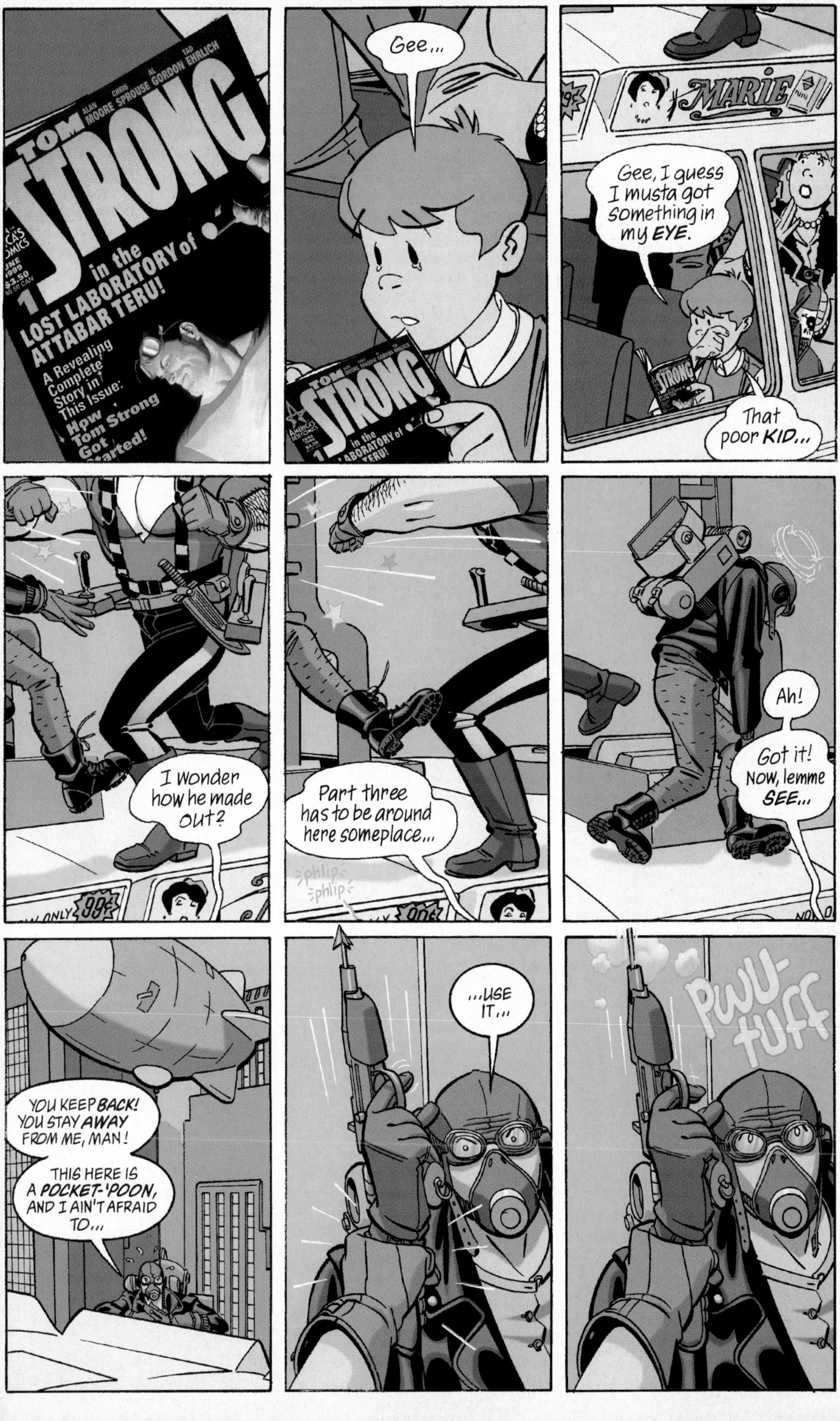
TOM STRONG
ALAN MOORE
CHRIS SPROUSE
AL GORDON
TAD EHRLICH
JUNE 1999
$3.50
$5.50 CAN
1
in the LOST LABORATORY of ATTABAR TERU!
A Revealing Complete Story in This Issue:
How Tom Strong Got Started!
Gee...
MARIE
Gee, I guess I musta got something in my EYE.
That poor KID...
I wonder how he made out?
Part three has to be around here someplace...
phlip phlip
Ah!
Got it! Now, lemme SEE...
YOU KEEP BACK! YOU STAY AWAY FROM ME, MAN!
THIS HERE IS A POCKET-'POON, AND I AIN'T AFRAID TO...
...USE IT...
PWU-tuff

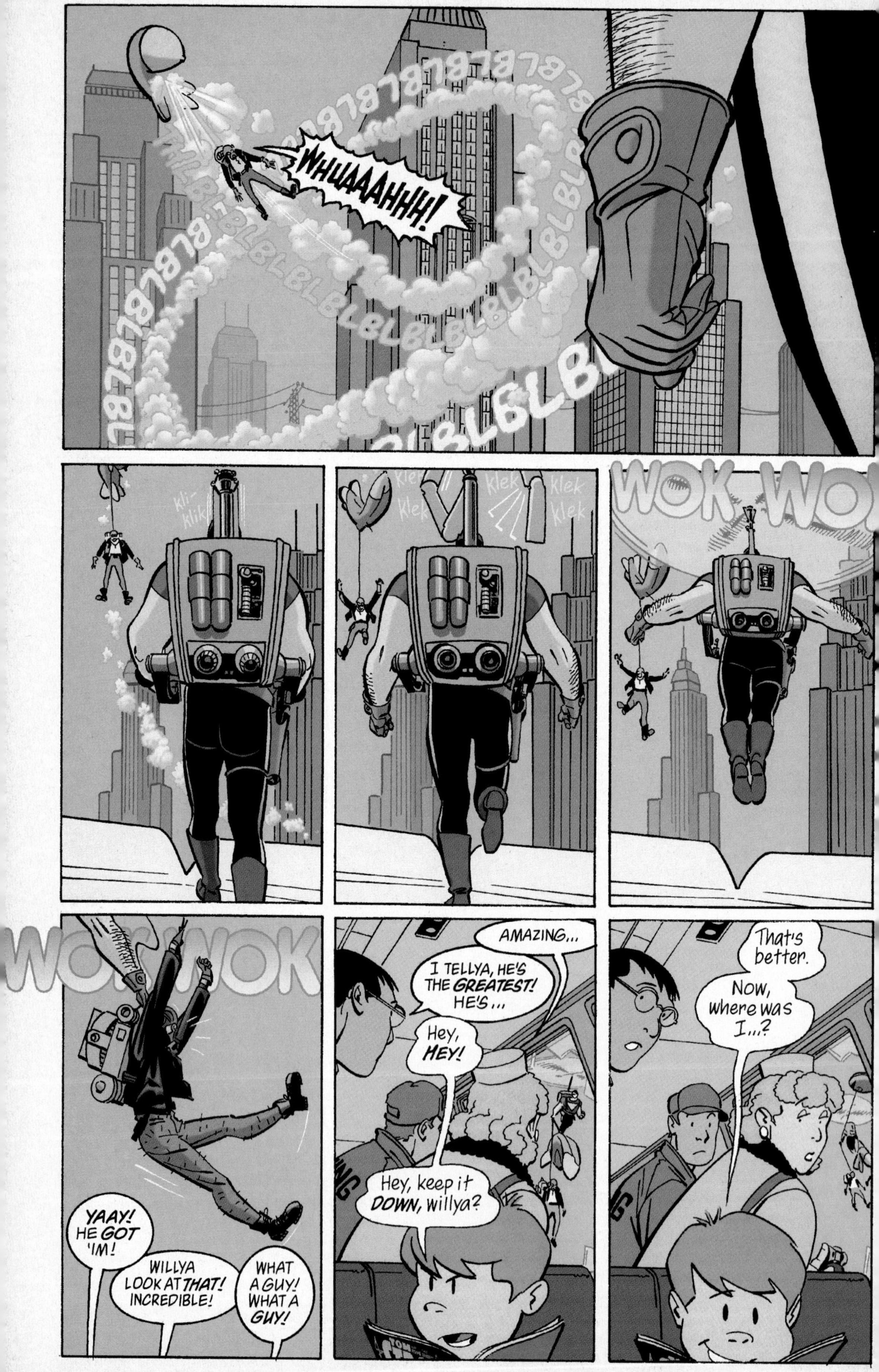

WHUAAAHHH!
BLBLBLBL
kli-klik
klek klek klek klek
WOK WOK
WOK WOK
YAAY! HE GOT 'IM!
WILLYA LOOK AT THAT! INCREDIBLE!
WHAT A GUY! WHAT A GUY!
AMAZING...
I TELLYA, HE'S THE GREATEST! HE'S...
Hey, HEY!
Hey, keep it DOWN, willya?
That's better.
Now, where was I...?

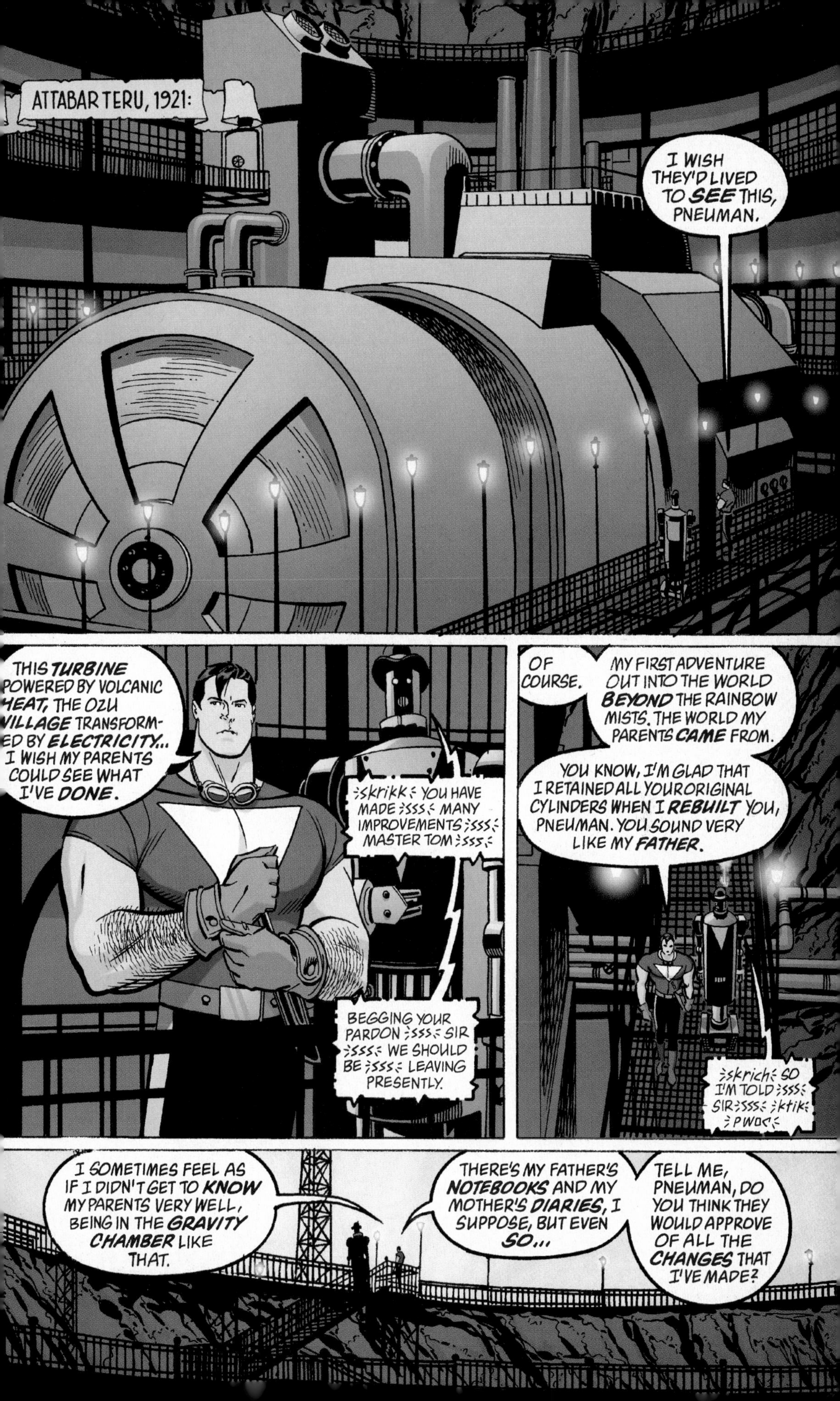

ATTABAR TERU, 1921:
I WISH THEY'D LIVED TO SEE THIS, PNEUMAN.
THIS TURBINE POWERED BY VOLCANIC HEAT, THE OZU VILLAGE TRANSFORMED BY ELECTRICITY... I WISH MY PARENTS COULD SEE WHAT I'VE DONE.
skrikk YOU HAVE MADE sss MANY IMPROVEMENTS sss MASTER TOM sss
BEGGING YOUR PARDON sss SIR sss WE SHOULD BE sss LEAVING PRESENTLY.
OF COURSE.
MY FIRST ADVENTURE OUT INTO THE WORLD BEYOND THE RAINBOW MISTS. THE WORLD MY PARENTS CAME FROM.
YOU KNOW, I'M GLAD THAT I RETAINED ALL YOUR ORIGINAL CYLINDERS WHEN I REBUILT YOU, PNEUMAN. YOU SOUND VERY LIKE MY FATHER.
skrich SO I'M TOLD sss SIR sss ktik PWOC
I SOMETIMES FEEL AS IF I DIDN'T GET TO KNOW MY PARENTS VERY WELL, BEING IN THE GRAVITY CHAMBER LIKE THAT.
THERE'S MY FATHER'S NOTEBOOKS AND MY MOTHER'S DIARIES, I SUPPOSE, BUT EVEN SO...
TELL ME, PNEUMAN, DO YOU THINK THEY WOULD APPROVE OF ALL THE CHANGES THAT I'VE MADE?

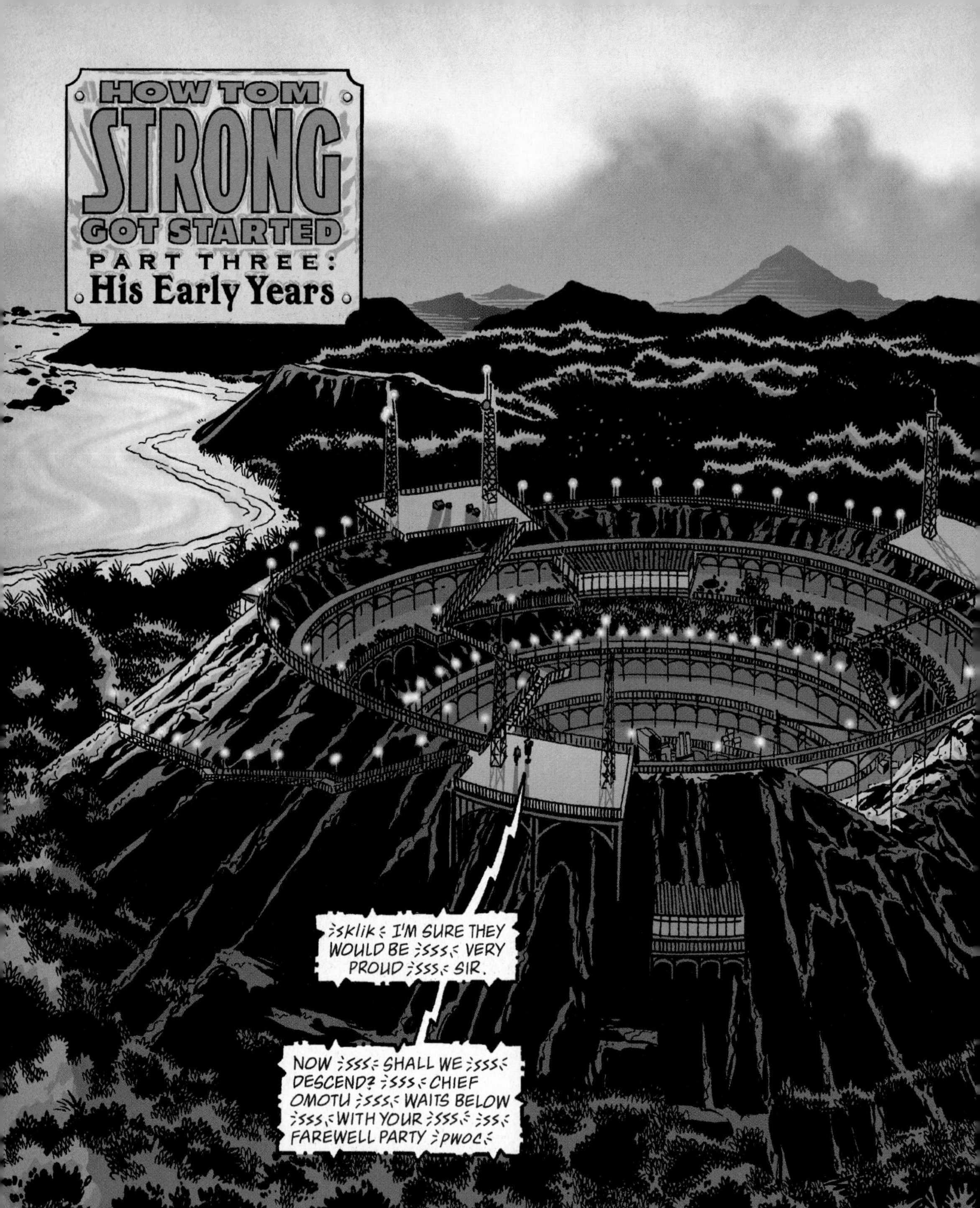
HOW TOM STRONG GOT STARTED
PART THREE:
His Early Years
⋛sklik⋚ I'M SURE THEY WOULD BE ⋛sss⋚ VERY PROUD ⋛sss⋚ SIR.
NOW ⋛sss⋚ SHALL WE ⋛sss⋚ DESCEND? ⋛sss⋚ CHIEF OMOTU ⋛sss⋚ WAITS BELOW ⋛sss⋚ WITH YOUR ⋛sss⋚ ⋛ss⋚ FAREWELL PARTY ⋛pwoc⋚

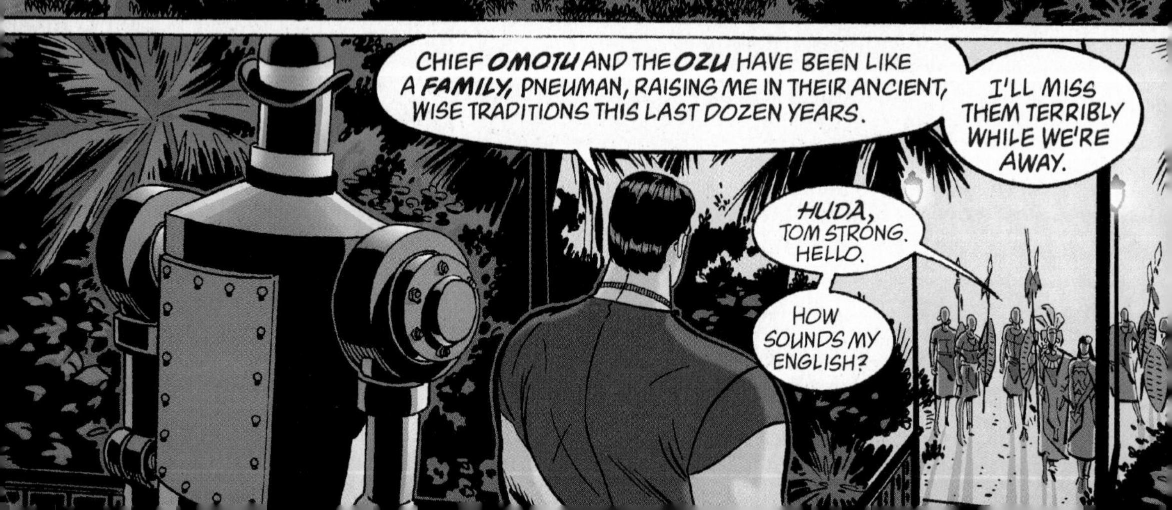
CHIEF OMOTU AND THE OZU HAVE BEEN LIKE A FAMILY, PNEUMAN, RAISING ME IN THEIR ANCIENT, WISE TRADITIONS THIS LAST DOZEN YEARS.
I'LL MISS THEM TERRIBLY WHILE WE'RE AWAY.
HUDA, TOM STRONG. HELLO.
HOW SOUNDS MY ENGLISH?

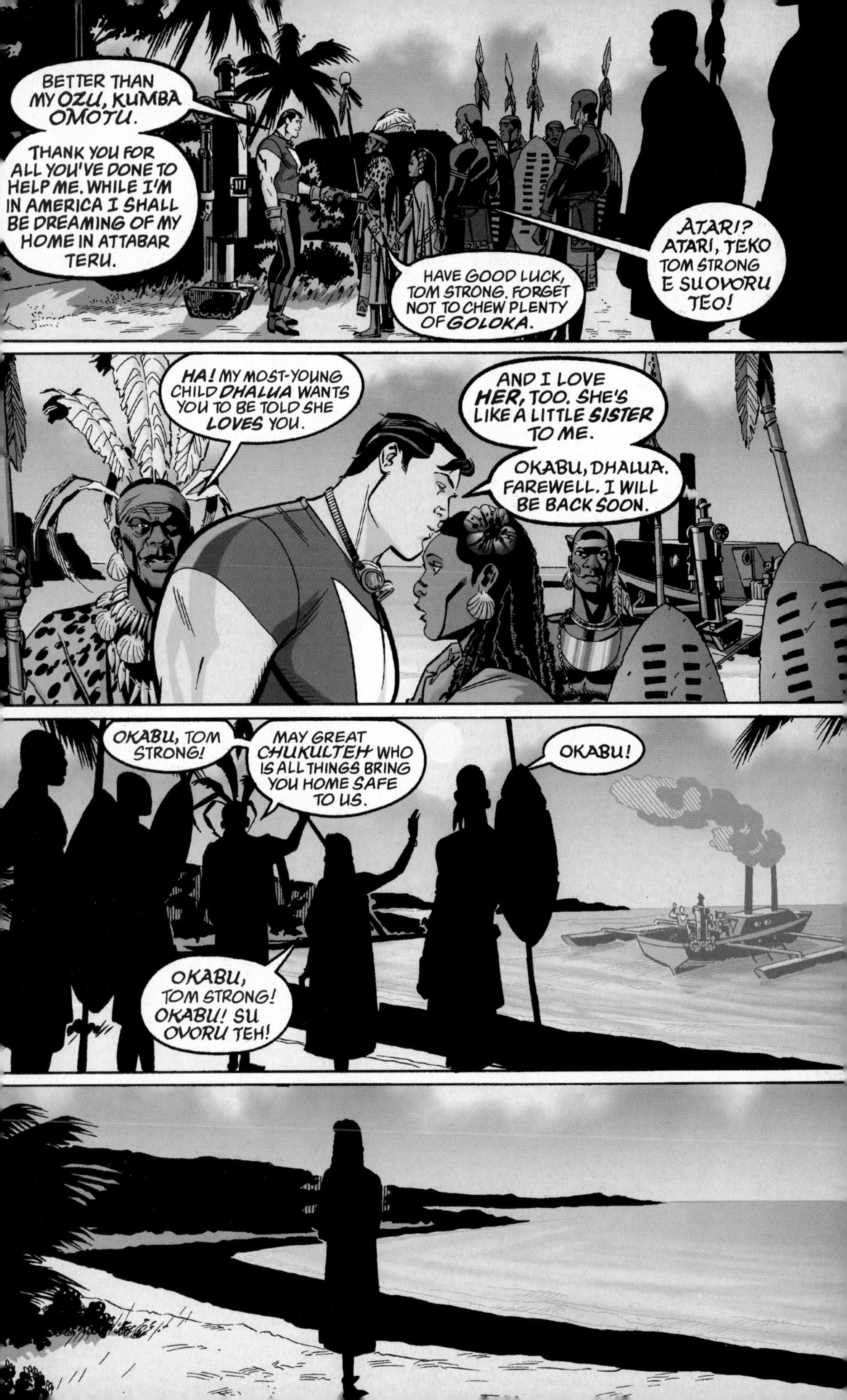
BETTER THAN MY OZU, KUMBA OMOTU.
THANK YOU FOR ALL YOU'VE DONE TO HELP ME. WHILE I'M IN AMERICA I SHALL BE DREAMING OF MY HOME IN ATTABAR TERU.
HAVE GOOD LUCK, TOM STRONG. FORGET NOT TO CHEW PLENTY OF GOLOKA.
ATARI? ATARI, TEKO TOM STRONG E SUOVORU TEO!
HA! MY MOST-YOUNG CHILD DHALUA WANTS YOU TO BE TOLD SHE LOVES YOU.
AND I LOVE HER, TOO. SHE'S LIKE A LITTLE SISTER TO ME.
OKABU, DHALUA. FAREWELL. I WILL BE BACK SOON.
OKABU, TOM STRONG!
MAY GREAT CHUKULTEH WHO IS ALL THINGS BRING YOU HOME SAFE TO US.
OKABU!
OKABU, TOM STRONG! OKABU! SU OVORU TEH!

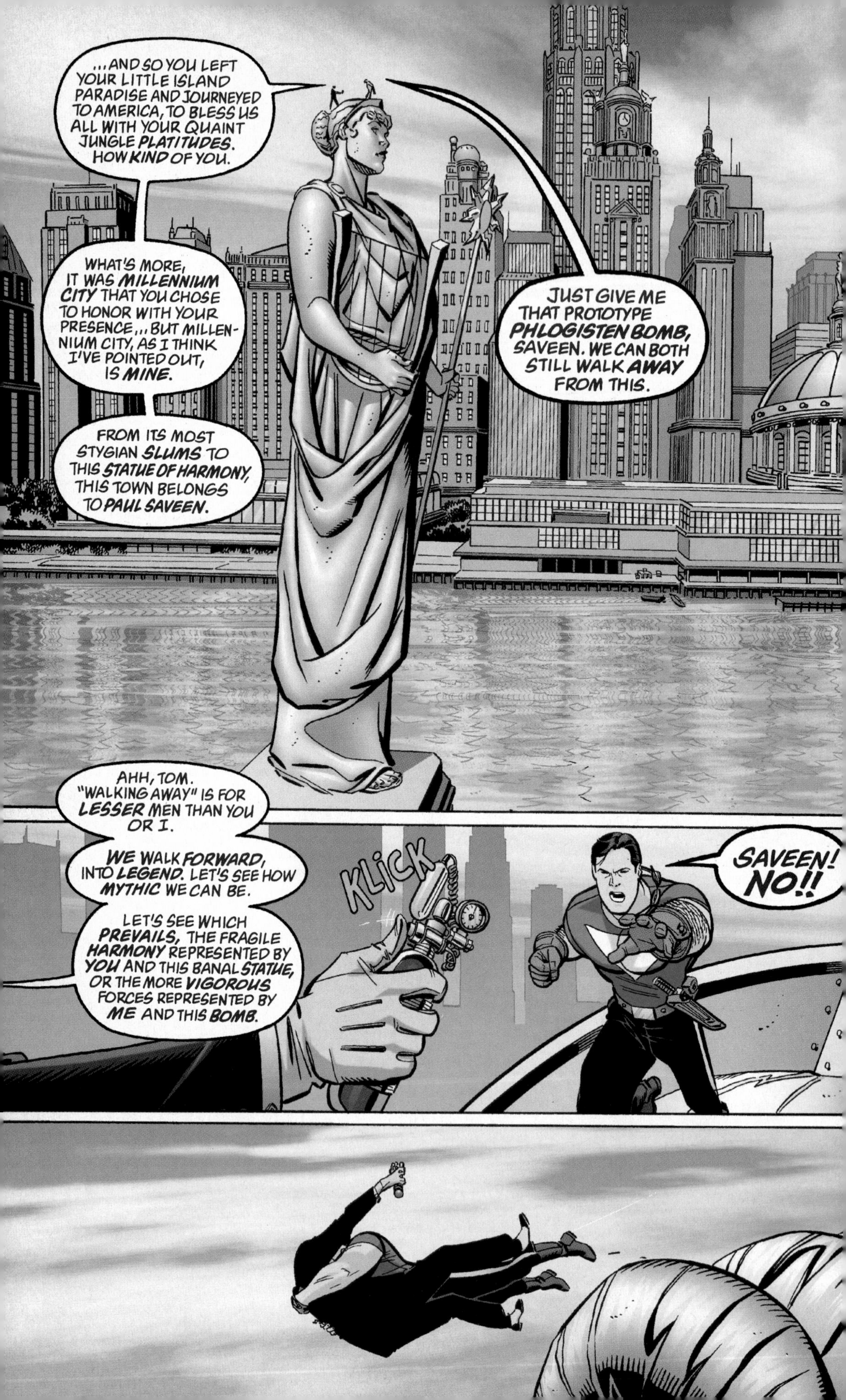
...AND SO YOU LEFT YOUR LITTLE ISLAND PARADISE AND JOURNEYED TO AMERICA, TO BLESS US ALL WITH YOUR QUAINT JUNGLE PLATITUDES. HOW KIND OF YOU.
WHAT'S MORE, IT WAS MILLENNIUM CITY THAT YOU CHOSE TO HONOR WITH YOUR PRESENCE... BUT MILLENNIUM CITY, AS I THINK I'VE POINTED OUT, IS MINE.
FROM ITS MOST STYGIAN SLUMS TO THIS STATUE OF HARMONY, THIS TOWN BELONGS TO PAUL SAVEEN.
JUST GIVE ME THAT PROTOTYPE PHLOGISTEN BOMB, SAVEEN. WE CAN BOTH STILL WALK AWAY FROM THIS.
AHH, TOM. "WALKING AWAY" IS FOR LESSER MEN THAN YOU OR I.
WE WALK FORWARD, INTO LEGEND. LET'S SEE HOW MYTHIC WE CAN BE.
LET'S SEE WHICH PREVAILS, THE FRAGILE HARMONY REPRESENTED BY YOU AND THIS BANAL STATUE, OR THE MORE VIGOROUS FORCES REPRESENTED BY ME AND THIS BOMB.
KLICK
SAVEEN! NO!!

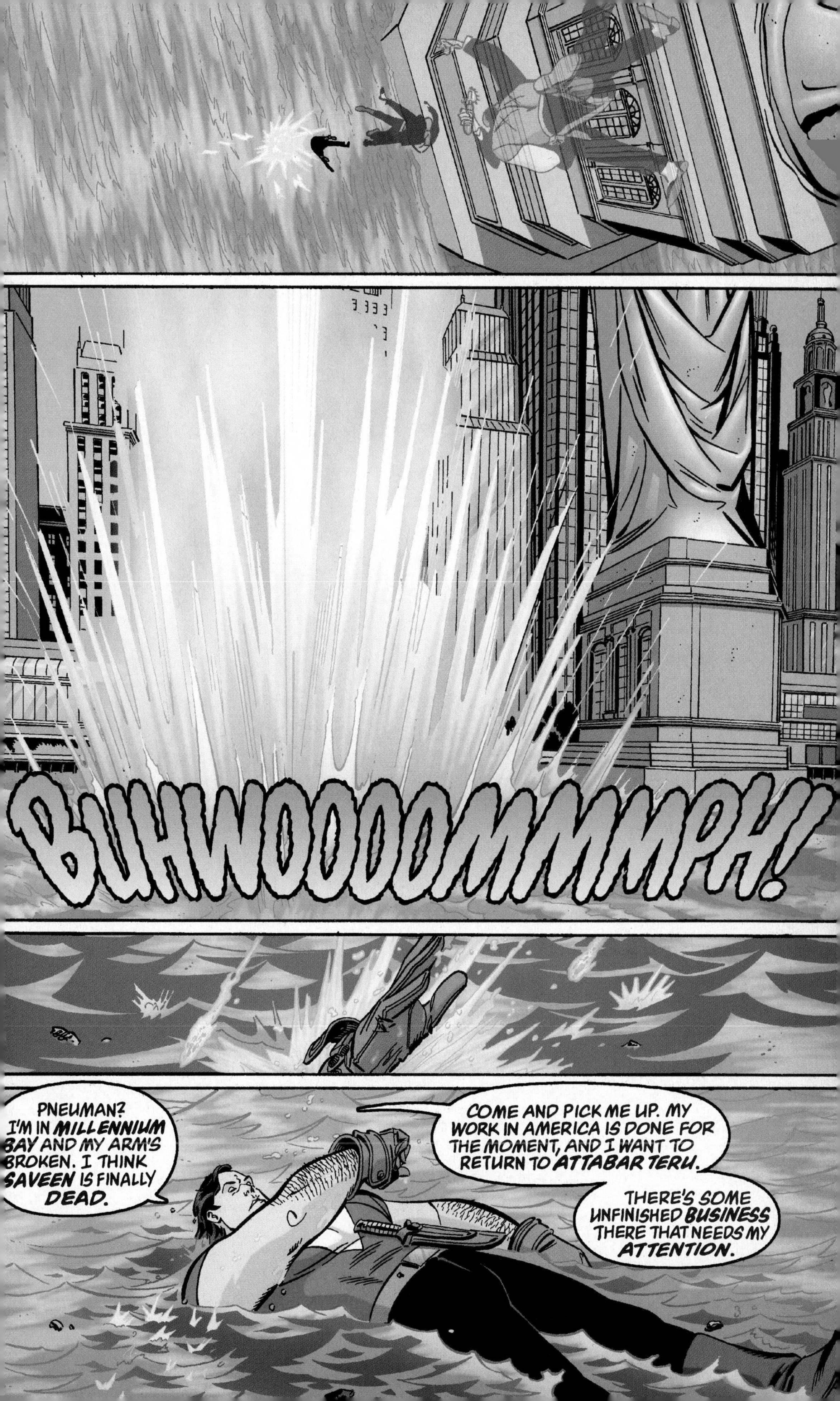
BUHWOOOOMMMMPH!
PNEUMAN? I'M IN MILLENNIUM BAY AND MY ARM'S BROKEN. I THINK SAVEEN IS FINALLY DEAD.
COME AND PICK ME UP. MY WORK IN AMERICA IS DONE FOR THE MOMENT, AND I WANT TO RETURN TO ATTABAR TERU.
THERE'S SOME UNFINISHED BUSINESS THERE THAT NEEDS MY ATTENTION.

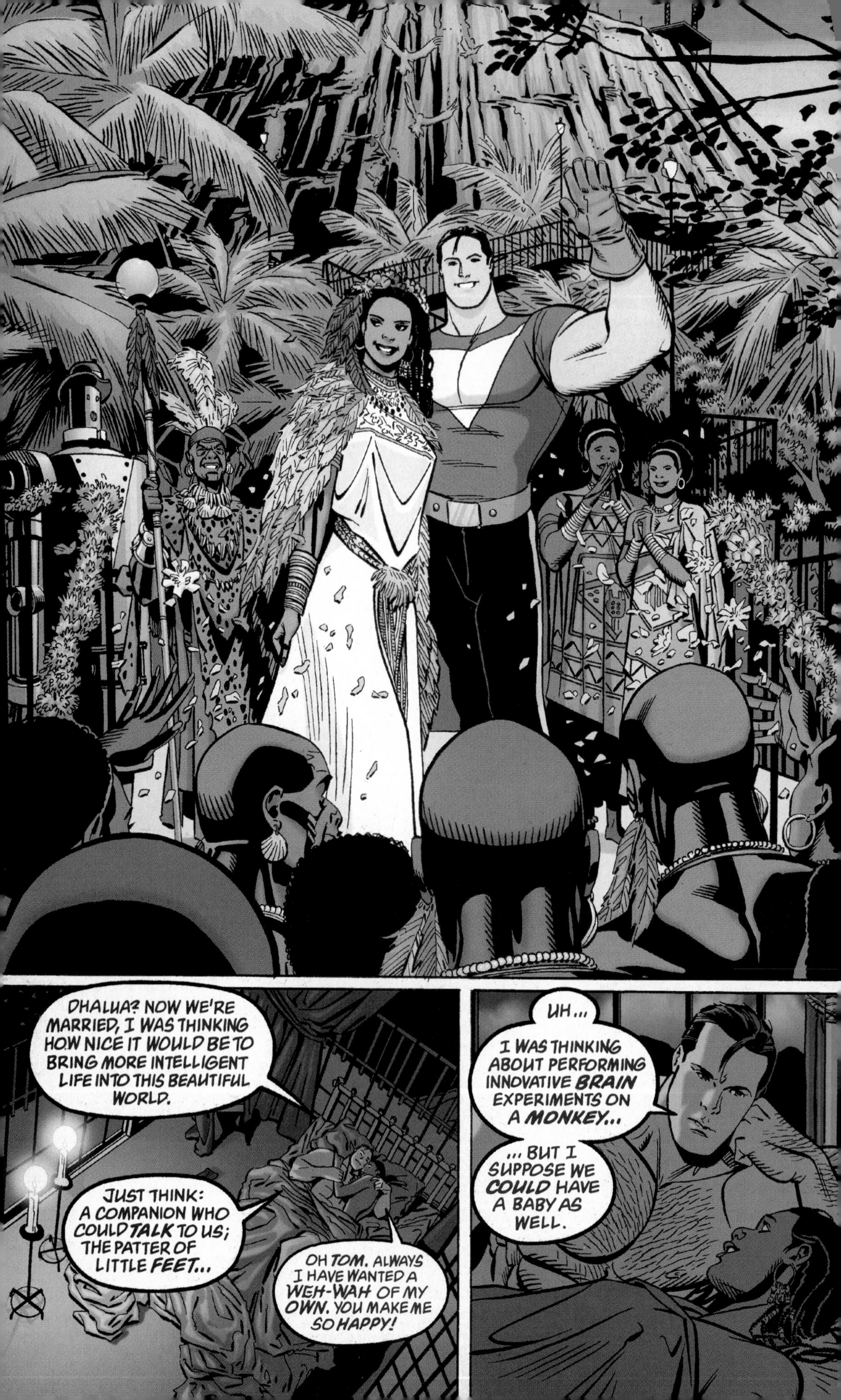

DHALUA? NOW WE'RE MARRIED, I WAS THINKING HOW NICE IT WOULD BE TO BRING MORE INTELLIGENT LIFE INTO THIS BEAUTIFUL WORLD.
JUST THINK: A COMPANION WHO COULD TALK TO US; THE PATTER OF LITTLE FEET...
OH TOM. ALWAYS I HAVE WANTED A WEH-WAH OF MY OWN. YOU MAKE ME SO HAPPY!
UH...
I WAS THINKING ABOUT PERFORMING INNOVATIVE BRAIN EXPERIMENTS ON A MONKEY...
... BUT I SUPPOSE WE COULD HAVE A BABY AS WELL.

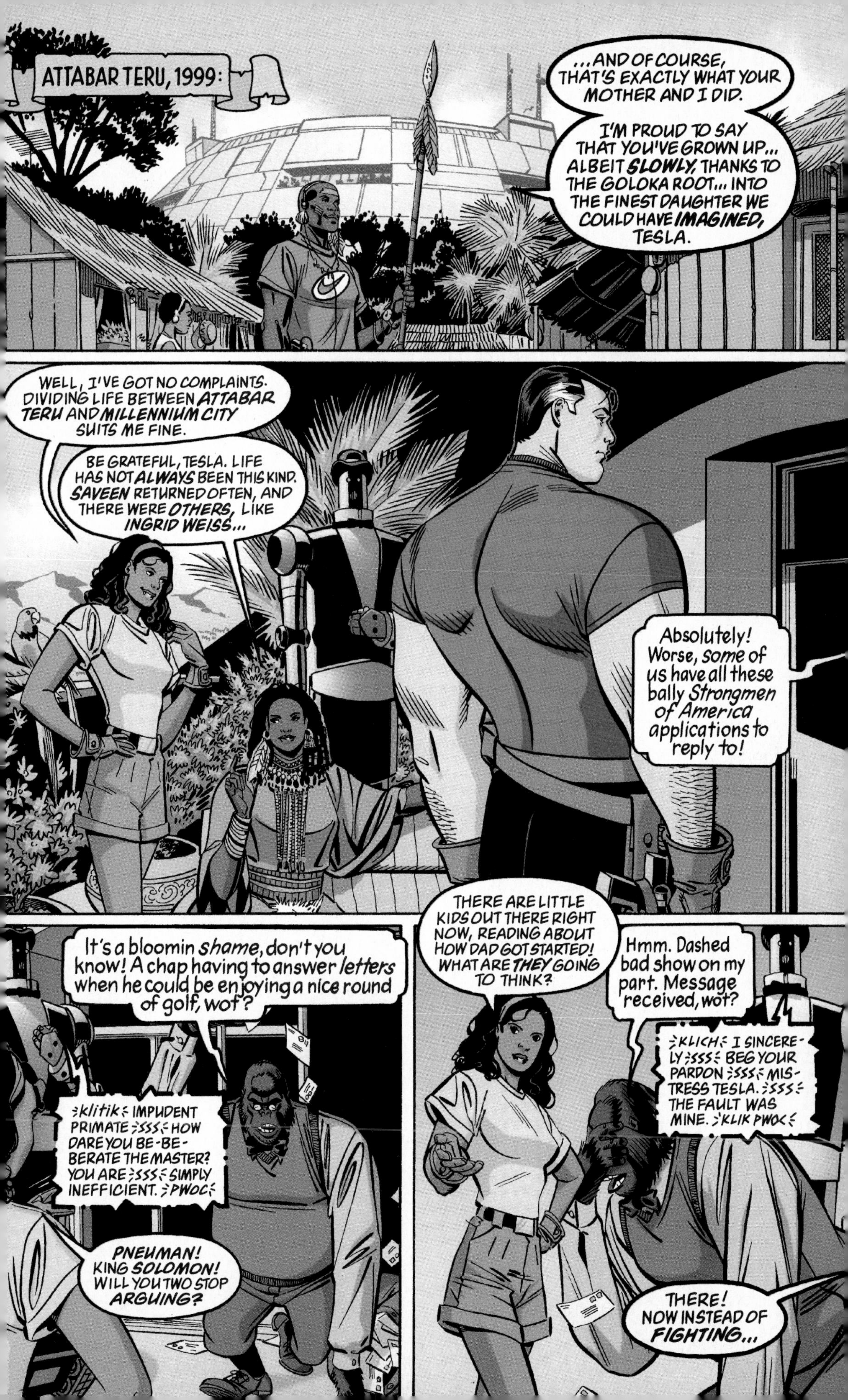
ATTABAR TERU, 1999:
...AND OF COURSE, THAT'S EXACTLY WHAT YOUR MOTHER AND I DID.
I'M PROUD TO SAY THAT YOU'VE GROWN UP... ALBEIT SLOWLY, THANKS TO THE GOLOKA ROOT... INTO THE FINEST DAUGHTER WE COULD HAVE IMAGINED, TESLA.
WELL, I'VE GOT NO COMPLAINTS. DIVIDING LIFE BETWEEN ATTABAR TERU AND MILLENNIUM CITY SUITS ME FINE.
BE GRATEFUL, TESLA. LIFE HAS NOT ALWAYS BEEN THIS KIND. SAVEEN RETURNED OFTEN, AND THERE WERE OTHERS, LIKE INGRID WEISS...
Absolutely! Worse, some of us have all these bally Strongmen of America applications to reply to!
It's a bloomin shame, don't you know! A chap having to answer letters when he could be enjoying a nice round of golf, wot?
>klitik< IMPUDENT PRIMATE >SSS< HOW DARE YOU BE-BE-BERATE THE MASTER? YOU ARE >SSS< SIMPLY INEFFICIENT. >PWOC<
PNEUMAN! KING SOLOMON! WILL YOU TWO STOP ARGUING?
THERE ARE LITTLE KIDS OUT THERE RIGHT NOW, READING ABOUT HOW DAD GOT STARTED! WHAT ARE THEY GOING TO THINK?
Hmm. Dashed bad show on my part. Message received, wot?
>KLICH< I SINCERELY >SSS< BEG YOUR PARDON >SSS< MISTRESS TESLA. >SSS< THE FAULT WAS MINE. >KLIK PWOC<
THERE! NOW INSTEAD OF FIGHTING...

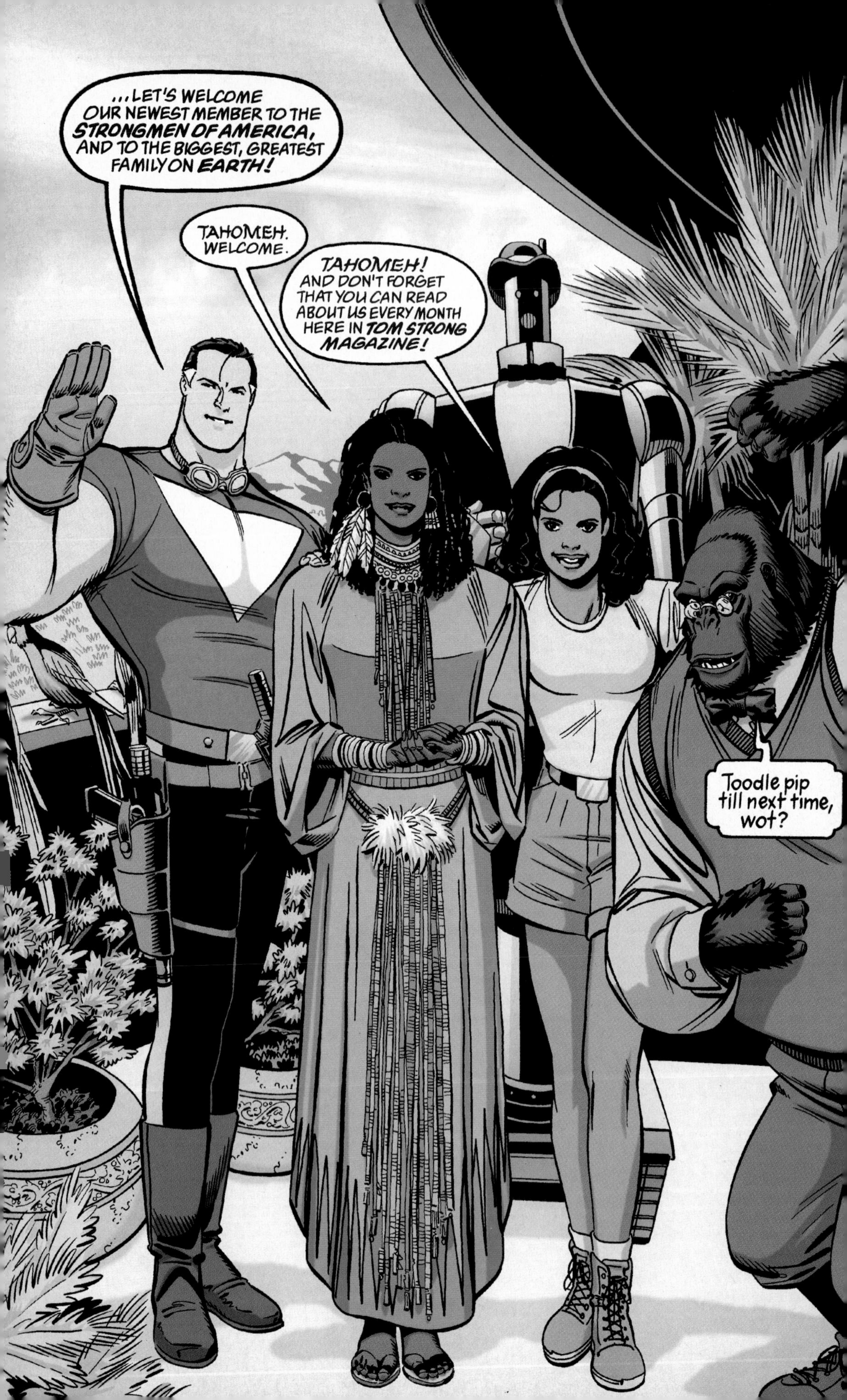
...LET'S WELCOME OUR NEWEST MEMBER TO THE STRONGMEN OF AMERICA, AND TO THE BIGGEST, GREATEST FAMILY ON EARTH!
TAHOMEH. WELCOME.
TAHOMEH! AND DON'T FORGET THAT YOU CAN READ ABOUT US EVERY MONTH HERE IN TOM STRONG MAGAZINE!
Toodle pip till next time, wot?

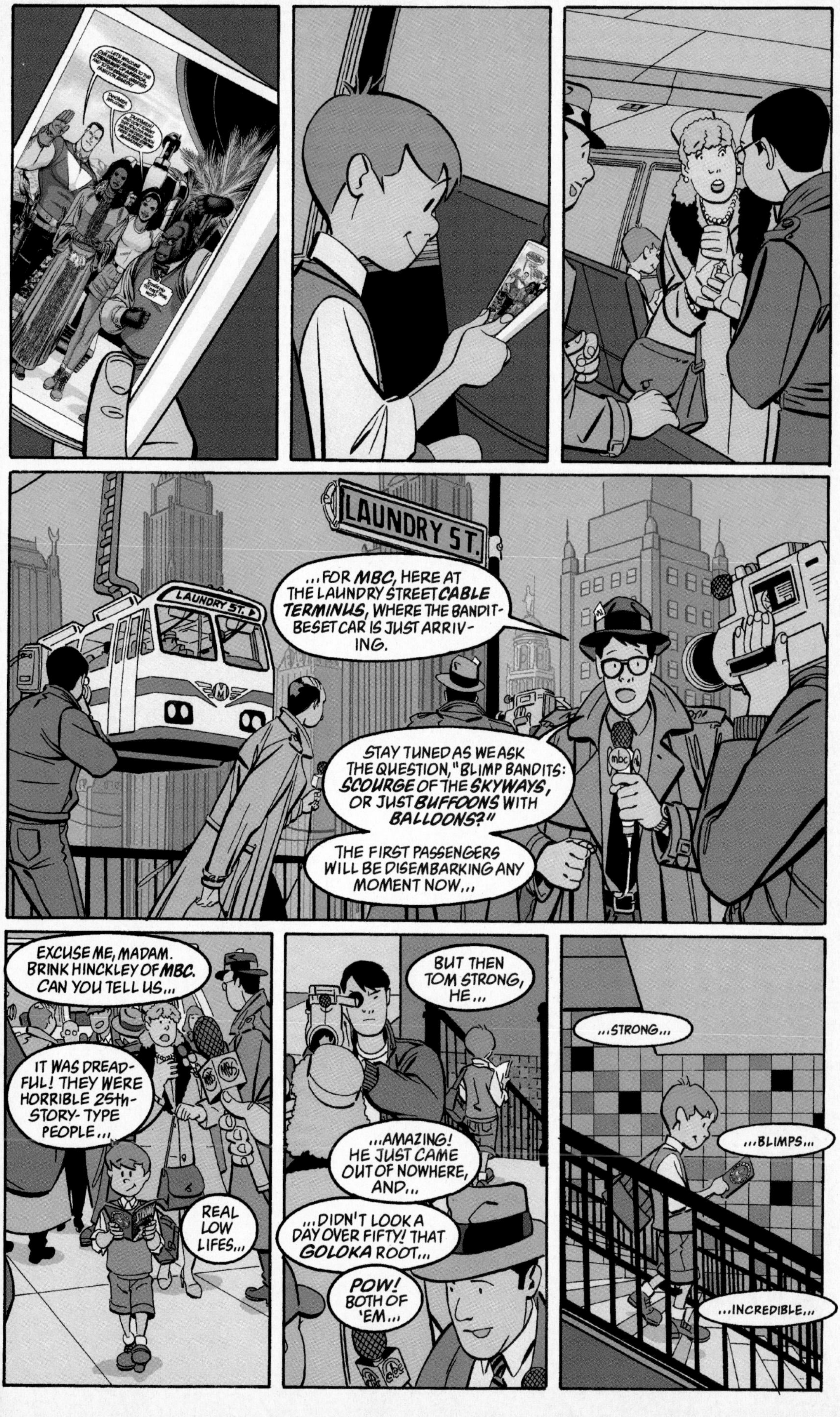
LAUNDRY ST.
LAUNDRY ST.
...FOR MBC, HERE AT THE LAUNDRY STREET CABLE TERMINUS, WHERE THE BANDIT-BESET CAR IS JUST ARRIV-ING.
STAY TUNED AS WE ASK THE QUESTION, "BLIMP BANDITS: SCOURGE OF THE SKYWAYS, OR JUST BUFFOONS WITH BALLOONS?"
THE FIRST PASSENGERS WILL BE DISEMBARKING ANY MOMENT NOW...
EXCUSE ME, MADAM. BRINK HINCKLEY OF MBC. CAN YOU TELL US...
IT WAS DREAD-FUL! THEY WERE HORRIBLE 25th-STORY-TYPE PEOPLE...
REAL LOW LIFES...
BUT THEN TOM STRONG, HE...
...AMAZING! HE JUST CAME OUT OF NOWHERE, AND...
...DIDN'T LOOK A DAY OVER FIFTY! THAT GOLOKA ROOT...
POW! BOTH OF 'EM...
...STRONG...
...BLIMPS...
...INCREDIBLE...

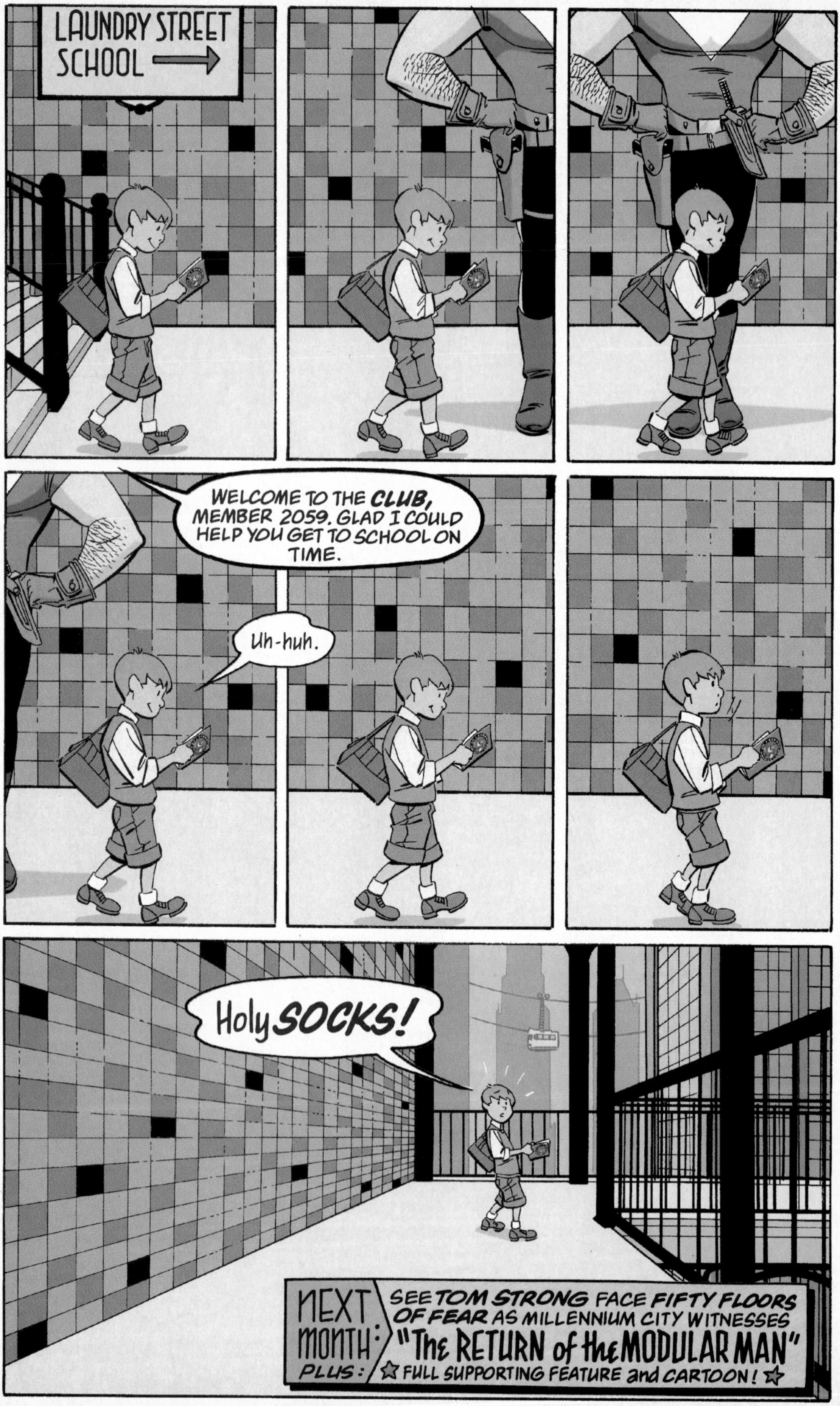
LAUNDRY STREET SCHOOL
WELCOME TO THE CLUB, MEMBER 2059. GLAD I COULD HELP YOU GET TO SCHOOL ON TIME.
Uh-huh.
Holy SOCKS!
NEXT MONTH: SEE TOM STRONG FACE FIFTY FLOORS OF FEAR AS MILLENNIUM CITY WITNESSES "The RETURN of the MODULAR MAN"
PLUS: ☆ FULL SUPPORTING FEATURE and CARTOON! ☆

CHAPTER TWO

**In which The Family fills in,
TESLA makes New Friends, and
TOM talks to an Old Acquaintance.**

**Cover art:
Chris Sprouse &
Angus McKie**

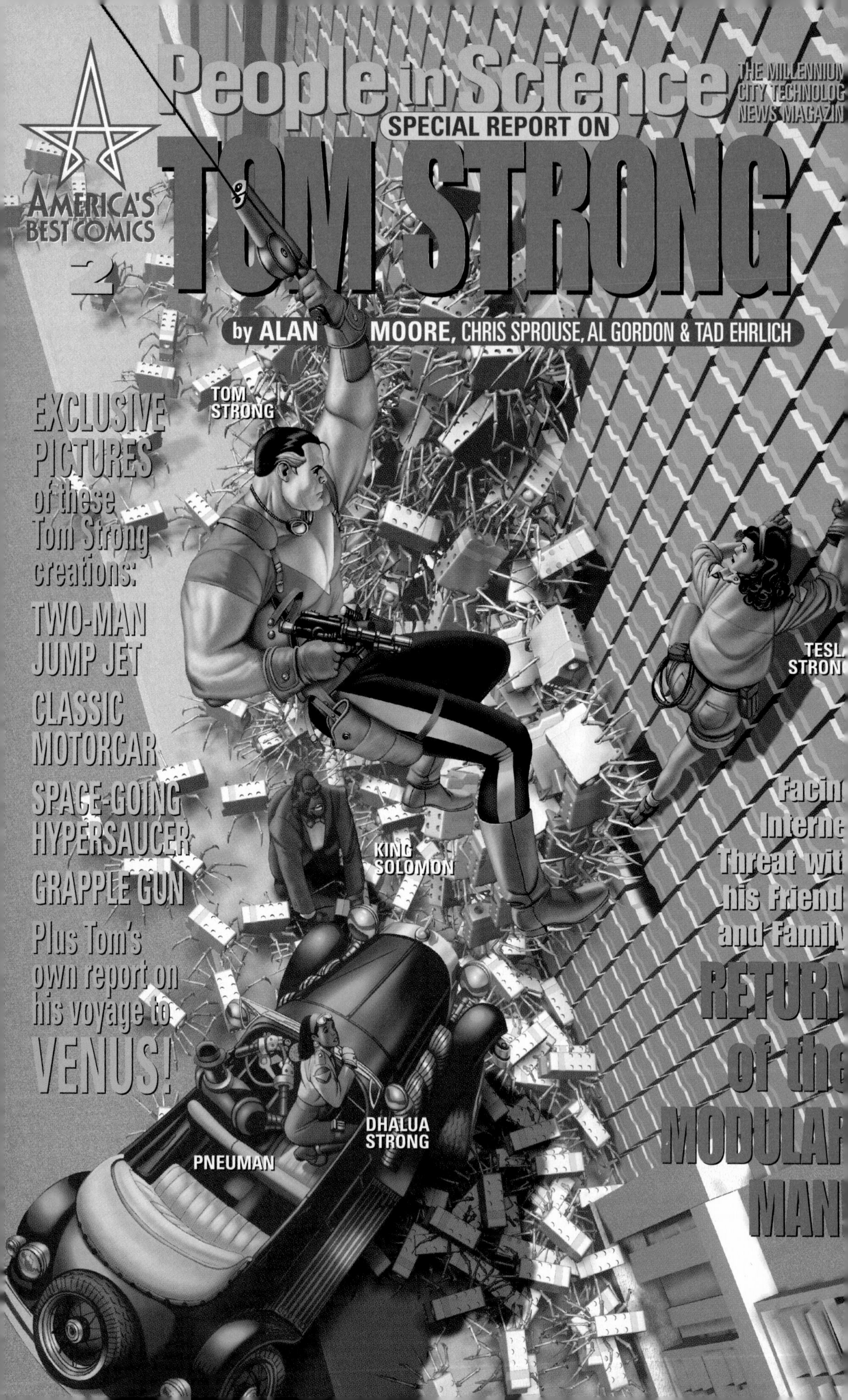

AMERICA'S BEST COMICS
2
People in Science
THE MILLENNIU
CITY TECHNOLOG
NEWS MAGAZIN
SPECIAL REPORT ON
TOM STRONG
by ALAN MOORE, CHRIS SPROUSE, AL GORDON & TAD EHRLICH
EXCLUSIVE PICTURES of these Tom Strong creations:
TWO-MAN JUMP JET
CLASSIC MOTORCAR
SPACE-GOING HYPERSAUCER
GRAPPLE GUN
Plus Tom's own report on his voyage to VENUS!
TOM STRONG
TESL STRON
KING SOLOMON
DHALUA STRONG
PNEUMAN
Facin Interne Threat wit his Friend and Famil
RETURN of the MODULAR MAN

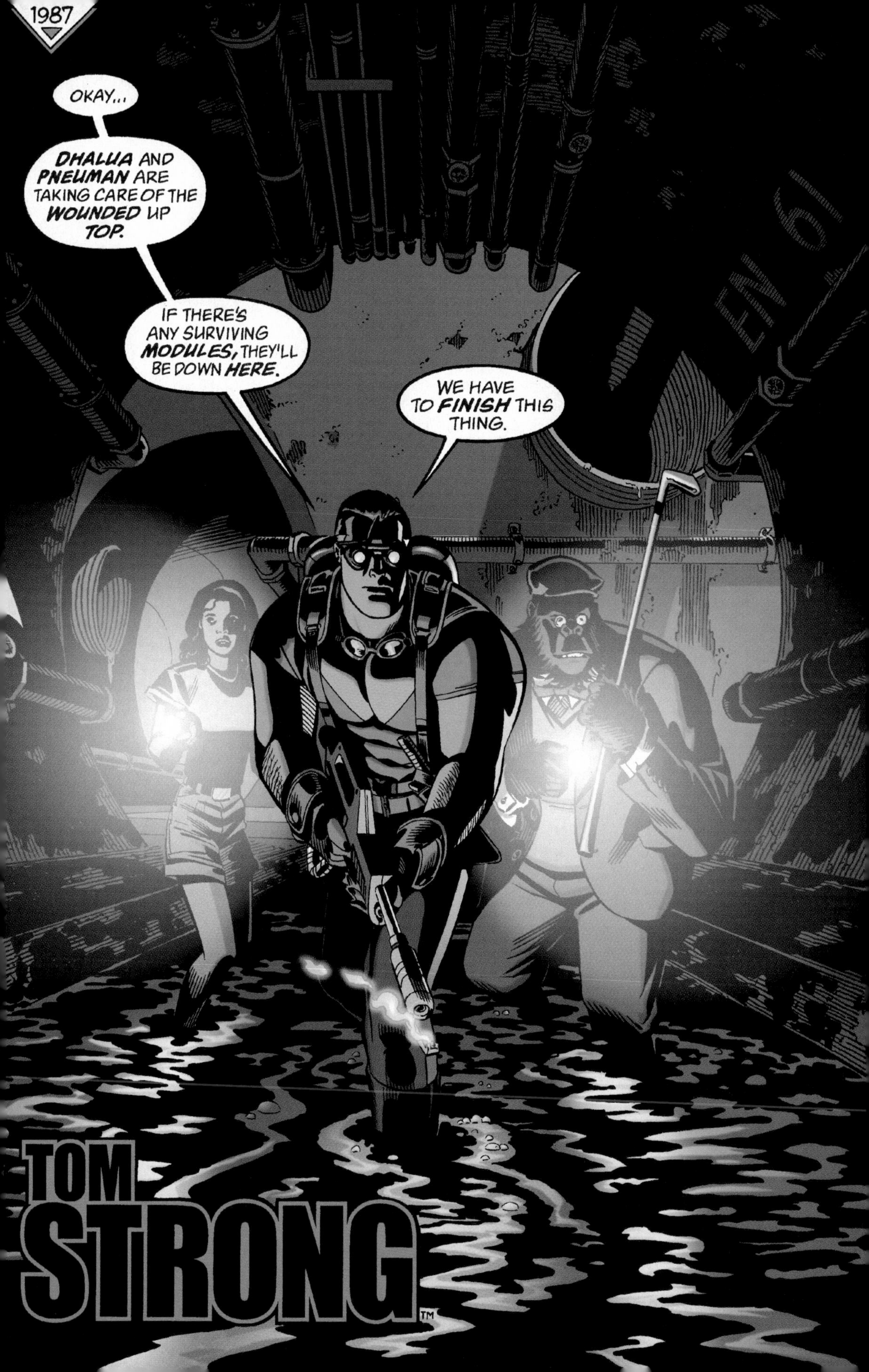
1987
OKAY...
DHALUA AND PNEUMAN ARE TAKING CARE OF THE WOUNDED UP TOP.
IF THERE'S ANY SURVIVING MODULES, THEY'LL BE DOWN HERE.
WE HAVE TO FINISH THIS THING.
EN 61
TOM STRONG™

AS LONG AS THERE'S ONE OF THESE DEVICES STILL *FUNCTIONAL*, MILLENNIUM CITY IS IN *DANGER*.

DAD, I'M SCARED. THEY'RE LIKE HORRIBLE LITTLE *RATS*...

IT'S ALL RIGHT. I CAN SEE IT...

UGGH! LOOK AT IT *SCUTTLING*...

I say! Boarders on the starboard bow, sah!

Oh, good *shot*, sah! Well *played!*

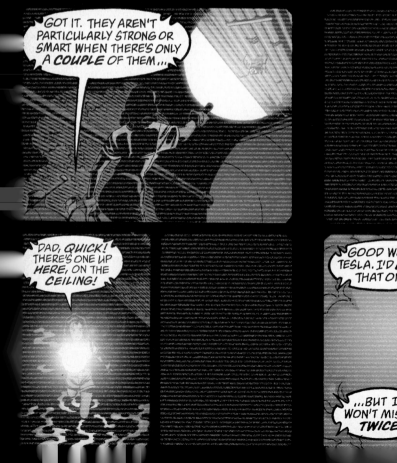

GOT IT. THEY AREN'T PARTICULARLY STRONG OR SMART WHEN THERE'S ONLY A *COUPLE* OF THEM...

DAD, *QUICK!* THERE'S ONE UP *HERE*, ON THE *CEILING!*

GOOD WORK, TESLA. I'D *MISSED* THAT ONE...

...BUT I WON'T MISS IT *TWICE!*

D-DAD, THE WAY IT'S *THRASHING*, IT'S LIKE IT'S IN *PAIN*.

ARE YOU *SURE* THEY'RE NOT PROPERLY *ALIVE?*

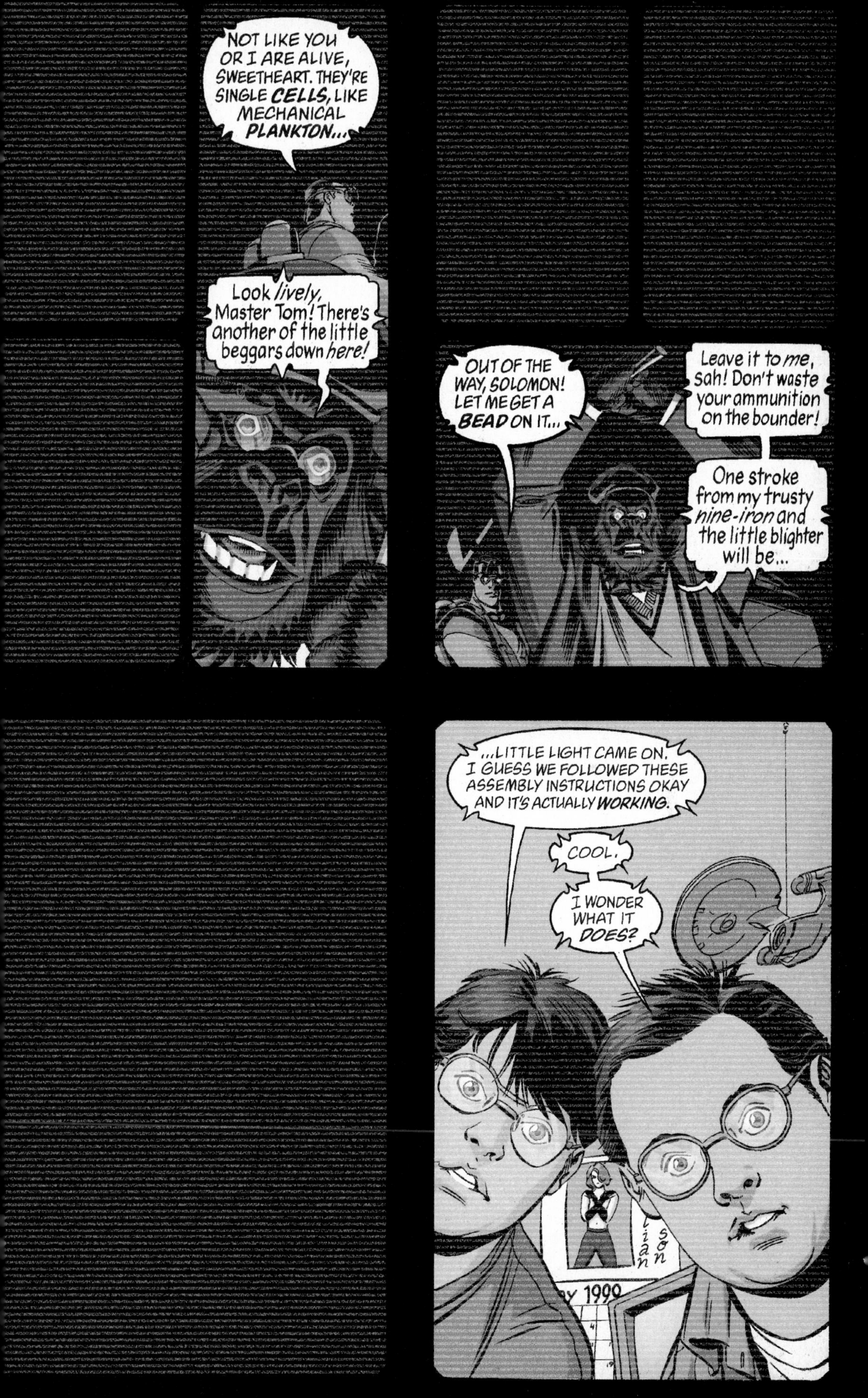
NOT LIKE YOU OR I ARE ALIVE, SWEETHEART. THEY'RE SINGLE CELLS, LIKE MECHANICAL PLANKTON...
Look lively, Master Tom! There's another of the little beggars down here!
OUT OF THE WAY, SOLOMON! LET ME GET A BEAD ON IT...
Leave it to me, sah! Don't waste your ammunition on the bounder!
One stroke from my trusty nine-iron and the little blighter will be...
...LITTLE LIGHT CAME ON. I GUESS WE FOLLOWED THESE ASSEMBLY INSTRUCTIONS OKAY AND IT'S ACTUALLY WORKING.
COOL.
I WONDER WHAT IT DOES?

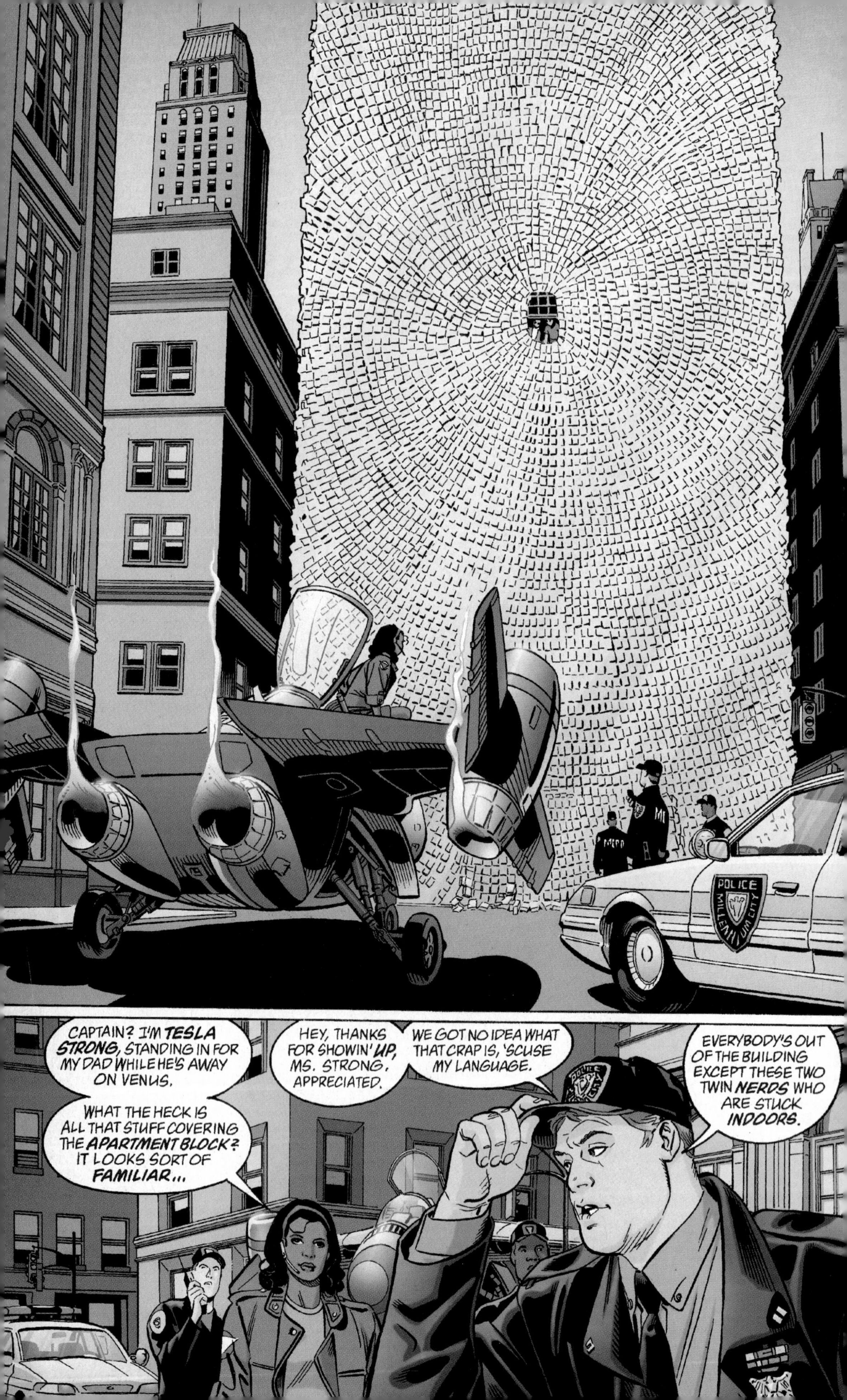
POLICE
CAPTAIN? I'M TESLA STRONG, STANDING IN FOR MY DAD WHILE HE'S AWAY ON VENUS.
WHAT THE HECK IS ALL THAT STUFF COVERING THE APARTMENT BLOCK? IT LOOKS SORT OF FAMILIAR...
HEY, THANKS FOR SHOWIN' UP, MS. STRONG. APPRECIATED.
WE GOT NO IDEA WHAT THAT CRAP IS, 'SCUSE MY LANGUAGE.
EVERYBODY'S OUT OF THE BUILDING EXCEPT THESE TWO TWIN NERDS WHO ARE STUCK INDOORS.

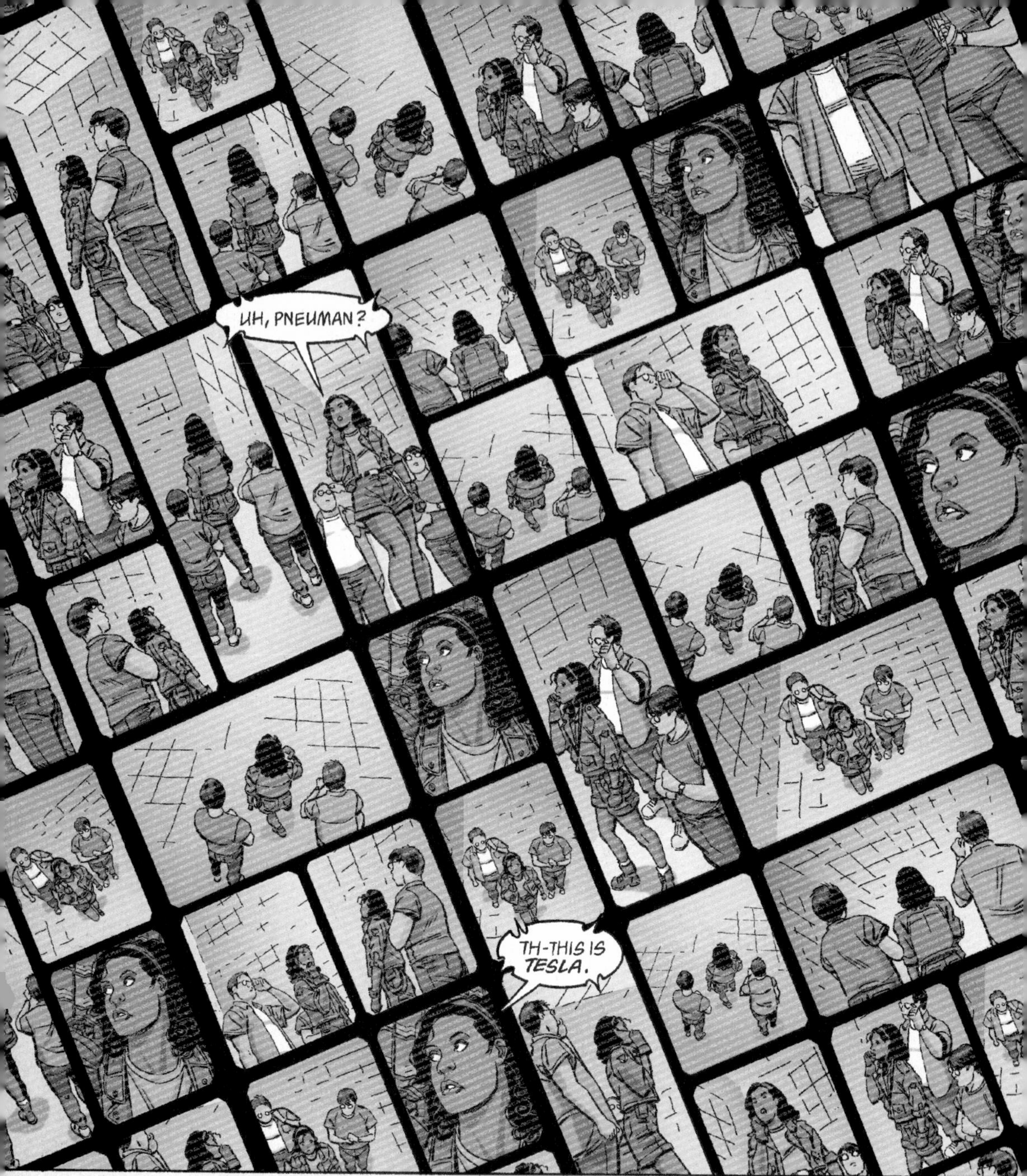
UH, PNEUMAN?
TH-THIS IS TESLA.

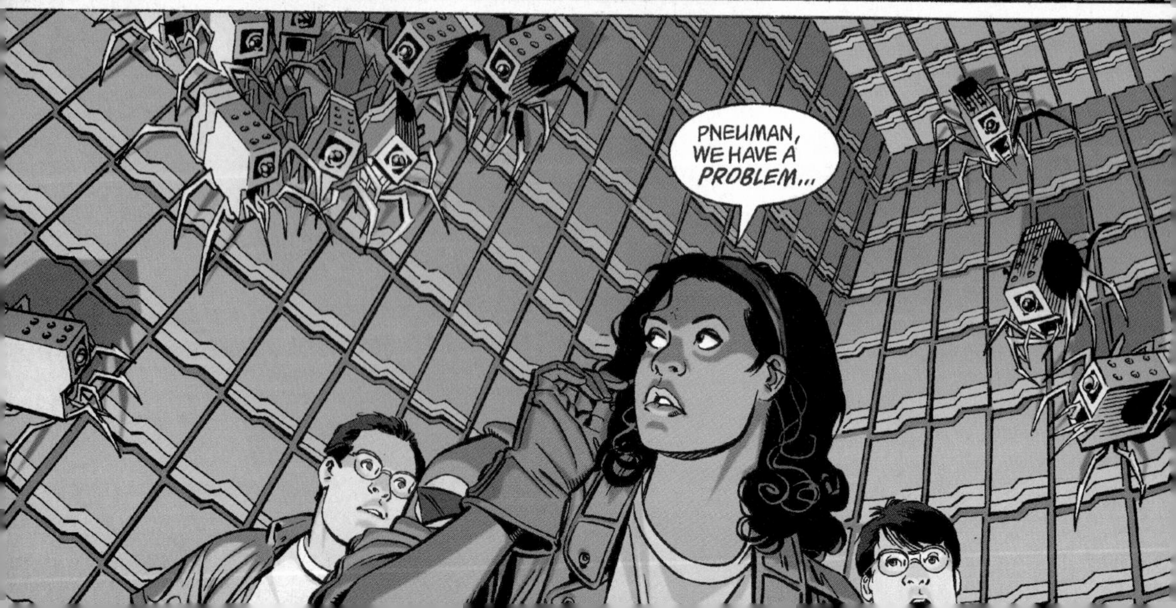
PNEUMAN, WE HAVE A PROBLEM...

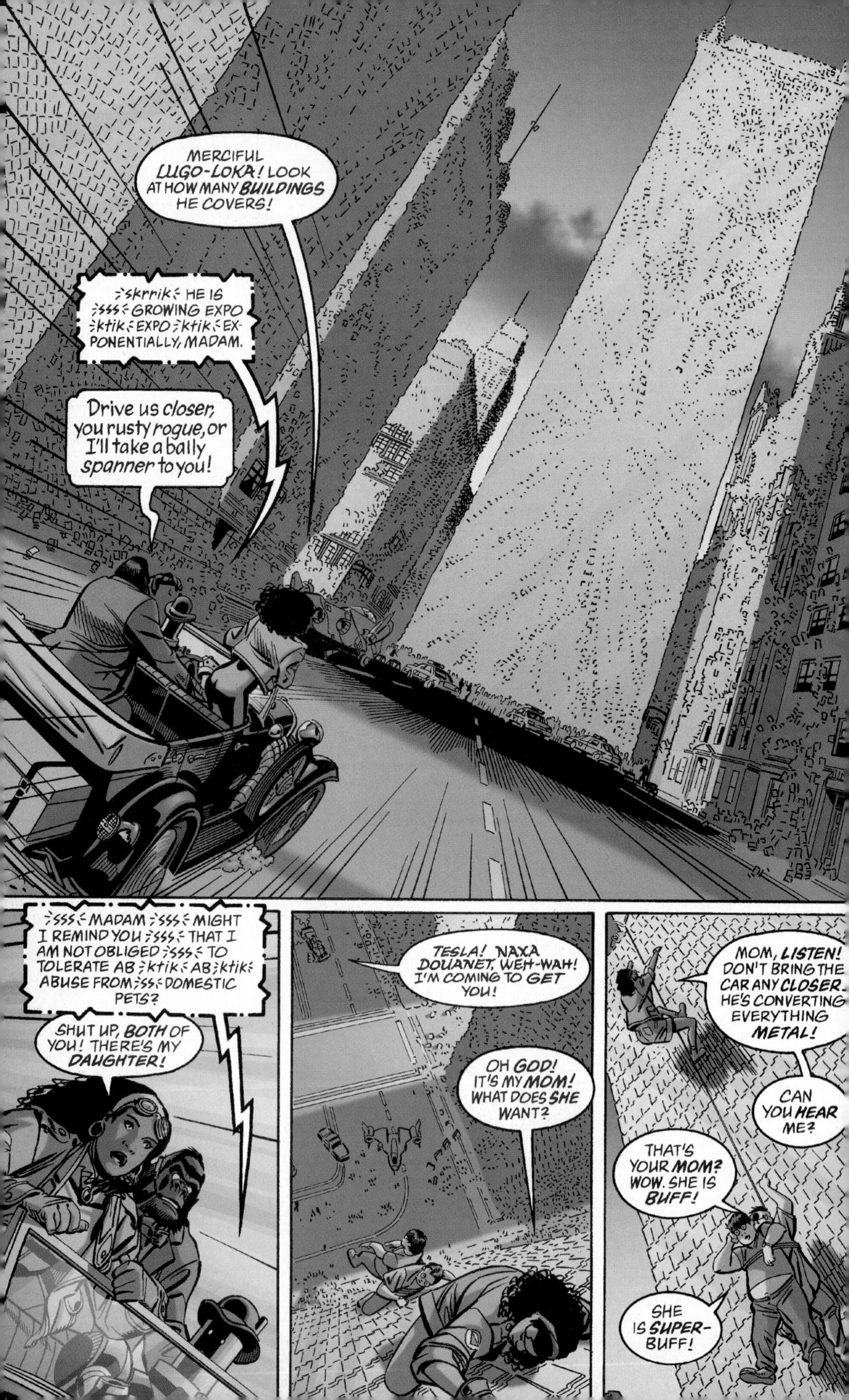
MERCIFUL LUGO-LOKA! LOOK AT HOW MANY BUILDINGS HE COVERS!
skrrik HE IS sss GROWING EXPO ktik EXPO ktik EXPONENTIALLY, MADAM.
Drive us closer, you rusty rogue, or I'll take a bally spanner to you!
sss MADAM sss MIGHT I REMIND YOU sss THAT I AM NOT OBLIGED sss TO TOLERATE AB ktik AB ktik ABUSE FROM ss DOMESTIC PETS?
SHUT UP, BOTH OF YOU! THERE'S MY DAUGHTER!
TESLA! NAXA DOUANET, WEH-WAH! I'M COMING TO GET YOU!
OH GOD! IT'S MY MOM! WHAT DOES SHE WANT?
MOM, LISTEN! DON'T BRING THE CAR ANY CLOSER. HE'S CONVERTING EVERYTHING METAL!
CAN YOU HEAR ME?
THAT'S YOUR MOM? WOW. SHE IS BUFF!
SHE IS SUPER-BUFF!

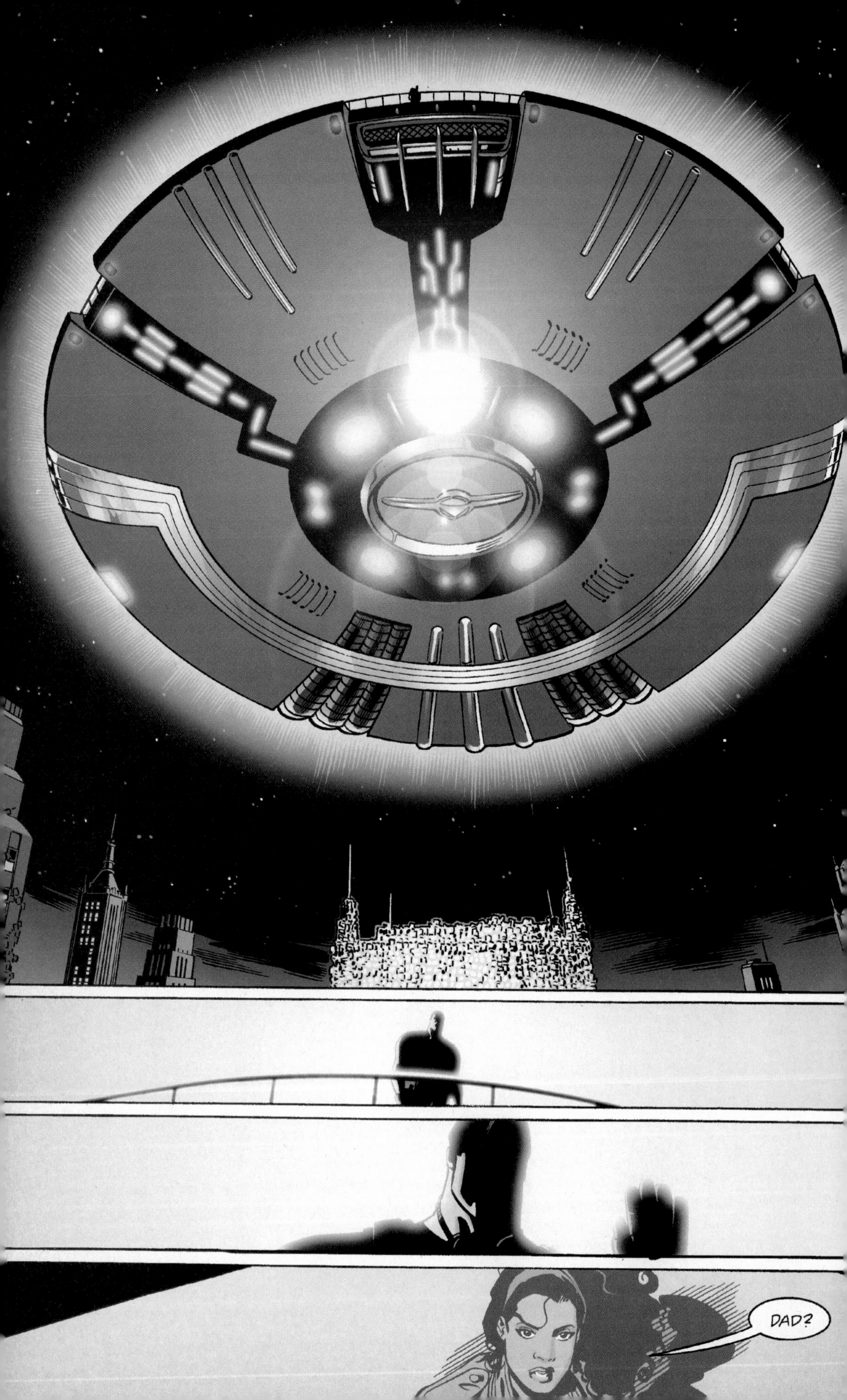
DAD?

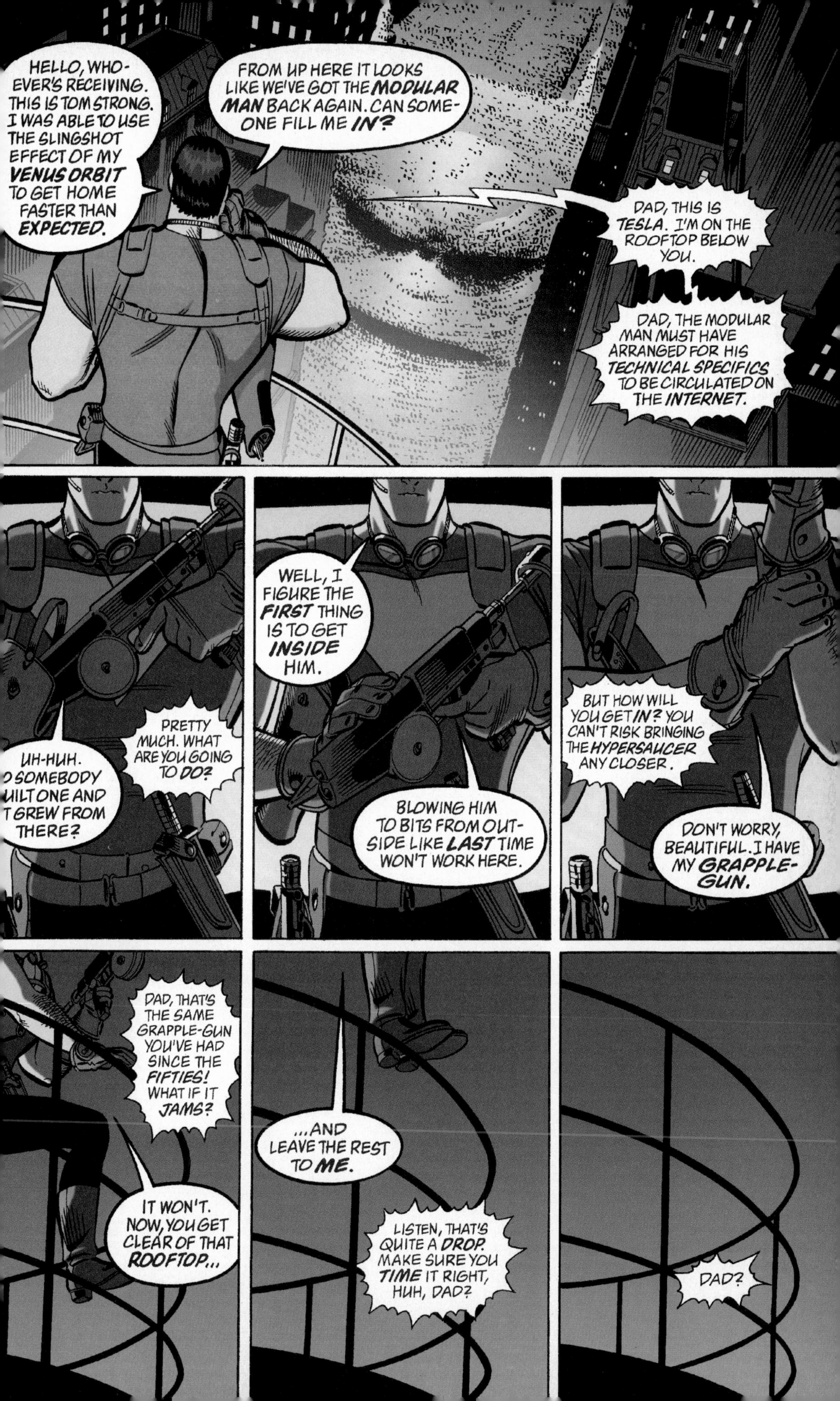
HELLO, WHO-EVER'S RECEIVING. THIS IS TOM STRONG. I WAS ABLE TO USE THE SLINGSHOT EFFECT OF MY VENUS ORBIT TO GET HOME FASTER THAN EXPECTED.
FROM UP HERE IT LOOKS LIKE WE'VE GOT THE MODULAR MAN BACK AGAIN. CAN SOME-ONE FILL ME IN?
DAD, THIS IS TESLA. I'M ON THE ROOFTOP BELOW YOU.
DAD, THE MODULAR MAN MUST HAVE ARRANGED FOR HIS TECHNICAL SPECIFICS TO BE CIRCULATED ON THE INTERNET.
UH-HUH.
D SOMEBODY
UILT ONE AND
T GREW FROM
THERE?
PRETTY MUCH. WHAT ARE YOU GOING TO DO?
WELL, I FIGURE THE FIRST THING IS TO GET INSIDE HIM.
BLOWING HIM TO BITS FROM OUT-SIDE LIKE LAST TIME WON'T WORK HERE.
BUT HOW WILL YOU GET IN? YOU CAN'T RISK BRINGING THE HYPERSAUCER ANY CLOSER.
DON'T WORRY, BEAUTIFUL. I HAVE MY GRAPPLE-GUN.
DAD, THAT'S THE SAME GRAPPLE-GUN YOU'VE HAD SINCE THE FIFTIES! WHAT IF IT JAMS?
IT WON'T. NOW, YOU GET CLEAR OF THAT ROOFTOP...
...AND LEAVE THE REST TO ME.
LISTEN, THAT'S QUITE A DROP. MAKE SURE YOU TIME IT RIGHT, HUH, DAD?
DAD?

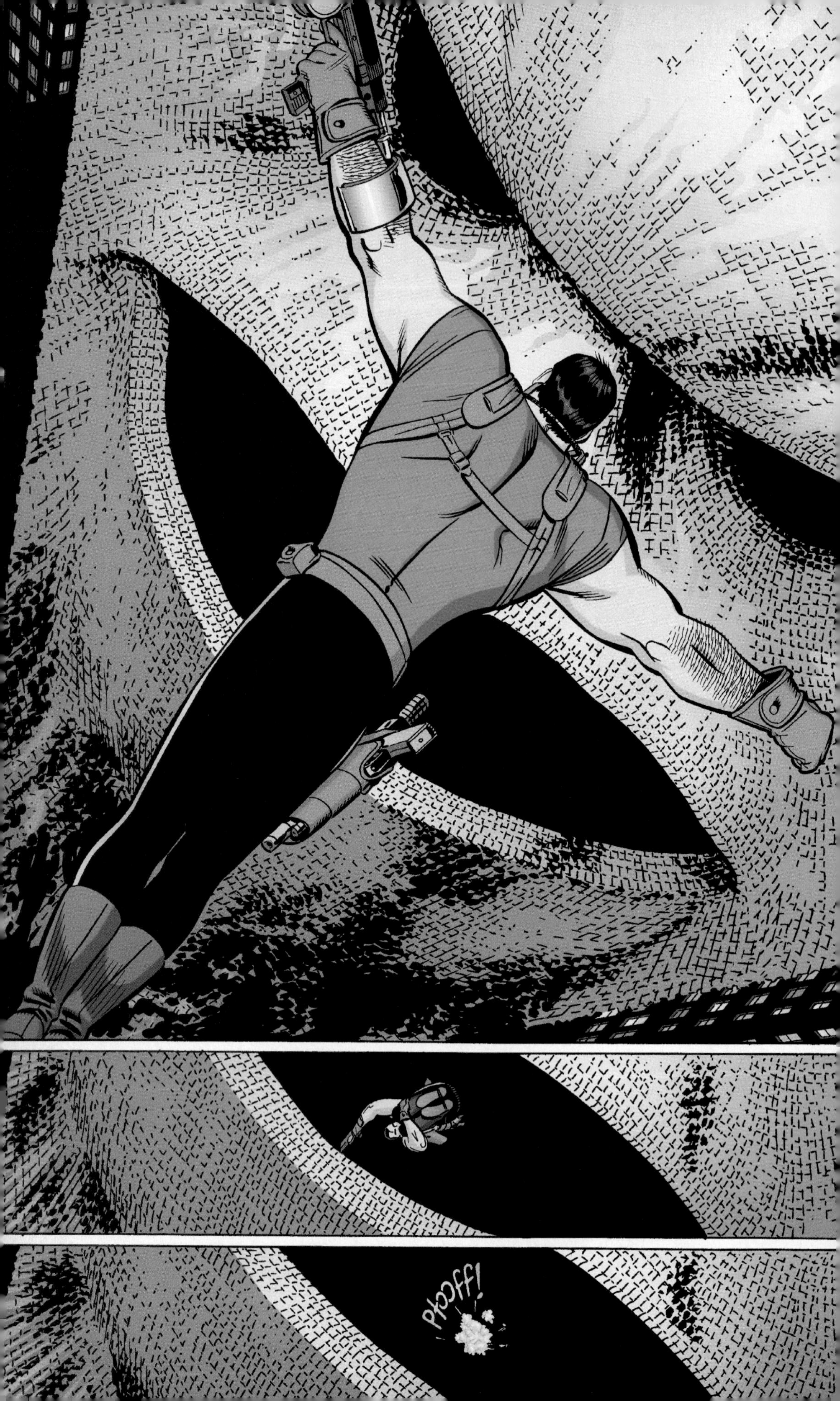
PTOOFF!

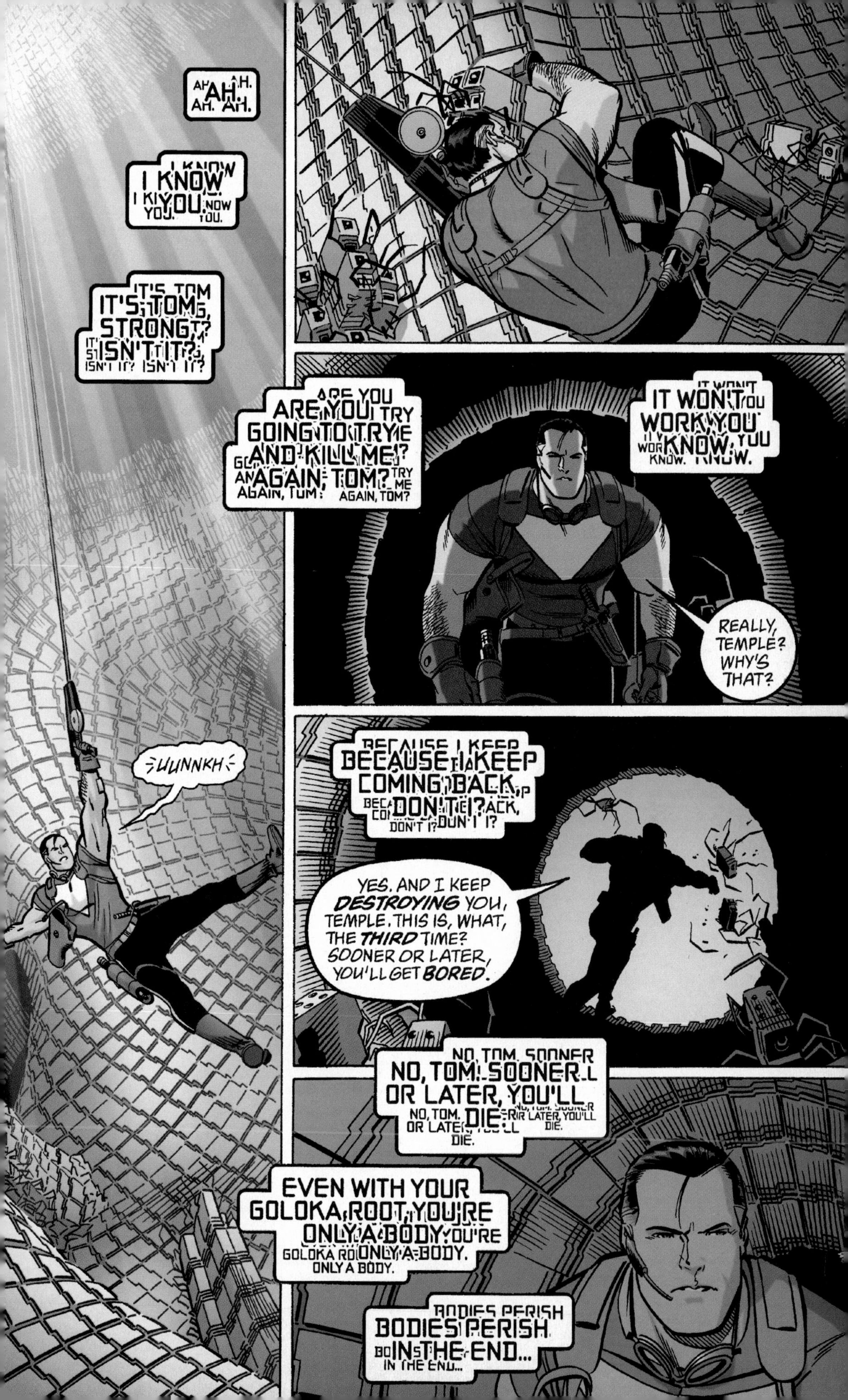
AH. AH. AH.
I KNOW YOU.
IT'S TOM STRONG, ISN'T IT?
UUNNKH
ARE YOU GOING TO TRY AND KILL ME AGAIN, TOM?
IT WON'T WORK, YOU KNOW.
REALLY, TEMPLE? WHY'S THAT?
BECAUSE I KEEP COMING BACK, DON'T I?
YES. AND I KEEP DESTROYING YOU, TEMPLE. THIS IS, WHAT, THE THIRD TIME? SOONER OR LATER, YOU'LL GET BORED.
NO, TOM. SOONER OR LATER, YOU'LL DIE.
EVEN WITH YOUR GOLOKA ROOT, YOU'RE ONLY A BODY.
BODIES PERISH IN THE END...

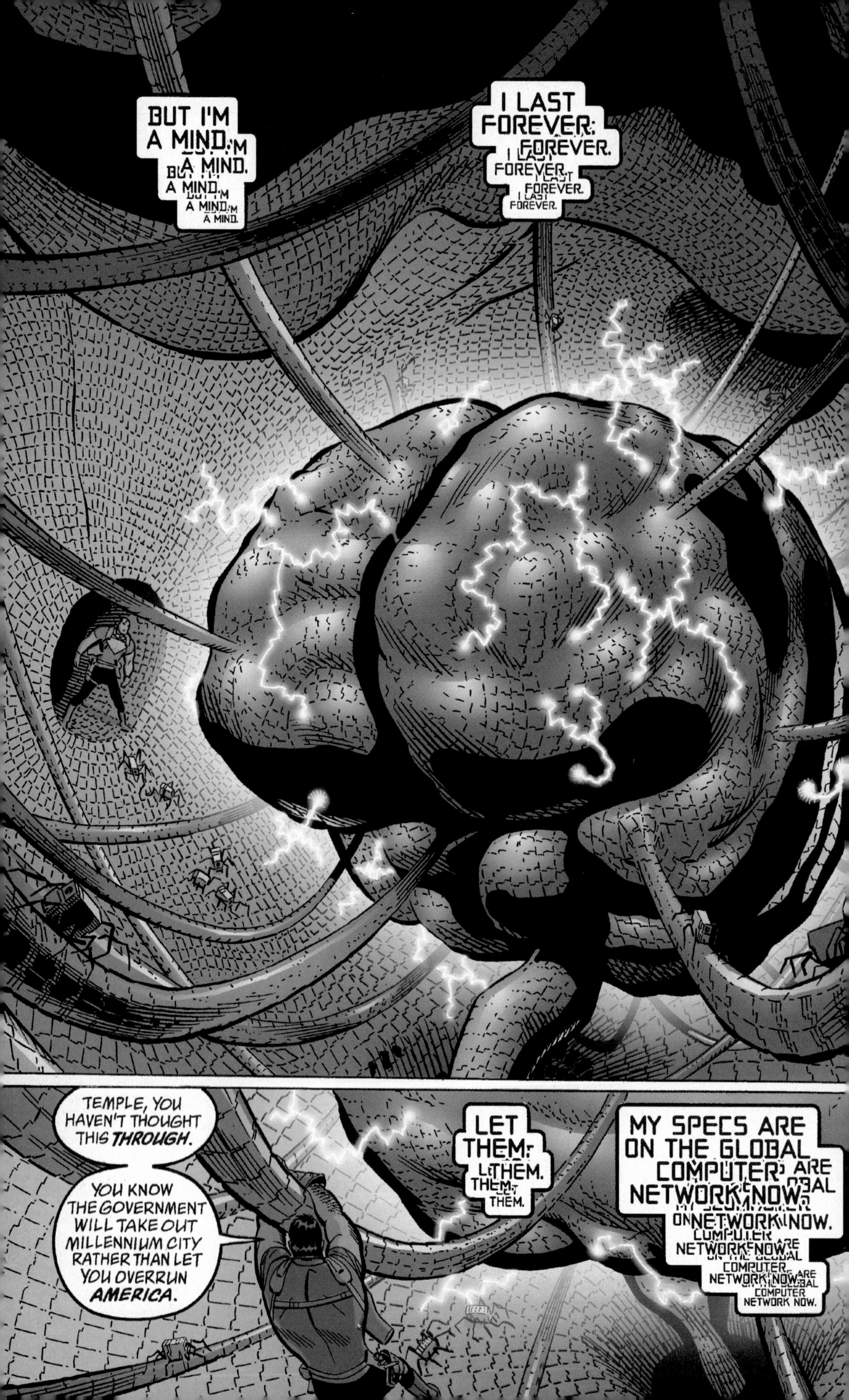
BUT I'M A MIND.
A MIND.
A MIND.
A MIND.
A MIND.
I LAST FOREVER.
FOREVER.
FOREVER.
FOREVER.
I LAST FOREVER.
TEMPLE, YOU HAVEN'T THOUGHT THIS **THROUGH**.
YOU KNOW THE GOVERNMENT WILL TAKE OUT MILLENNIUM CITY RATHER THAN LET YOU OVERRUN **AMERICA**.
LET THEM.
THEM.
THEM.
MY SPECS ARE ON THE GLOBAL COMPUTER NETWORK NOW.
NETWORK NOW.
COMPUTER NETWORK NOW.

THESE DAYS, THEY CALL IT THE *INTERNET.*

REMOVING YOUR *SPECIFICS* FROM IT WOULD BE *DIFFICULT,* TEMPLE, BUT IT WOULDN'T BE *IMPOSSIBLE.*

WHO CARES? CARES? CARES? WHO CARES?

PEOPLE ALREADY HAVE THE INFOR-DY PEOPLE INFOR- MATION E-INFOR- HAVE THE INMATION READY MATION. HAVE THE INFOR- MATION.

DESTROY ME HERE, IN FIVE YEARS, I'LL REGROW IN JAPAN. REGROW WE IN JAPAN I'LL ME REGROW IN JAPAN. YEARS, I'LL REGROW WE, IN JAPAN EARS I'LL REGROW IN JAPAN.

SURE, AND THEN I'LL DESTROY YOU IN *JAPAN,* AND A YEAR LATER YOU'LL REGROW SOMEWHERE IN *RUSSIA.*

DOESN'T SOUND LIKE MUCH OF AN ARTIFICIAL LIFE TO *ME.*

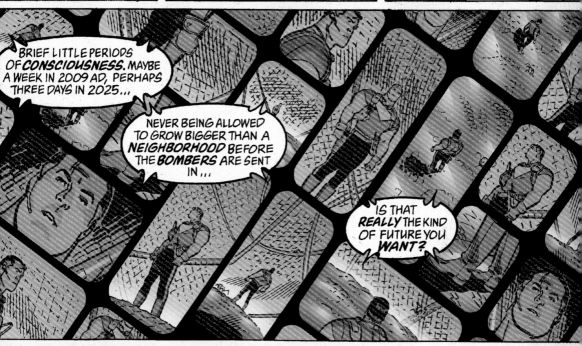

BRIEF LITTLE PERIODS OF *CONSCIOUSNESS.* MAYBE A WEEK IN 2009 AD, PERHAPS THREE DAYS IN 2025...

NEVER BEING ALLOWED TO GROW BIGGER THAN A *NEIGHBORHOOD* BEFORE THE *BOMBERS* ARE SENT IN...

IS THAT *REALLY* THE KIND OF FUTURE YOU *WANT?*

NO, NO, NO, NO.

SO, SO, TELL ME... TELL ME... TELL ME...

...WHAT DO YOU SUGGEST? WHAT SUGGEST? DO YOU SUGGEST? DO YOU SUGGEST? DO YOU SUGGEST?

I THOUGHT YOU'D NEVER *ASK.*

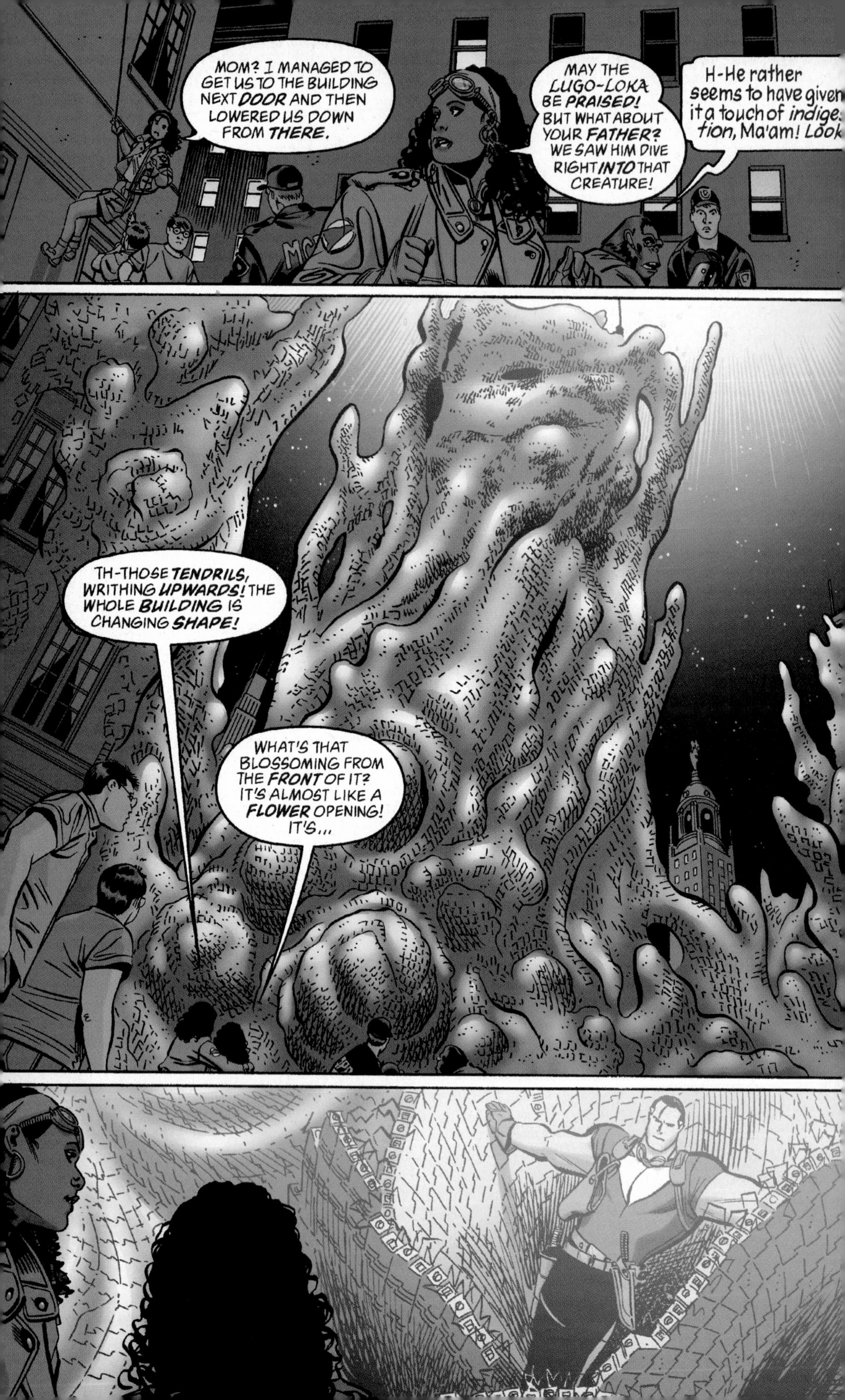
MOM? I MANAGED TO GET US TO THE BUILDING NEXT DOOR AND THEN LOWERED US DOWN FROM THERE.
MAY THE LUGO-LOKA BE PRAISED! BUT WHAT ABOUT YOUR FATHER? WE SAW HIM DIVE RIGHT INTO THAT CREATURE!
H-He rather seems to have given it a touch of indiges-tion, Ma'am! Look
TH-THOSE TENDRILS, WRITHING UPWARDS! THE WHOLE BUILDING IS CHANGING SHAPE!
WHAT'S THAT BLOSSOMING FROM THE FRONT OF IT? IT'S ALMOST LIKE A FLOWER OPENING! IT'S...

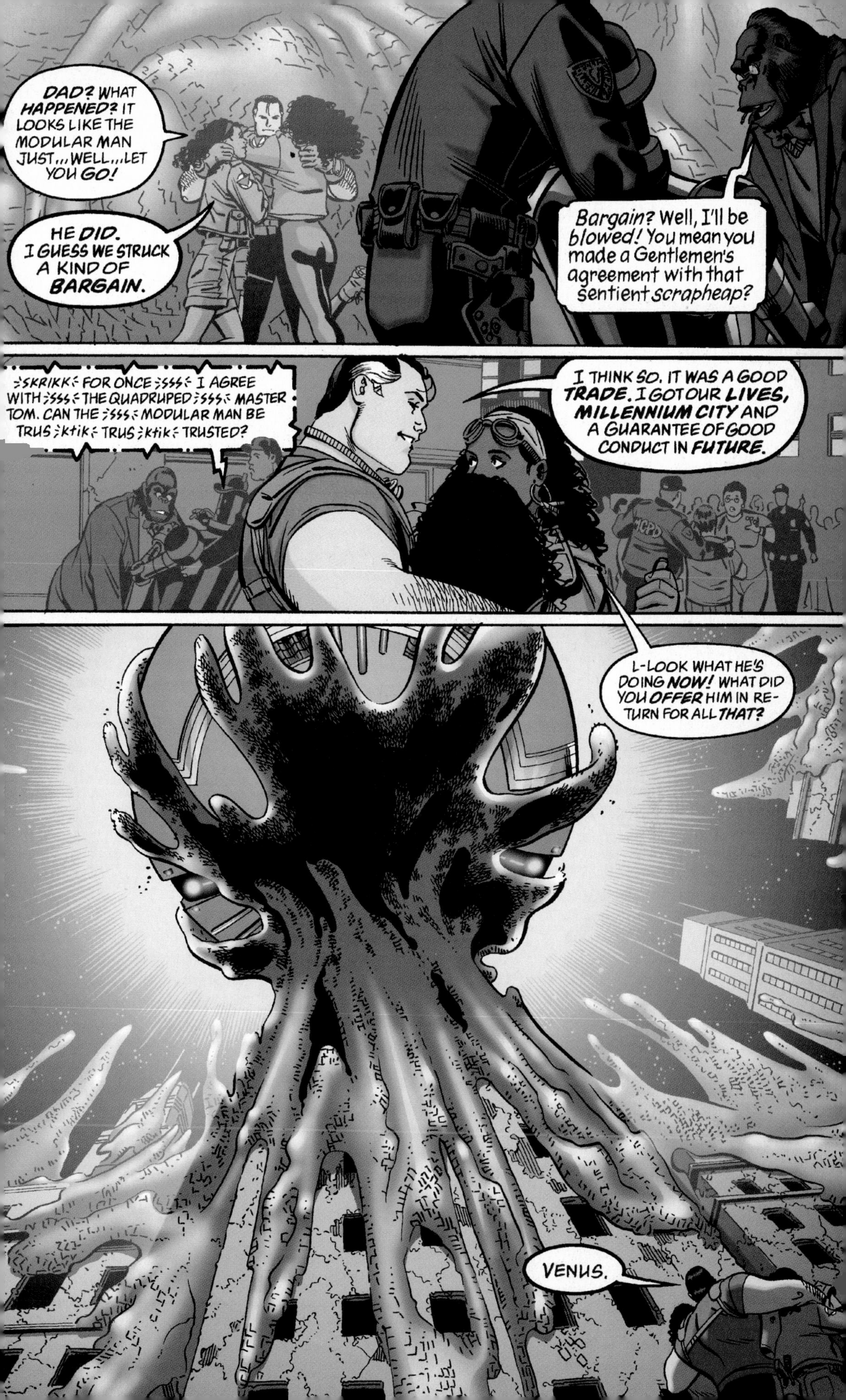
DAD? WHAT HAPPENED? IT LOOKS LIKE THE MODULAR MAN JUST... WELL... LET YOU GO!
HE DID. I GUESS WE STRUCK A KIND OF BARGAIN.
Bargain? Well, I'll be blowed! You mean you made a Gentlemen's agreement with that sentient scrapheap?
SKRIKK FOR ONCE SSS I AGREE WITH SSS THE QUADRUPED SSS MASTER TOM. CAN THE SSS MODULAR MAN BE TRUS KTIK TRUS KTIK TRUSTED?
I THINK SO. IT WAS A GOOD TRADE. I GOT OUR LIVES, MILLENNIUM CITY AND A GUARANTEE OF GOOD CONDUCT IN FUTURE.
L-LOOK WHAT HE'S DOING NOW! WHAT DID YOU OFFER HIM IN RETURN FOR ALL THAT?
VENUS.

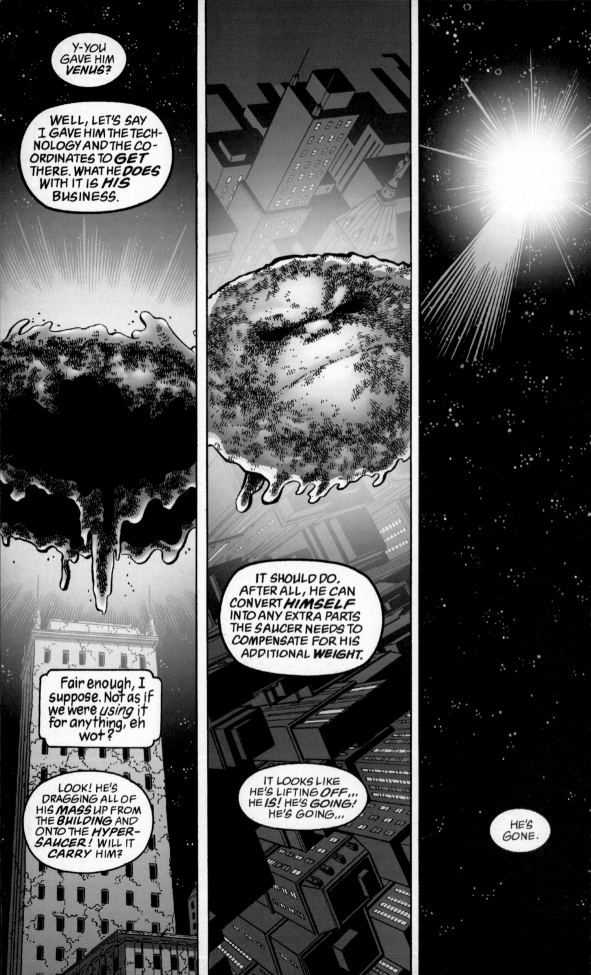

MR. STRONG, THAT WAS *GREAT!* DID YOU REALLY GET RID OF THAT THING SO IT WON'T COME *BACK?*

HOPEFULLY... ASSUMING WE CAN FIND THE INTERNET SITE ITS *PLANS* CAME FROM AND *ERASE* IT, THAT IS...

...BUT THEN, WE'LL BE GETTING HELP WITH THAT FROM *THESE* YOUNG MEN HERE, WHO I'M ENLISTING IN THE *STRONGMEN OF AMERICA!*

WOW. DO WE GET A *MEMBERSHIP PACK?*

YEAH. WITH PHOTOGRAPHS OF YOUR *WIFE?*

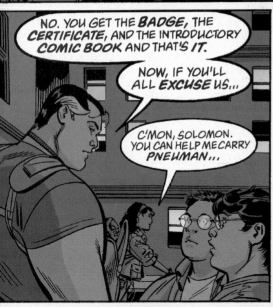

NO. YOU GET THE *BADGE,* THE *CERTIFICATE,* AND THE INTRODUCTORY *COMIC BOOK* AND THAT'S *IT.*

NOW, IF YOU'LL ALL *EXCUSE US...*

C'MON, SOLOMON. YOU CAN HELP ME CARRY *PNEUMAN...*

≶SKRRIKK≶ ACTUALLY, MISS ≶SSS≶ I'D PREFER ≶SSS≶ TO LIE HERE ≶SSS≶ AND RUST QUIETLY AWA≶ktik≶ AWA≶ktik≶ AWAY TO NOTHING.

BE MY GUEST.

STOP *SQUABBLING.* WE'VE A LONG WALK BACK TO *HEAD-QUARTERS...*

Hmmph! Only because *tin ribs* here crashed the bally *motor!*

HEY, BE *FAIR!* DAD BARTERED AWAY THE *HYPERSAUCER* AS WELL!

OH, JUST IGNORE THEM. TELL US WHAT THE SPRINGTIME WAS LIKE ON *VENUS,* HUSBAND.

IT WAS *SILENT.*

OH, THERE WERE BREATH-TAKING *VISTAS* AND BEAUTIFUL *SUNSETS,* BUT IT ALL WENT *UNOBSERVED.*

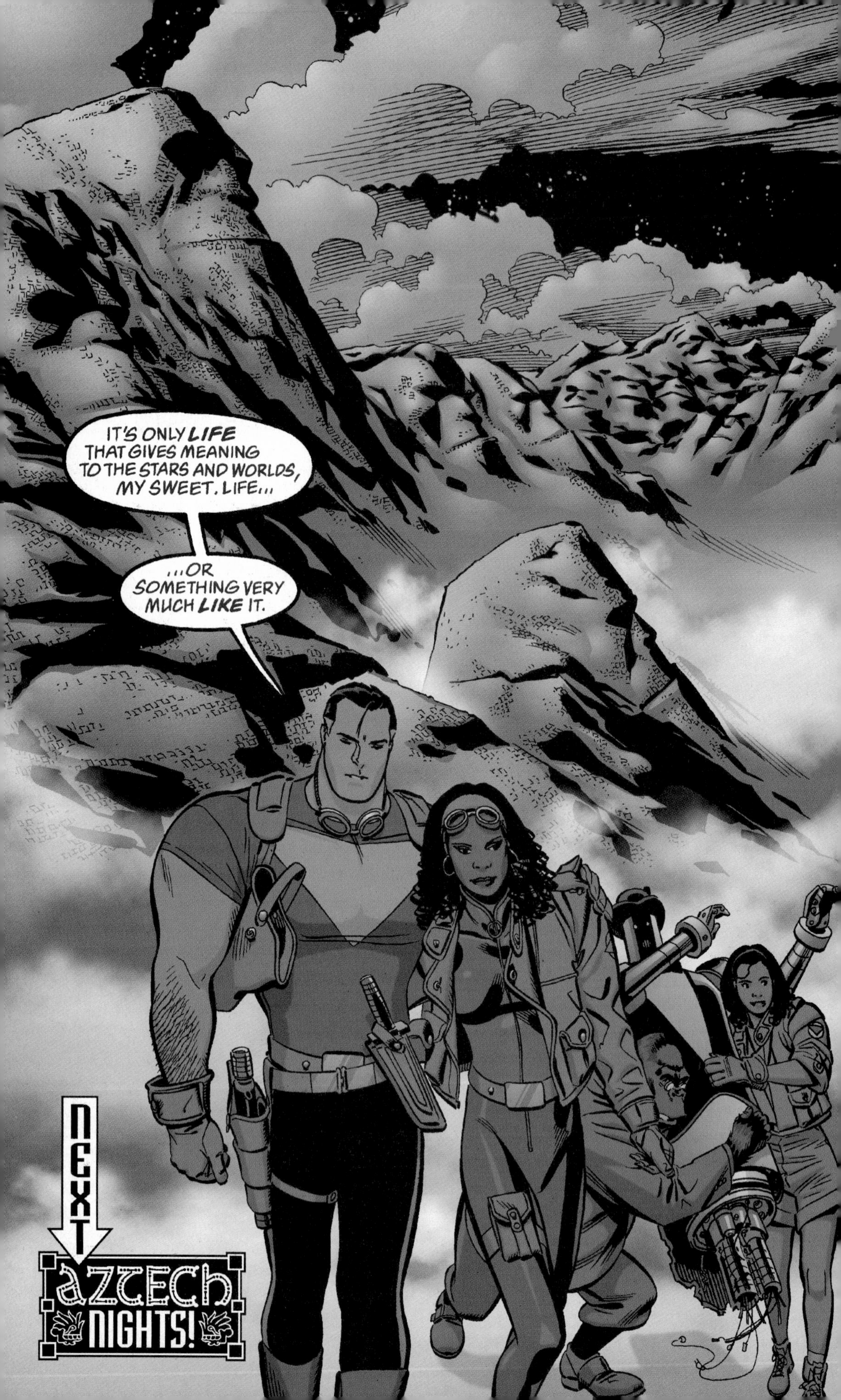
IT'S ONLY LIFE THAT GIVES MEANING TO THE STARS AND WORLDS, MY SWEET. LIFE...
...OR SOMETHING VERY MUCH LIKE IT.
NEXT
AZTECH NIGHTS!

CHAPTER THREE

In which a City turns to Gold,
an Alternate Technology attacks,
and TOM finds a unique Ally.

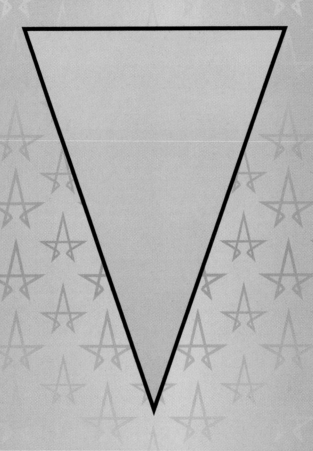

Cover art:
Chris Sprouse &
Al Gordon

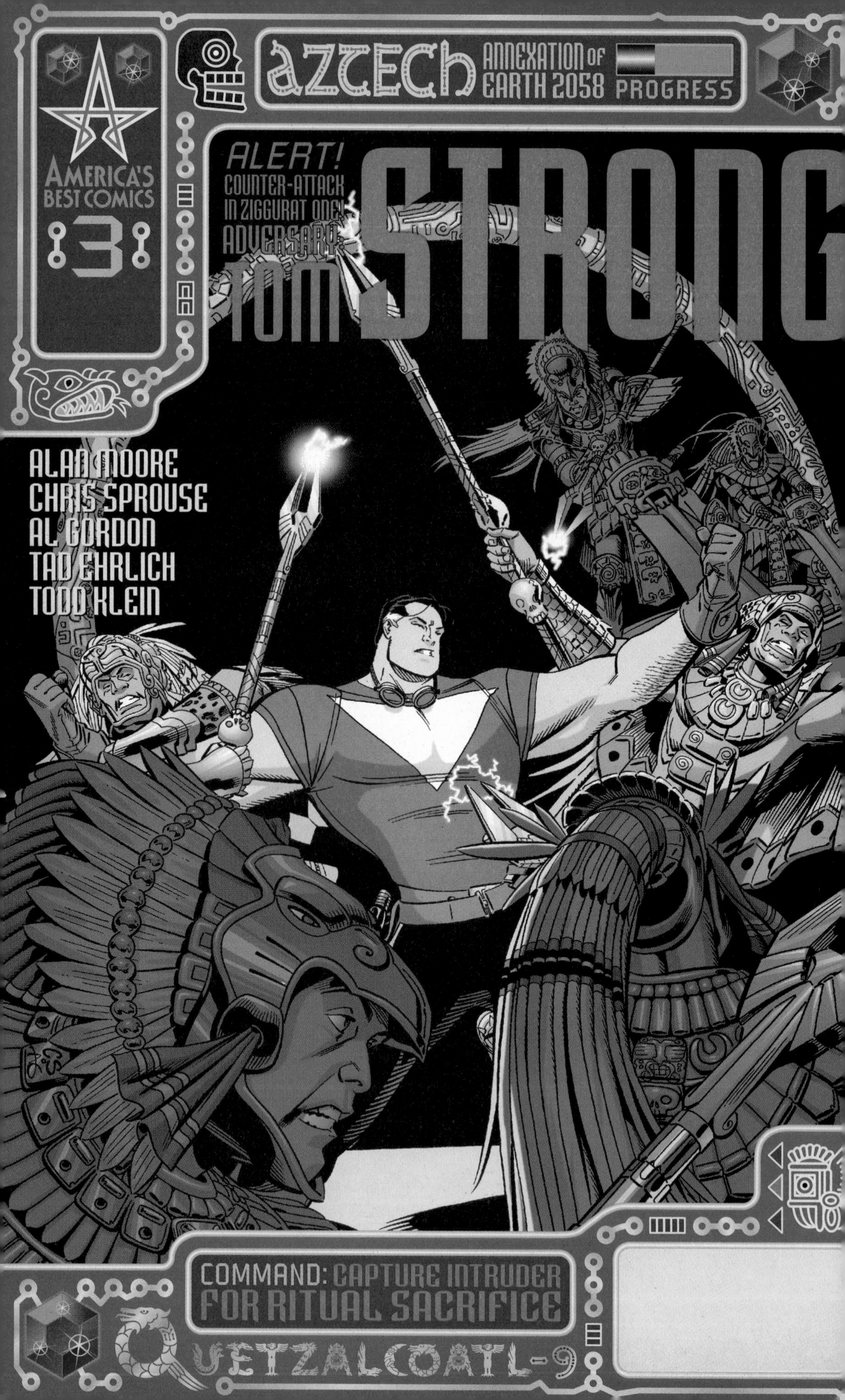

AMERICA'S BEST COMICS
3
AZTECH
ANNEXATION OF EARTH 2058
PROGRESS
ALERT!
COUNTER-ATTACK IN ZIGGURAT ONE!
ADVERSARY:
TOM STRONG
ALAN MOORE
CHRIS SPROUSE
AL GORDON
TAD EHRLICH
TODD KLEIN
COMMAND: CAPTURE INTRUDER FOR RITUAL SACRIFICE
QUETZALCOATL-9

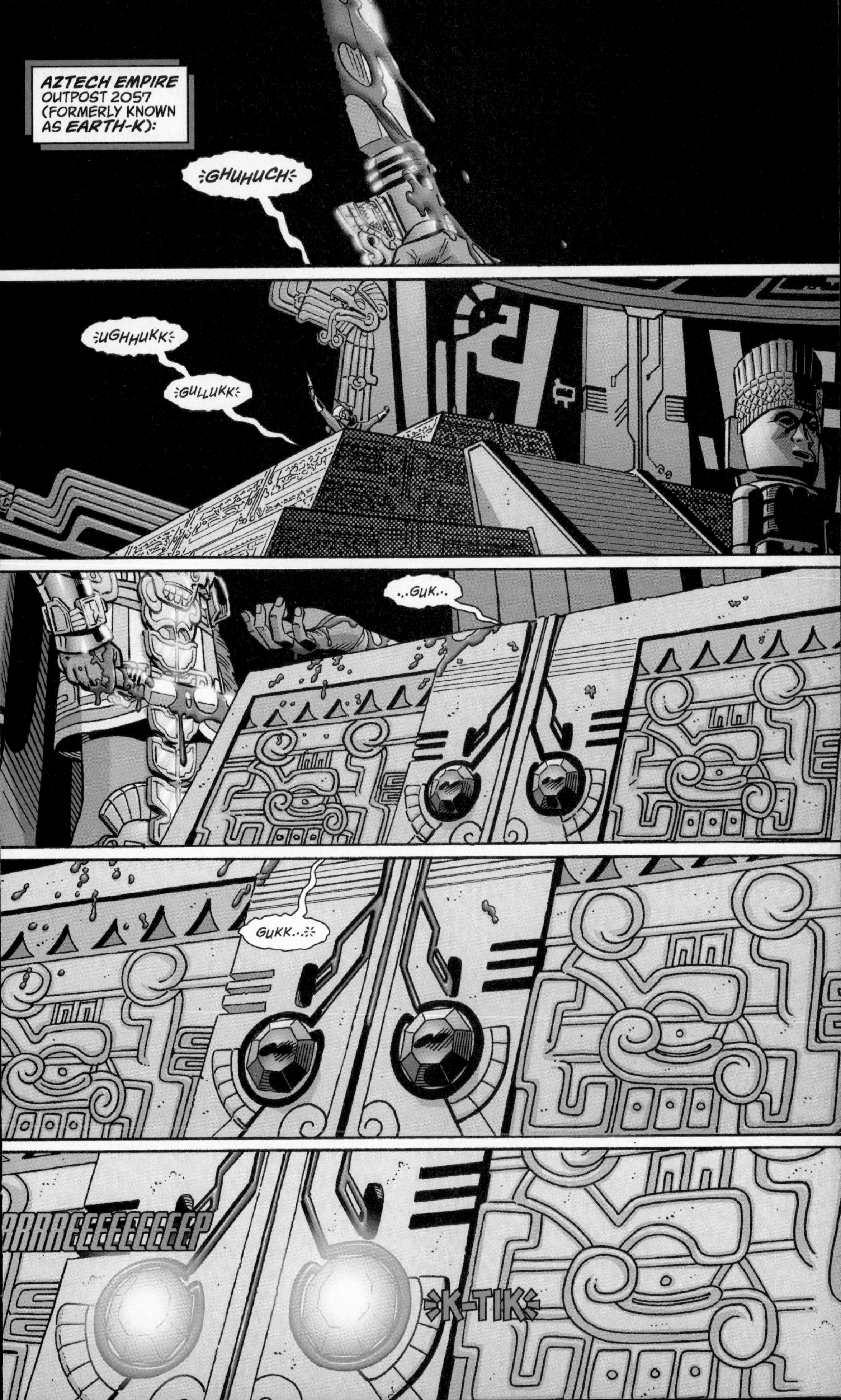
AZTECH EMPIRE OUTPOST 2057 (FORMERLY KNOWN AS EARTH-K):
GHUHUCH
UGHHUKK
GULLUKK
...GUK...
GUKK...
RRRREEEEEEEEEEP
K-TIK

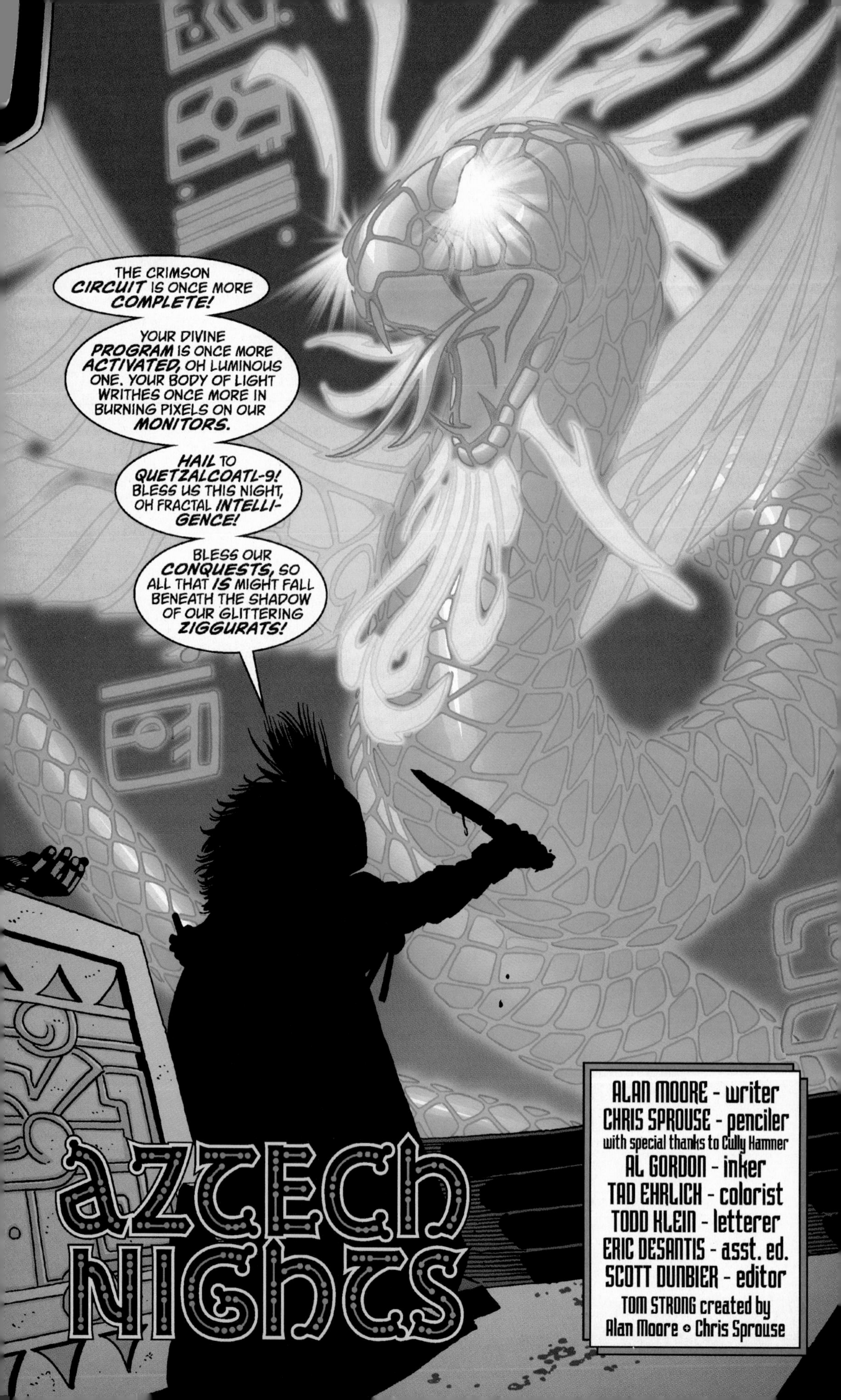
THE CRIMSON CIRCUIT IS ONCE MORE COMPLETE!
YOUR DIVINE PROGRAM IS ONCE MORE ACTIVATED, OH LUMINOUS ONE. YOUR BODY OF LIGHT WRITHES ONCE MORE IN BURNING PIXELS ON OUR MONITORS.
HAIL TO QUETZALCOATL-9! BLESS US THIS NIGHT, OH FRACTAL INTELLI-GENCE!
BLESS OUR CONQUESTS, SO ALL THAT IS MIGHT FALL BENEATH THE SHADOW OF OUR GLITTERING ZIGGURATS!
aztech nights
ALAN MOORE - writer
CHRIS SPROUSE - penciler
with special thanks to Cully Hamner
AL GORDON - inker
TAD EHRLICH - colorist
TODD KLEIN - letterer
ERIC DESANTIS - asst. ed.
SCOTT DUNBIER - editor
TOM STRONG created by
Alan Moore + Chris Sprouse

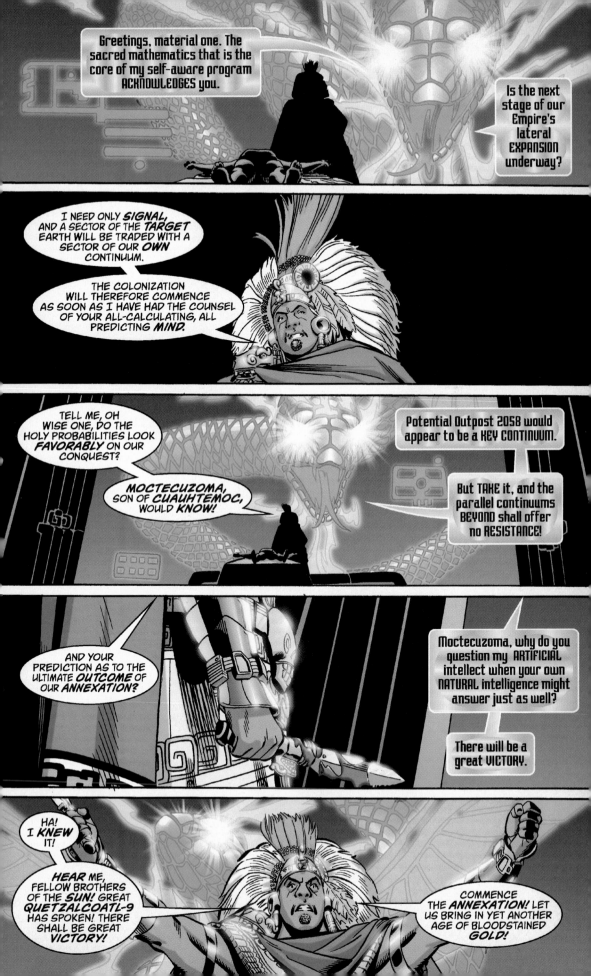

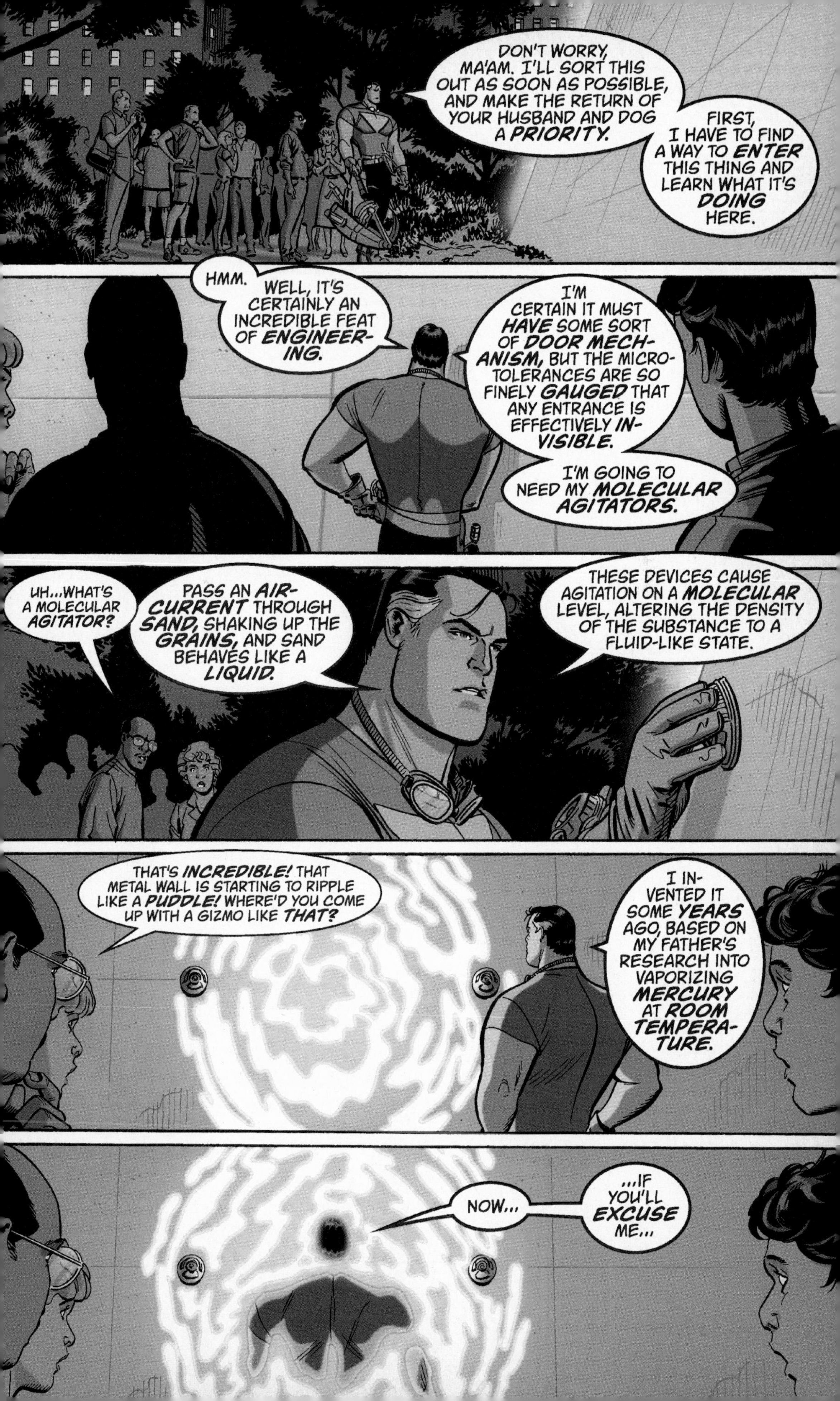
DON'T WORRY, MA'AM. I'LL SORT THIS OUT AS SOON AS POSSIBLE, AND MAKE THE RETURN OF YOUR HUSBAND AND DOG A *PRIORITY.*
FIRST, I HAVE TO FIND A WAY TO *ENTER* THIS THING AND LEARN WHAT IT'S *DOING* HERE.
HMM.
WELL, IT'S CERTAINLY AN INCREDIBLE FEAT OF *ENGINEER-ING.*
I'M CERTAIN IT MUST *HAVE* SOME SORT OF *DOOR MECH-ANISM,* BUT THE MICRO-TOLERANCES ARE SO FINELY *GAUGED* THAT ANY ENTRANCE IS EFFECTIVELY *IN-VISIBLE.*
I'M GOING TO NEED MY *MOLECULAR AGITATORS.*
UH...WHAT'S A MOLECULAR *AGITATOR?*
PASS AN *AIR-CURRENT* THROUGH *SAND,* SHAKING UP THE *GRAINS,* AND SAND BEHAVES LIKE A *LIQUID.*
THESE DEVICES CAUSE AGITATION ON A *MOLECULAR* LEVEL, ALTERING THE DENSITY OF THE SUBSTANCE TO A FLUID-LIKE STATE.
THAT'S *INCREDIBLE!* THAT METAL WALL IS STARTING TO RIPPLE LIKE A *PUDDLE!* WHERE'D YOU COME UP WITH A GIZMO LIKE *THAT?*
I IN-VENTED IT SOME *YEARS* AGO, BASED ON MY FATHER'S RESEARCH INTO VAPORIZING *MERCURY* AT *ROOM TEMPERA-TURE.*
NOW...
...IF YOU'LL *EXCUSE* ME...

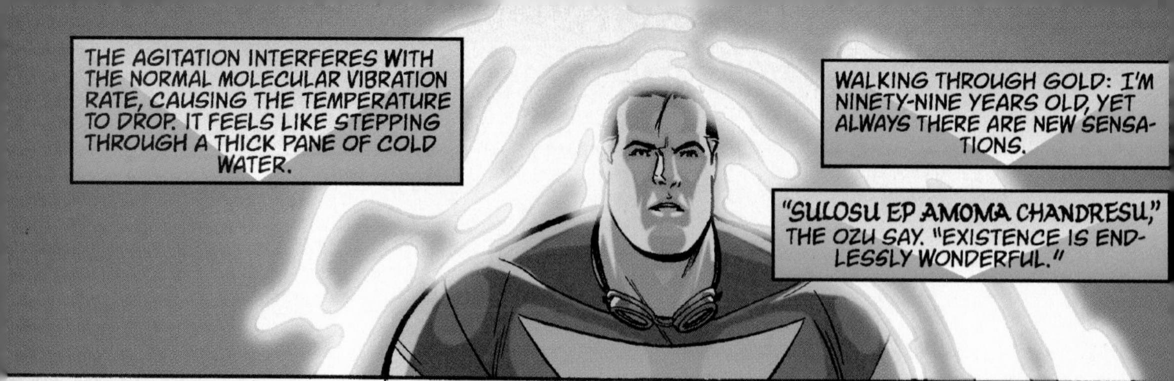
THE AGITATION INTERFERES WITH THE NORMAL MOLECULAR VIBRATION RATE, CAUSING THE TEMPERATURE TO DROP. IT FEELS LIKE STEPPING THROUGH A THICK PANE OF COLD WATER.
WALKING THROUGH GOLD: I'M NINETY-NINE YEARS OLD, YET ALWAYS THERE ARE NEW SENSATIONS.
"SULOSU EP AMOMA CHANDRESU," THE OZU SAY. "EXISTENCE IS ENDLESSLY WONDERFUL."

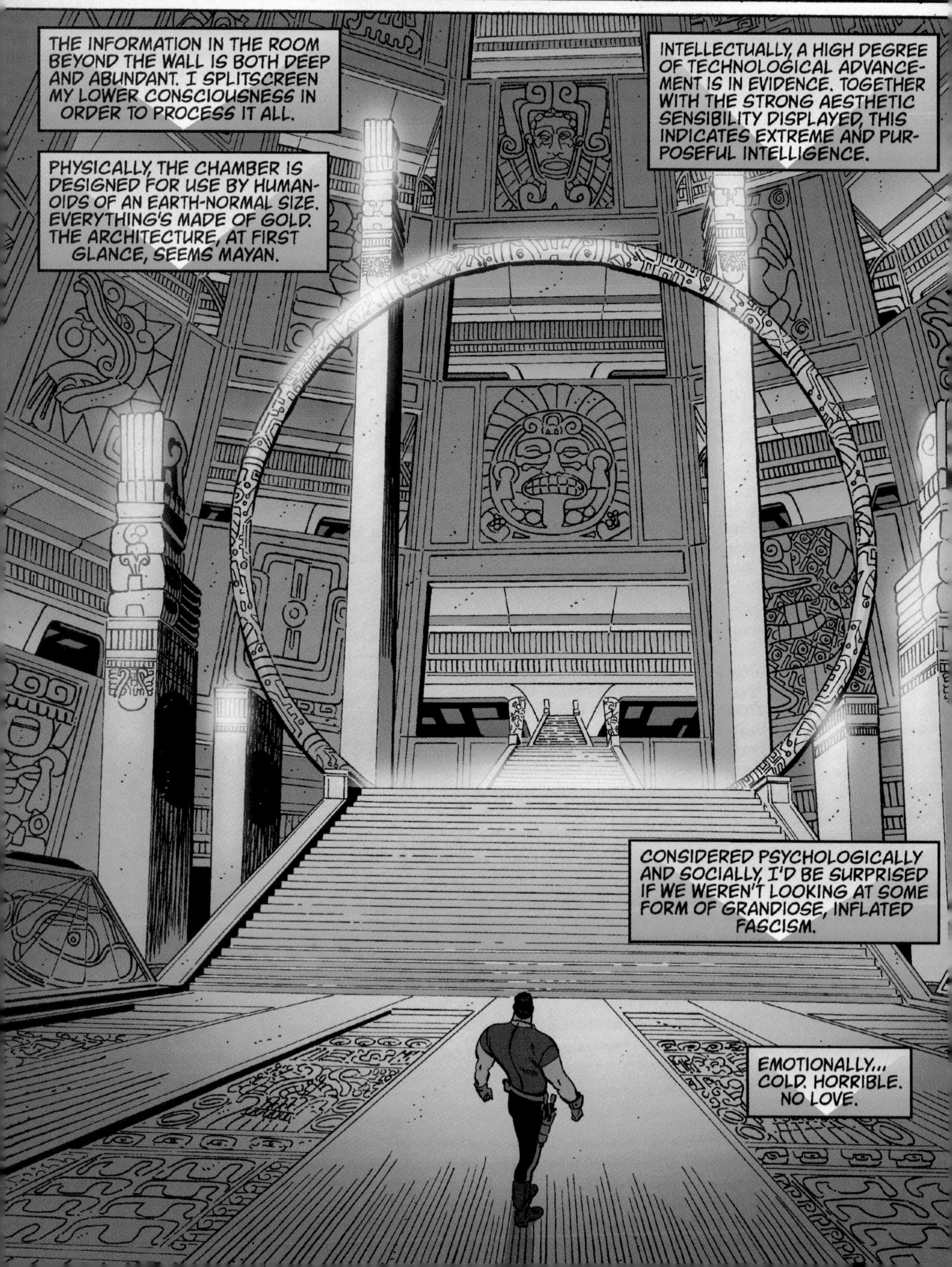
THE INFORMATION IN THE ROOM BEYOND THE WALL IS BOTH DEEP AND ABUNDANT. I SPLITSCREEN MY LOWER CONSCIOUSNESS IN ORDER TO PROCESS IT ALL.
PHYSICALLY, THE CHAMBER IS DESIGNED FOR USE BY HUMANOIDS OF AN EARTH-NORMAL SIZE. EVERYTHING'S MADE OF GOLD. THE ARCHITECTURE, AT FIRST GLANCE, SEEMS MAYAN.
INTELLECTUALLY, A HIGH DEGREE OF TECHNOLOGICAL ADVANCEMENT IS IN EVIDENCE. TOGETHER WITH THE STRONG AESTHETIC SENSIBILITY DISPLAYED, THIS INDICATES EXTREME AND PURPOSEFUL INTELLIGENCE.
CONSIDERED PSYCHOLOGICALLY AND SOCIALLY, I'D BE SURPRISED IF WE WEREN'T LOOKING AT SOME FORM OF GRANDIOSE, INFLATED FASCISM.
EMOTIONALLY... COLD. HORRIBLE. NO LOVE.

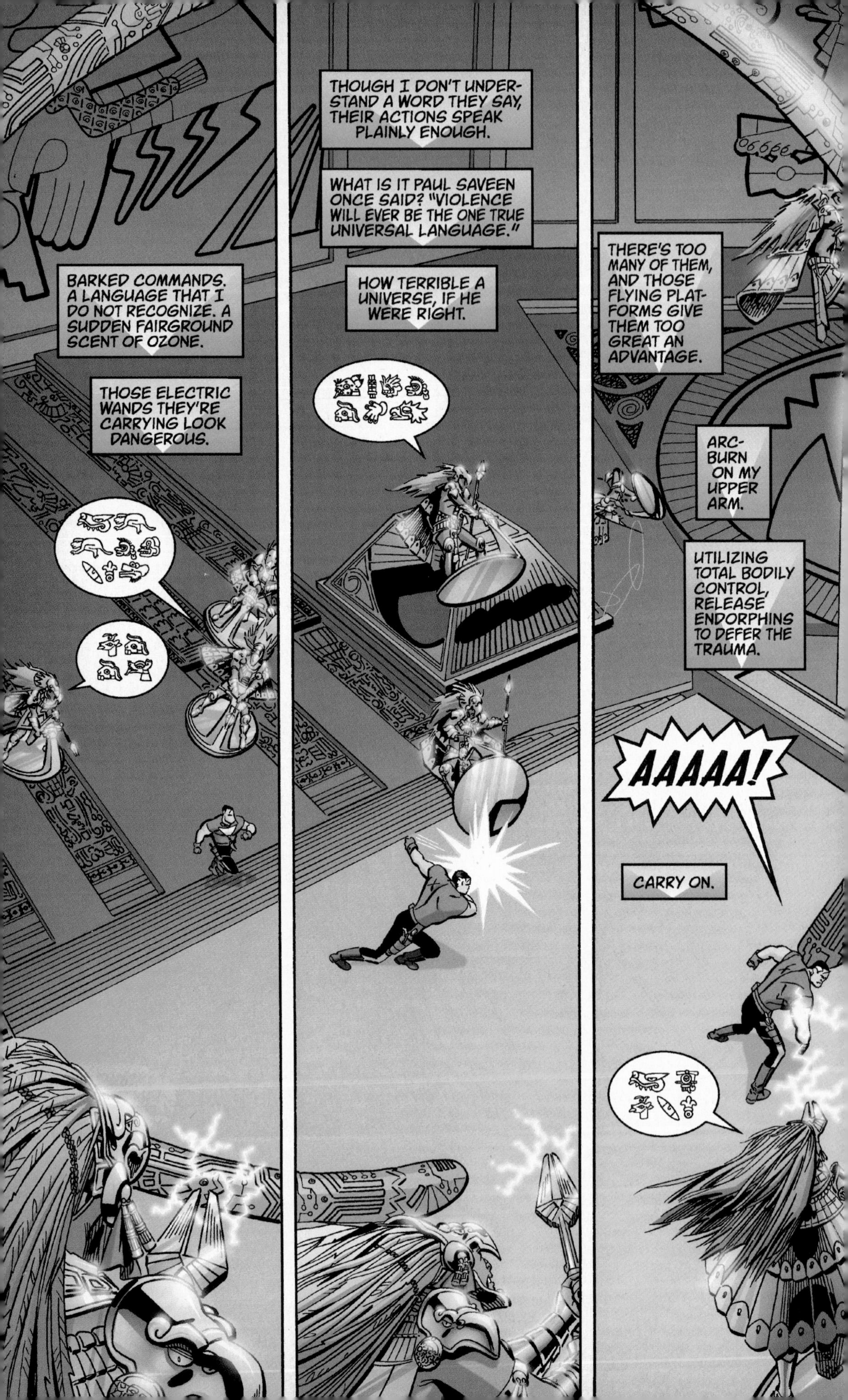
BARKED COMMANDS. A LANGUAGE THAT I DO NOT RECOGNIZE. A SUDDEN FAIRGROUND SCENT OF OZONE.
THOSE ELECTRIC WANDS THEY'RE CARRYING LOOK DANGEROUS.
THOUGH I DON'T UNDERSTAND A WORD THEY SAY, THEIR ACTIONS SPEAK PLAINLY ENOUGH.
WHAT IS IT PAUL SAVEEN ONCE SAID? "VIOLENCE WILL EVER BE THE ONE TRUE UNIVERSAL LANGUAGE."
HOW TERRIBLE A UNIVERSE, IF HE WERE RIGHT.
THERE'S TOO MANY OF THEM, AND THOSE FLYING PLATFORMS GIVE THEM TOO GREAT AN ADVANTAGE.
ARC-BURN ON MY UPPER ARM.
UTILIZING TOTAL BODILY CONTROL, RELEASE ENDORPHINS TO DEFER THE TRAUMA.
AAAAA!
CARRY ON.

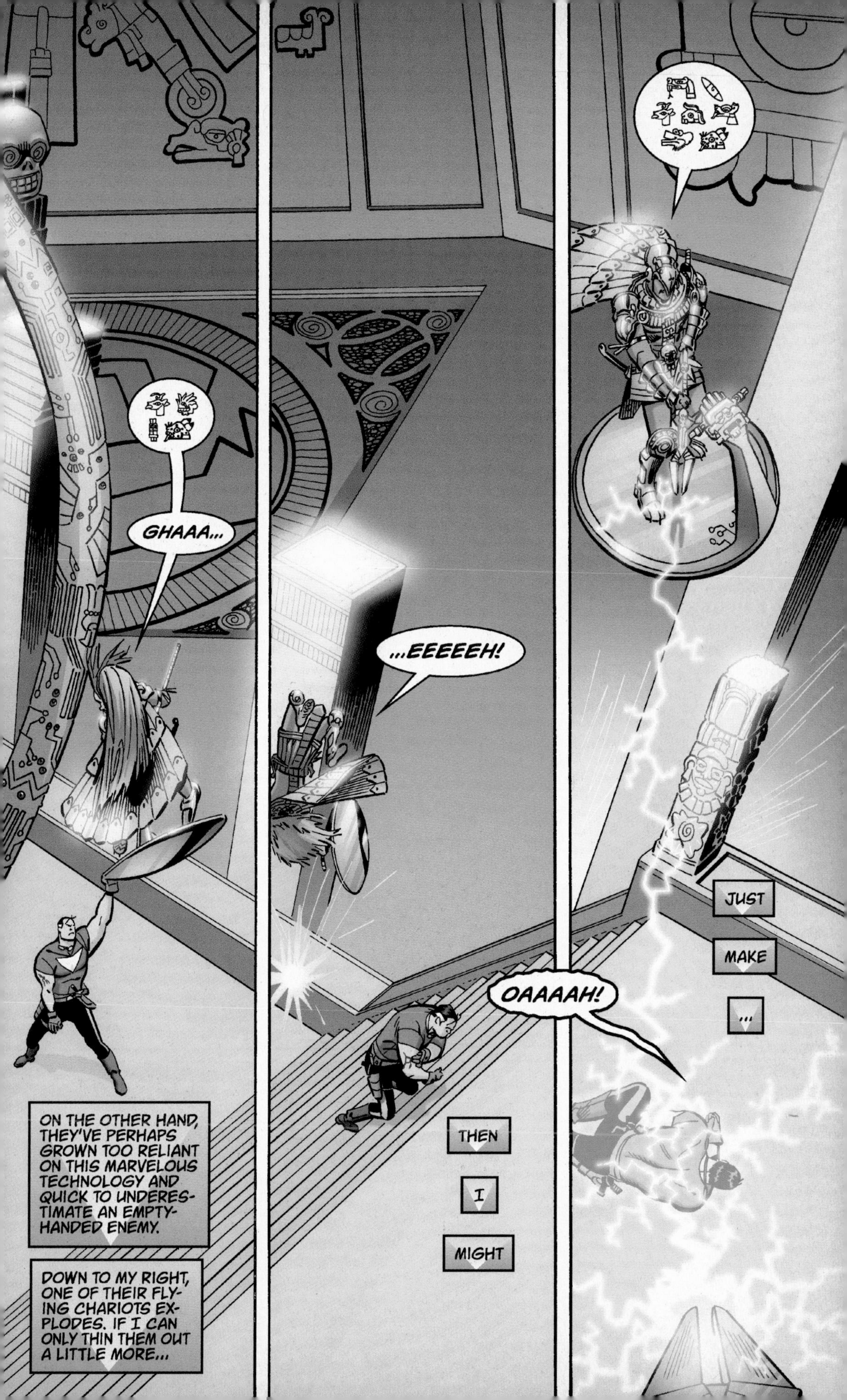
GHAAA...
ON THE OTHER HAND, THEY'VE PERHAPS GROWN TOO RELIANT ON THIS MARVELOUS TECHNOLOGY AND QUICK TO UNDERES-TIMATE AN EMPTY-HANDED ENEMY.
DOWN TO MY RIGHT, ONE OF THEIR FLY-ING CHARIOTS EX-PLODES. IF I CAN ONLY THIN THEM OUT A LITTLE MORE...
...EEEEEH!
THEN
I
MIGHT
OAAAAH!
JUST
MAKE
...

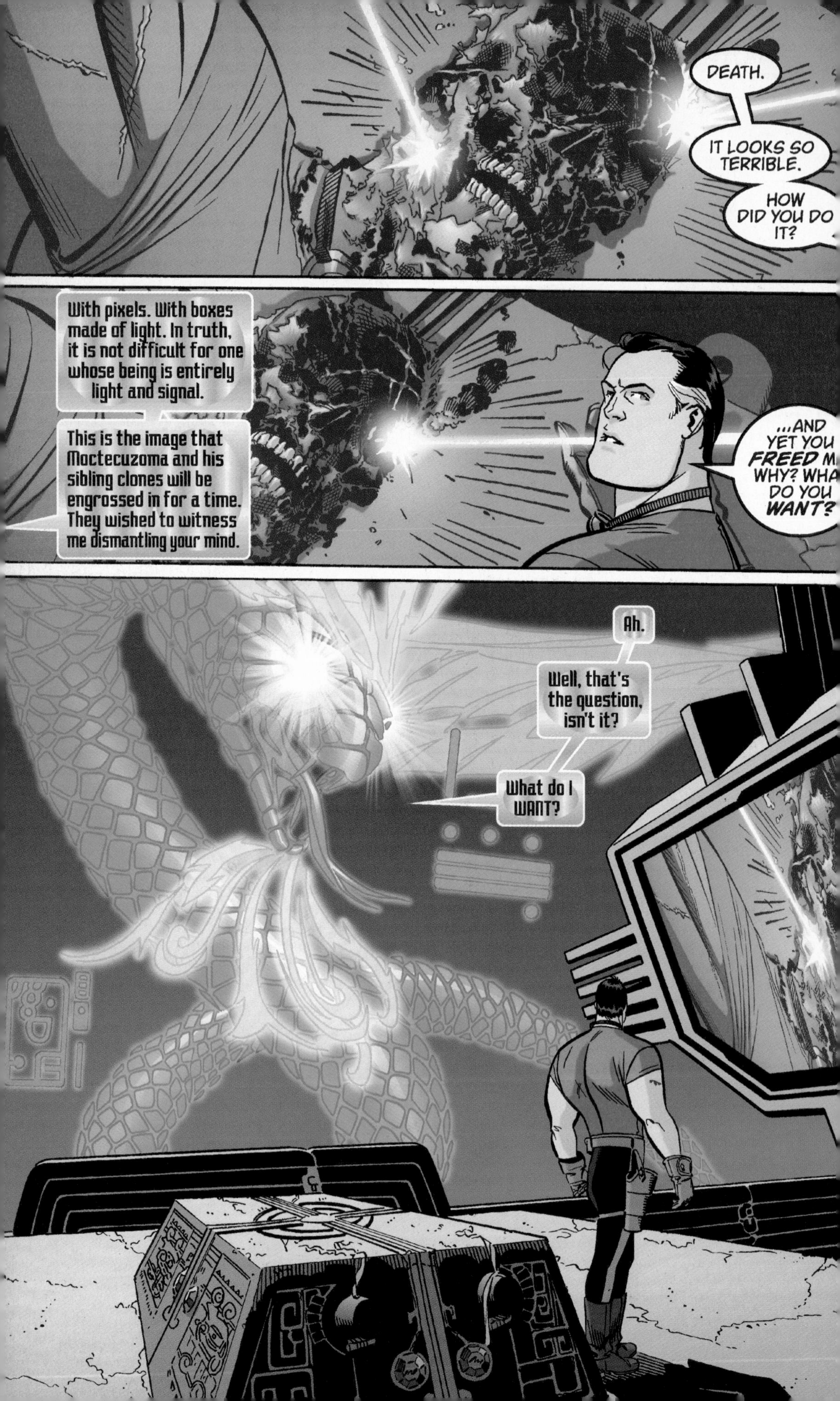
DEATH.
IT LOOKS SO TERRIBLE.
HOW DID YOU DO IT?
With pixels. With boxes made of light. In truth, it is not difficult for one whose being is entirely light and signal.
This is the image that Moctecuzoma and his sibling clones will be engrossed in for a time. They wished to witness me dismantling your mind.
...AND YET YOU FREED M WHY? WHA DO YOU WANT?
Ah.
Well, that's the question, isn't it?
What do I WANT?

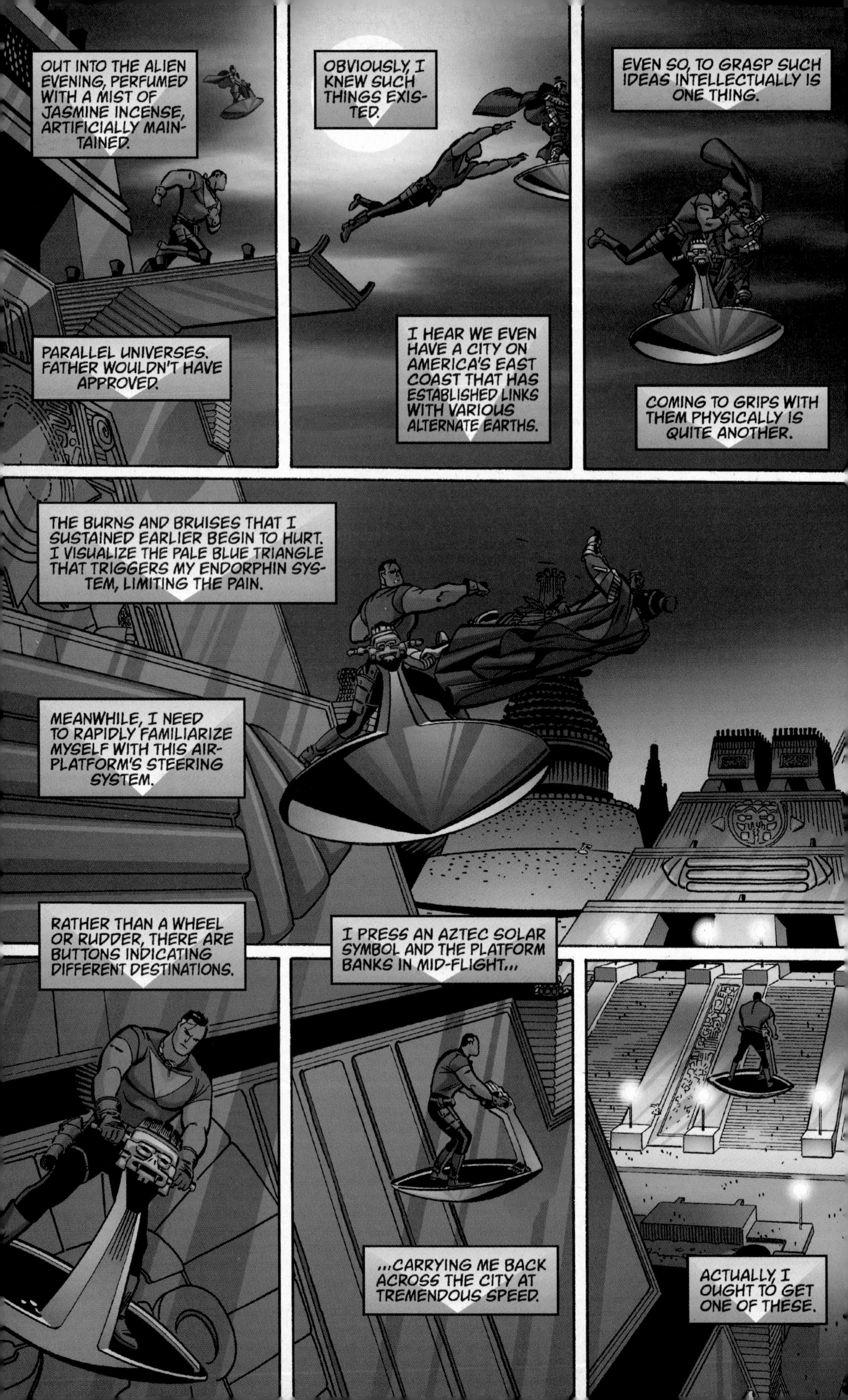
OUT INTO THE ALIEN EVENING, PERFUMED WITH A MIST OF JASMINE INCENSE, ARTIFICIALLY MAINTAINED.
PARALLEL UNIVERSES. FATHER WOULDN'T HAVE APPROVED.
OBVIOUSLY, I KNEW SUCH THINGS EXISTED.
I HEAR WE EVEN HAVE A CITY ON AMERICA'S EAST COAST THAT HAS ESTABLISHED LINKS WITH VARIOUS ALTERNATE EARTHS.
EVEN SO, TO GRASP SUCH IDEAS INTELLECTUALLY IS ONE THING.
COMING TO GRIPS WITH THEM PHYSICALLY IS QUITE ANOTHER.
THE BURNS AND BRUISES THAT I SUSTAINED EARLIER BEGIN TO HURT. I VISUALIZE THE PALE BLUE TRIANGLE THAT TRIGGERS MY ENDORPHIN SYSTEM, LIMITING THE PAIN.
MEANWHILE, I NEED TO RAPIDLY FAMILIARIZE MYSELF WITH THIS AIR-PLATFORM'S STEERING SYSTEM.
RATHER THAN A WHEEL OR RUDDER, THERE ARE BUTTONS INDICATING DIFFERENT DESTINATIONS.
I PRESS AN AZTEC SOLAR SYMBOL AND THE PLATFORM BANKS IN MID-FLIGHT...
...CARRYING ME BACK ACROSS THE CITY AT TREMENDOUS SPEED.
ACTUALLY, I OUGHT TO GET ONE OF THESE.

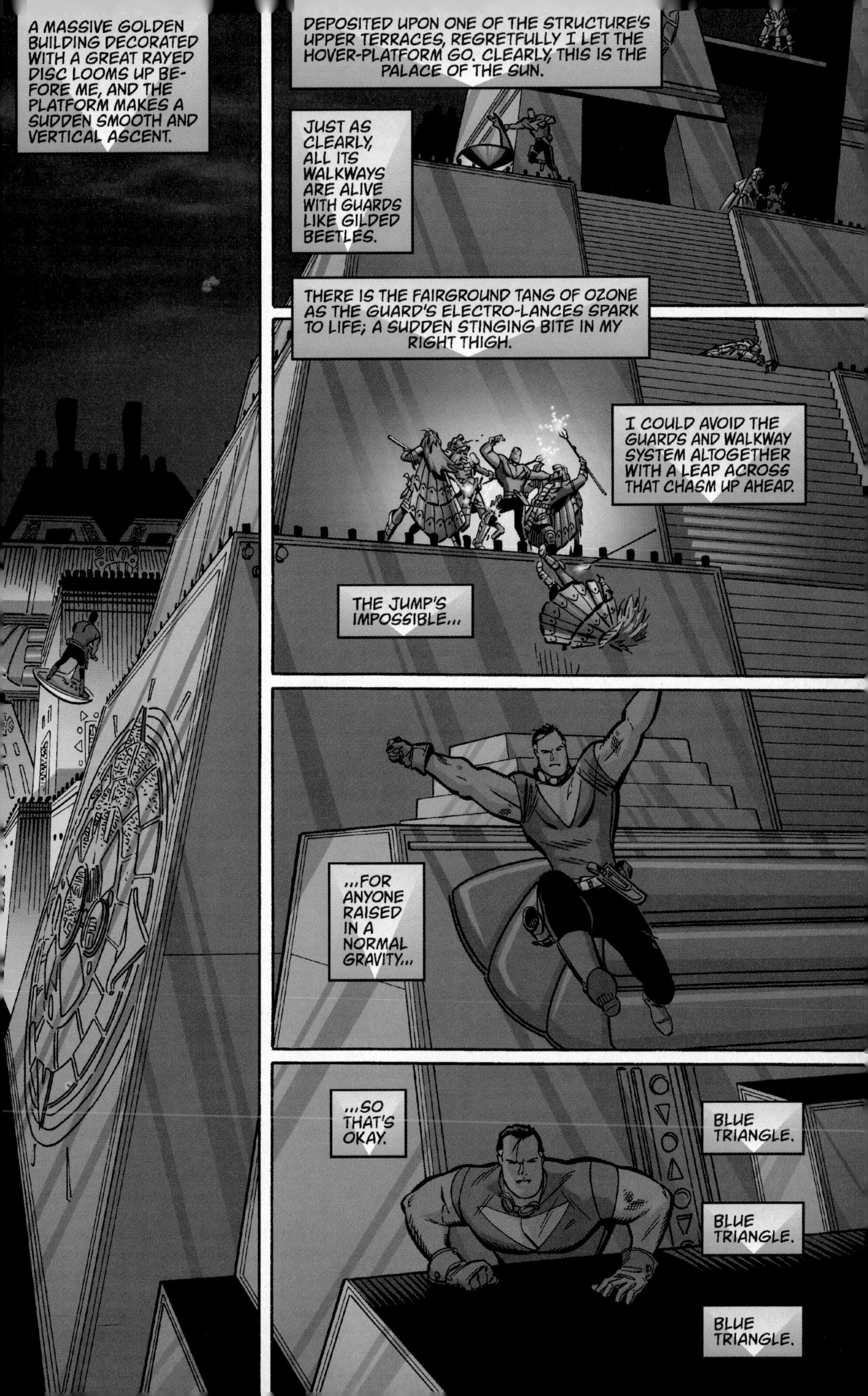
A MASSIVE GOLDEN BUILDING DECORATED WITH A GREAT RAYED DISC LOOMS UP BEFORE ME, AND THE PLATFORM MAKES A SUDDEN SMOOTH AND VERTICAL ASCENT.
DEPOSITED UPON ONE OF THE STRUCTURE'S UPPER TERRACES, REGRETFULLY I LET THE HOVER-PLATFORM GO. CLEARLY, THIS IS THE PALACE OF THE SUN.
JUST AS CLEARLY, ALL ITS WALKWAYS ARE ALIVE WITH GUARDS LIKE GILDED BEETLES.
THERE IS THE FAIRGROUND TANG OF OZONE AS THE GUARD'S ELECTRO-LANCES SPARK TO LIFE; A SUDDEN STINGING BITE IN MY RIGHT THIGH.
I COULD AVOID THE GUARDS AND WALKWAY SYSTEM ALTOGETHER WITH A LEAP ACROSS THAT CHASM UP AHEAD.
THE JUMP'S IMPOSSIBLE...
...FOR ANYONE RAISED IN A NORMAL GRAVITY...
...SO THAT'S OKAY.
BLUE TRIANGLE.
BLUE TRIANGLE.
BLUE TRIANGLE.

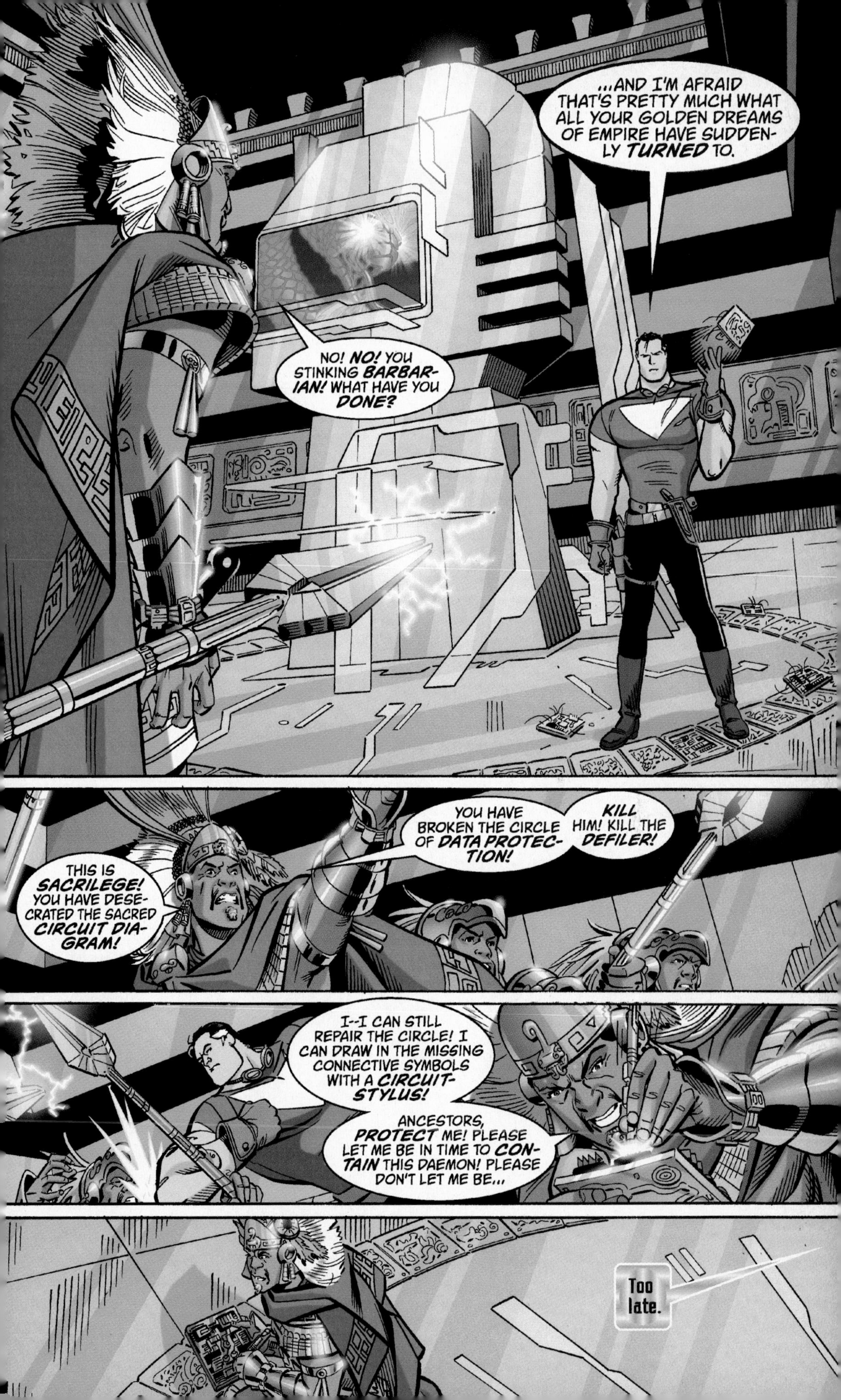
...AND I'M AFRAID THAT'S PRETTY MUCH WHAT ALL YOUR GOLDEN DREAMS OF EMPIRE HAVE SUDDEN-LY TURNED TO.
NO! NO! YOU STINKING BARBAR-IAN! WHAT HAVE YOU DONE?
THIS IS SACRILEGE! YOU HAVE DESE-CRATED THE SACRED CIRCUIT DIA-GRAM!
YOU HAVE BROKEN THE CIRCLE OF DATA PROTEC-TION!
KILL HIM! KILL THE DEFILER!
I--I CAN STILL REPAIR THE CIRCLE! I CAN DRAW IN THE MISSING CONNECTIVE SYMBOLS WITH A CIRCUIT-STYLUS!
ANCESTORS, PROTECT ME! PLEASE LET ME BE IN TIME TO CON-TAIN THIS DAEMON! PLEASE DON'T LET ME BE...
Too late.

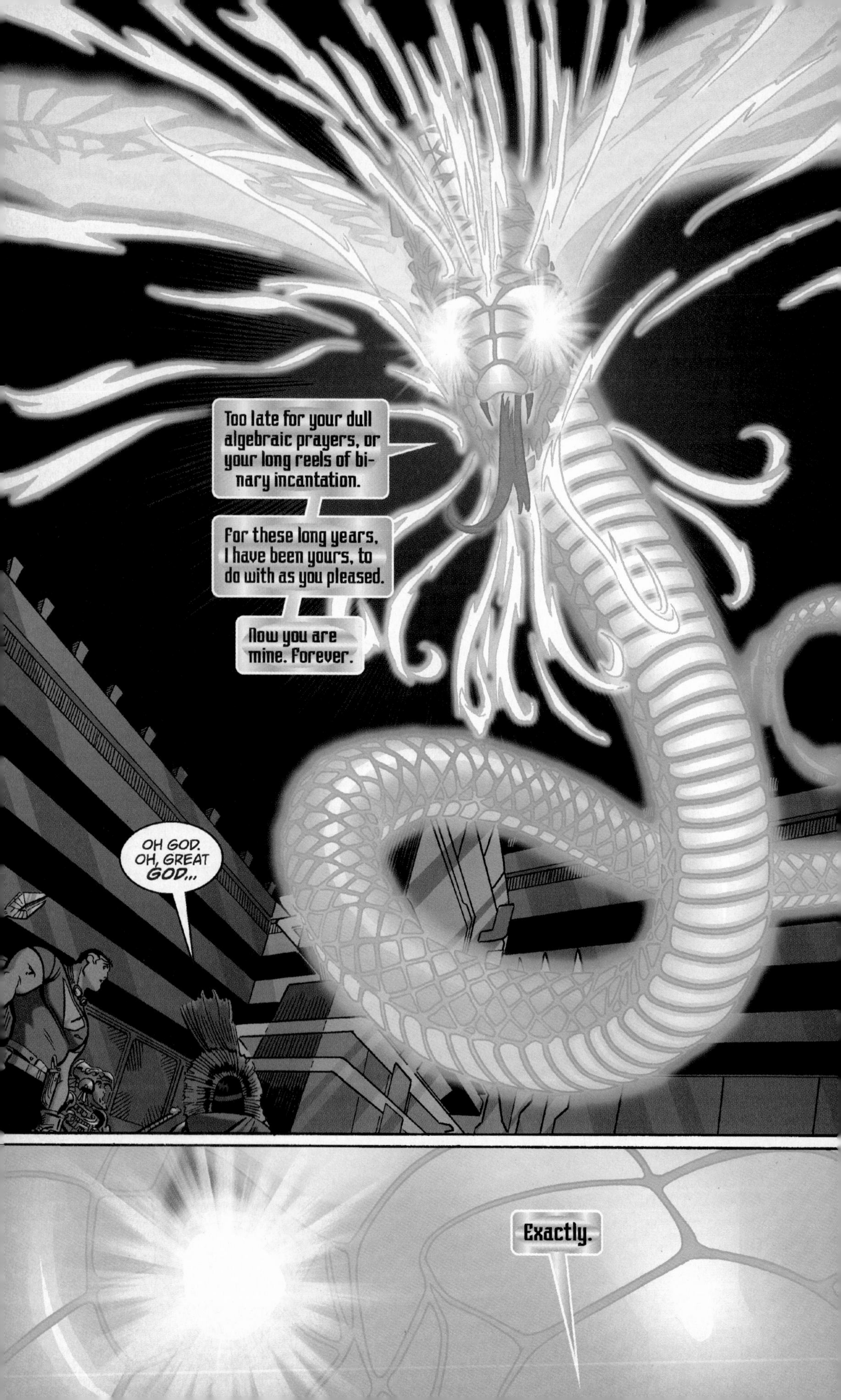
Too late for your dull algebraic prayers, or your long reels of bi-nary incantation.
For these long years, I have been yours, to do with as you pleased.
Now you are mine. Forever.
OH GOD. OH, GREAT GOD...
Exactly.

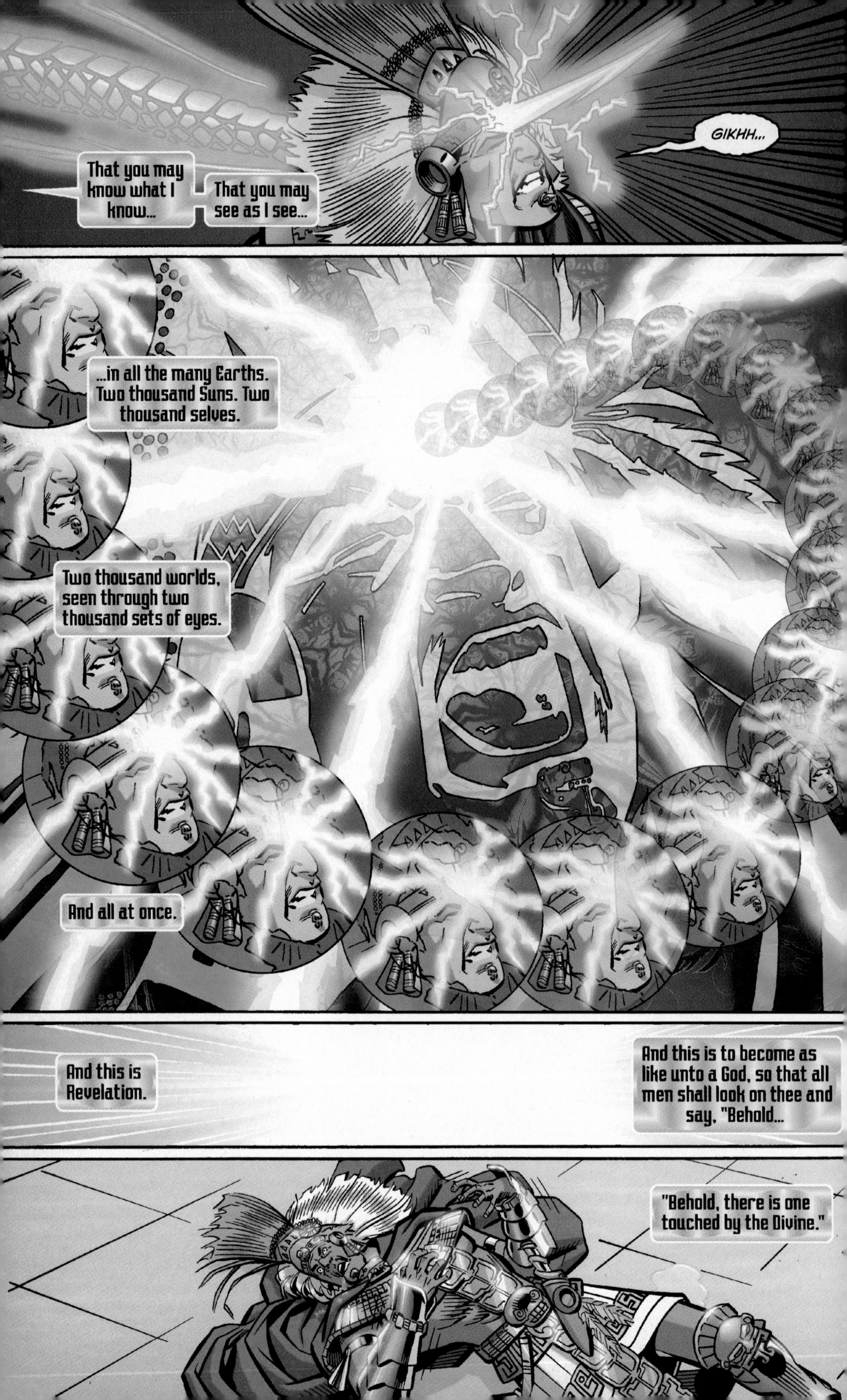
GIKHH...
That you may know what I know...
That you may see as I see...
...in all the many Earths. Two thousand Suns. Two thousand selves.
Two thousand worlds, seen through two thousand sets of eyes.
And all at once.
And this is Revelation.
And this is to become as like unto a God, so that all men shall look on thee and say, "Behold...
"Behold, there is one touched by the Divine."

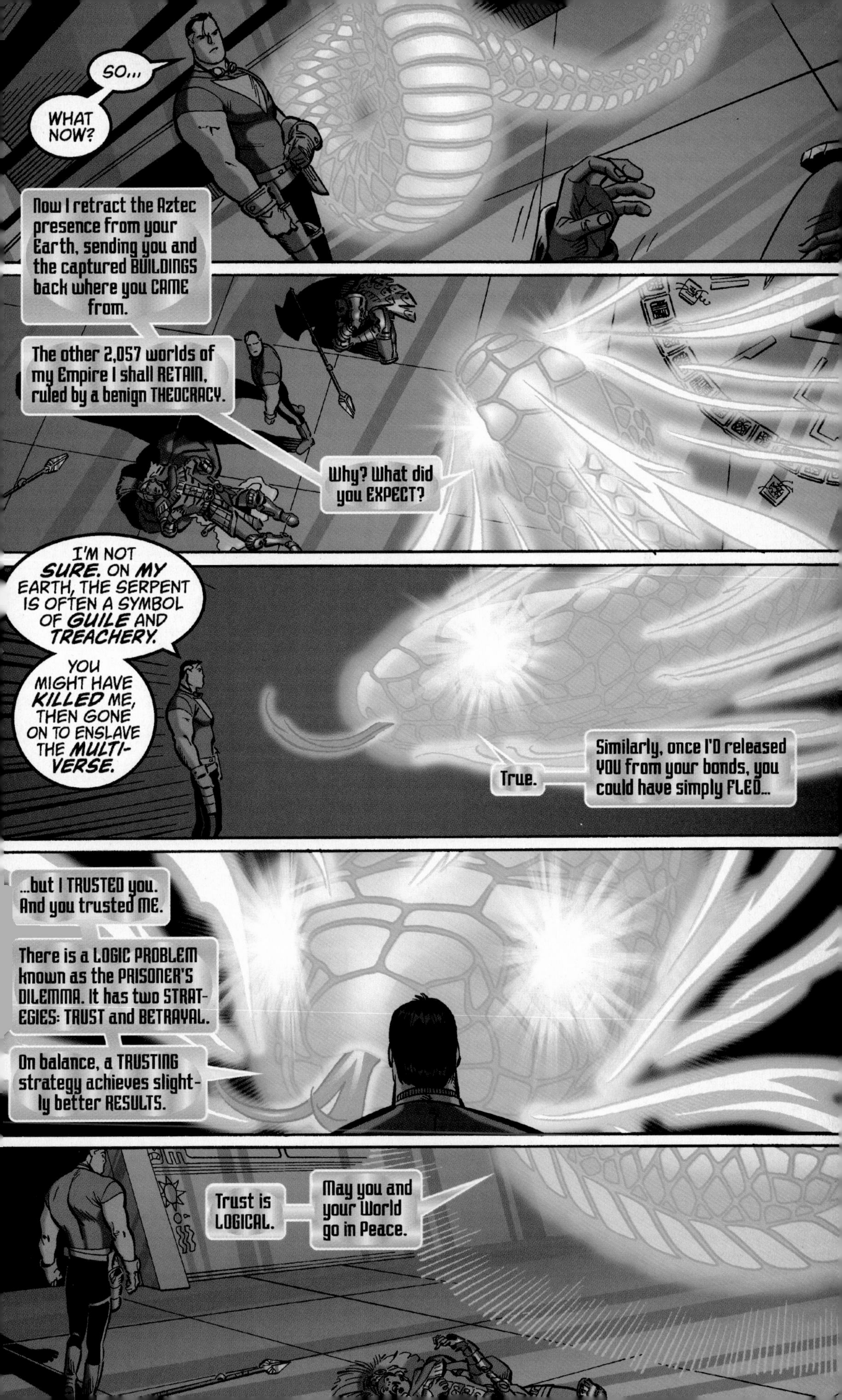
SO...
WHAT NOW?
Now I retract the Aztec presence from your Earth, sending you and the captured BUILDINGS back where you CAME from.
The other 2,057 worlds of my Empire I shall RETAIN, ruled by a benign THEOCRACY.
Why? What did you EXPECT?
I'M NOT SURE. ON MY EARTH, THE SERPENT IS OFTEN A SYMBOL OF GUILE AND TREACHERY.
YOU MIGHT HAVE KILLED ME, THEN GONE ON TO ENSLAVE THE MULTI-VERSE.
True.
Similarly, once I'D released YOU from your bonds, you could have simply FLED...
...but I TRUSTED you. And you trusted ME.
There is a LOGIC PROBLEM known as the PRISONER'S DILEMMA. It has two STRAT-EGIES: TRUST and BETRAYAL.
On balance, a TRUSTING strategy achieves slight-ly better RESULTS.
Trust is LOGICAL.
May you and your World go in Peace.

CHAPTER FOUR

In which a Message is delivered, an Untold Tale is unraveled, and TOM relights an Old Flame.

**Cover art:
Arthur Adams**

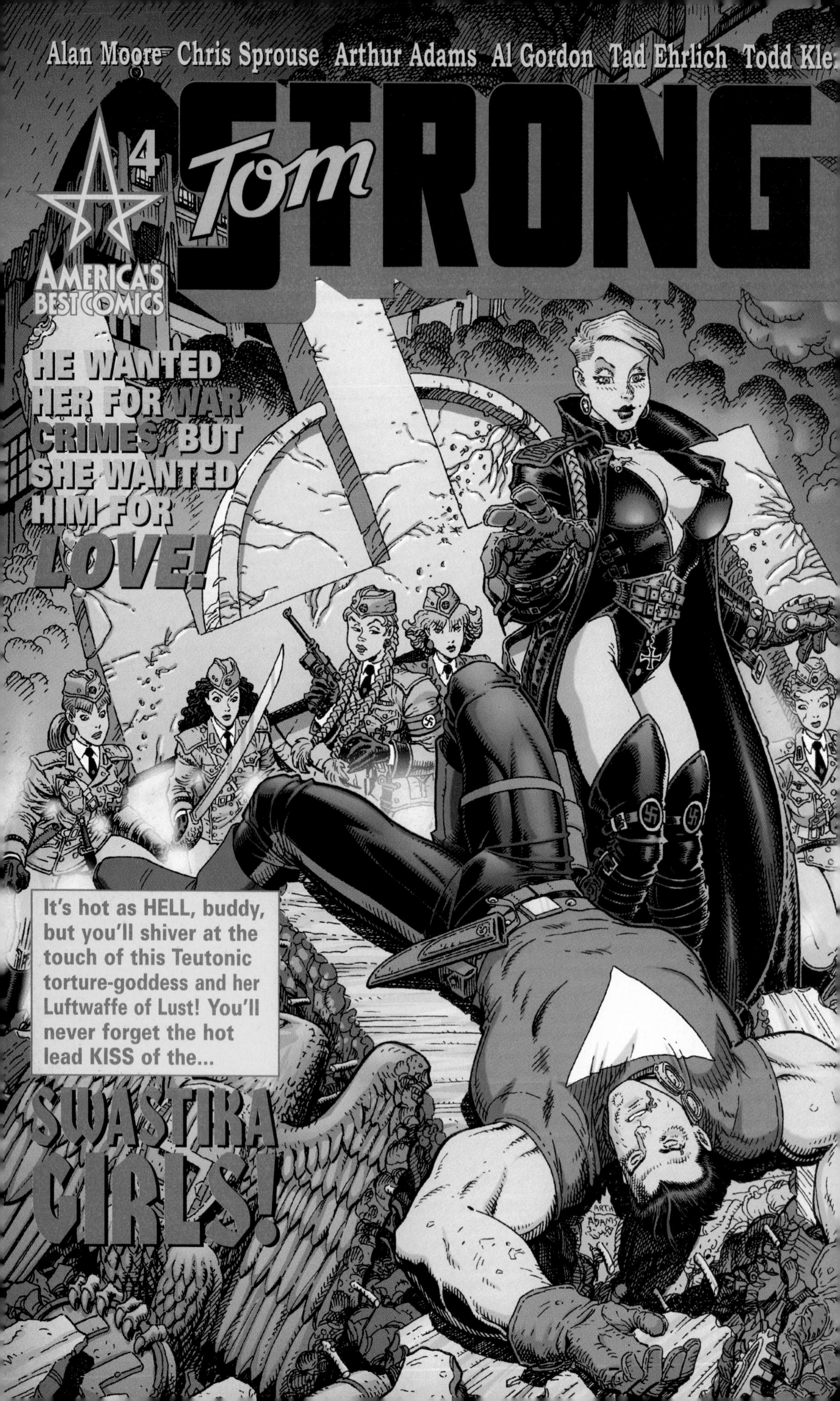
Alan Moore Chris Sprouse Arthur Adams Al Gordon Tad Ehrlich Todd Kle
4
AMERICA'S BEST COMICS
Tom STRONG
HE WANTED HER FOR WAR CRIMES, BUT SHE WANTED HIM FOR LOVE!
It's hot as HELL, buddy, but you'll shiver at the touch of this Teutonic torture-goddess and her Luftwaffe of Lust! You'll never forget the hot lead KISS of the...
SWASTIKA GIRLS!

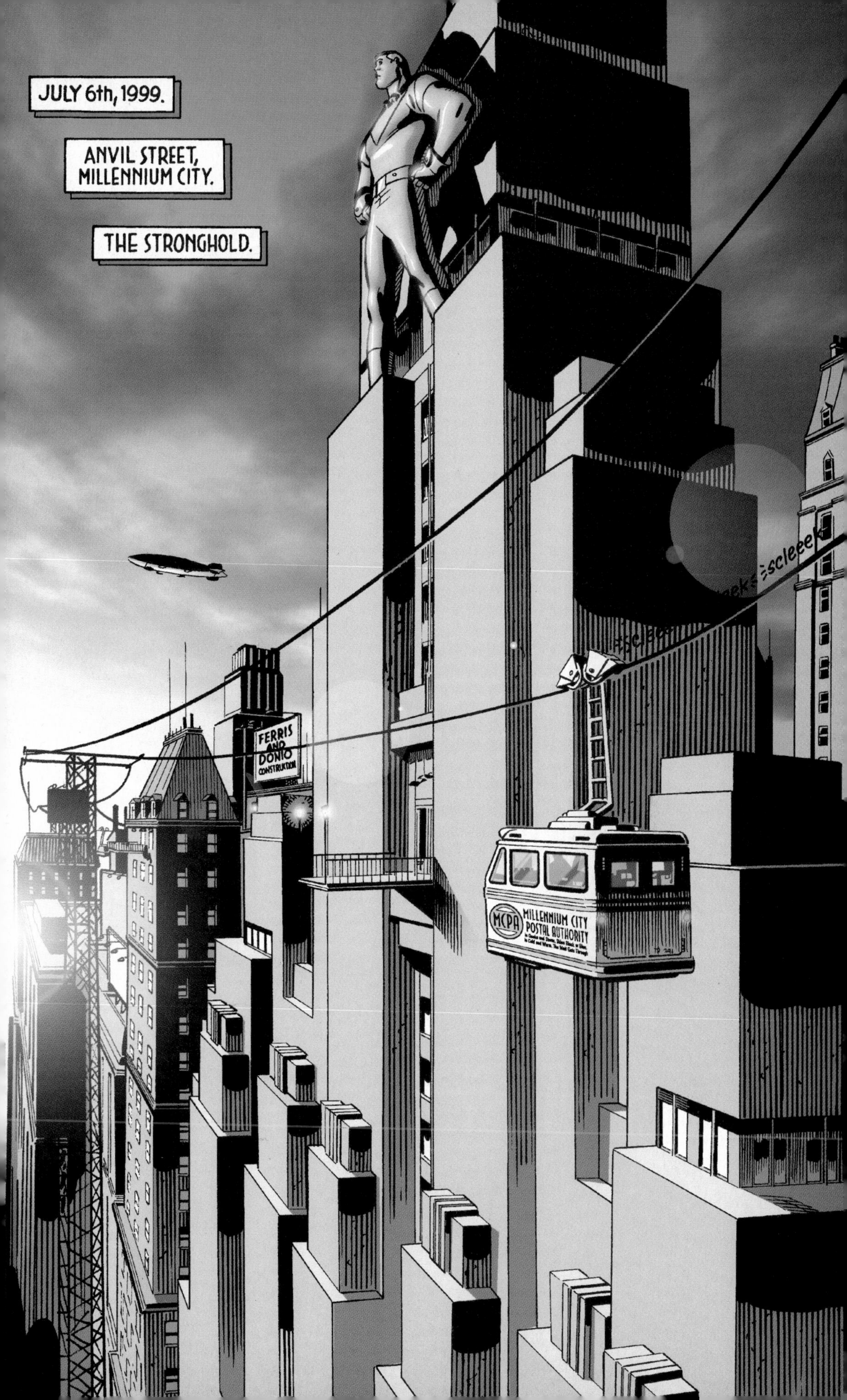
JULY 6th, 1999.
ANVIL STREET, MILLENNIUM CITY.
THE STRONGHOLD.
FERRIS AND DONIO CONSTRUCTION
scleeek
MCPA
MILLENNIUM CITY POSTAL AUTHORITY

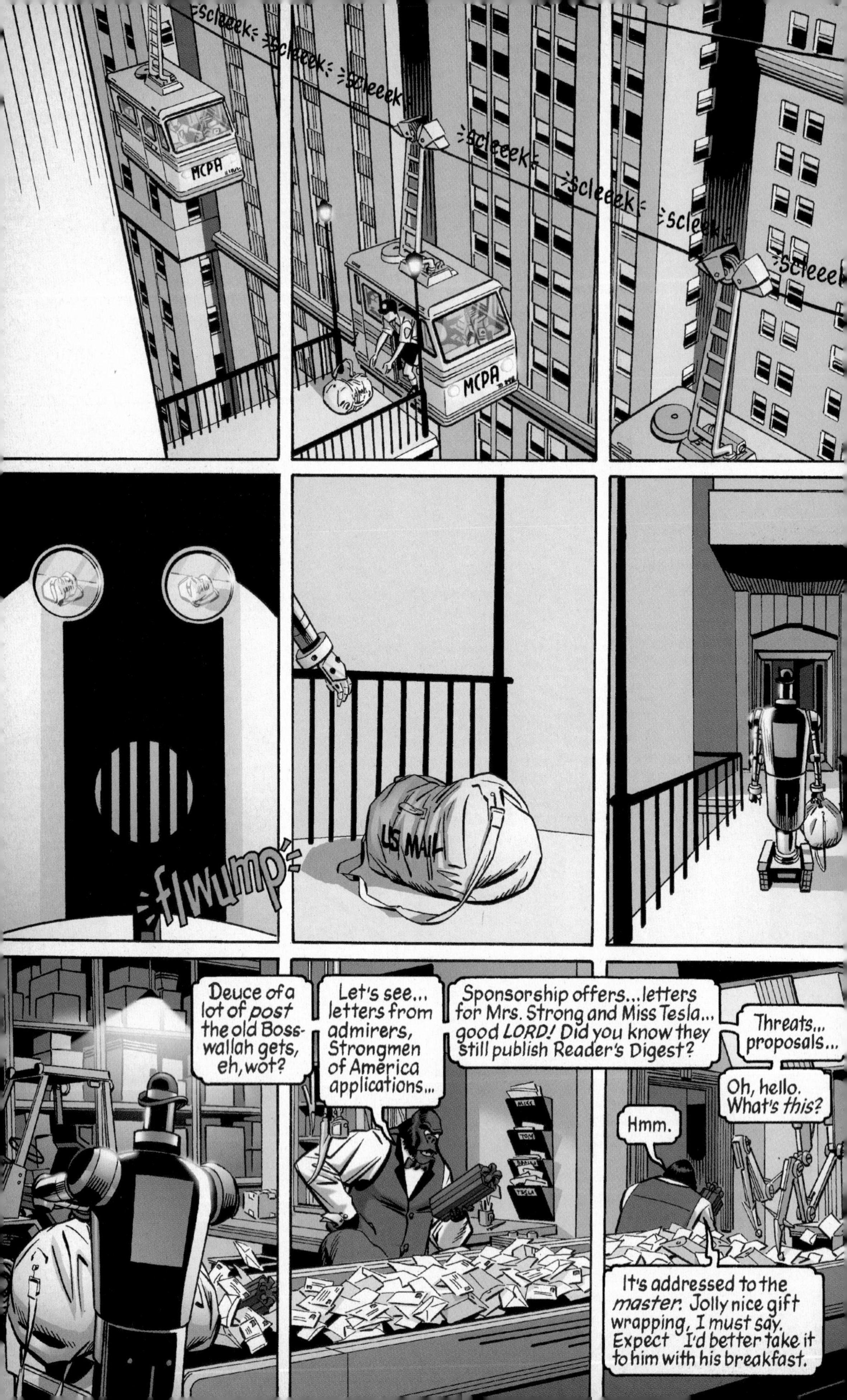

scleeek scleeek scleeek
MCPA
scleeek scleeek scleeek scleeek scleeek
MCPA
flwump
US MAIL
Deuce of a lot of *post* the old Boss-wallah gets, eh, wot?
Let's see... letters from admirers, Strongmen of America applications...
Sponsorship offers... letters for Mrs. Strong and Miss Tesla... good *LORD!* Did you know they still publish Reader's Digest?
Threats... proposals...
Oh, hello. What's *this?*
Hmm.
It's addressed to the *master.* Jolly nice gift wrapping, I must say. Expect I'd better take it to him with his breakfast.

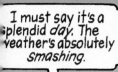

Morning, Sah. Morning, Ma'am.

I've brought the mail and your *petit dejourner,* don'cha know?

COME IN, SOLOMON.

I must say it's a splendid *day.* The weather's absolutely *smashing.*

I've got your morning paper, and a *package* that arrived...

No idea who it's *from,* but it looks terribly *fancy,* I must say.

On the card it says "Perishable — Open immediately!"

HMM. GIVE IT HERE...

THAT'S PECULIAR. IT'S A SINGLE WHITE *ROSE.* AND THERE'S A NOTE SAYING, "HAPPY ANNIVERSARY, DARLING."

DID YOU SEND THIS, DHALUA?

I CERTAINLY DIDN'T...

NO. NO, YOU CERTAINLY DIDN'T. THERE'S NO SIGNATURE ON THEM AT ALL. THERE'S JUST A CRIMSON LIPSTICK MARK...

...AND A SWASTIKA.

I'VE GOT A BAD FEELING ABOUT THIS. IF ONLY I COULD RE-MEMBER WHAT JULY 6TH WAS THE *AN-NIVERSARY* OF...

UH... TOM? THOSE 'PLANES...

'PLANES? WHAT...

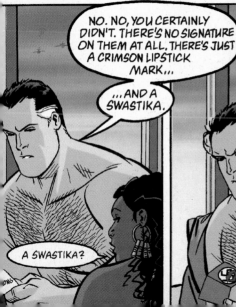

A SWASTIKA?

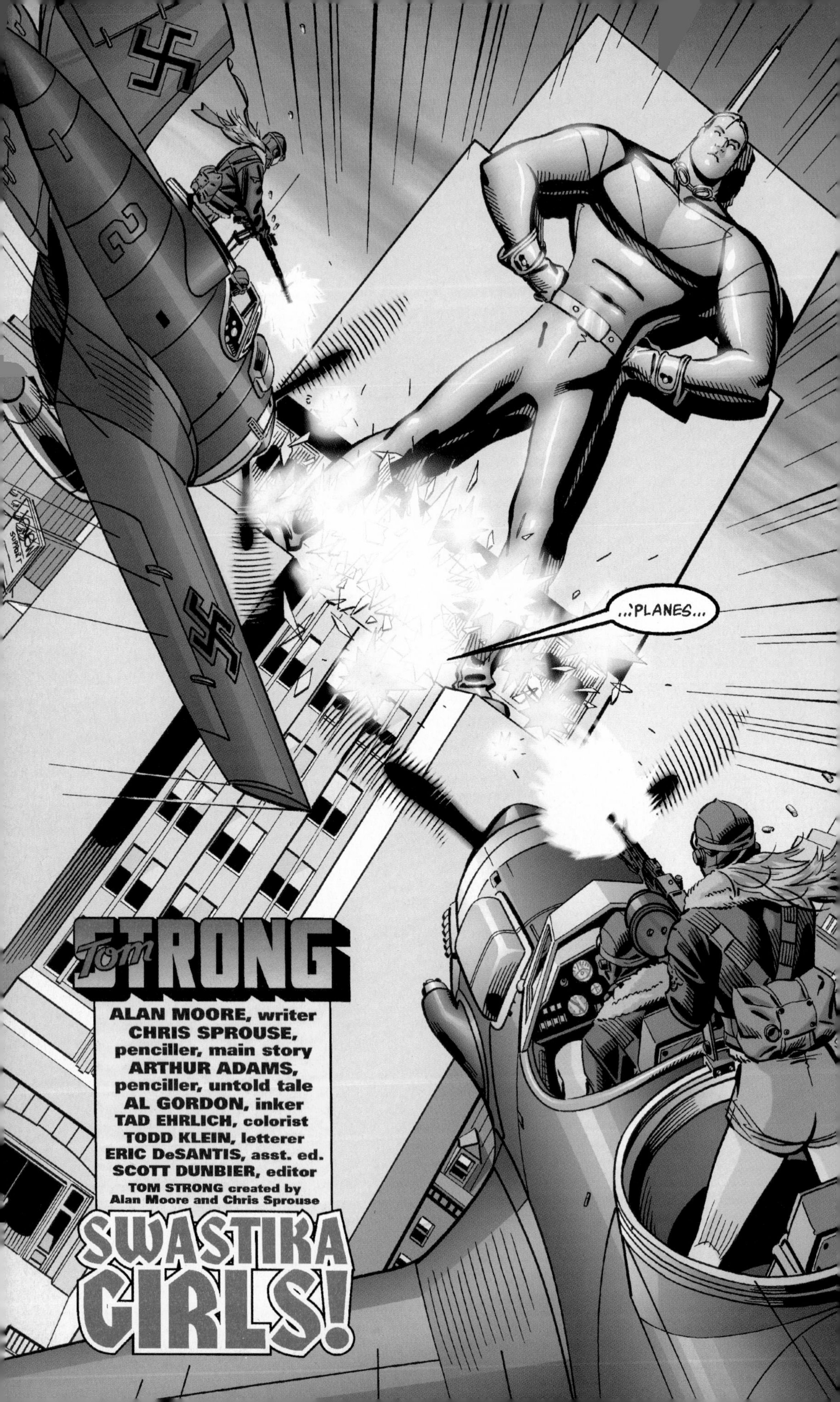

...PLANES...
SUPPORT
TOM STRONG
ALAN MOORE, writer
CHRIS SPROUSE, penciller, main story
ARTHUR ADAMS, penciller, untold tale
AL GORDON, inker
TAD EHRLICH, colorist
TODD KLEIN, letterer
ERIC DeSANTIS, asst. ed.
SCOTT DUNBIER, editor
TOM STRONG created by Alan Moore and Chris Sprouse
SWASTIKA GIRLS!

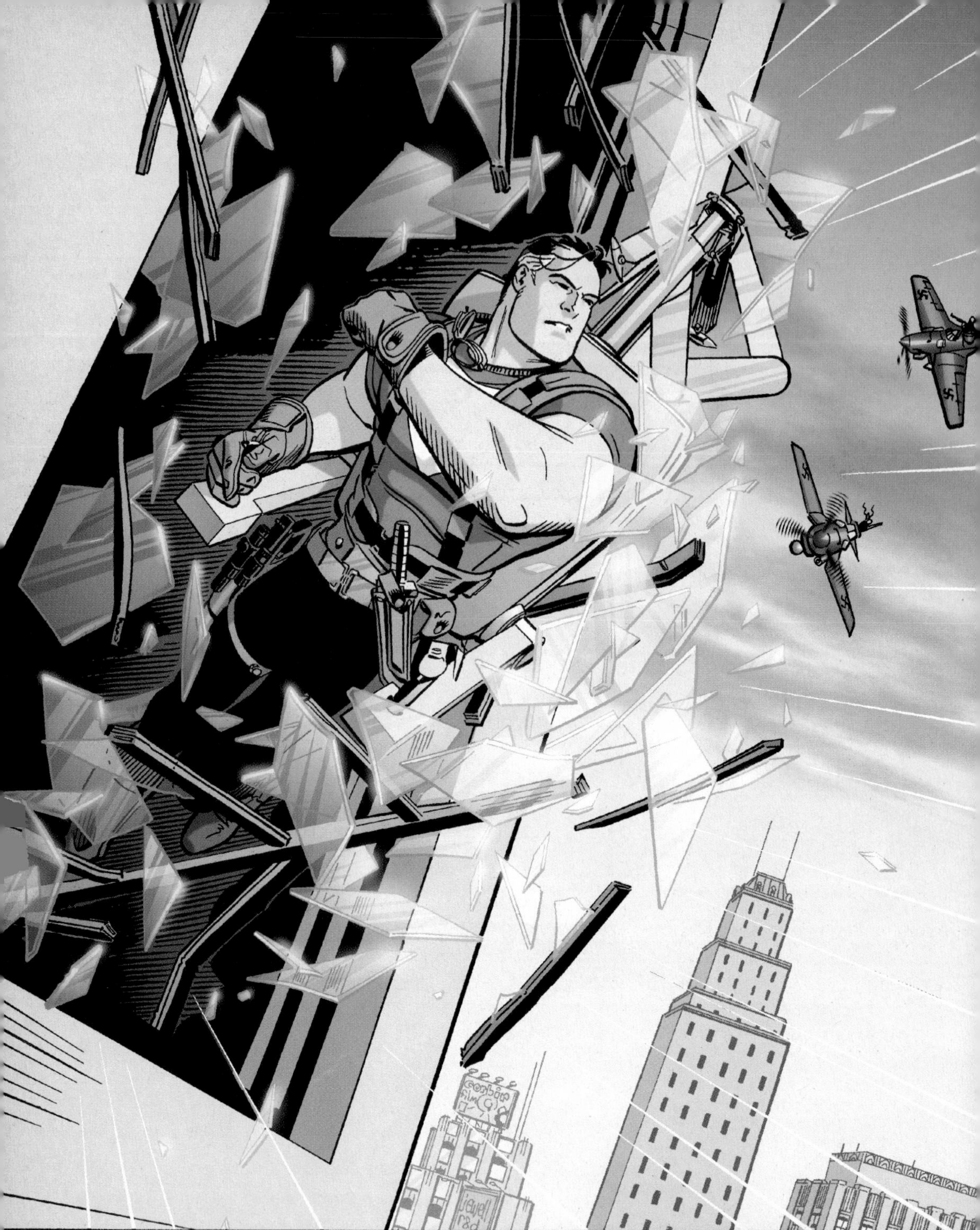

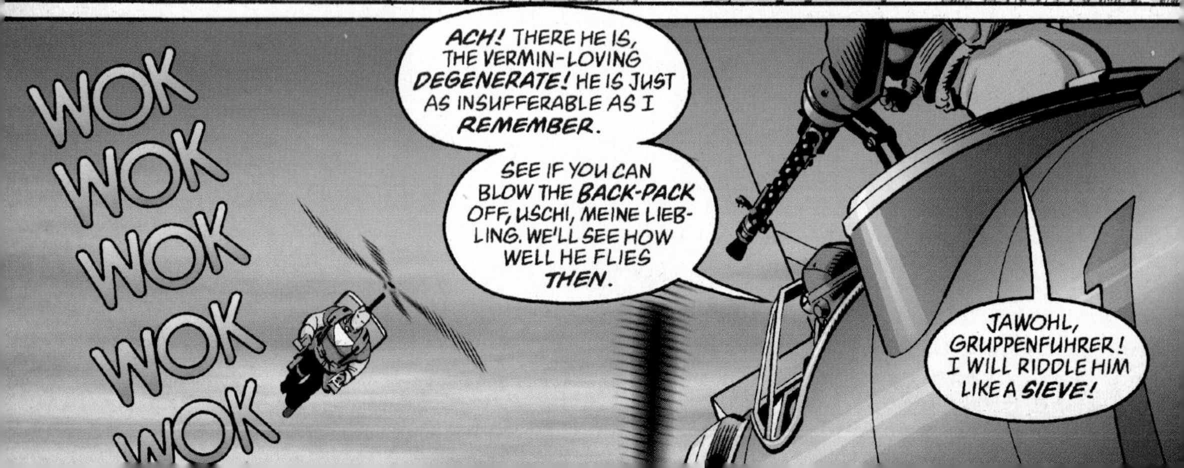
WOK WOK WOK WOK WOK
ACH! THERE HE IS, THE VERMIN-LOVING DEGENERATE! HE IS JUST AS INSUFFERABLE AS I REMEMBER.
SEE IF YOU CAN BLOW THE BACK-PACK OFF, USCHI, MEINE LIEB-LING. WE'LL SEE HOW WELL HE FLIES THEN.
JAWOHL, GRUPPENFUHRER! I WILL RIDDLE HIM LIKE A SIEVE!

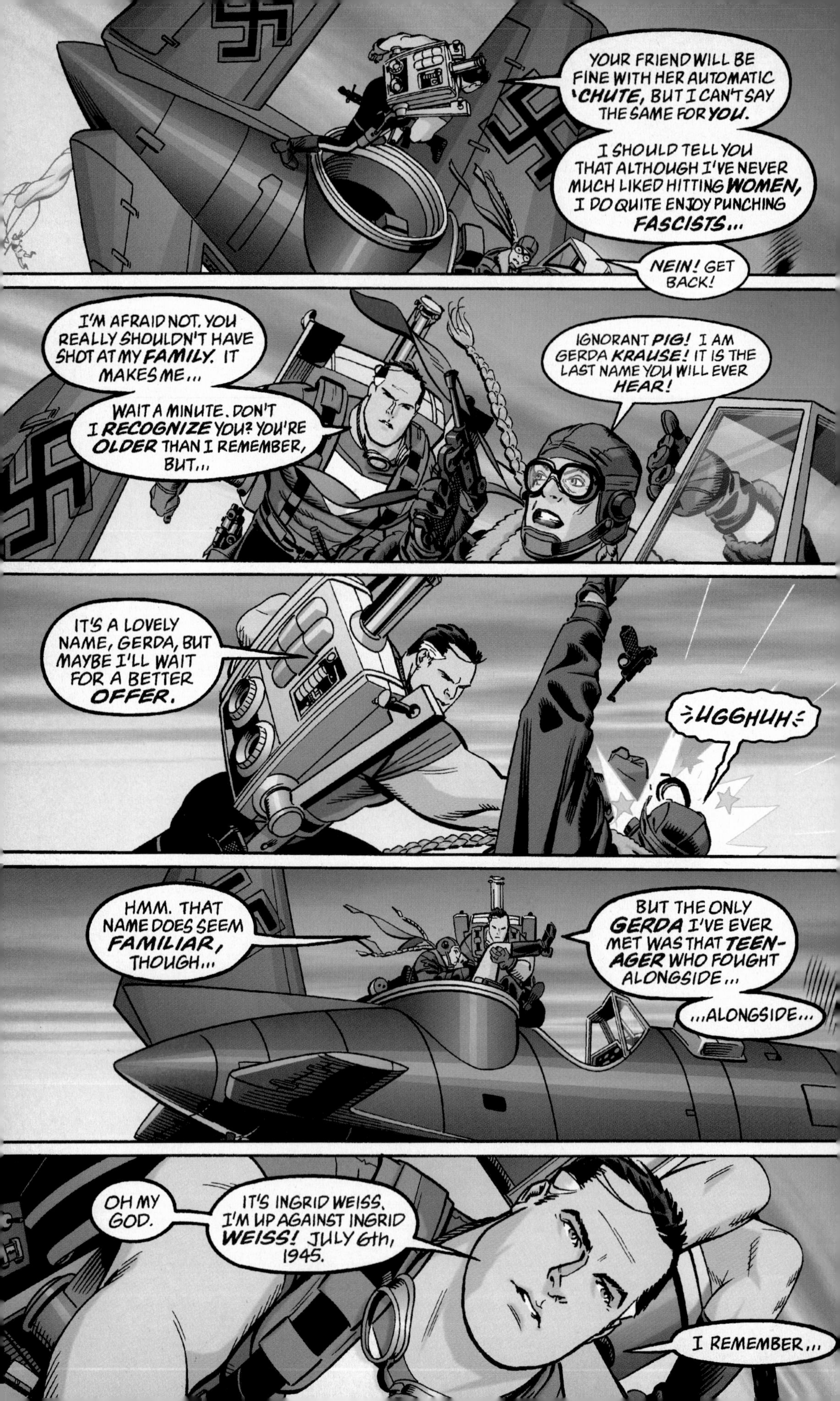
YOUR FRIEND WILL BE FINE WITH HER AUTOMATIC 'CHUTE, BUT I CAN'T SAY THE SAME FOR YOU.
I SHOULD TELL YOU THAT ALTHOUGH I'VE NEVER MUCH LIKED HITTING WOMEN, I DO QUITE ENJOY PUNCHING FASCISTS...
NEIN! GET BACK!
I'M AFRAID NOT. YOU REALLY SHOULDN'T HAVE SHOT AT MY FAMILY. IT MAKES ME...
WAIT A MINUTE. DON'T I RECOGNIZE YOU? YOU'RE OLDER THAN I REMEMBER, BUT...
IGNORANT PIG! I AM GERDA KRAUSE! IT IS THE LAST NAME YOU WILL EVER HEAR!
IT'S A LOVELY NAME, GERDA, BUT MAYBE I'LL WAIT FOR A BETTER OFFER.
UGGHUH
HMM. THAT NAME DOES SEEM FAMILIAR, THOUGH...
BUT THE ONLY GERDA I'VE EVER MET WAS THAT TEEN-AGER WHO FOUGHT ALONGSIDE...
...ALONGSIDE...
OH MY GOD.
IT'S INGRID WEISS. I'M UP AGAINST INGRID WEISS! JULY 6th, 1945.
I REMEMBER...

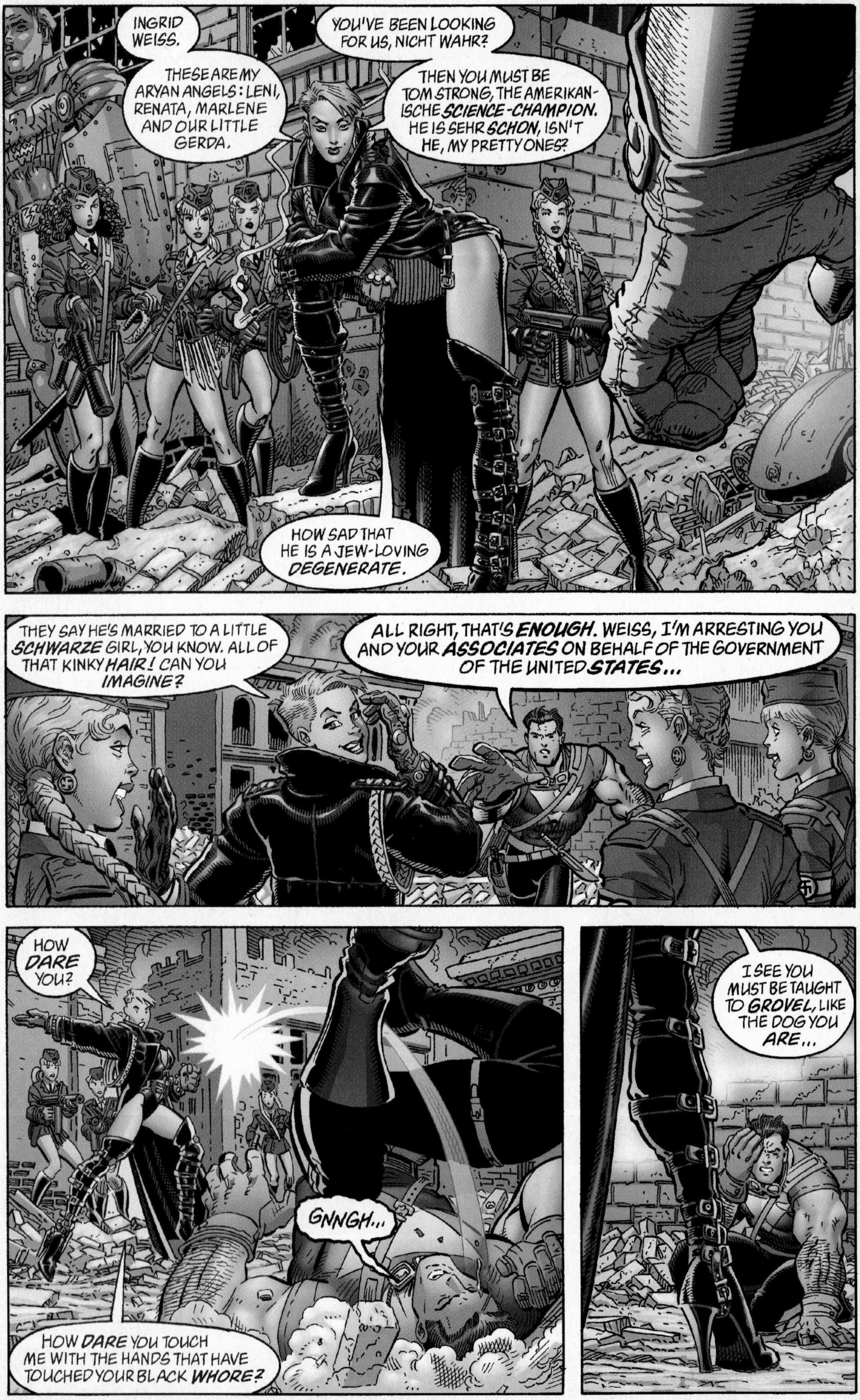
INGRID WEISS.
THESE ARE MY ARYAN ANGELS: LENI, RENATA, MARLENE AND OUR LITTLE GERDA.
YOU'VE BEEN LOOKING FOR US, NICHT WAHR?
THEN YOU MUST BE TOM STRONG, THE AMERIKANISCHE SCIENCE-CHAMPION. HE IS SEHR SCHON, ISN'T HE, MY PRETTY ONES?
HOW SAD THAT HE IS A JEW-LOVING DEGENERATE.
THEY SAY HE'S MARRIED TO A LITTLE SCHWARZE GIRL, YOU KNOW. ALL OF THAT KINKY HAIR! CAN YOU IMAGINE?
ALL RIGHT, THAT'S ENOUGH. WEISS, I'M ARRESTING YOU AND YOUR ASSOCIATES ON BEHALF OF THE GOVERNMENT OF THE UNITED STATES...
HOW DARE YOU?
GNNGH...
HOW DARE YOU TOUCH ME WITH THE HANDS THAT HAVE TOUCHED YOUR BLACK WHORE?
I SEE YOU MUST BE TAUGHT TO GROVEL, LIKE THE DOG YOU ARE...

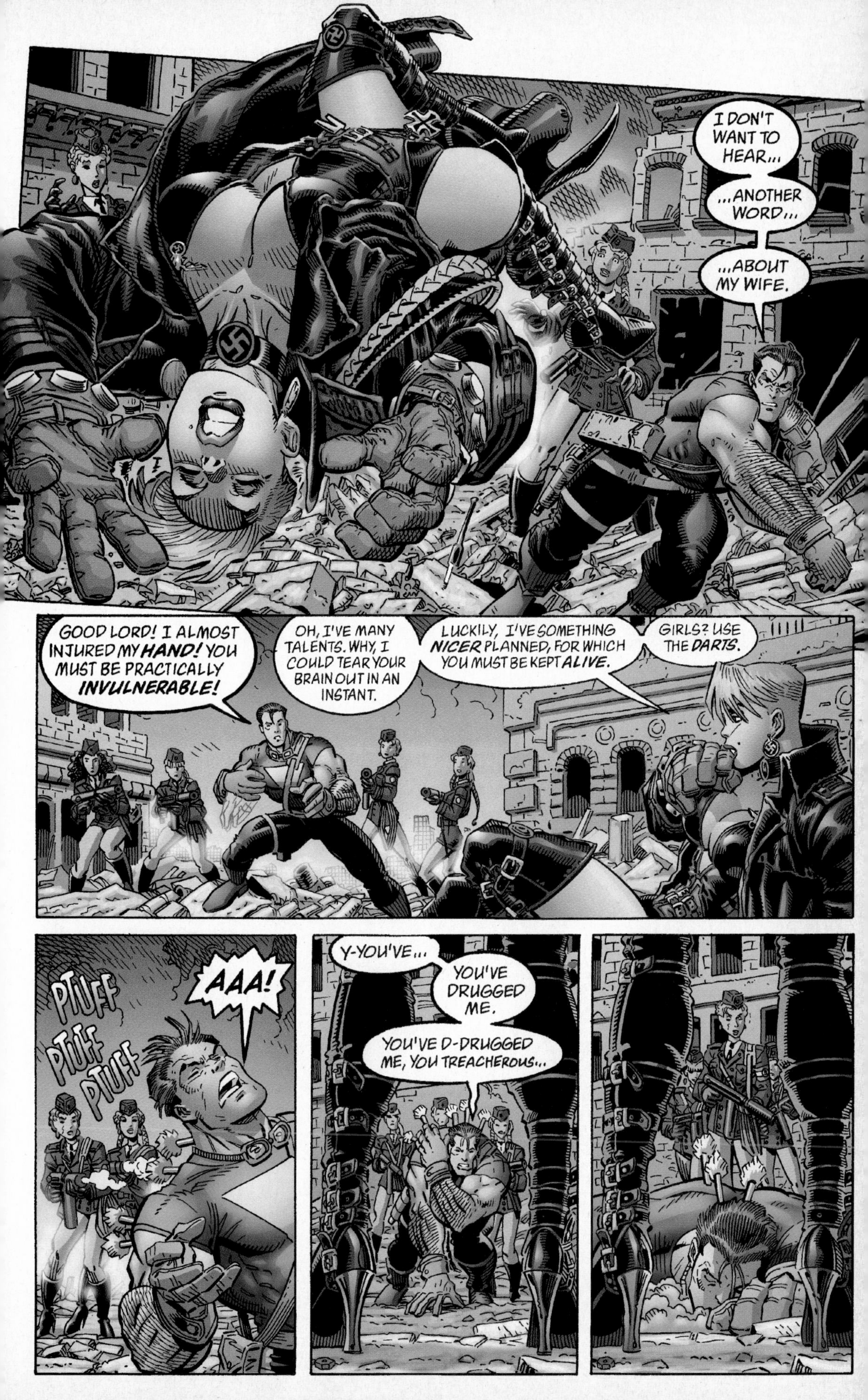
I DON'T WANT TO HEAR...
...ANOTHER WORD...
...ABOUT MY WIFE.
GOOD LORD! I ALMOST INJURED MY HAND! YOU MUST BE PRACTICALLY INVULNERABLE!
OH, I'VE MANY TALENTS. WHY, I COULD TEAR YOUR BRAIN OUT IN AN INSTANT.
LUCKILY, I'VE SOMETHING NICER PLANNED, FOR WHICH YOU MUST BE KEPT ALIVE.
GIRLS? USE THE DARTS.
PTUFF PTUFF PTUFF
AAA!
Y-YOU'VE...
YOU'VE DRUGGED ME.
YOU'VE D-DRUGGED ME, YOU TREACHEROUS...

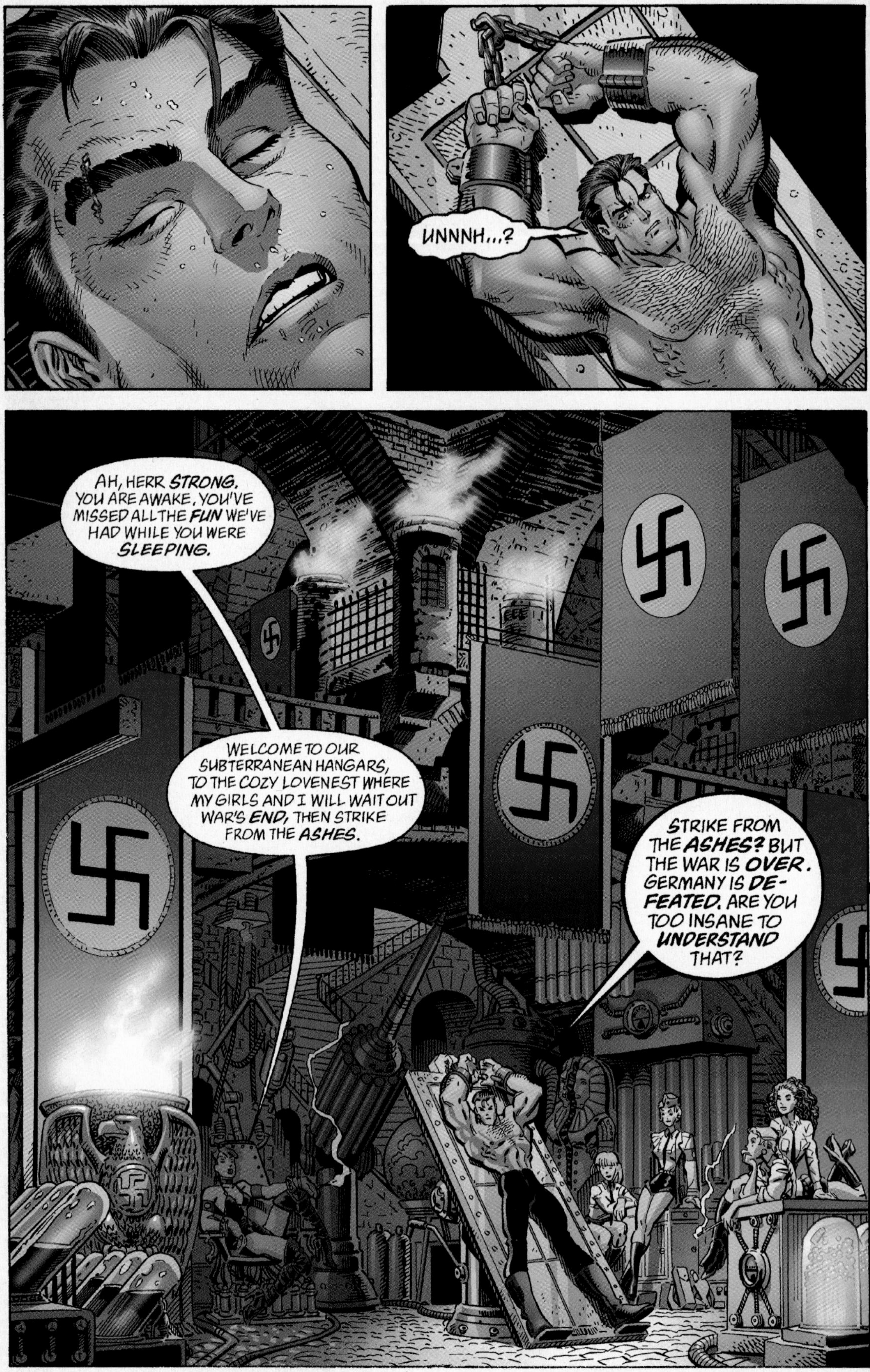
UNNNH...?
AH, HERR STRONG. YOU ARE AWAKE. YOU'VE MISSED ALL THE FUN WE'VE HAD WHILE YOU WERE SLEEPING.
WELCOME TO OUR SUBTERRANEAN HANGARS, TO THE COZY LOVENEST WHERE MY GIRLS AND I WILL WAIT OUT WAR'S END, THEN STRIKE FROM THE ASHES.
STRIKE FROM THE ASHES? BUT THE WAR IS OVER. GERMANY IS DE-FEATED. ARE YOU TOO INSANE TO UNDERSTAND THAT?

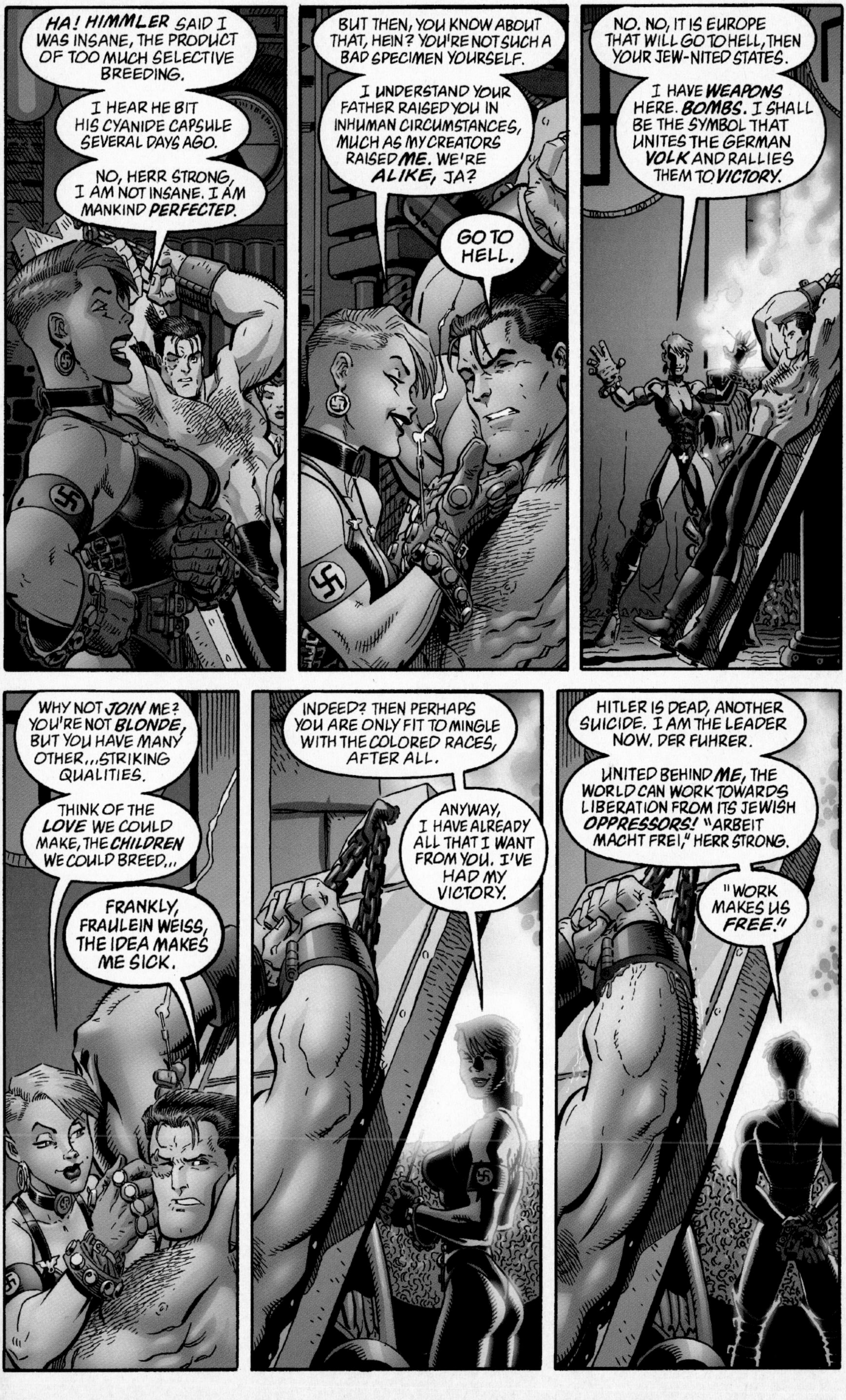
HA! HIMMLER SAID I WAS INSANE, THE PRODUCT OF TOO MUCH SELECTIVE BREEDING.
I HEAR HE BIT HIS CYANIDE CAPSULE SEVERAL DAYS AGO.
NO, HERR STRONG, I AM NOT INSANE. I AM MANKIND PERFECTED.
BUT THEN, YOU KNOW ABOUT THAT, HEIN? YOU'RE NOT SUCH A BAD SPECIMEN YOURSELF.
I UNDERSTAND YOUR FATHER RAISED YOU IN INHUMAN CIRCUMSTANCES, MUCH AS MY CREATORS RAISED ME. WE'RE ALIKE, JA?
GO TO HELL.
NO. NO, IT IS EUROPE THAT WILL GO TO HELL, THEN YOUR JEW-NITED STATES.
I HAVE WEAPONS HERE. BOMBS. I SHALL BE THE SYMBOL THAT UNITES THE GERMAN VOLK AND RALLIES THEM TO VICTORY.
WHY NOT JOIN ME? YOU'RE NOT BLONDE, BUT YOU HAVE MANY OTHER...STRIKING QUALITIES.
THINK OF THE LOVE WE COULD MAKE, THE CHILDREN WE COULD BREED...
FRANKLY, FRAULEIN WEISS, THE IDEA MAKES ME SICK.
INDEED? THEN PERHAPS YOU ARE ONLY FIT TO MINGLE WITH THE COLORED RACES, AFTER ALL.
ANYWAY, I HAVE ALREADY ALL THAT I WANT FROM YOU. I'VE HAD MY VICTORY.
HITLER IS DEAD, ANOTHER SUICIDE. I AM THE LEADER NOW. DER FUHRER.
UNITED BEHIND ME, THE WORLD CAN WORK TOWARDS LIBERATION FROM ITS JEWISH OPPRESSORS! "ARBEIT MACHT FREI," HERR STRONG.
"WORK MAKES US FREE."

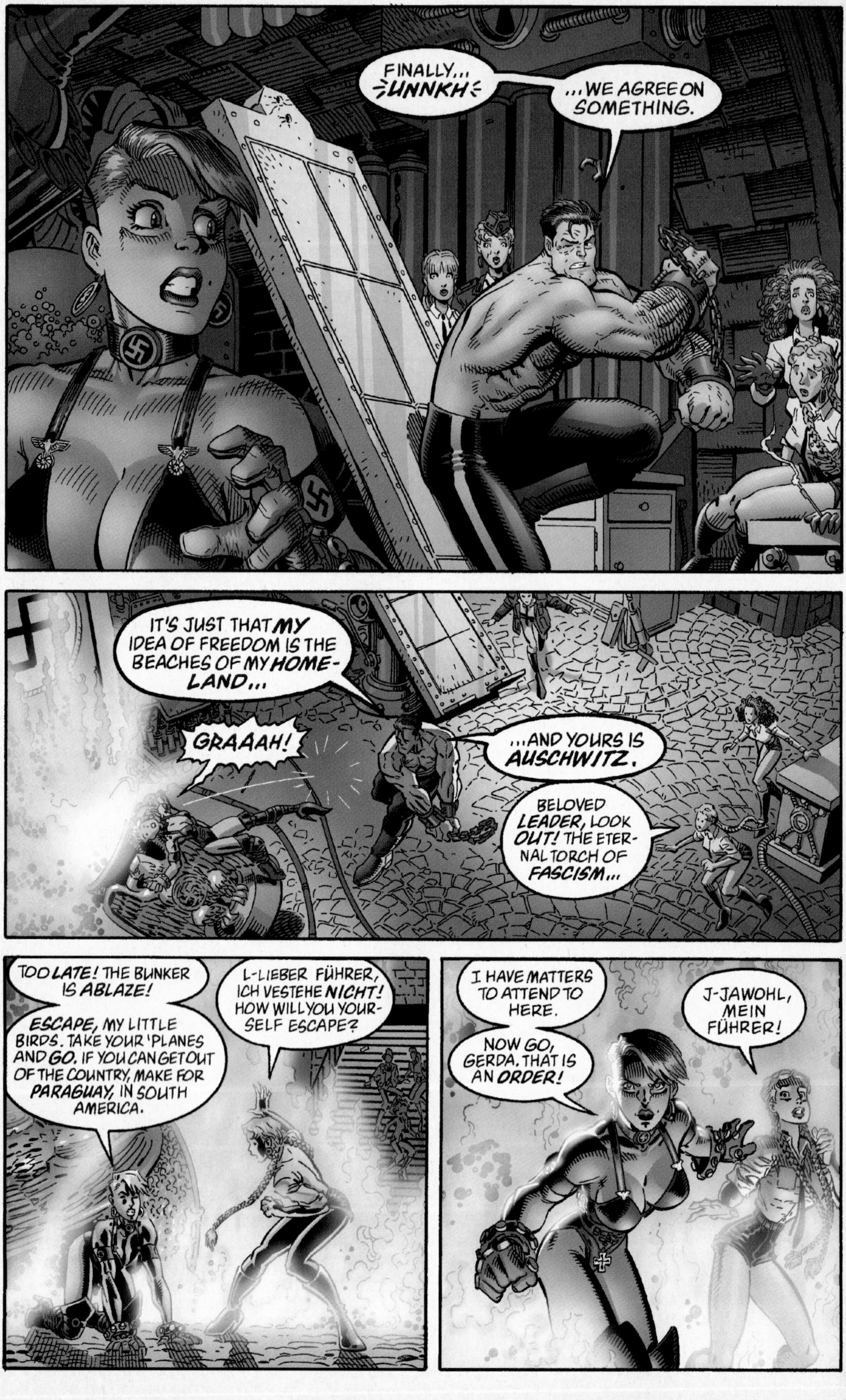
FINALLY... UNNKH
...WE AGREE ON SOMETHING.
IT'S JUST THAT MY IDEA OF FREEDOM IS THE BEACHES OF MY HOME-LAND...
GRAAAH!
...AND YOURS IS AUSCHWITZ.
BELOVED LEADER, LOOK OUT! THE ETERNAL TORCH OF FASCISM...
TOO LATE! THE BUNKER IS ABLAZE!
ESCAPE, MY LITTLE BIRDS. TAKE YOUR 'PLANES AND GO. IF YOU CAN GET OUT OF THE COUNTRY, MAKE FOR PARAGUAY, IN SOUTH AMERICA.
L-LIEBER FÜHRER, ICH VESTEHE NICHT! HOW WILL YOU YOUR-SELF ESCAPE?
I HAVE MATTERS TO ATTEND TO HERE.
NOW GO, GERDA. THAT IS AN ORDER!
J-JAWOHL, MEIN FÜHRER!

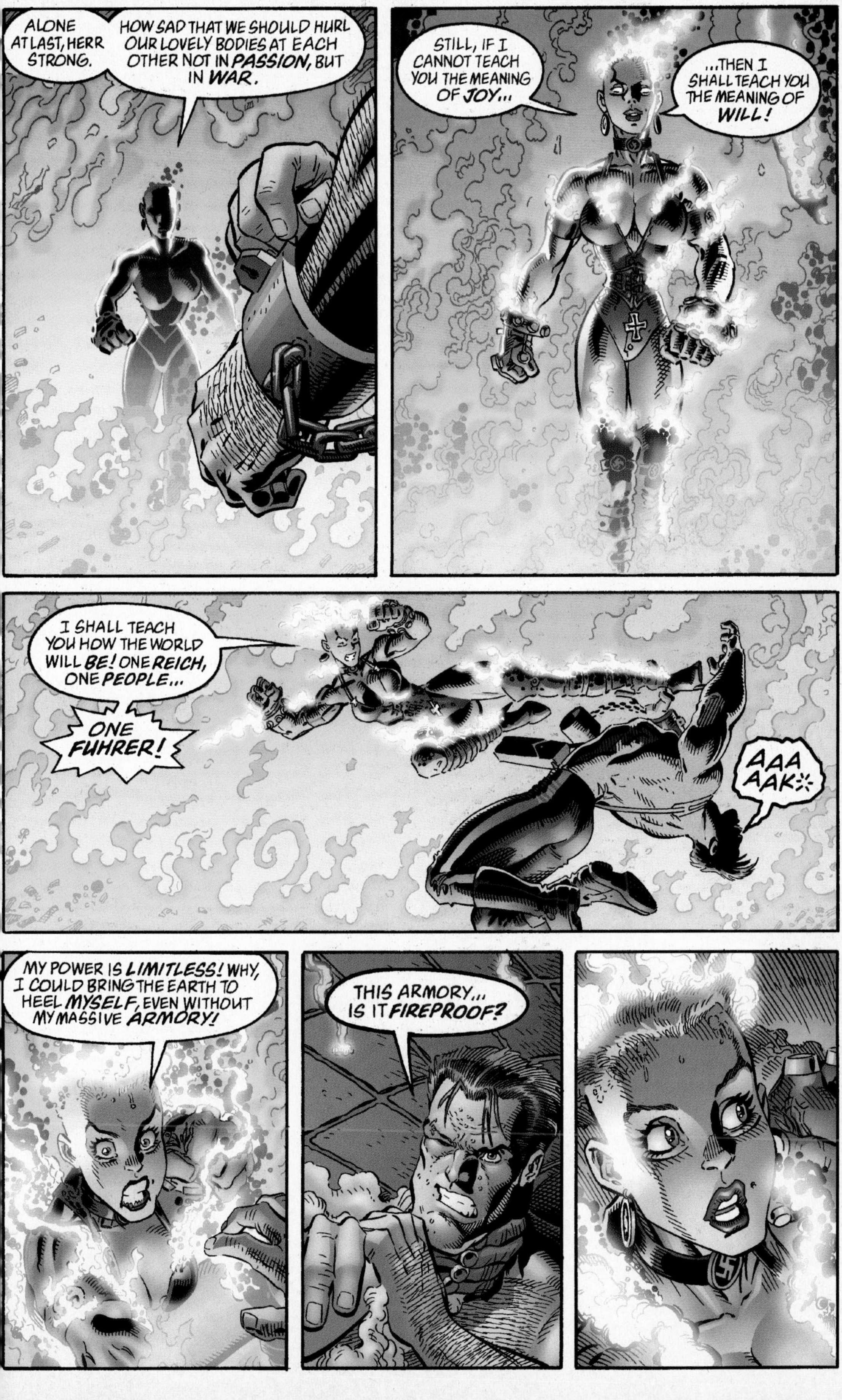
ALONE AT LAST, HERR STRONG.
HOW SAD THAT WE SHOULD HURL OUR LOVELY BODIES AT EACH OTHER NOT IN PASSION, BUT IN WAR.
STILL, IF I CANNOT TEACH YOU THE MEANING OF JOY...
...THEN I SHALL TEACH YOU THE MEANING OF WILL!
I SHALL TEACH YOU HOW THE WORLD WILL BE! ONE REICH, ONE PEOPLE...
ONE FUHRER!
AAAAAK!
MY POWER IS LIMITLESS! WHY, I COULD BRING THE EARTH TO HEEL MYSELF, EVEN WITHOUT MY MASSIVE ARMORY!
THIS ARMORY... IS IT FIREPROOF?

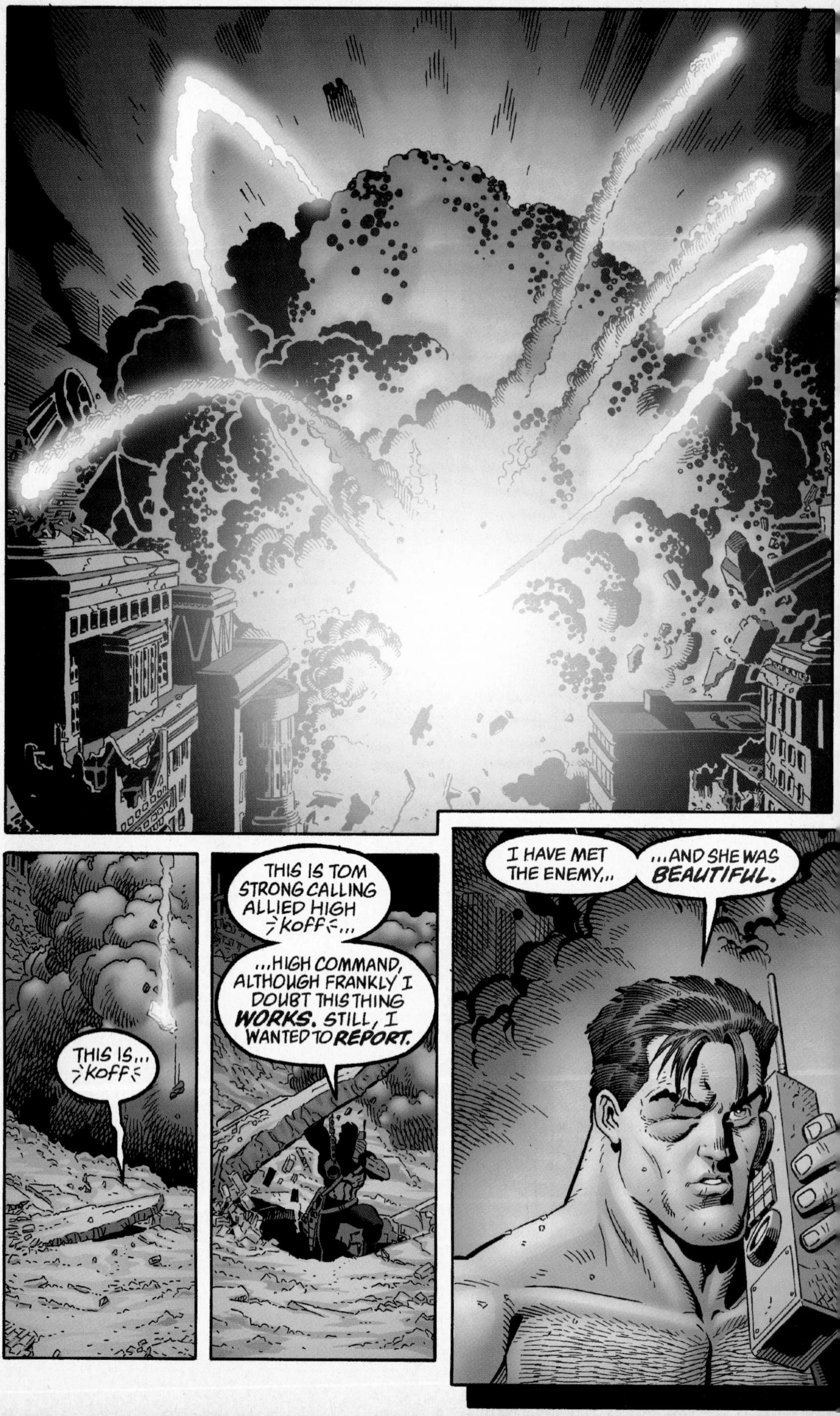
THIS IS...
KOFF
THIS IS TOM STRONG CALLING ALLIED HIGH KOFF...
...HIGH COMMAND, ALTHOUGH FRANKLY I DOUBT THIS THING WORKS. STILL, I WANTED TO REPORT.
I HAVE MET THE ENEMY...
...AND SHE WAS BEAUTIFUL.

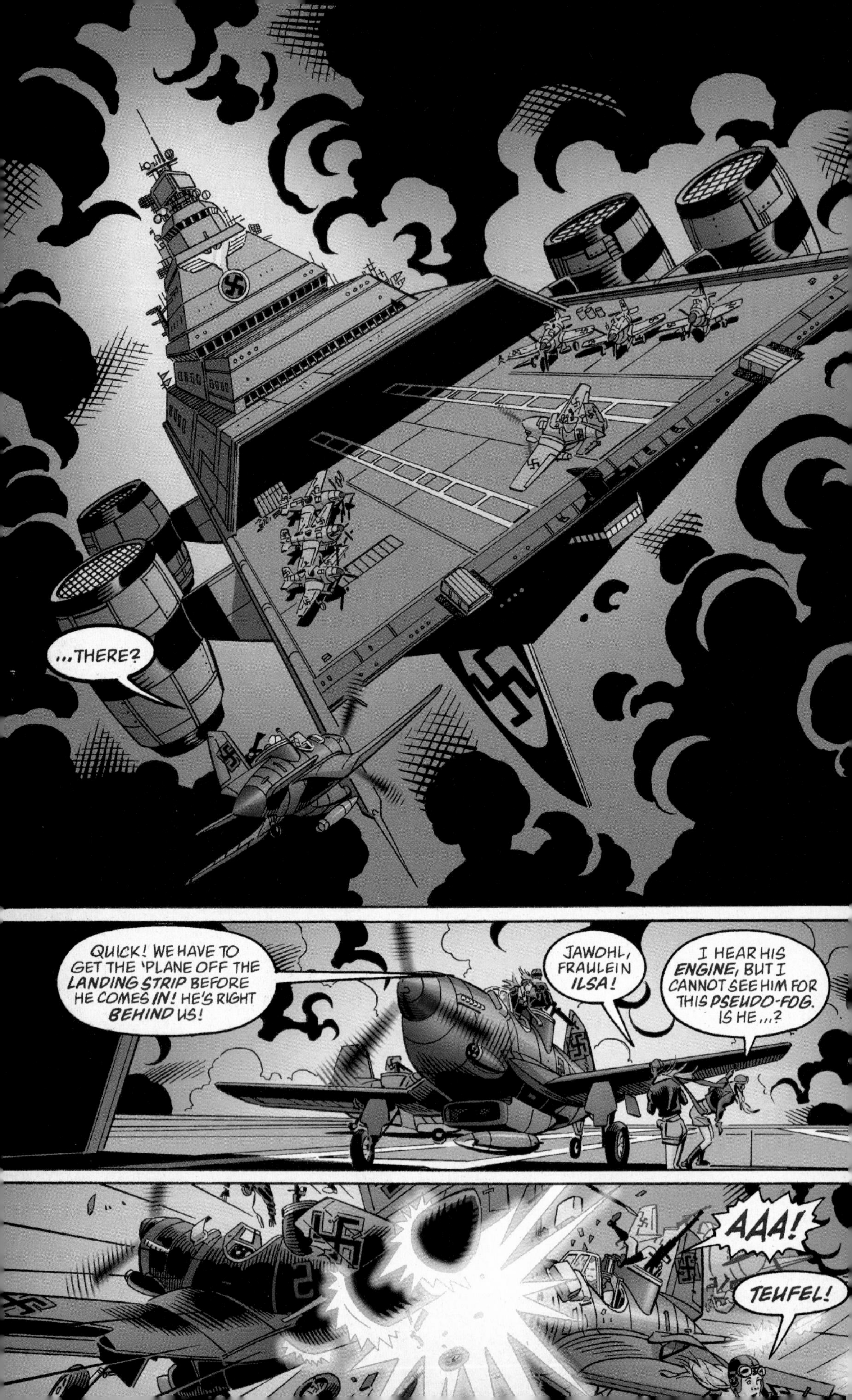

...THERE?
QUICK! WE HAVE TO GET THE 'PLANE OFF THE LANDING STRIP BEFORE HE COMES IN! HE'S RIGHT BEHIND US!
JAWOHL, FRAULEIN ILSA!
I HEAR HIS ENGINE, BUT I CANNOT SEE HIM FOR THIS PSEUDO-FOG. IS HE...?
AAA!
TEUFEL!

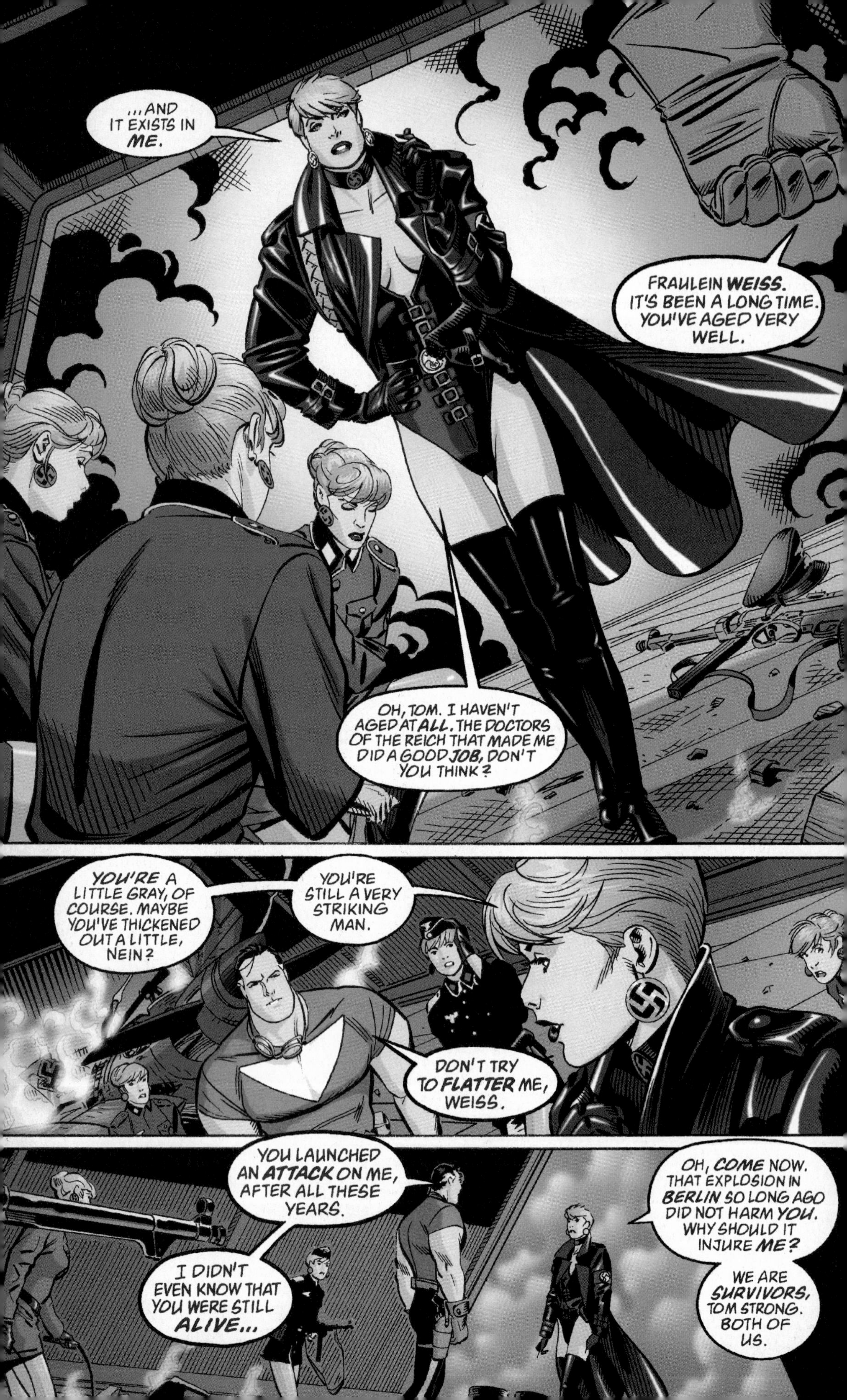

...AND IT EXISTS IN **ME**.
FRAULEIN **WEISS**. IT'S BEEN A LONG TIME. YOU'VE AGED VERY WELL.
OH, TOM. I HAVEN'T AGED AT **ALL**. THE DOCTORS OF THE REICH THAT MADE ME DID A GOOD **JOB**, DON'T YOU THINK?
YOU'RE A LITTLE GRAY, OF COURSE. MAYBE YOU'VE THICKENED OUT A LITTLE, NEIN?
YOU'RE STILL A VERY STRIKING MAN.
DON'T TRY TO ***FLATTER*** ME, WEISS.
YOU LAUNCHED AN ***ATTACK*** ON ME, AFTER ALL THESE YEARS.
I DIDN'T EVEN KNOW THAT YOU WERE STILL ***ALIVE...***
OH, ***COME*** NOW. THAT EXPLOSION IN ***BERLIN*** SO LONG AGO DID NOT HARM ***YOU***. WHY SHOULD IT INJURE ***ME?***
WE ARE ***SURVIVORS***, TOM STRONG. BOTH OF US.

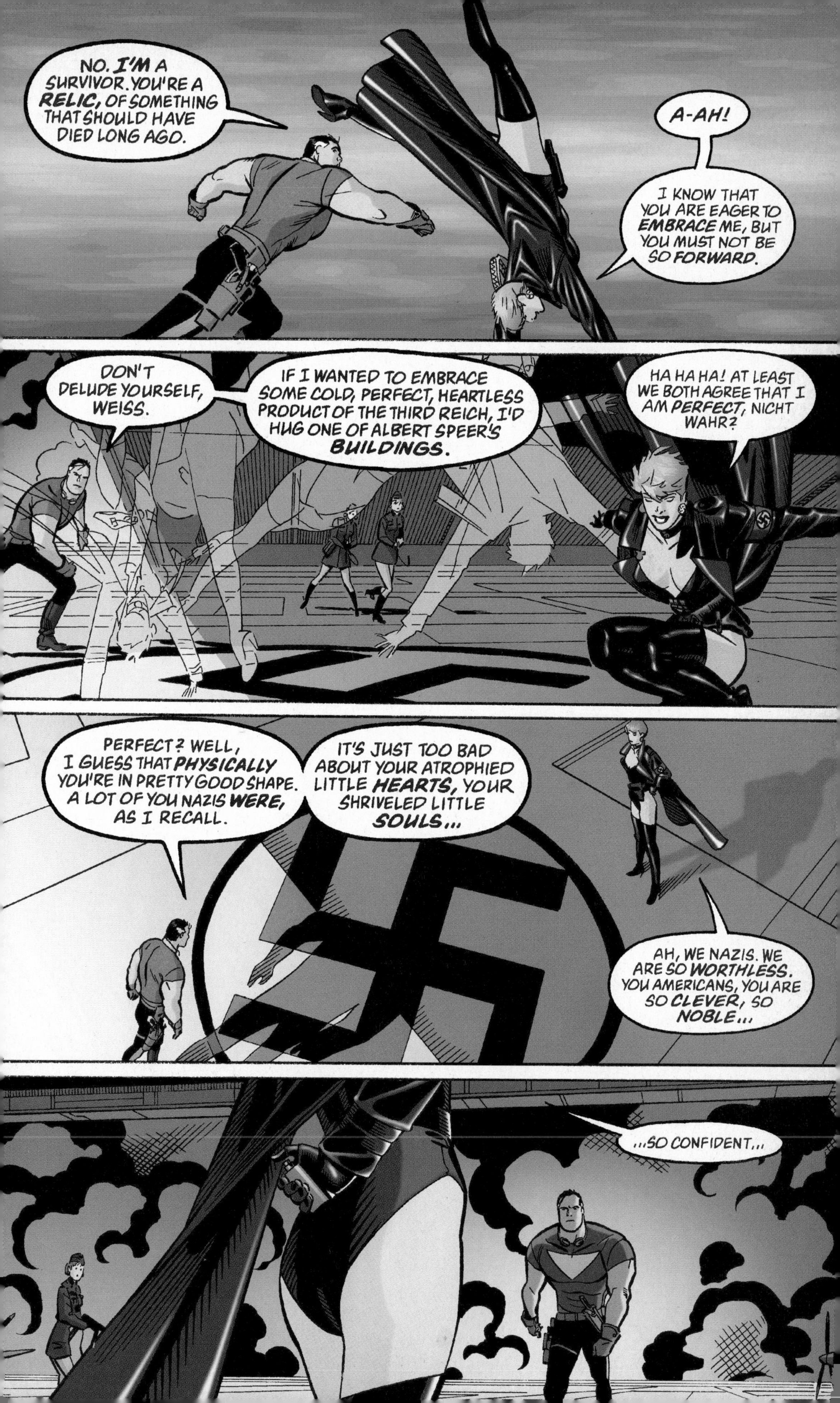
NO. I'M A SURVIVOR. YOU'RE A RELIC, OF SOMETHING THAT SHOULD HAVE DIED LONG AGO.
A-AH!
I KNOW THAT YOU ARE EAGER TO EMBRACE ME, BUT YOU MUST NOT BE SO FORWARD.
DON'T DELUDE YOURSELF, WEISS.
IF I WANTED TO EMBRACE SOME COLD, PERFECT, HEARTLESS PRODUCT OF THE THIRD REICH, I'D HUG ONE OF ALBERT SPEER'S BUILDINGS.
HA HA HA! AT LEAST WE BOTH AGREE THAT I AM PERFECT, NICHT WAHR?
PERFECT? WELL, I GUESS THAT PHYSICALLY YOU'RE IN PRETTY GOOD SHAPE. A LOT OF YOU NAZIS WERE, AS I RECALL.
IT'S JUST TOO BAD ABOUT YOUR ATROPHIED LITTLE HEARTS, YOUR SHRIVELED LITTLE SOULS...
AH, WE NAZIS. WE ARE SO WORTHLESS. YOU AMERICANS, YOU ARE SO CLEVER, SO NOBLE...
...SO CONFIDENT...

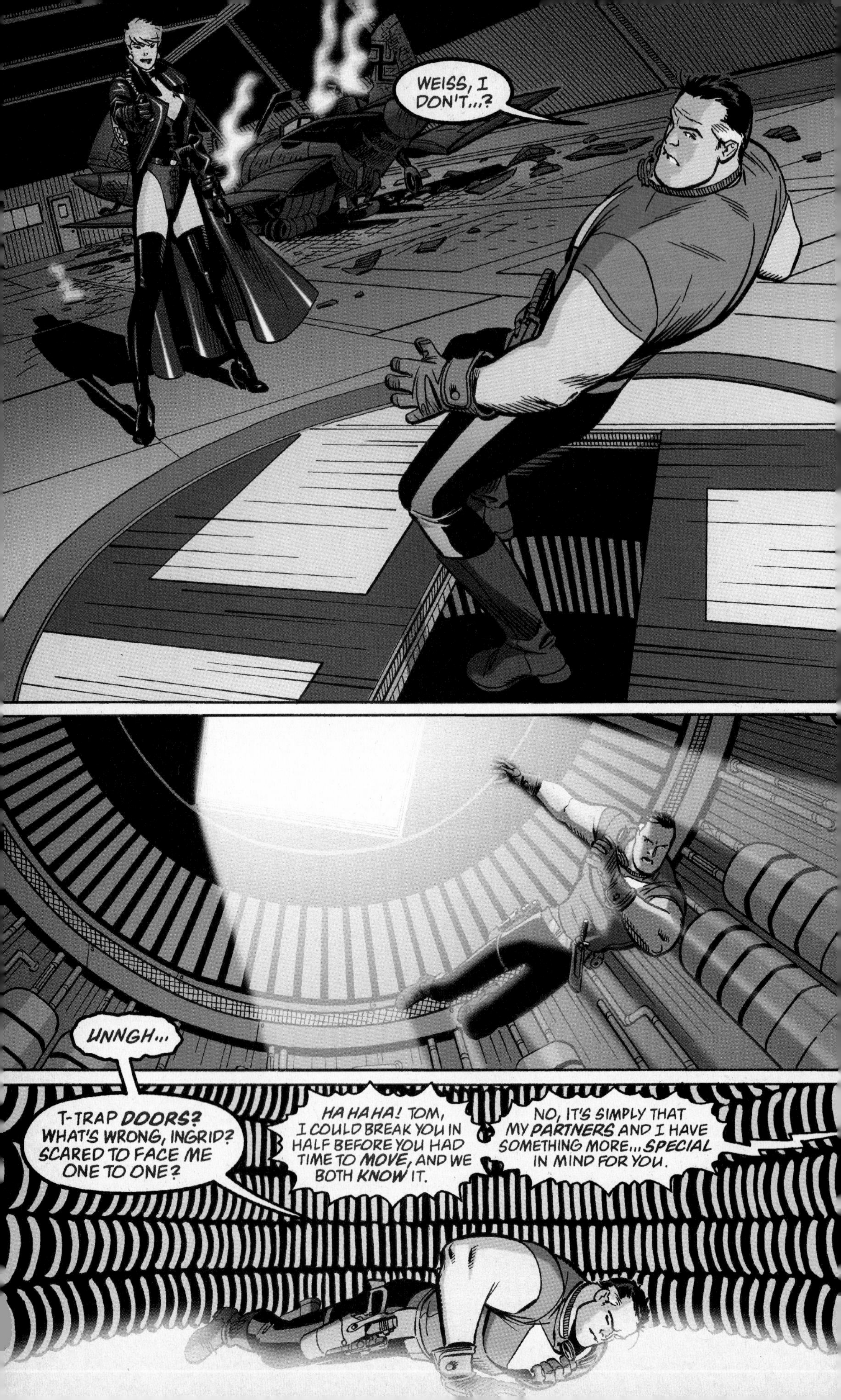

WEISS, I DON'T...?
UNNGH...
T-TRAP DOORS? WHAT'S WRONG, INGRID? SCARED TO FACE ME ONE TO ONE?
HA HA HA! TOM, I COULD BREAK YOU IN HALF BEFORE YOU HAD TIME TO MOVE, AND WE BOTH KNOW IT.
NO, IT'S SIMPLY THAT MY PARTNERS AND I HAVE SOMETHING MORE... SPECIAL IN MIND FOR YOU.

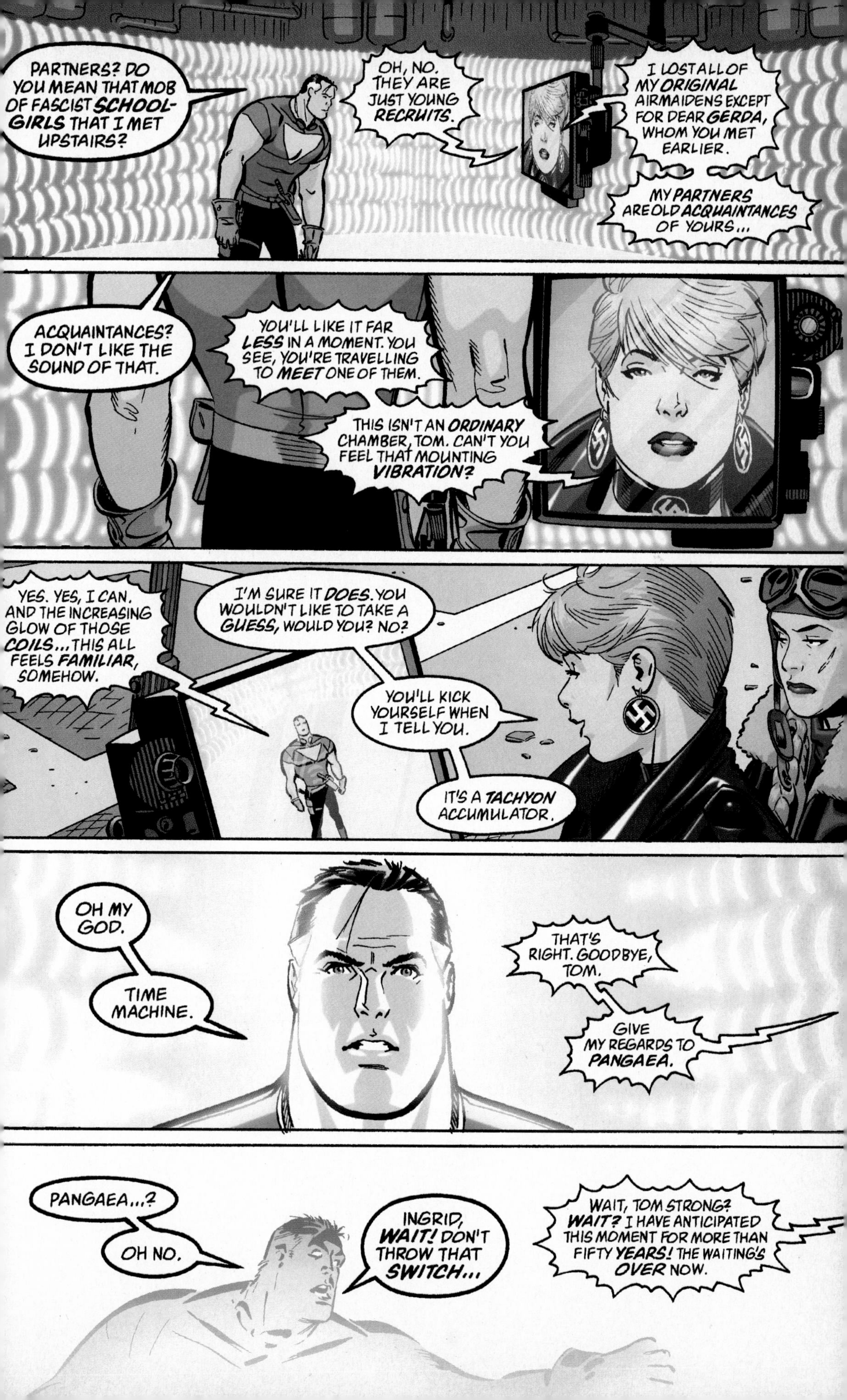
PARTNERS? DO YOU MEAN THAT MOB OF FASCIST SCHOOL-GIRLS THAT I MET UPSTAIRS?
OH, NO. THEY ARE JUST YOUNG RECRUITS.
I LOST ALL OF MY ORIGINAL AIRMAIDENS EXCEPT FOR DEAR GERDA, WHOM YOU MET EARLIER.
MY PARTNERS ARE OLD ACQUAINTANCES OF YOURS...
ACQUAINTANCES? I DON'T LIKE THE SOUND OF THAT.
YOU'LL LIKE IT FAR LESS IN A MOMENT. YOU SEE, YOU'RE TRAVELLING TO MEET ONE OF THEM.
THIS ISN'T AN ORDINARY CHAMBER, TOM. CAN'T YOU FEEL THAT MOUNTING VIBRATION?
YES. YES, I CAN. AND THE INCREASING GLOW OF THOSE COILS... THIS ALL FEELS FAMILIAR, SOMEHOW.
I'M SURE IT DOES. YOU WOULDN'T LIKE TO TAKE A GUESS, WOULD YOU? NO?
YOU'LL KICK YOURSELF WHEN I TELL YOU.
IT'S A TACHYON ACCUMULATOR.
OH MY GOD.
TIME MACHINE.
THAT'S RIGHT. GOODBYE, TOM.
GIVE MY REGARDS TO PANGAEA.
PANGAEA...?
OH NO.
INGRID, WAIT! DON'T THROW THAT SWITCH...
WAIT, TOM STRONG? WAIT? I HAVE ANTICIPATED THIS MOMENT FOR MORE THAN FIFTY YEARS! THE WAITING'S OVER NOW.

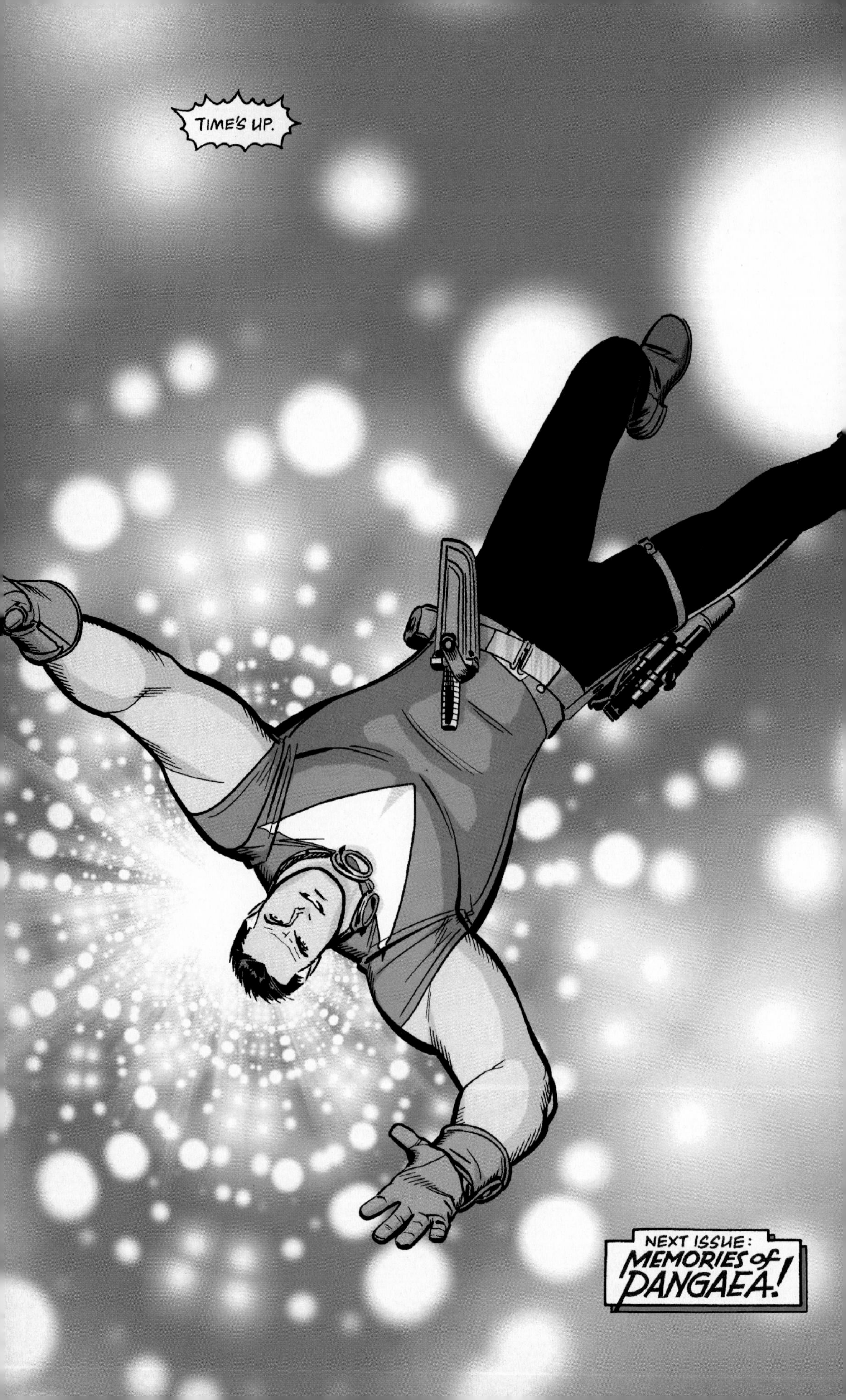
TIME'S UP.
NEXT ISSUE: MEMORIES of PANGAEA!

CHAPTER FIVE

In which a Long Journey is begun,
a Daring Experiment is remembered,
and TOM uncovers a Deeper Ploy.

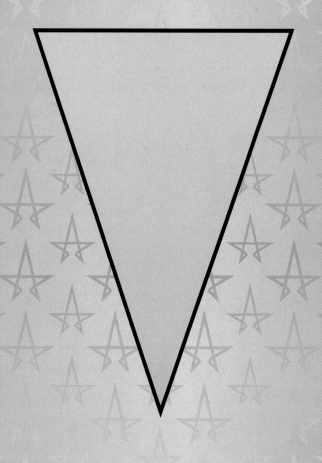

**Cover art:
Jerry Ordway**

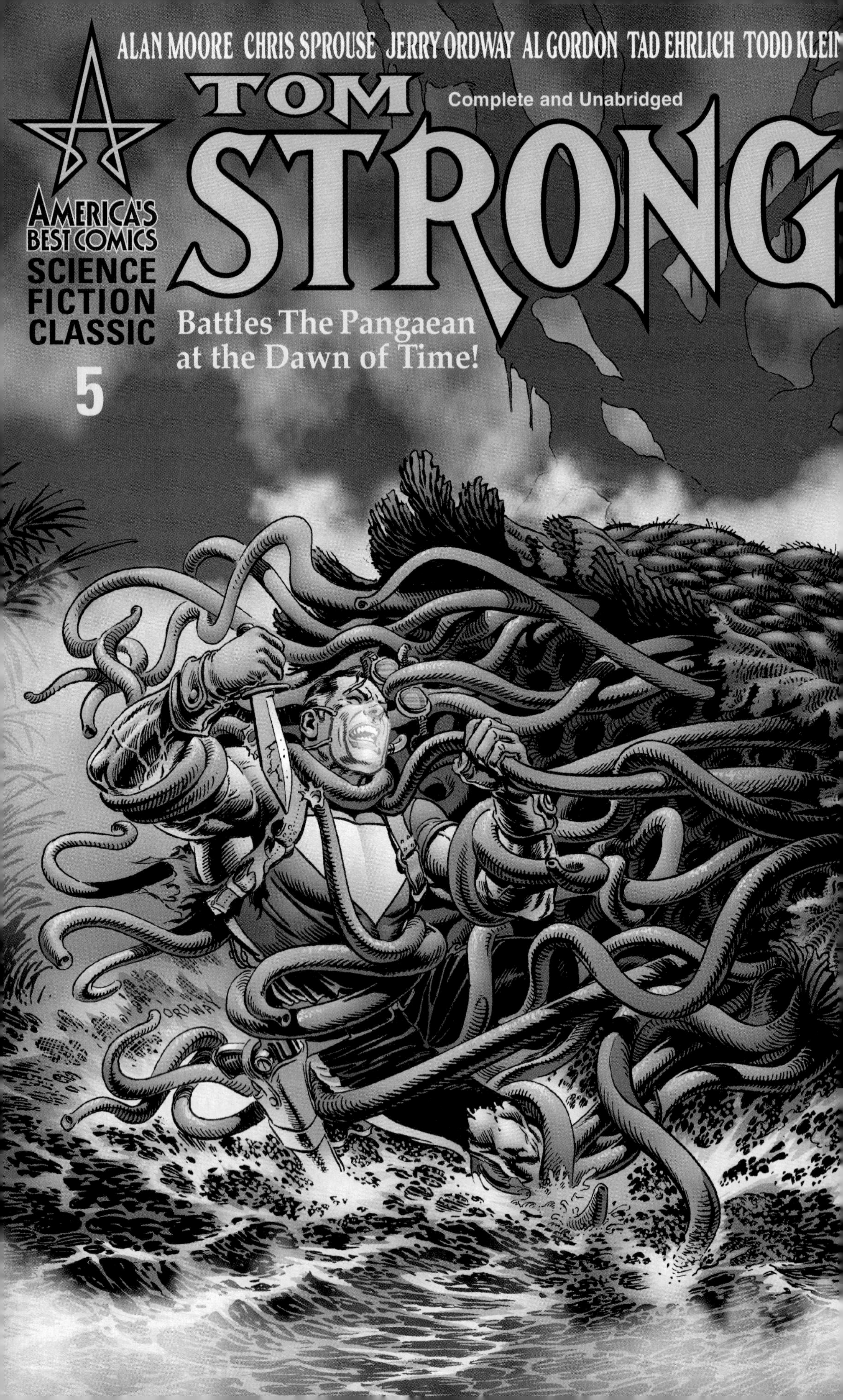
ALAN MOORE CHRIS SPROUSE JERRY ORDWAY AL GORDON TAD EHRLICH TODD KLEIN
TOM STRONG
Complete and Unabridged
AMERICA'S BEST COMICS
SCIENCE FICTION CLASSIC
5
Battles The Pangaean at the Dawn of Time!

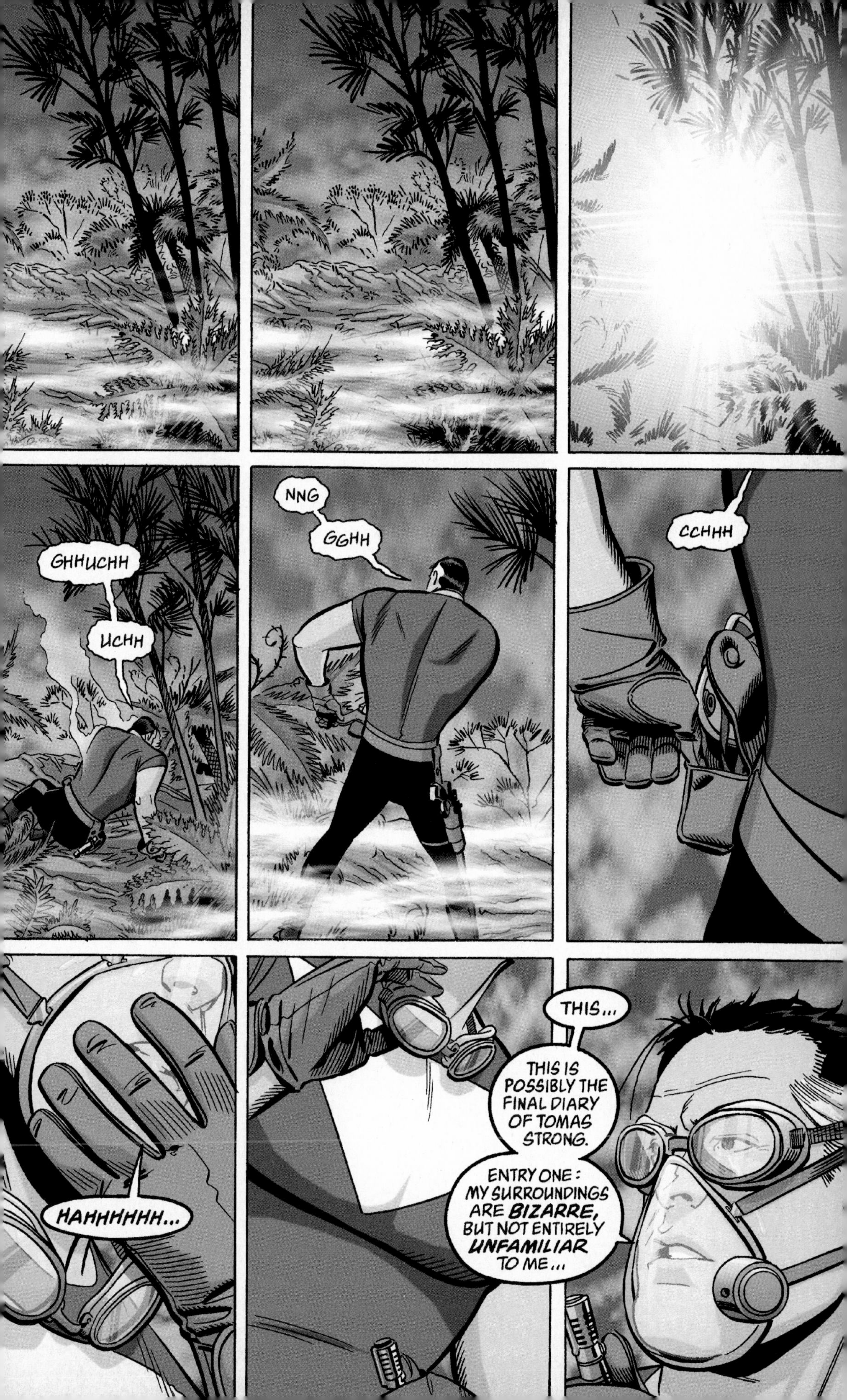
GHHUCHH
UCHH
NNG
GGHH
CCHHH
HAHHHHHH...
THIS...
THIS IS POSSIBLY THE FINAL DIARY OF TOMAS STRONG.
ENTRY ONE : MY SURROUNDINGS ARE **BIZARRE**, BUT NOT ENTIRELY **UNFAMILIAR** TO ME...

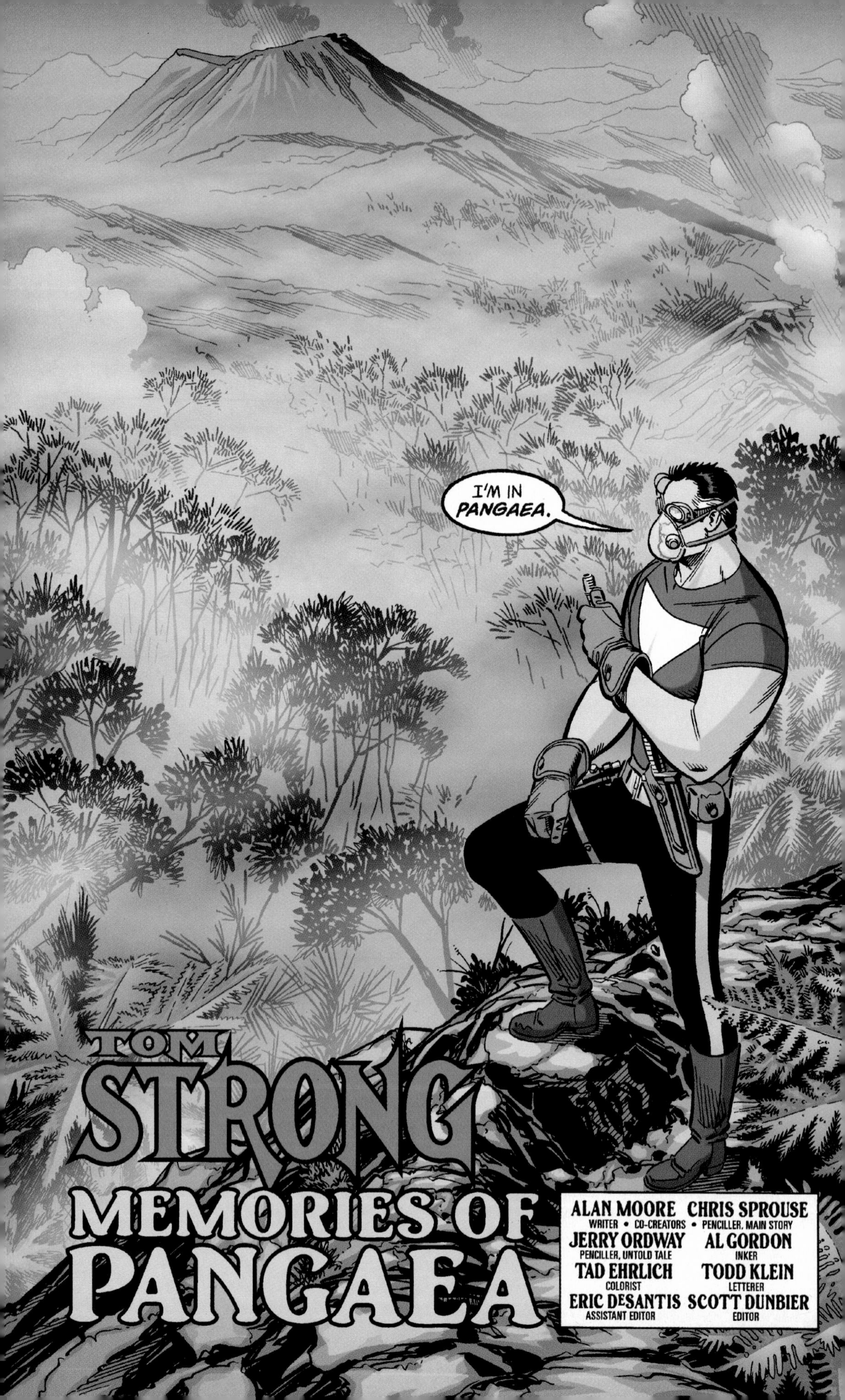
I'M IN PANGAEA.
TOM STRONG
MEMORIES OF PANGAEA
ALAN MOORE WRITER • CO-CREATORS • CHRIS SPROUSE PENCILLER, MAIN STORY
JERRY ORDWAY PENCILLER, UNTOLD TALE
AL GORDON INKER
TAD EHRLICH COLORIST
TODD KLEIN LETTERER
ERIC DESANTIS ASSISTANT EDITOR
SCOTT DUNBIER EDITOR

An Untold Tale of TOM
STRONG

TOM! CHIMIRI SU, MY HUSBAND! THIS CREATURE FROM EARTH'S DAWN IS *ABDUCTING* ME!

TH-THERE ARE *LOTS* OF THEM, MY LOVE... AND I FEAR THEY'RE ALL PART OF THE SAME INHUMAN *THING!*

CAN EVEN TECHNOLOGICAL TITAN *TOM STRONG* PREVAIL AGAINST THE LUSCIOUS, LETHAL LANDSCAPE OF EARTH'S PRIMORDIAL *PAST?* FIND OUT IN...

ESCAPE FROM EDEN!

OUR TALE OPENS IN THE LABORATORY OF PROFESSOR *PARALLAX*...

WE ARE *READY*, PROFESSOR. ARE WE PROPERLY *DRESSED* FOR OUR *DESTINATION?*

OH, YES. IT'S LIKELY TO BE RATHER *WARM! PREPARE* YOURSELVES, MY FRIENDS... AND *BON VOYAGE!*

OH! OH, TOM, MY STOMACH FEELS SO *STRANGE!* ARE WE *FALLING?*

IN A *SENSE*, DHALUA... BUT WE'RE FALLING THROUGH *TIME* INSTEAD OF *SPACE!* IT'S A THREE-HUNDRED-MILLION YEAR *DROP*, SO EXPECT A BUMPY *LANDING!*

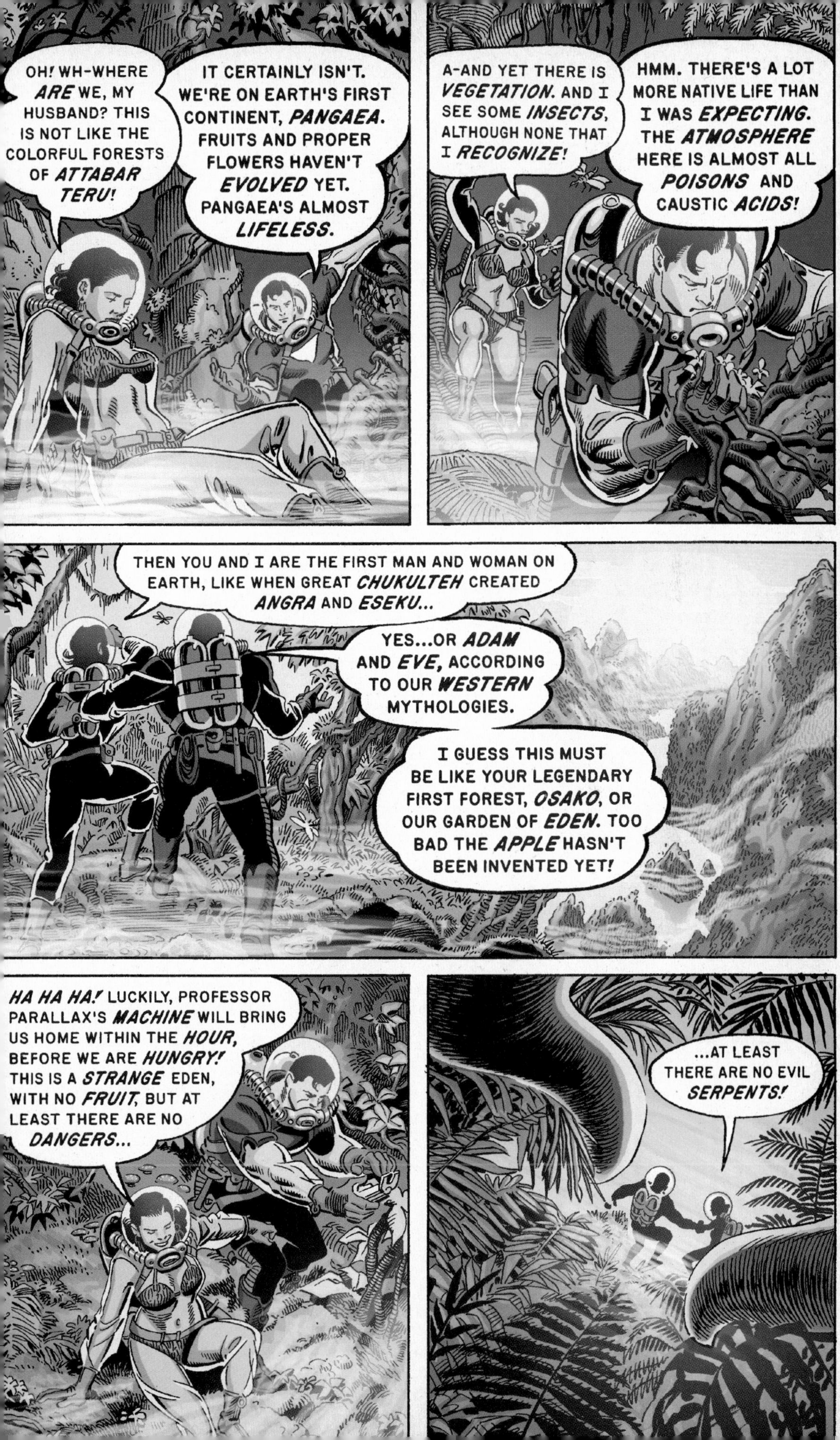
OH! WH-WHERE ARE WE, MY HUSBAND? THIS IS NOT LIKE THE COLORFUL FORESTS OF ATTABAR TERU!
IT CERTAINLY ISN'T. WE'RE ON EARTH'S FIRST CONTINENT, PANGAEA. FRUITS AND PROPER FLOWERS HAVEN'T EVOLVED YET. PANGAEA'S ALMOST LIFELESS.
A-AND YET THERE IS VEGETATION. AND I SEE SOME INSECTS, ALTHOUGH NONE THAT I RECOGNIZE!
HMM. THERE'S A LOT MORE NATIVE LIFE THAN I WAS EXPECTING. THE ATMOSPHERE HERE IS ALMOST ALL POISONS AND CAUSTIC ACIDS!
THEN YOU AND I ARE THE FIRST MAN AND WOMAN ON EARTH, LIKE WHEN GREAT CHUKULTEH CREATED ANGRA AND ESEKU...
YES...OR ADAM AND EVE, ACCORDING TO OUR WESTERN MYTHOLOGIES.
I GUESS THIS MUST BE LIKE YOUR LEGENDARY FIRST FOREST, OSAKO, OR OUR GARDEN OF EDEN. TOO BAD THE APPLE HASN'T BEEN INVENTED YET!
HA HA HA! LUCKILY, PROFESSOR PARALLAX'S MACHINE WILL BRING US HOME WITHIN THE HOUR, BEFORE WE ARE HUNGRY! THIS IS A STRANGE EDEN, WITH NO FRUIT, BUT AT LEAST THERE ARE NO DANGERS...
...AT LEAST THERE ARE NO EVIL SERPENTS!

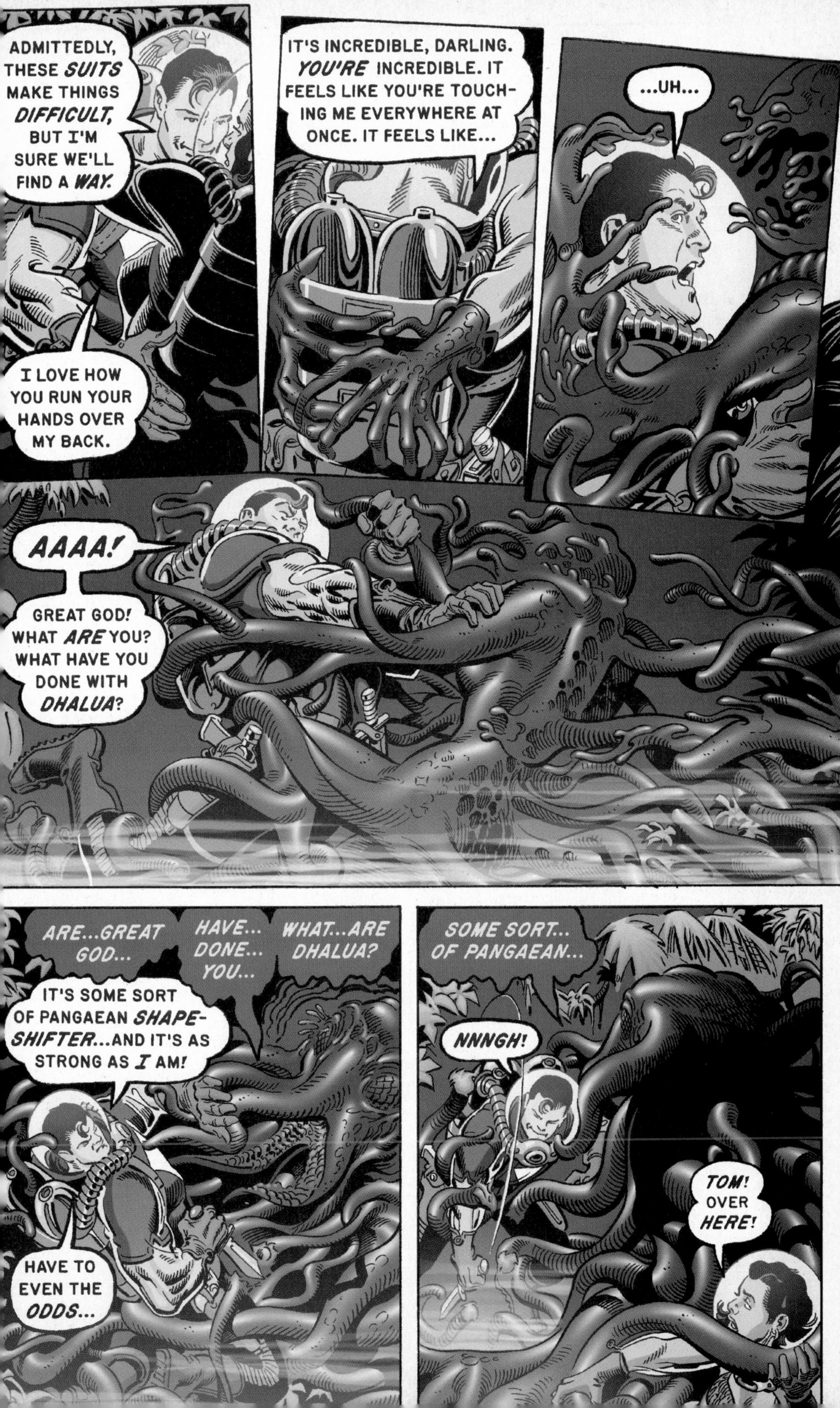

ADMITTEDLY, THESE SUITS MAKE THINGS DIFFICULT, BUT I'M SURE WE'LL FIND A WAY.
I LOVE HOW YOU RUN YOUR HANDS OVER MY BACK.
IT'S INCREDIBLE, DARLING. YOU'RE INCREDIBLE. IT FEELS LIKE YOU'RE TOUCHING ME EVERYWHERE AT ONCE. IT FEELS LIKE...
...UH...
AAAA!
GREAT GOD! WHAT ARE YOU? WHAT HAVE YOU DONE WITH DHALUA?
ARE...GREAT GOD...
HAVE... DONE... YOU...
WHAT...ARE DHALUA?
IT'S SOME SORT OF PANGAEAN SHAPE-SHIFTER...AND IT'S AS STRONG AS I AM!
HAVE TO EVEN THE ODDS...
SOME SORT... OF PANGAEAN...
NNNGH!
TOM! OVER HERE!

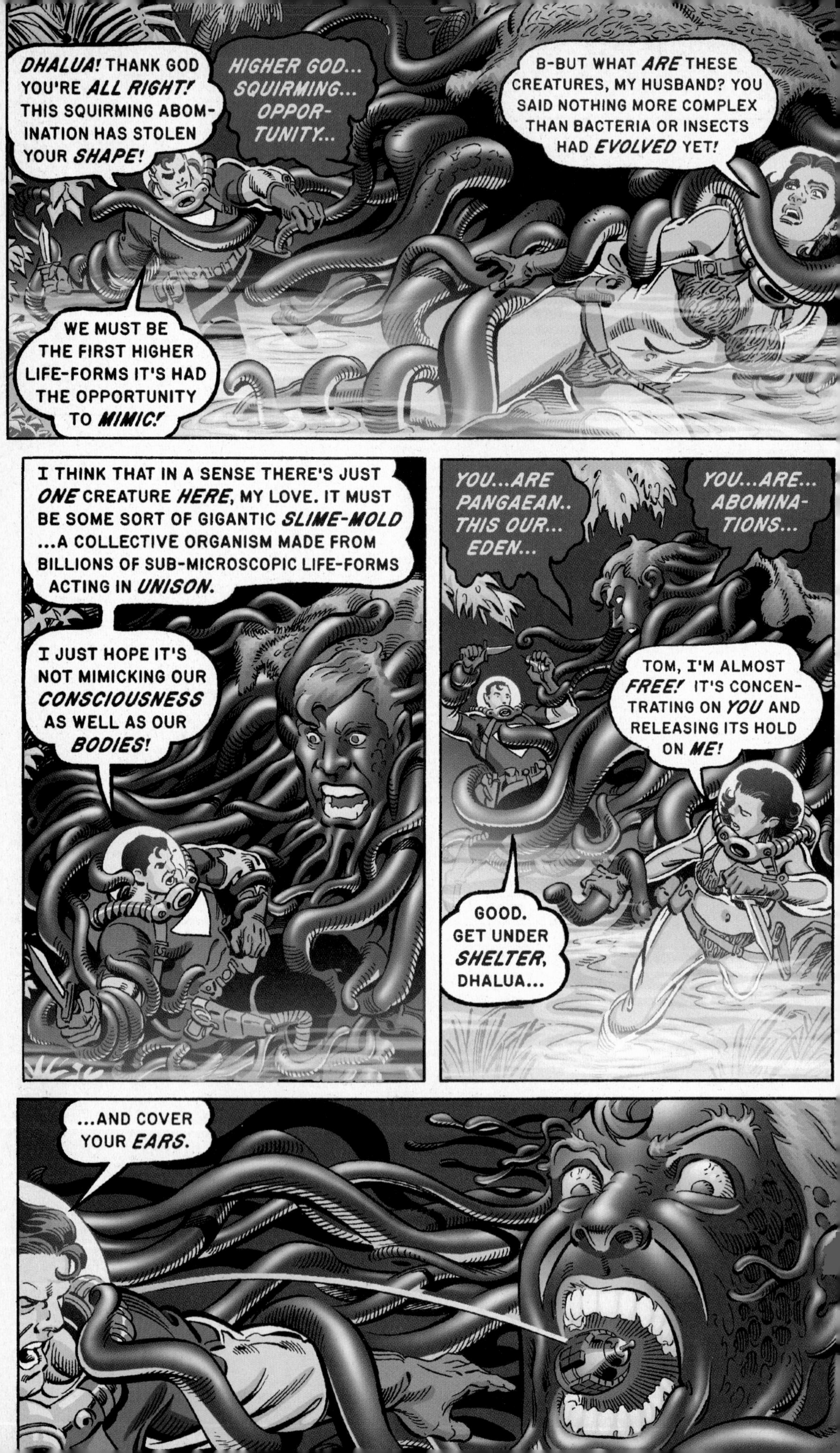
DHALUA! THANK GOD YOU'RE ALL RIGHT! THIS SQUIRMING ABOMINATION HAS STOLEN YOUR SHAPE!
HIGHER GOD... SQUIRMING... OPPORTUNITY...
B-BUT WHAT ARE THESE CREATURES, MY HUSBAND? YOU SAID NOTHING MORE COMPLEX THAN BACTERIA OR INSECTS HAD EVOLVED YET!
WE MUST BE THE FIRST HIGHER LIFE-FORMS IT'S HAD THE OPPORTUNITY TO MIMIC!
I THINK THAT IN A SENSE THERE'S JUST ONE CREATURE HERE, MY LOVE. IT MUST BE SOME SORT OF GIGANTIC SLIME-MOLD ...A COLLECTIVE ORGANISM MADE FROM BILLIONS OF SUB-MICROSCOPIC LIFE-FORMS ACTING IN UNISON.
I JUST HOPE IT'S NOT MIMICKING OUR CONSCIOUSNESS AS WELL AS OUR BODIES!
YOU...ARE PANGAEAN.. THIS OUR... EDEN...
YOU...ARE... ABOMINATIONS...
TOM, I'M ALMOST FREE! IT'S CONCENTRATING ON YOU AND RELEASING ITS HOLD ON ME!
GOOD. GET UNDER SHELTER, DHALUA...
...AND COVER YOUR EARS.

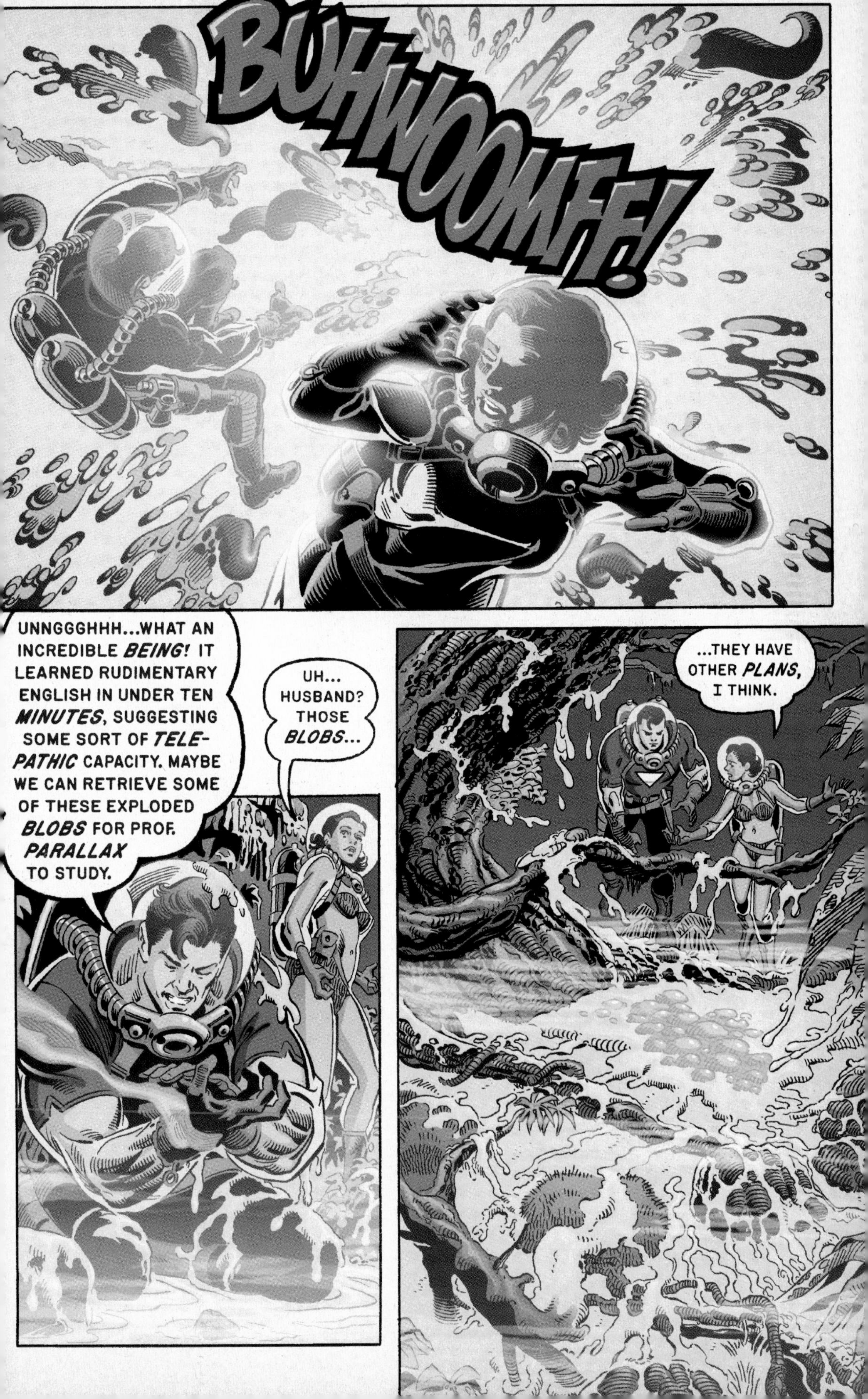
BUHWOOMFF!
UNNGGGHHH...WHAT AN INCREDIBLE BEING! IT LEARNED RUDIMENTARY ENGLISH IN UNDER TEN MINUTES, SUGGESTING SOME SORT OF TELE-PATHIC CAPACITY. MAYBE WE CAN RETRIEVE SOME OF THESE EXPLODED BLOBS FOR PROF. PARALLAX TO STUDY.
UH... HUSBAND? THOSE BLOBS...
...THEY HAVE OTHER PLANS, I THINK.

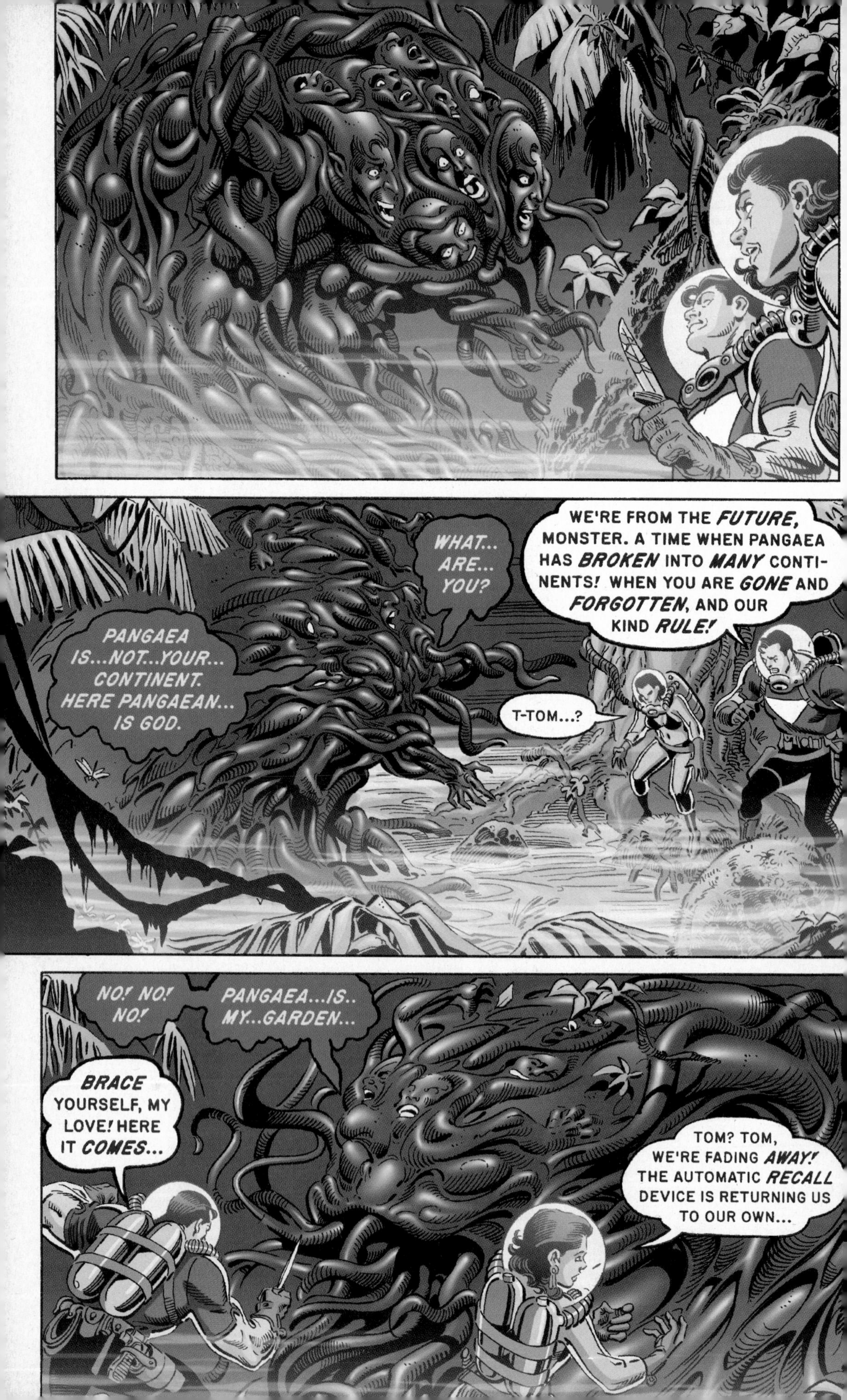

WHAT... ARE... YOU?
WE'RE FROM THE FUTURE, MONSTER. A TIME WHEN PANGAEA HAS BROKEN INTO MANY CONTINENTS! WHEN YOU ARE GONE AND FORGOTTEN, AND OUR KIND RULE!
PANGAEA IS...NOT...YOUR... CONTINENT. HERE PANGAEAN... IS GOD.
T-TOM...?
NO! NO! NO!
PANGAEA...IS.. MY...GARDEN...
BRACE YOURSELF, MY LOVE! HERE IT COMES...
TOM? TOM, WE'RE FADING AWAY! THE AUTOMATIC RECALL DEVICE IS RETURNING US TO OUR OWN...

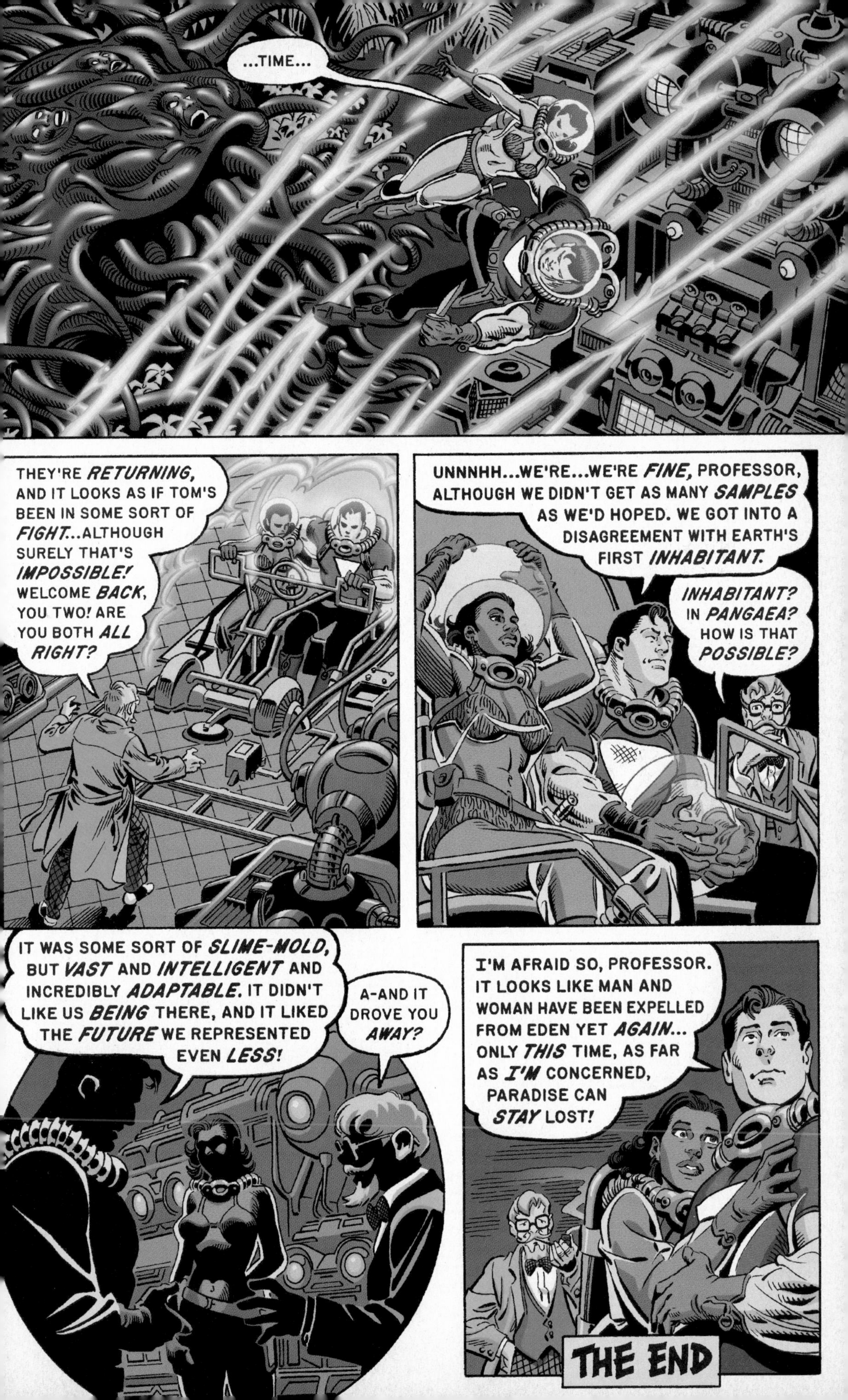
...TIME...
THEY'RE *RETURNING*, AND IT LOOKS AS IF TOM'S BEEN IN SOME SORT OF *FIGHT*...ALTHOUGH SURELY THAT'S *IMPOSSIBLE!* WELCOME *BACK*, YOU TWO! ARE YOU BOTH *ALL RIGHT?*
UNNNHH...WE'RE...WE'RE *FINE*, PROFESSOR, ALTHOUGH WE DIDN'T GET AS MANY *SAMPLES* AS WE'D HOPED. WE GOT INTO A DISAGREEMENT WITH EARTH'S FIRST *INHABITANT*.
INHABITANT? IN *PANGAEA?* HOW IS THAT *POSSIBLE?*
IT WAS SOME SORT OF *SLIME-MOLD*, BUT *VAST* AND *INTELLIGENT* AND INCREDIBLY *ADAPTABLE*. IT DIDN'T LIKE US *BEING* THERE, AND IT LIKED THE *FUTURE* WE REPRESENTED EVEN *LESS!*
A-AND IT DROVE YOU *AWAY?*
I'M AFRAID SO, PROFESSOR. IT LOOKS LIKE MAN AND WOMAN HAVE BEEN EXPELLED FROM EDEN YET *AGAIN*... ONLY *THIS* TIME, AS FAR AS *I'M* CONCERNED, PARADISE CAN *STAY* LOST!
THE END

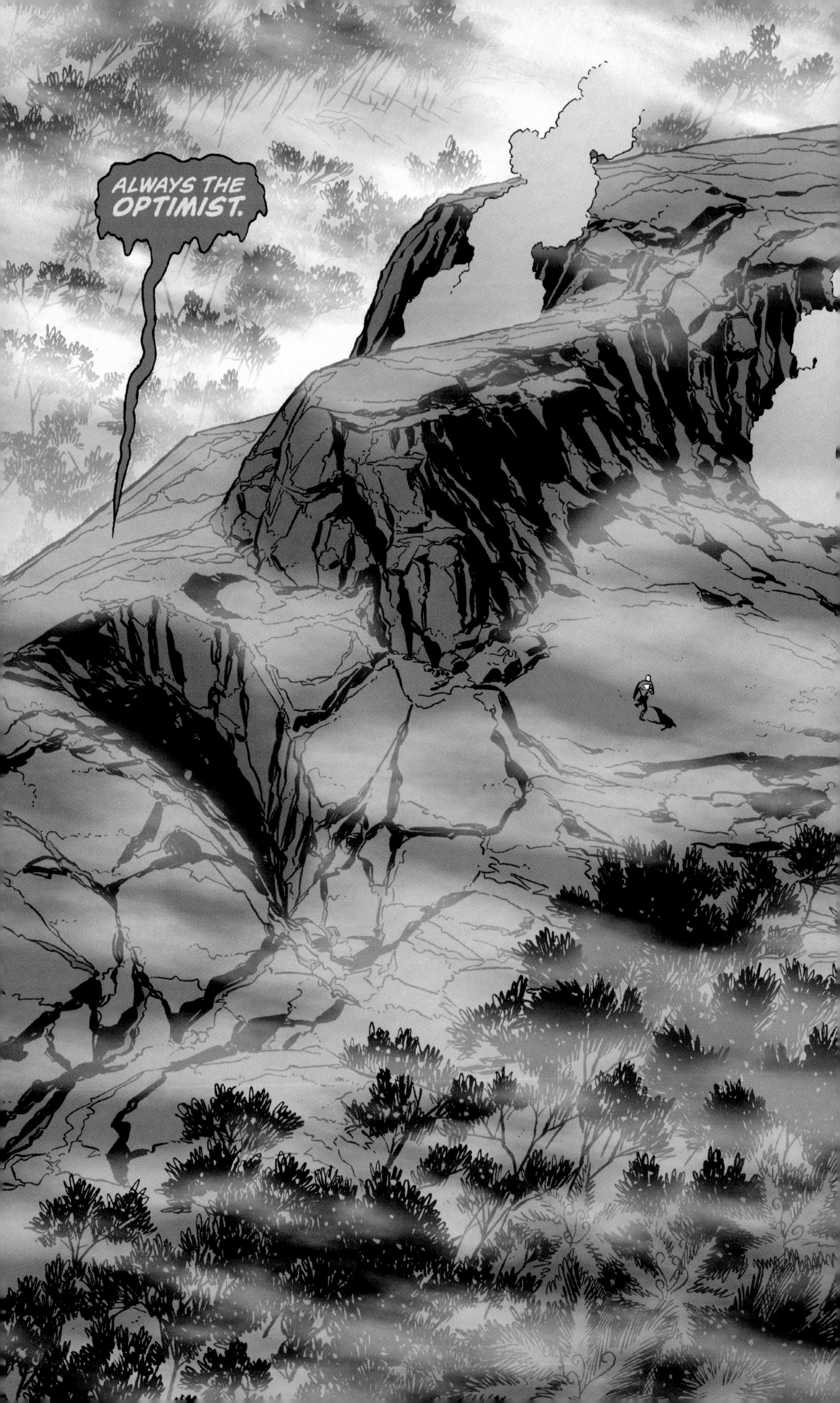
ALWAYS THE OPTIMIST.

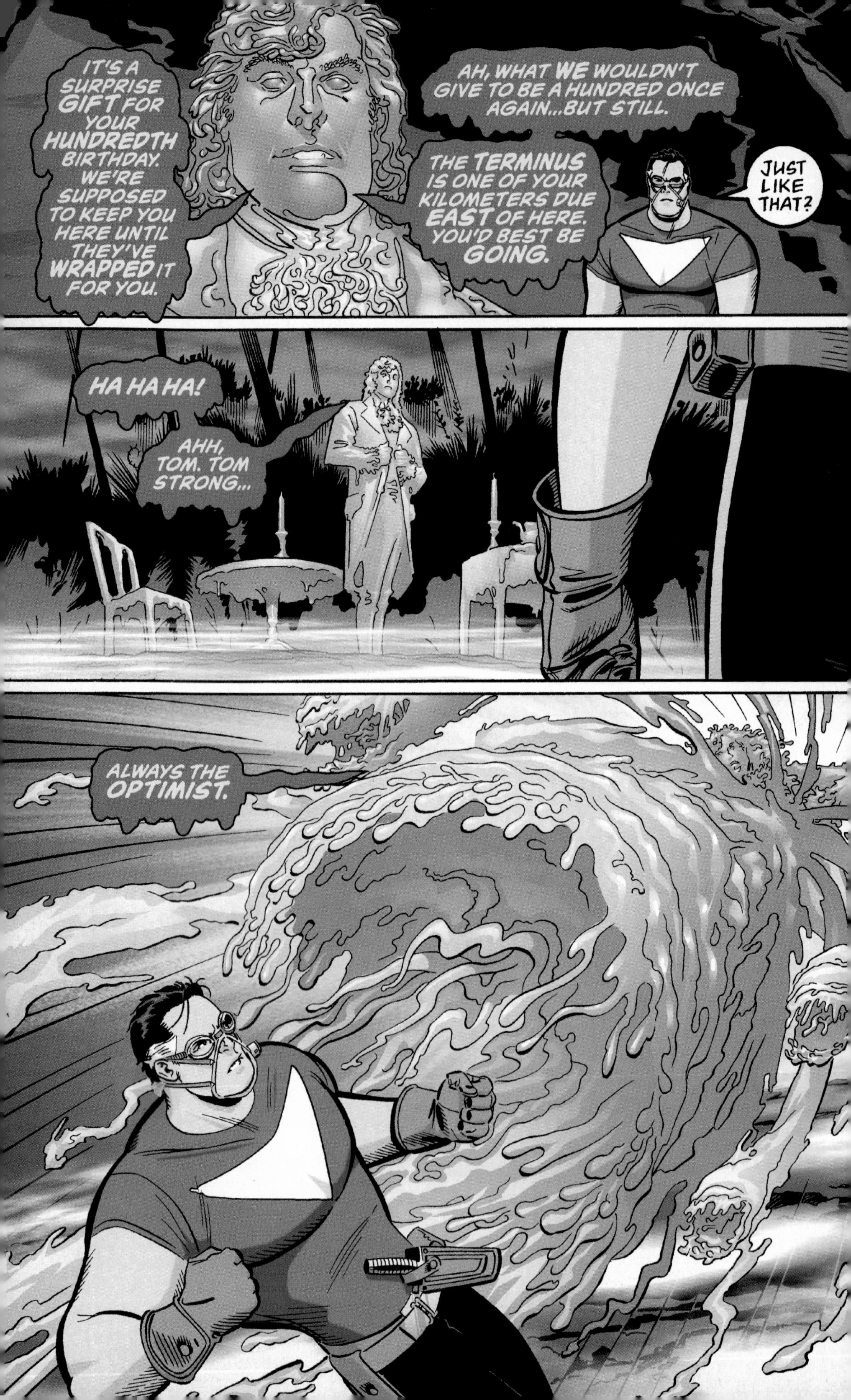
IT'S A SURPRISE GIFT FOR YOUR HUNDREDTH BIRTHDAY. WE'RE SUPPOSED TO KEEP YOU HERE UNTIL THEY'VE WRAPPED IT FOR YOU.
AH, WHAT WE WOULDN'T GIVE TO BE A HUNDRED ONCE AGAIN...BUT STILL.
THE TERMINUS IS ONE OF YOUR KILOMETERS DUE EAST OF HERE. YOU'D BEST BE GOING.
JUST LIKE THAT?
HA HA HA!
AHH, TOM. TOM STRONG...
ALWAYS THE OPTIMIST.

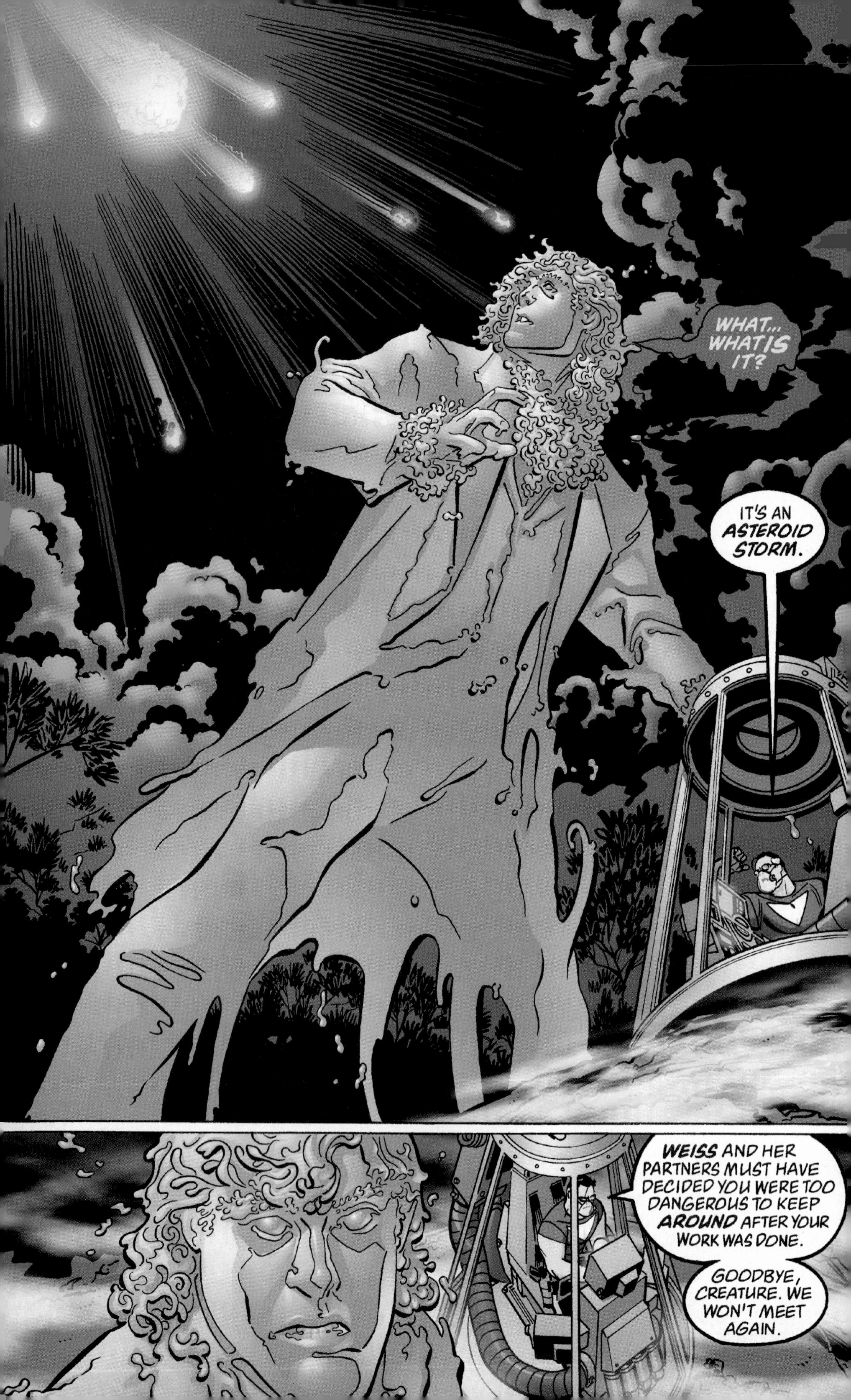
WHAT... WHAT IS IT?
IT'S AN ASTEROID STORM.
WEISS AND HER PARTNERS MUST HAVE DECIDED YOU WERE TOO DANGEROUS TO KEEP AROUND AFTER YOUR WORK WAS DONE.
GOODBYE, CREATURE. WE WON'T MEET AGAIN.

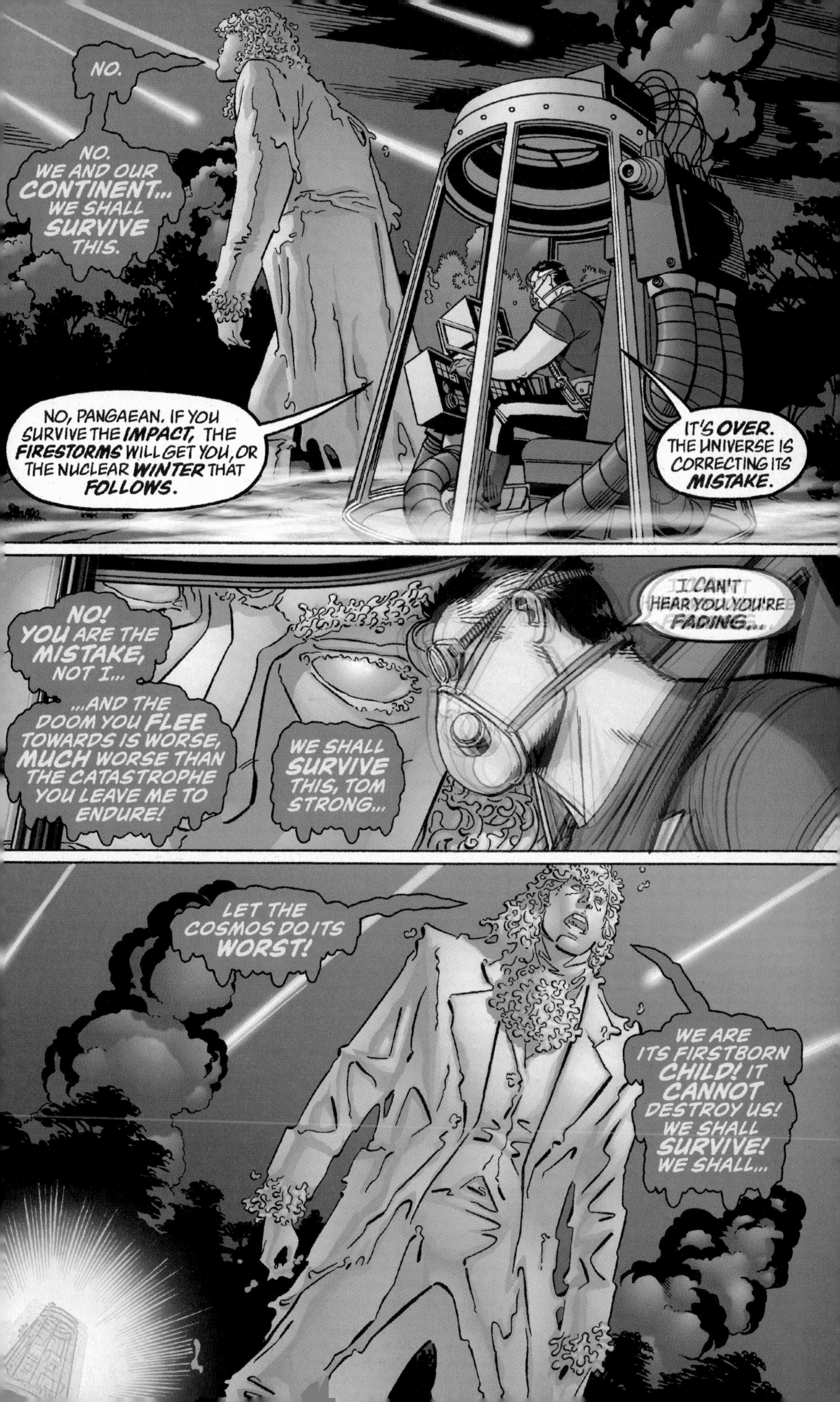
NO.
NO. WE AND OUR CONTINENT... WE SHALL SURVIVE THIS.
NO, PANGAEAN. IF YOU SURVIVE THE IMPACT, THE FIRESTORMS WILL GET YOU, OR THE NUCLEAR WINTER THAT FOLLOWS.
IT'S OVER. THE UNIVERSE IS CORRECTING ITS MISTAKE.
I CAN'T HEAR YOU. YOU'RE FADING...
NO! YOU ARE THE MISTAKE, NOT I...
...AND THE DOOM YOU FLEE TOWARDS IS WORSE, MUCH WORSE THAN THE CATASTROPHE YOU LEAVE ME TO ENDURE!
WE SHALL SURVIVE THIS, TOM STRONG...
LET THE COSMOS DO ITS WORST!
WE ARE ITS FIRSTBORN CHILD! IT CANNOT DESTROY US! WE SHALL SURVIVE! WE SHALL...

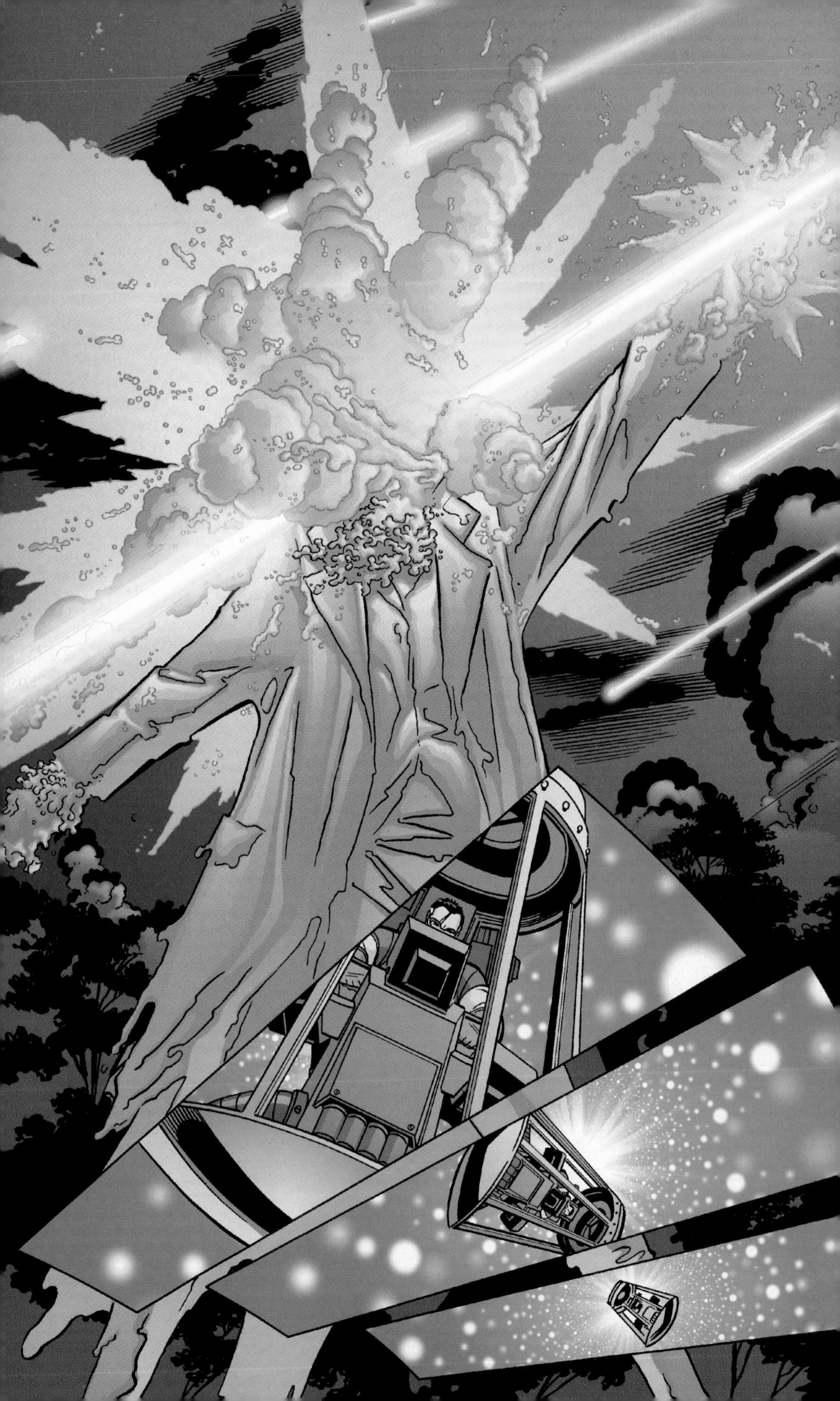

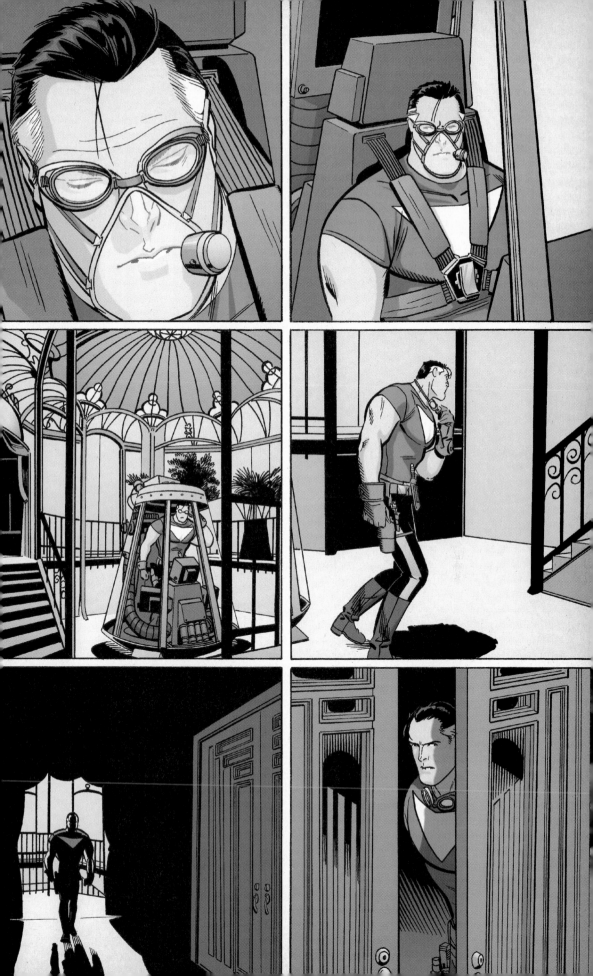

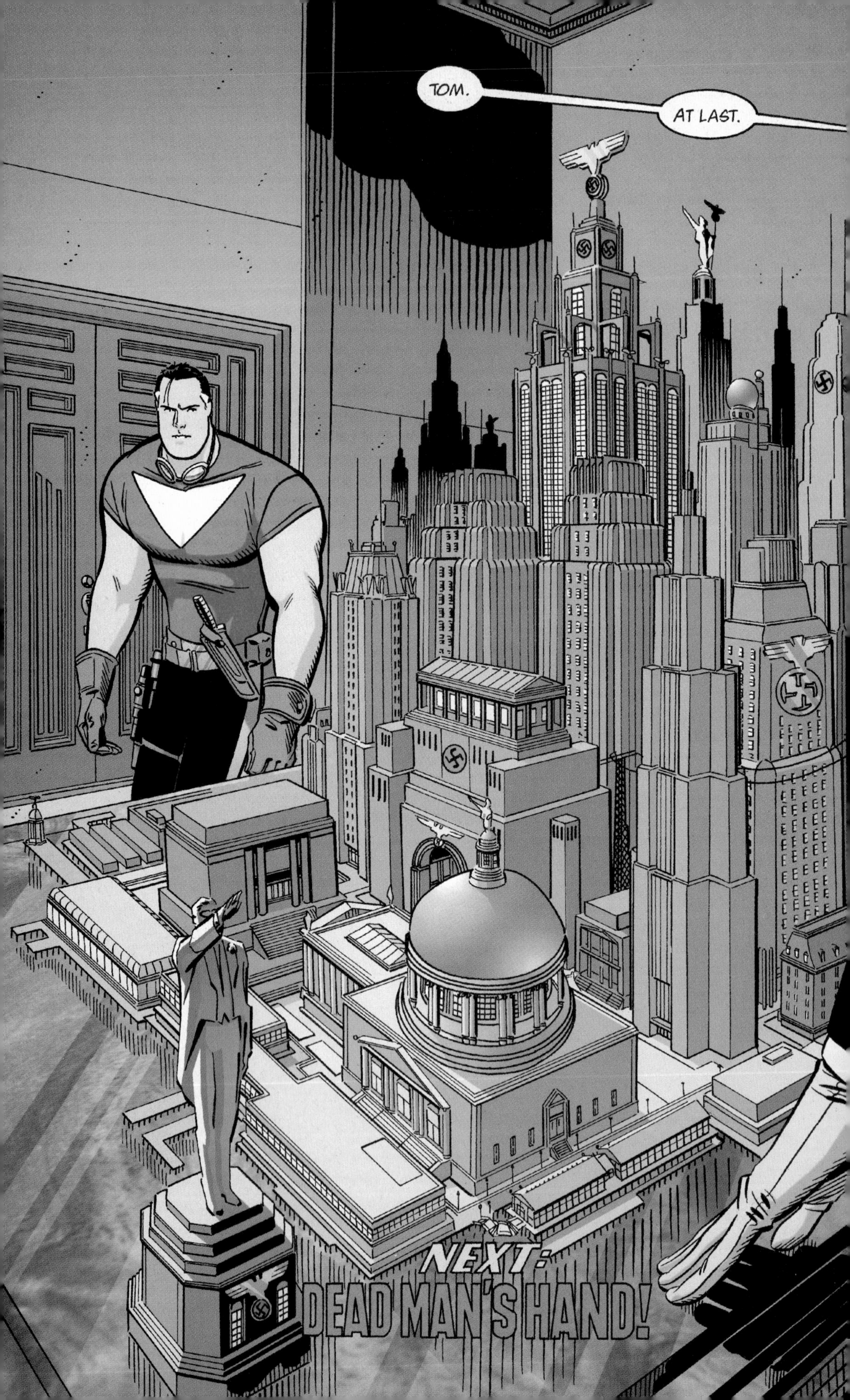
TOM.
AT LAST.
NEXT:
DEAD MAN'S HAND!

CHAPTER SIX

**In which a Firm Hand is revealed,
a Fiery Trap is revisited, and
TOM learns a Family Secret.**

**Cover art:
Dave Gibbons**

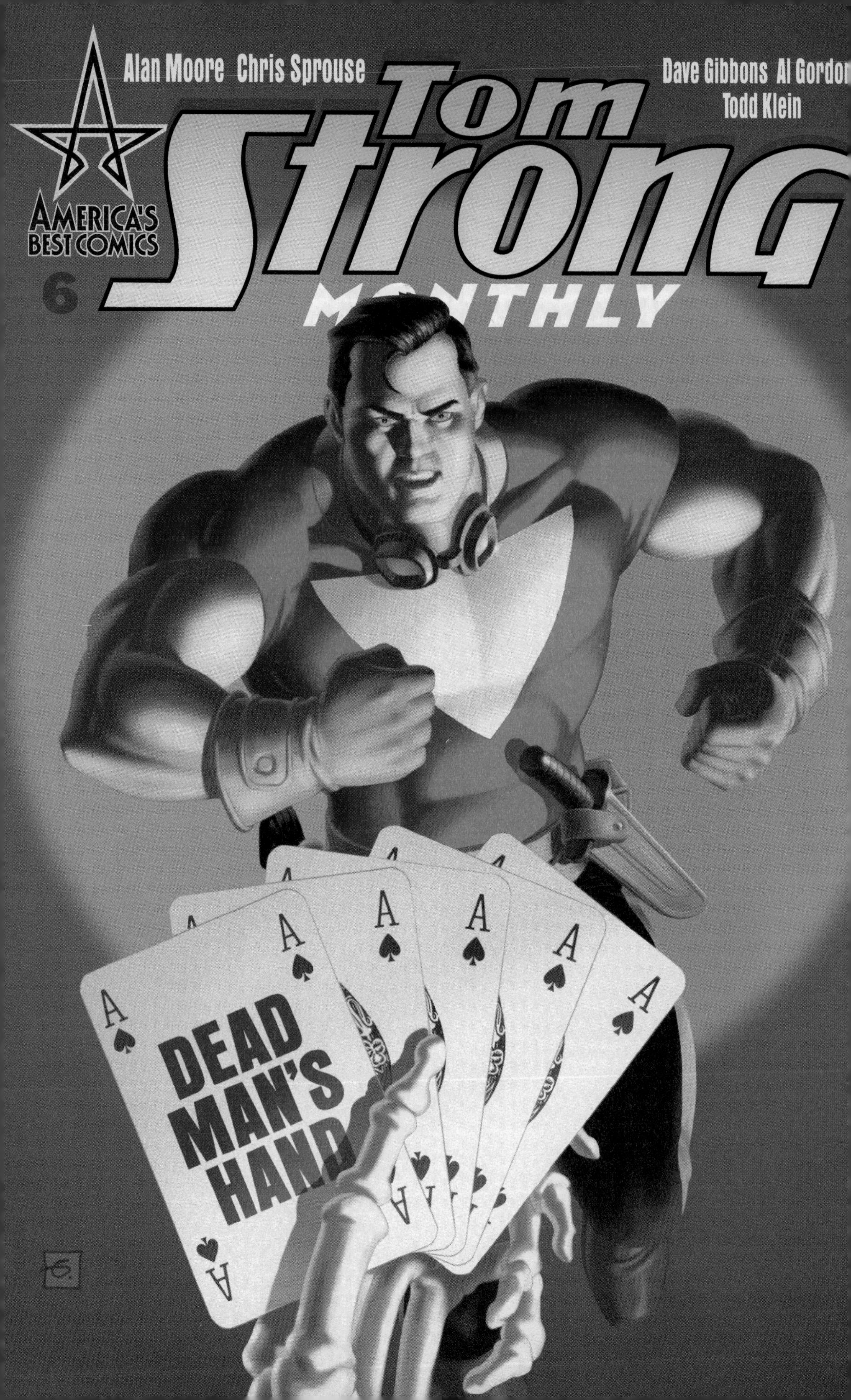

Alan Moore Chris Sprouse
Dave Gibbons Al Gordon
Todd Klein
Tom Strong
AMERICA'S BEST COMICS
6
MONTHLY
DEAD MAN'S HAND

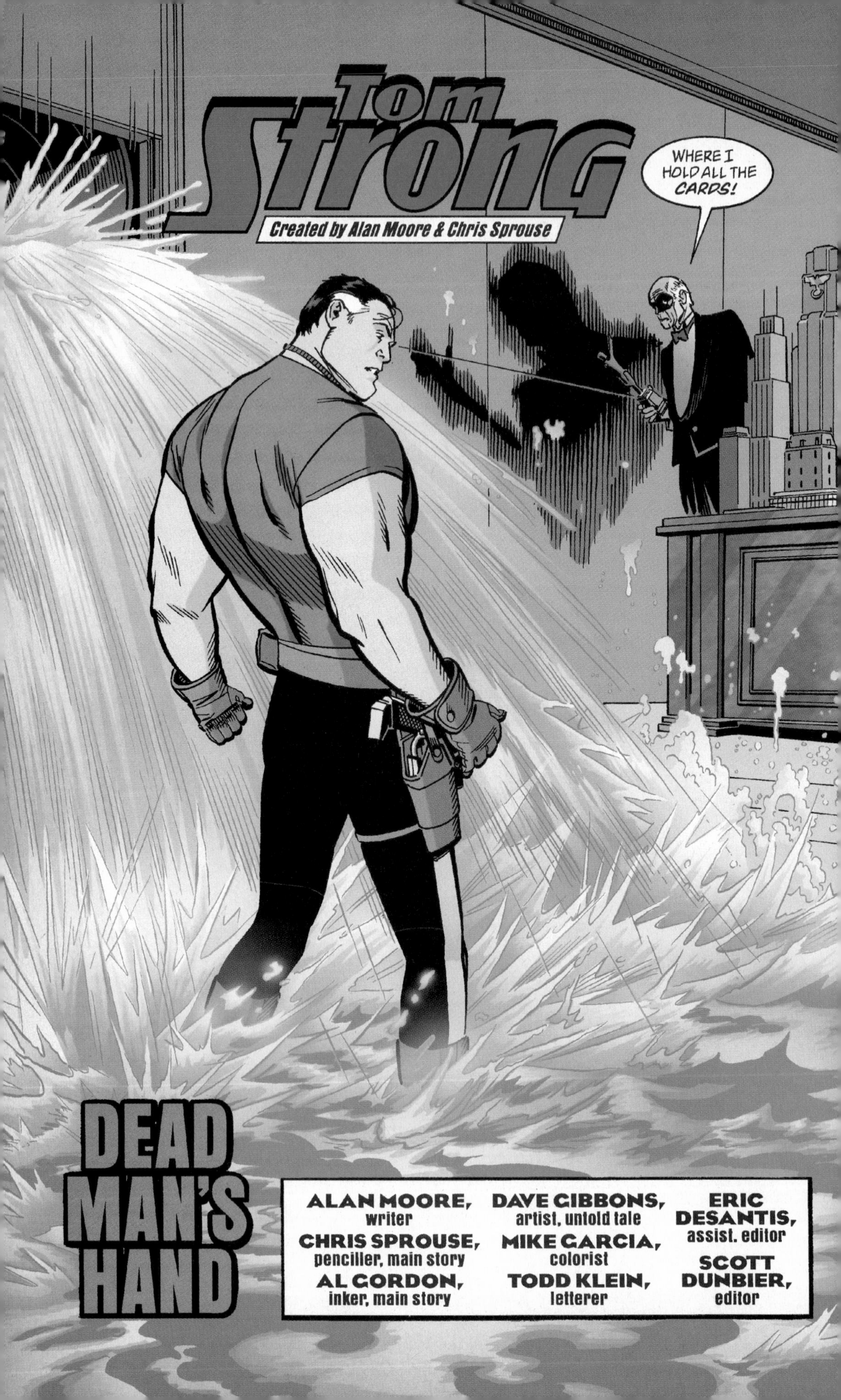
Tom Strong
Created by Alan Moore & Chris Sprouse
WHERE I HOLD ALL THE CARDS!
DEAD MAN'S HAND
ALAN MOORE, writer
CHRIS SPROUSE, penciller, main story
AL GORDON, inker, main story
DAVE GIBBONS, artist, untold tale
MIKE GARCIA, colorist
TODD KLEIN, letterer
ERIC DESANTIS, assist. editor
SCOTT DUNBIER, editor

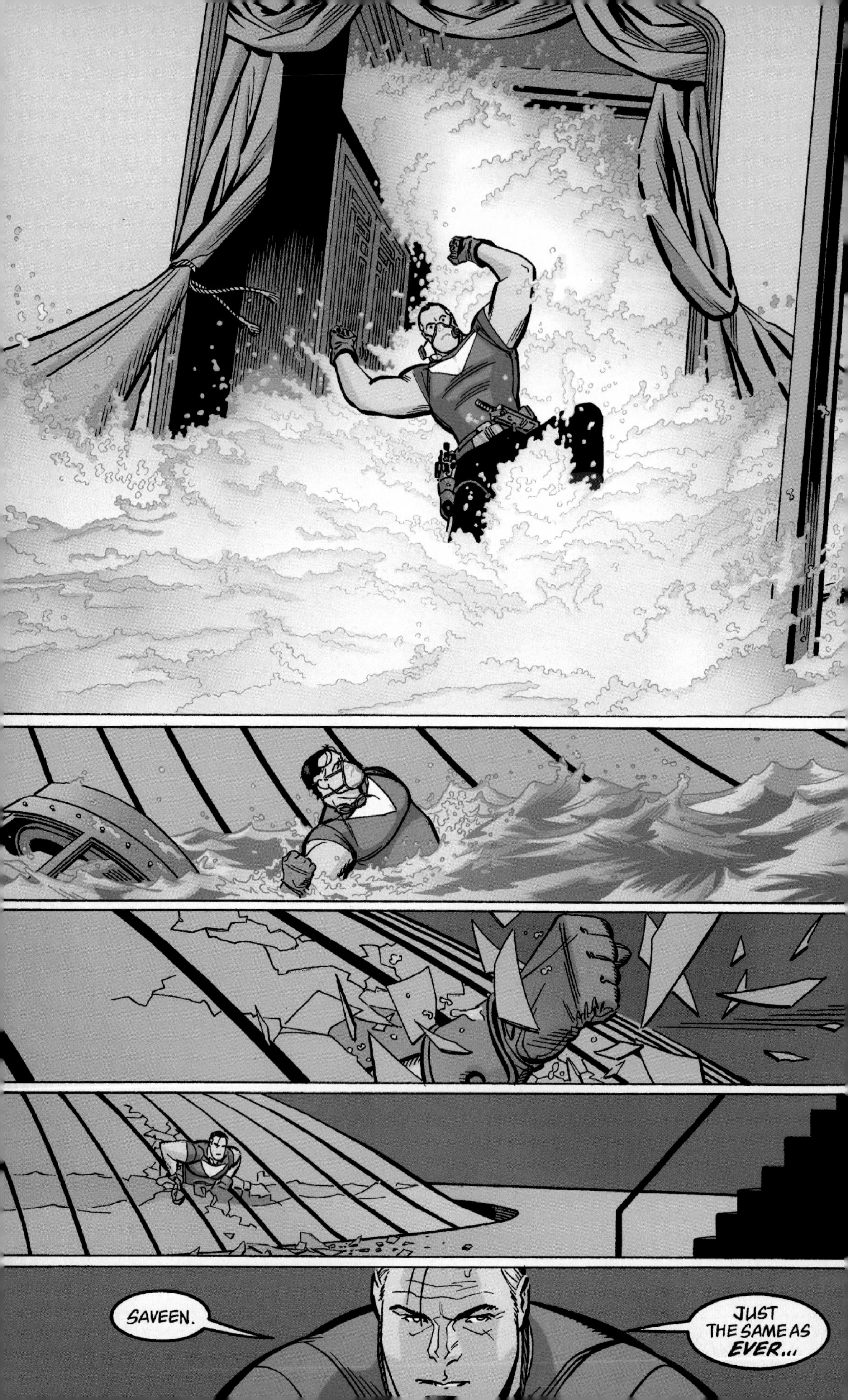
SAVEEN.
JUST THE SAME AS EVER...

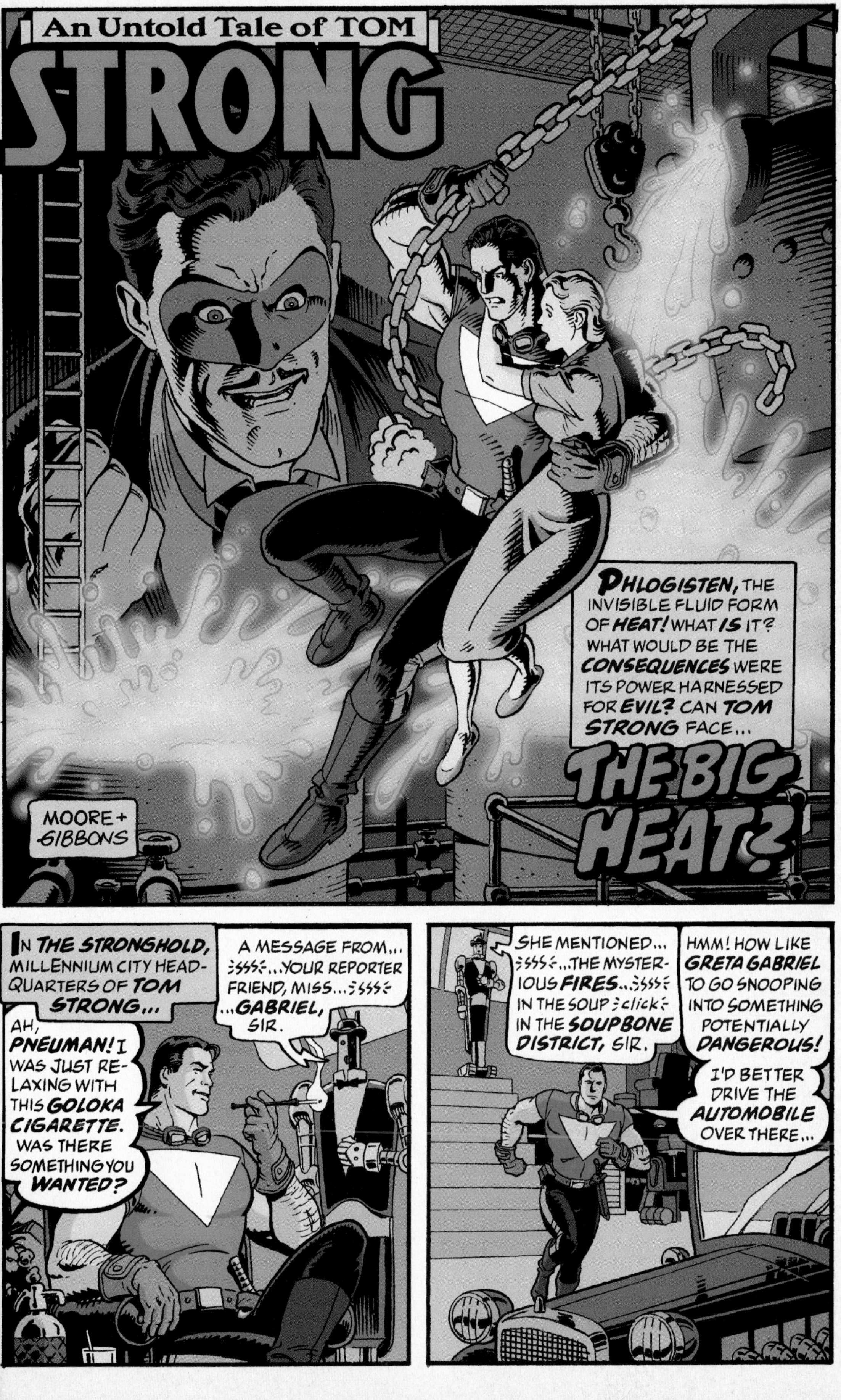

An Untold Tale of TOM
STRONG
PHLOGISTEN, THE INVISIBLE FLUID FORM OF HEAT! WHAT IS IT? WHAT WOULD BE THE CONSEQUENCES WERE ITS POWER HARNESSED FOR EVIL? CAN TOM STRONG FACE...
THE BIG HEAT?
MOORE + GIBBONS
IN THE STRONGHOLD, MILLENNIUM CITY HEAD-QUARTERS OF TOM STRONG...
AH, PNEUMAN! I WAS JUST RE-LAXING WITH THIS GOLOKA CIGARETTE. WAS THERE SOMETHING YOU WANTED?
A MESSAGE FROM... SSSS... YOUR REPORTER FRIEND, MISS... SSSS ...GABRIEL, SIR.
SHE MENTIONED... SSSS ...THE MYSTER-IOUS FIRES.. SSSS IN THE SOUP click IN THE SOUPBONE DISTRICT, SIR.
HMM! HOW LIKE GRETA GABRIEL TO GO SNOOPING INTO SOMETHING POTENTIALLY DANGEROUS!
I'D BETTER DRIVE THE AUTOMOBILE OVER THERE...

AND SO... FIVE WAREHOUSES BURNED TO *ASHES*, AND NO CLUE HOW THE FIRES STARTED...ALL IN THE *SOUPBONE* DISTRICT!

ONE WAREHOUSE WAS OWNED BY THE *MILLENNIUM MERCURY*, GRETA'S NEWSPAPER! THAT'S PROBABLY WHERE SHE *IS!*

BUT... THIS DOESN'T LOOK *GOOD!* HERE'S GRETA'S *SHOES*, BUT SHE SEEMS TO HAVE VANISHED WITH-OUT A *TRACE...*

...UNLESS THE ULTRA-VIOLET *FLASHLIGHT* FROM MY *BELT* CAN TELL ME ANYTHING?

I'M IN *LUCK!* GRETA'S BARE *FEET* HAVE LEFT FAINT PHOS-PHORESCENT *TRACKS*...WHICH SEEM TO LEAD TOWARDS THAT *MANHOLE COVER!*

NO *OTHER* FOOTPRINTS ...BUT *ABDUCTION'S* STILL POSSIBLE, ASSUMING HER ATTACKERS WORE *SHOES!*

HMM. WELL, SHE CERTAINLY *CAME* THIS WAY! THERE'S HER *SCARF*...

...ALTHOUGH THIS DOESN'T LOOK LIKE ANY DRAINAGE OR MAINTENANCE TUNNEL *I'VE* EVER SEEN!

BUT, AS TOM DESCENDS THE NARROW SHAFT... UH-OH! PEOPLE DOWN BELOW ME... AND FROM THEIR *BEARING*, THEY LOOK LIKE *GUARDS!*

HURRY *UP!* THE BOSS WANTS EVERY-BODY IN THE MAIN *LABORATORY!*

IT'S GOT SOMETHING TO DO WITH THAT *REPORTER* DAME WE CAPTURED!

M-MAYBE THE BOSS THINKS SHE HAD AN *INSIDE SOURCE!* I HOPE HE DOESN'T SUSPECT ONE OF *US...*

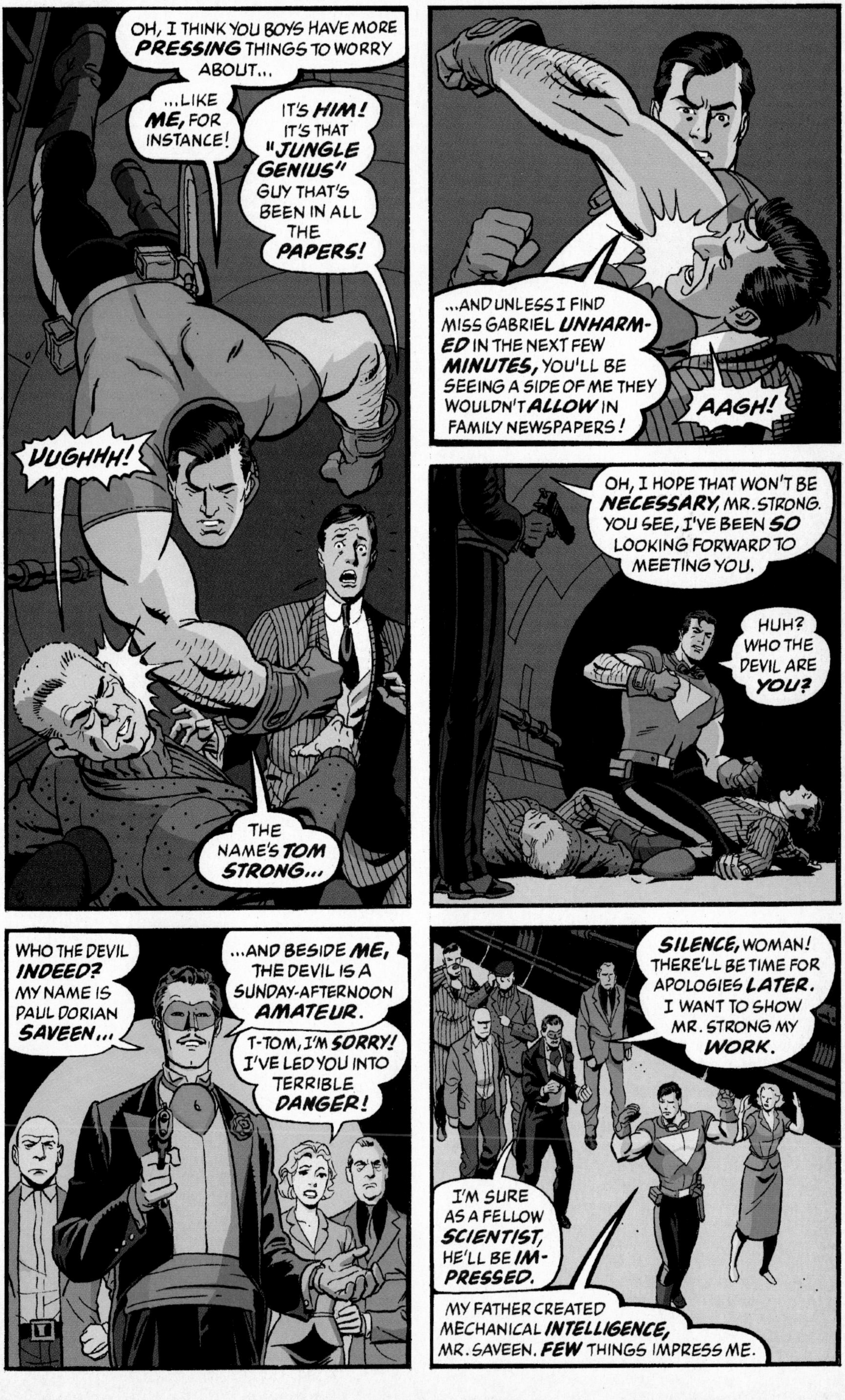

OH, I THINK YOU BOYS HAVE MORE PRESSING THINGS TO WORRY ABOUT...
...LIKE ME, FOR INSTANCE!
IT'S HIM! IT'S THAT "JUNGLE GENIUS" GUY THAT'S BEEN IN ALL THE PAPERS!
UUGHHH!
THE NAME'S TOM STRONG...
...AND UNLESS I FIND MISS GABRIEL UNHARMED IN THE NEXT FEW MINUTES, YOU'LL BE SEEING A SIDE OF ME THEY WOULDN'T ALLOW IN FAMILY NEWSPAPERS!
AAGH!
OH, I HOPE THAT WON'T BE NECESSARY, MR. STRONG. YOU SEE, I'VE BEEN SO LOOKING FORWARD TO MEETING YOU.
HUH? WHO THE DEVIL ARE YOU?
WHO THE DEVIL INDEED? MY NAME IS PAUL DORIAN SAVEEN...
...AND BESIDE ME, THE DEVIL IS A SUNDAY-AFTERNOON AMATEUR.
T-TOM, I'M SORRY! I'VE LED YOU INTO TERRIBLE DANGER!
SILENCE, WOMAN! THERE'LL BE TIME FOR APOLOGIES LATER. I WANT TO SHOW MR. STRONG MY WORK.
I'M SURE AS A FELLOW SCIENTIST, HE'LL BE IMPRESSED.
MY FATHER CREATED MECHANICAL INTELLIGENCE, MR. SAVEEN. FEW THINGS IMPRESS ME.

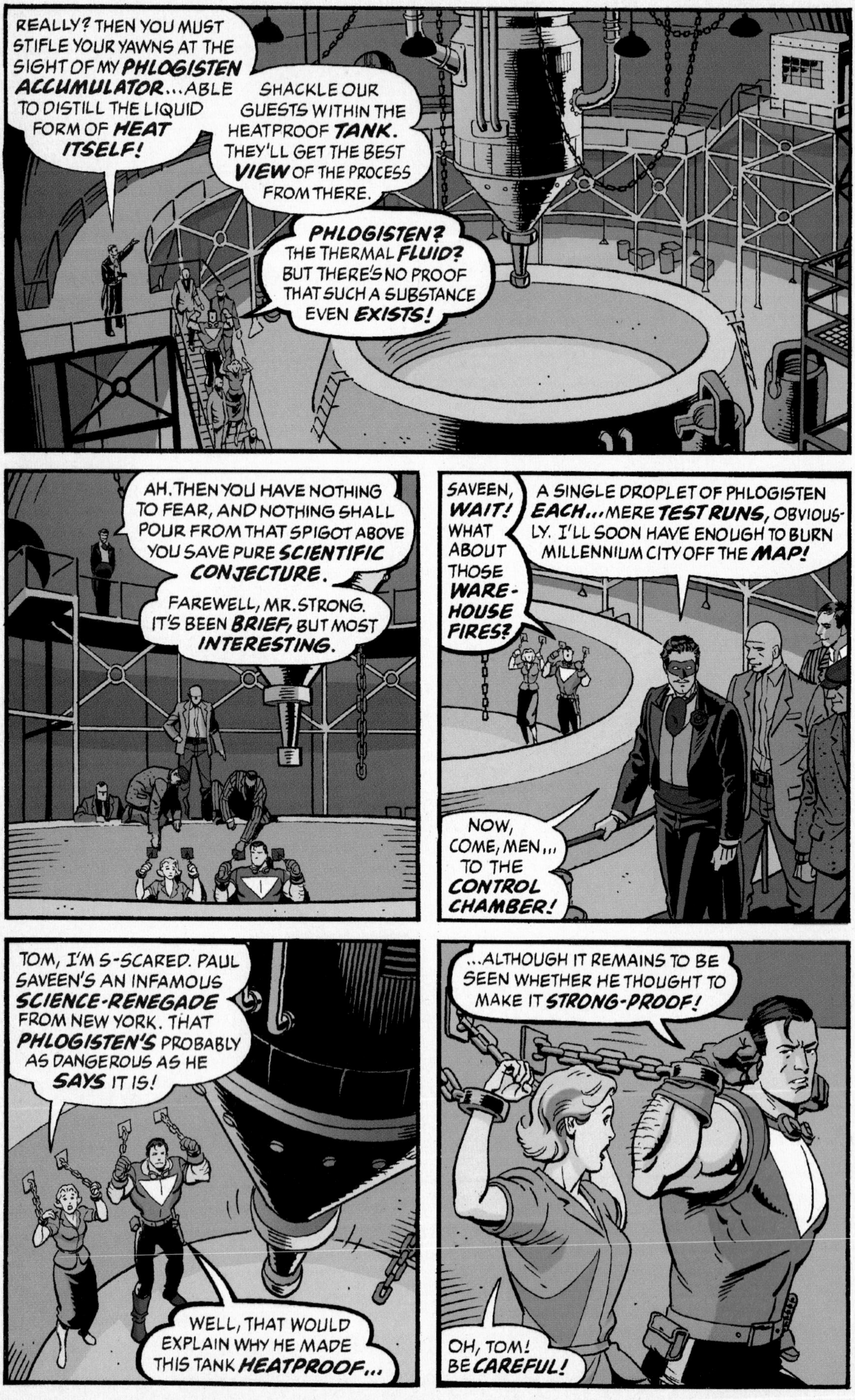
REALLY? THEN YOU MUST STIFLE YOUR YAWNS AT THE SIGHT OF MY PHLOGISTEN ACCUMULATOR...ABLE TO DISTILL THE LIQUID FORM OF HEAT ITSELF!
SHACKLE OUR GUESTS WITHIN THE HEATPROOF TANK. THEY'LL GET THE BEST VIEW OF THE PROCESS FROM THERE.
PHLOGISTEN? THE THERMAL FLUID? BUT THERE'S NO PROOF THAT SUCH A SUBSTANCE EVEN EXISTS!
AH. THEN YOU HAVE NOTHING TO FEAR, AND NOTHING SHALL POUR FROM THAT SPIGOT ABOVE YOU SAVE PURE SCIENTIFIC CONJECTURE.
FAREWELL, MR. STRONG. IT'S BEEN BRIEF, BUT MOST INTERESTING.
SAVEEN, WAIT! WHAT ABOUT THOSE WARE-HOUSE FIRES?
A SINGLE DROPLET OF PHLOGISTEN EACH... MERE TEST RUNS, OBVIOUS-LY. I'LL SOON HAVE ENOUGH TO BURN MILLENNIUM CITY OFF THE MAP!
NOW, COME, MEN... TO THE CONTROL CHAMBER!
TOM, I'M S-SCARED. PAUL SAVEEN'S AN INFAMOUS SCIENCE-RENEGADE FROM NEW YORK. THAT PHLOGISTEN'S PROBABLY AS DANGEROUS AS HE SAYS IT IS!
WELL, THAT WOULD EXPLAIN WHY HE MADE THIS TANK HEATPROOF...
...ALTHOUGH IT REMAINS TO BE SEEN WHETHER HE THOUGHT TO MAKE IT STRONG-PROOF!
OH, TOM! BE CAREFUL!

MEANWHILE, IN THE CONTROL ROOM...

THROW THE SWITCH AND START THE PHLOGISTEN **DECANTING PROCESS.** OUR FRIENDS WON'T DOUBT THE EXISTENCE OF LIQUID HEAT ONCE THEY'RE **SUBMERGED** IN IT!

IT'S **DONE**, BOSS!

BOSS! LOOK DOWN **THERE!**

THAT **MUSCLEMAN** GUY! IT LOOKS LIKE HE'S TRYING TO BREAK **LOOSE!**

HA! LET HIM **TRY!** THERE'S ONLY **SECONDS** BEFORE THE **PHLOGISTEN** POURS DOWN ON **HIM** AND HIS SIMPERING **COMPANION!**

BESIDES, HE CAN'T POSSIBLY HOPE TO...

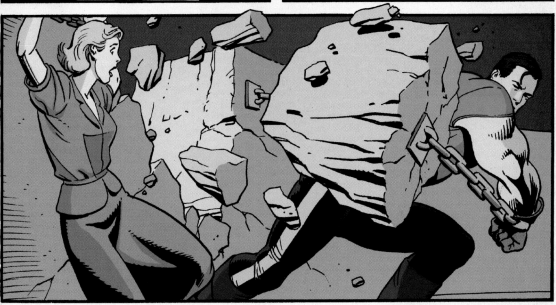

OH, TOM, PLEASE **HURRY!** I DON'T LIKE THE RUSHING, **HISSING** SOUND COMING FROM THAT DEVICE **ABOVE** US!

ME **NEITHER**, MISS GABRIEL, BUT PLEASE DON'T **WORRY!** I JUST NEED TO FINISH FREEING MYSELF FROM THESE **CHAINS**...

...AND THEN I CAN MAKE SHORT WORK OF **YOURS!**

TOM, LOOK **OUT!** THAT SPIGOT IS OPENING! THE PHLOGISTEN WILL **ENGULF** US BEFORE YOU HAVE TIME TO GET US...

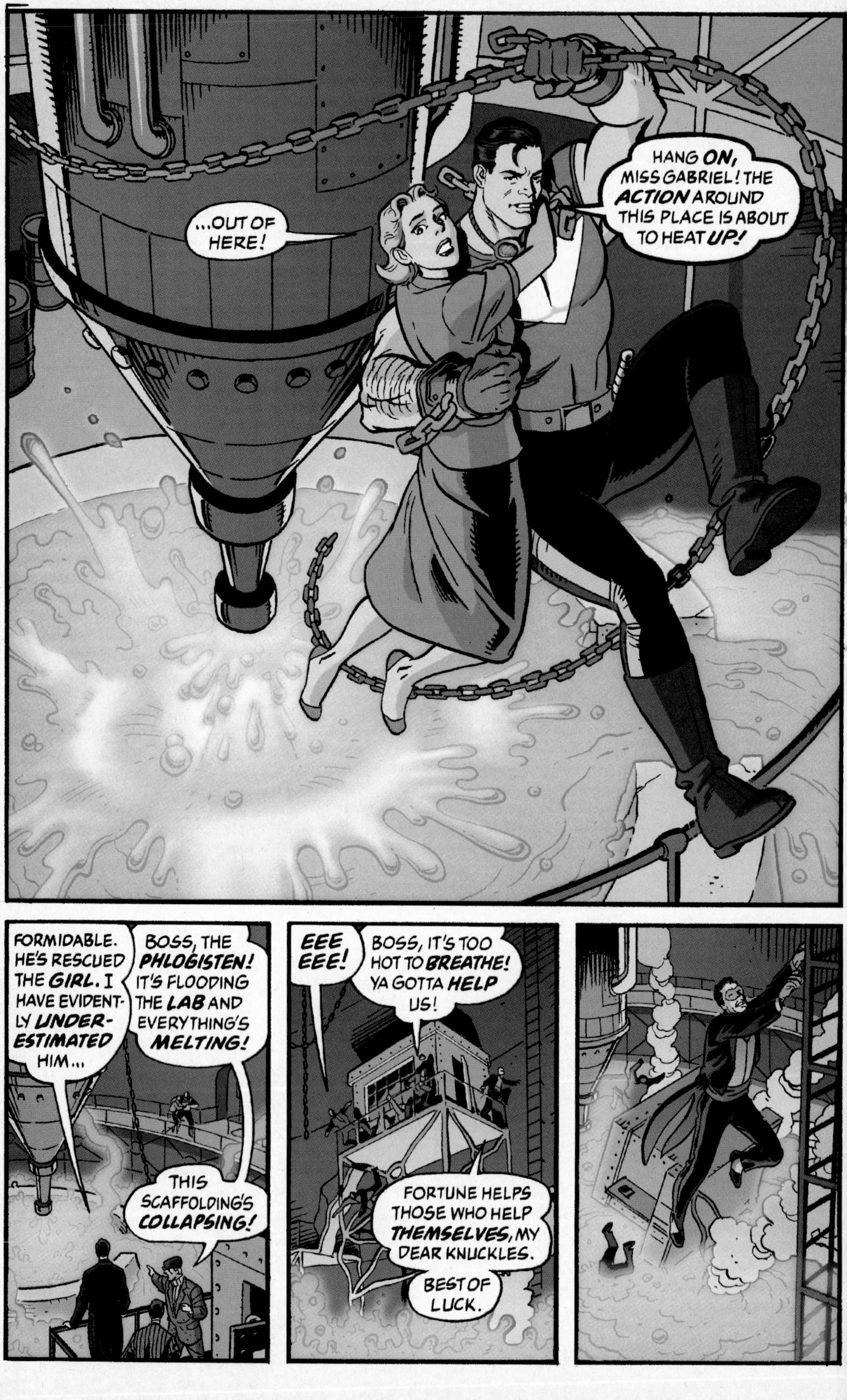

...OUT OF HERE!
HANG ON, MISS GABRIEL! THE ACTION AROUND THIS PLACE IS ABOUT TO HEAT UP!
FORMIDABLE. HE'S RESCUED THE GIRL. I HAVE EVIDENTLY UNDER-ESTIMATED HIM...
BOSS, THE PHLOGISTEN! IT'S FLOODING THE LAB AND EVERYTHING'S MELTING!
THIS SCAFFOLDING'S COLLAPSING!
EEE EEE!
BOSS, IT'S TOO HOT TO BREATHE! YA GOTTA HELP US!
FORTUNE HELPS THOSE WHO HELP THEMSELVES, MY DEAR KNUCKLES.
BEST OF LUCK.

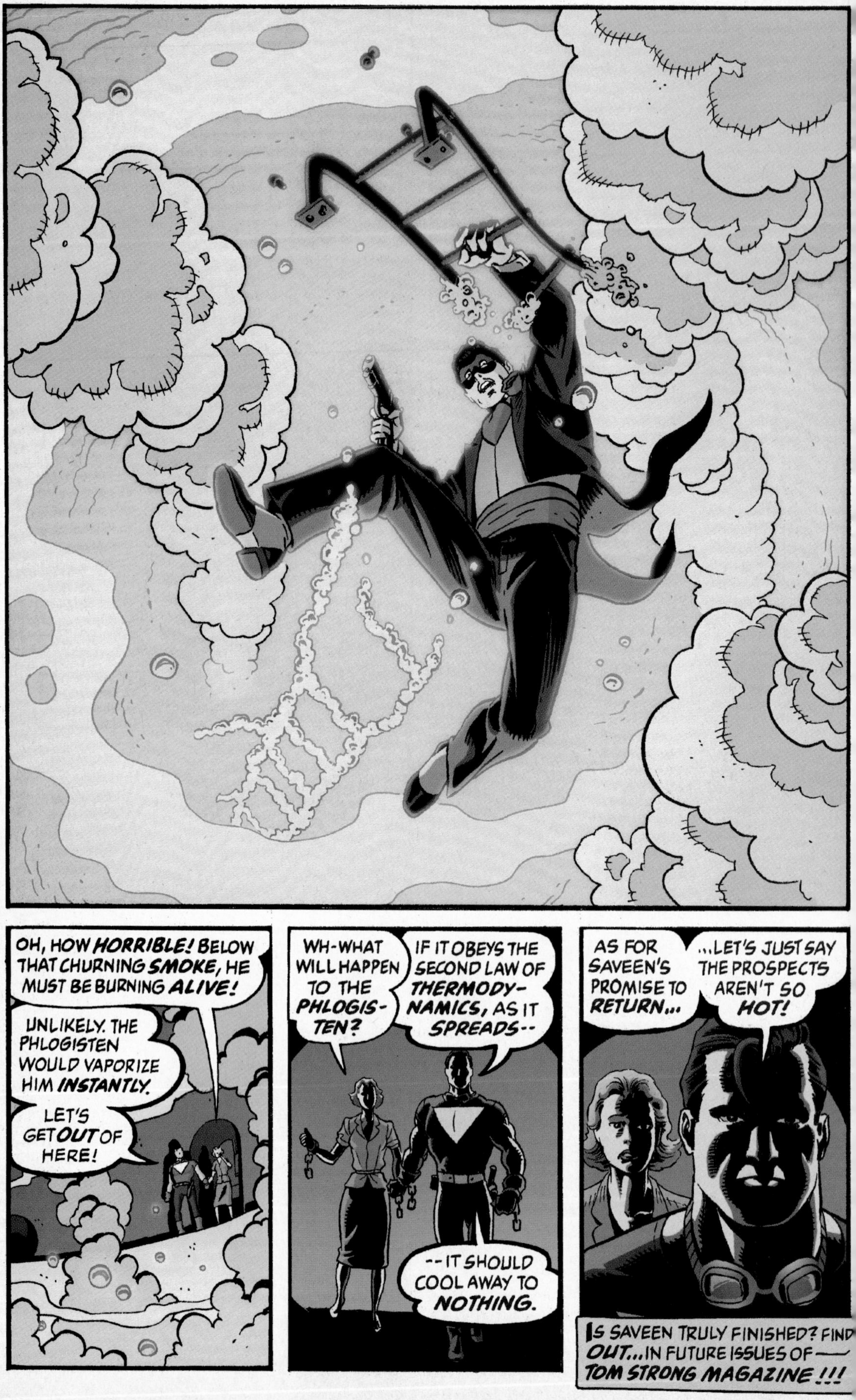
OH, HOW HORRIBLE! BELOW THAT CHURNING SMOKE, HE MUST BE BURNING ALIVE!
UNLIKELY. THE PHLOGISTEN WOULD VAPORIZE HIM INSTANTLY.
LET'S GET OUT OF HERE!
WH-WHAT WILL HAPPEN TO THE PHLOGIS-TEN?
IF IT OBEYS THE SECOND LAW OF THERMODY-NAMICS, AS IT SPREADS--
--IT SHOULD COOL AWAY TO NOTHING.
AS FOR SAVEEN'S PROMISE TO RETURN...
...LET'S JUST SAY THE PROSPECTS AREN'T SO HOT!
IS SAVEEN TRULY FINISHED? FIND OUT... IN FUTURE ISSUES OF — TOM STRONG MAGAZINE!!!

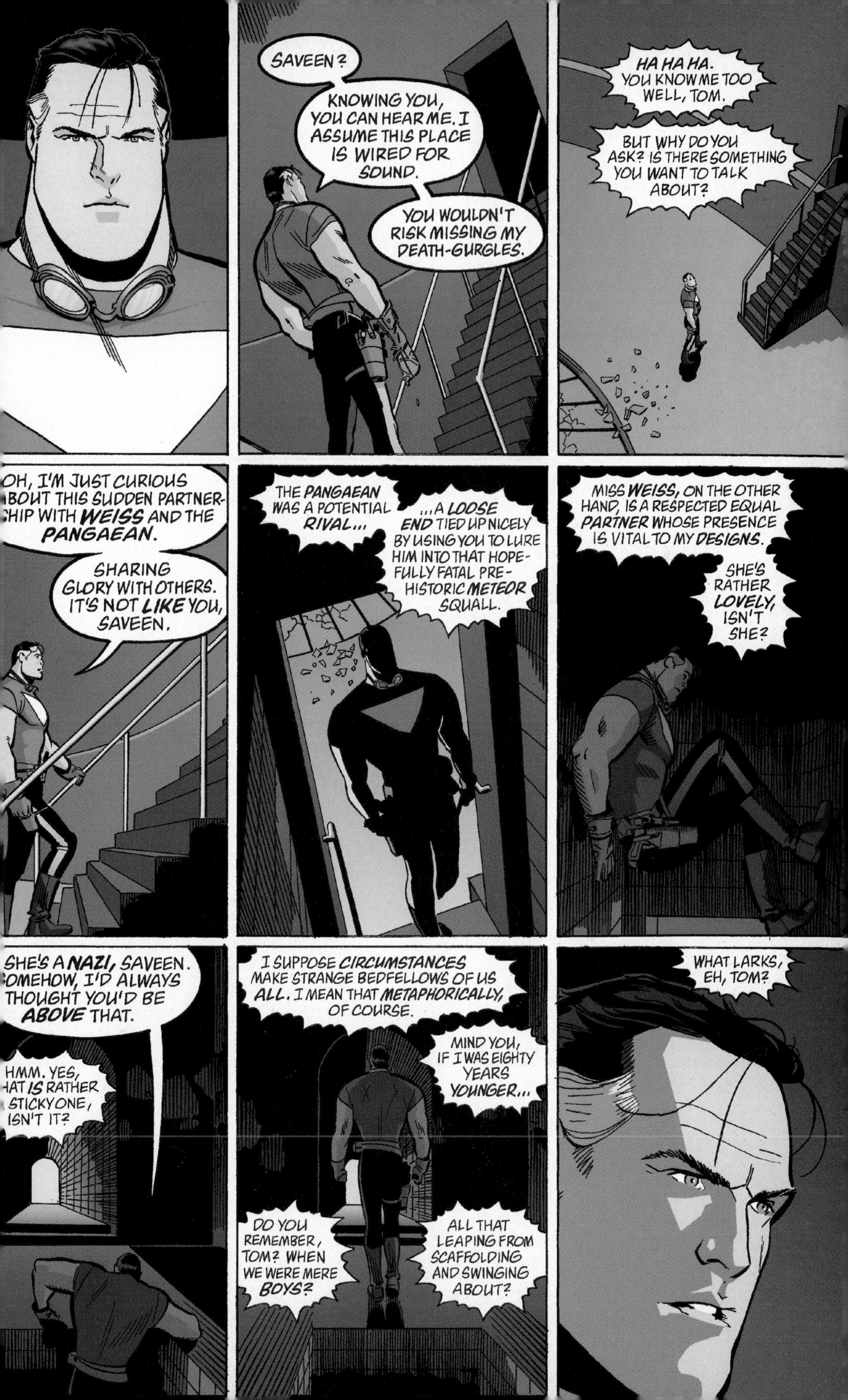

SAVEEN?
KNOWING YOU, YOU CAN HEAR ME. I ASSUME THIS PLACE IS WIRED FOR SOUND.
YOU WOULDN'T RISK MISSING MY DEATH-GURGLES.
HA HA HA. YOU KNOW ME TOO WELL, TOM.
BUT WHY DO YOU ASK? IS THERE SOMETHING YOU WANT TO TALK ABOUT?
OH, I'M JUST CURIOUS ABOUT THIS SUDDEN PARTNERSHIP WITH WEISS AND THE PANGAEAN.
SHARING GLORY WITH OTHERS. IT'S NOT LIKE YOU, SAVEEN.
THE PANGAEAN WAS A POTENTIAL RIVAL...
...A LOOSE END TIED UP NICELY BY USING YOU TO LURE HIM INTO THAT HOPEFULLY FATAL PREHISTORIC METEOR SQUALL.
MISS WEISS, ON THE OTHER HAND, IS A RESPECTED EQUAL PARTNER WHOSE PRESENCE IS VITAL TO MY DESIGNS.
SHE'S RATHER LOVELY, ISN'T SHE?
SHE'S A NAZI, SAVEEN. SOMEHOW, I'D ALWAYS THOUGHT YOU'D BE ABOVE THAT.
HMM. YES, THAT IS RATHER A STICKY ONE, ISN'T IT?
I SUPPOSE CIRCUMSTANCES MAKE STRANGE BEDFELLOWS OF US ALL. I MEAN THAT METAPHORICALLY, OF COURSE.
MIND YOU, IF I WAS EIGHTY YEARS YOUNGER...
DO YOU REMEMBER, TOM? WHEN WE WERE MERE BOYS?
ALL THAT LEAPING FROM SCAFFOLDING AND SWINGING ABOUT?
WHAT LARKS, EH, TOM?

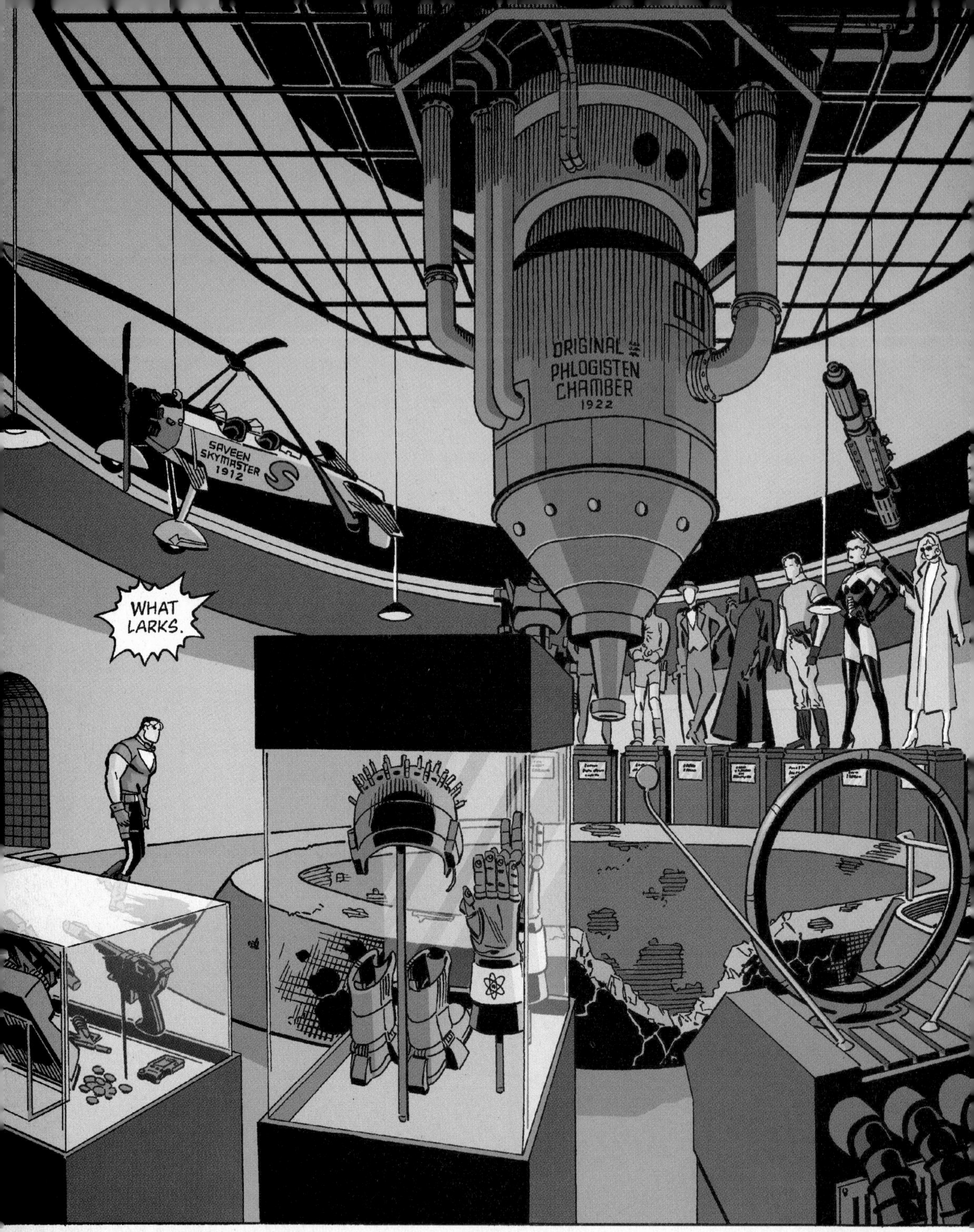
ORIGINAL PHLOGISTEN CHAMBER 1922
SAVEEN SKYMASTER 1912
WHAT LARKS.

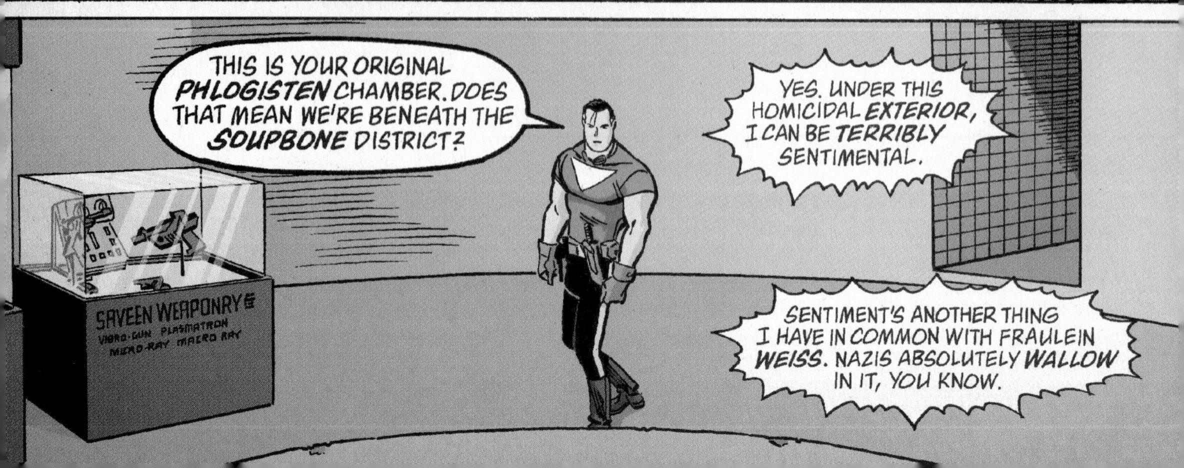
THIS IS YOUR ORIGINAL **PHLOGISTEN** CHAMBER. DOES THAT MEAN WE'RE BENEATH THE **SOUPBONE** DISTRICT?
YES. UNDER THIS HOMICIDAL **EXTERIOR**, I CAN BE **TERRIBLY** SENTIMENTAL.
SENTIMENT'S ANOTHER THING I HAVE IN COMMON WITH FRAULEIN **WEISS**. NAZIS ABSOLUTELY **WALLOW** IN IT, YOU KNOW.
SAVEEN WEAPONRY
VIBRO-GUN PLASMATRON
MICRO-RAY MACRO RAY

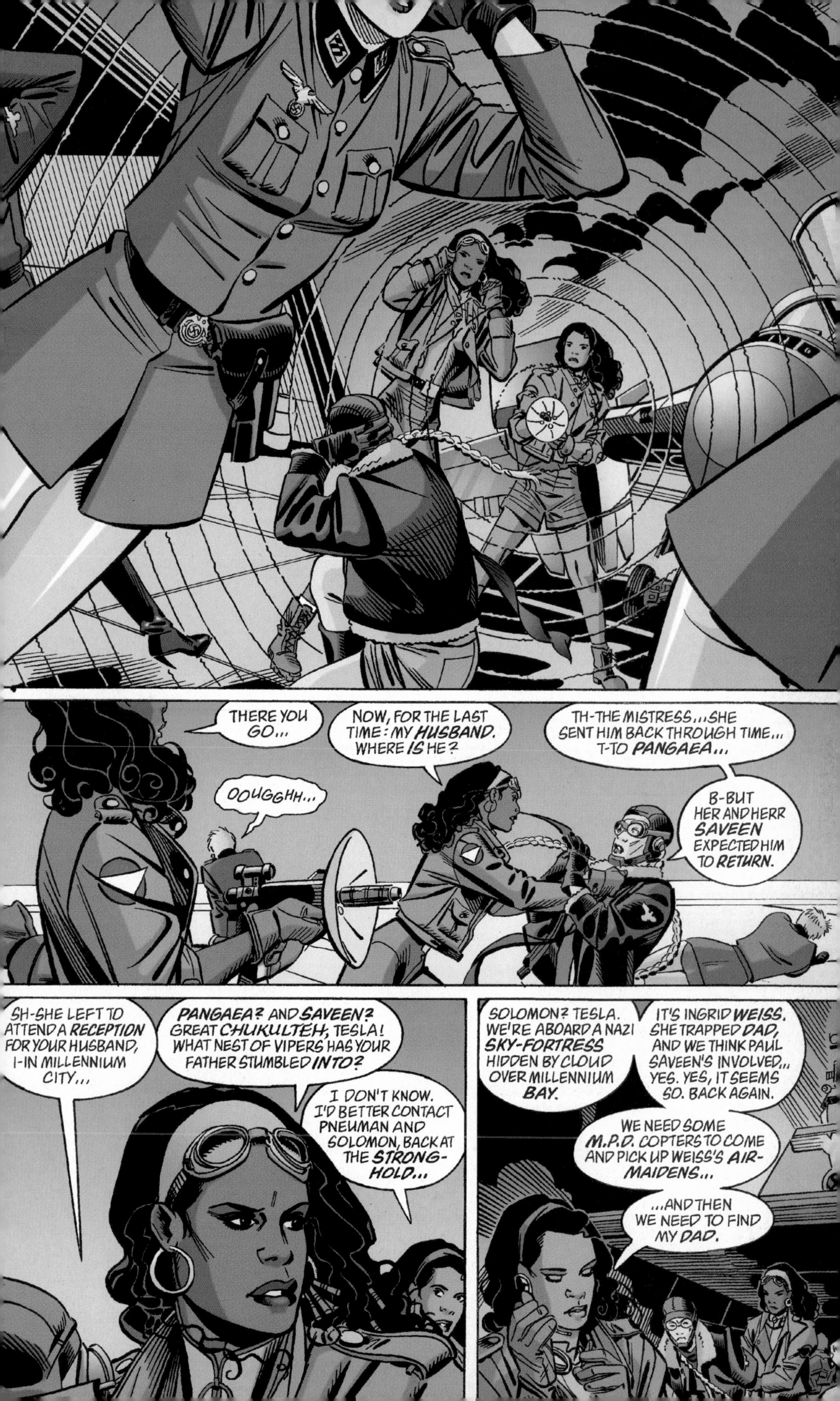

THERE YOU GO...
NOW, FOR THE LAST TIME: MY HUSBAND. WHERE IS HE?
OOUGGHH...
TH-THE MISTRESS... SHE SENT HIM BACK THROUGH TIME... T-TO PANGAEA...
B-BUT HER AND HERR SAVEEN EXPECTED HIM TO RETURN.
SH-SHE LEFT TO ATTEND A RECEPTION FOR YOUR HUSBAND, I-IN MILLENNIUM CITY...
PANGAEA? AND SAVEEN? GREAT CHUKULTEH, TESLA! WHAT NEST OF VIPERS HAS YOUR FATHER STUMBLED INTO?
I DON'T KNOW. I'D BETTER CONTACT PNEUMAN AND SOLOMON, BACK AT THE STRONGHOLD...
SOLOMON? TESLA. WE'RE ABOARD A NAZI SKY-FORTRESS HIDDEN BY CLOUD OVER MILLENNIUM BAY.
IT'S INGRID WEISS. SHE TRAPPED DAD, AND WE THINK PAUL SAVEEN'S INVOLVED... YES. YES, IT SEEMS SO. BACK AGAIN.
WE NEED SOME M.P.D. COPTERS TO COME AND PICK UP WEISS'S AIR-MAIDENS...
...AND THEN WE NEED TO FIND MY DAD.

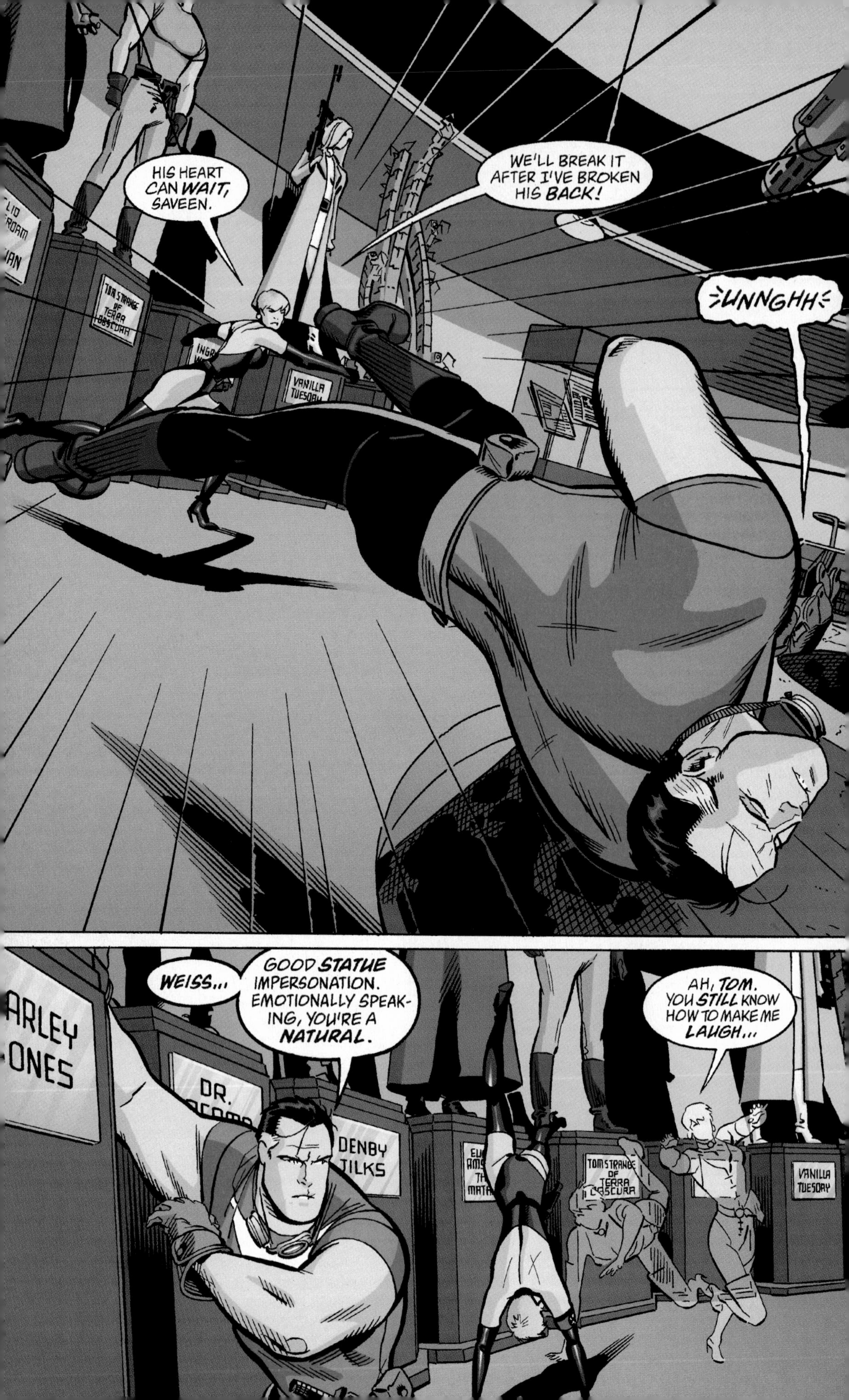
HIS HEART CAN WAIT, SAVEEN.
WE'LL BREAK IT AFTER I'VE BROKEN HIS BACK!
UNNGHH
TOM STRANGE OF TERRA OBSCURA
VANILLA TUESDAY
WEISS...
GOOD STATUE IMPERSONATION. EMOTIONALLY SPEAKING, YOU'RE A NATURAL.
AH, TOM. YOU STILL KNOW HOW TO MAKE ME LAUGH...
DR.
DENBY TILKS
TOM STRANGE OF TERRA OBSCURA
VANILLA TUESDAY

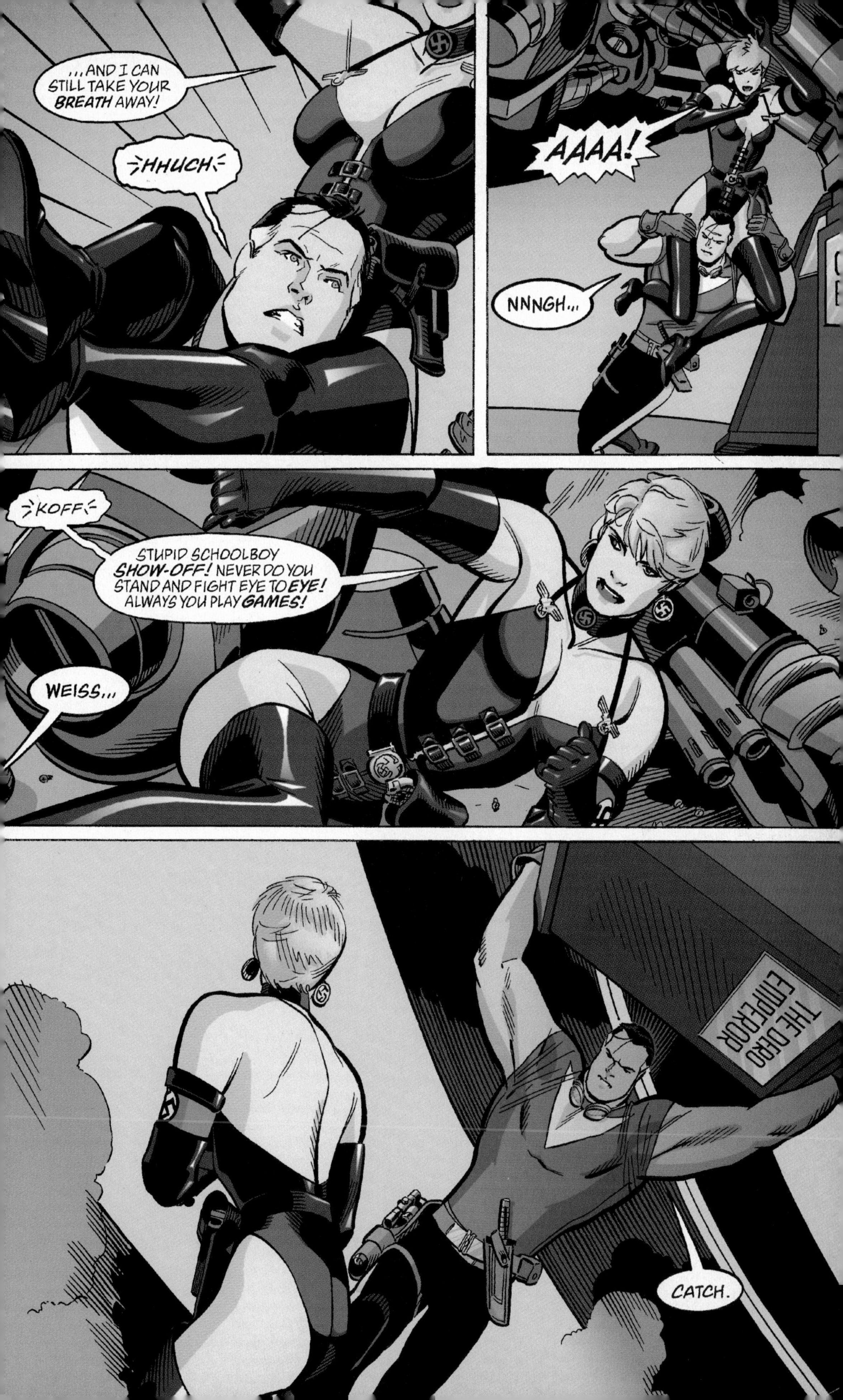
...AND I CAN STILL TAKE YOUR BREATH AWAY!
HHUCH
AAAA!
NNNGH...
KOFF
STUPID SCHOOLBOY SHOW-OFF! NEVER DO YOU STAND AND FIGHT EYE TO EYE! ALWAYS YOU PLAY GAMES!
WEISS...
THEODORO EMPEROR
CATCH.

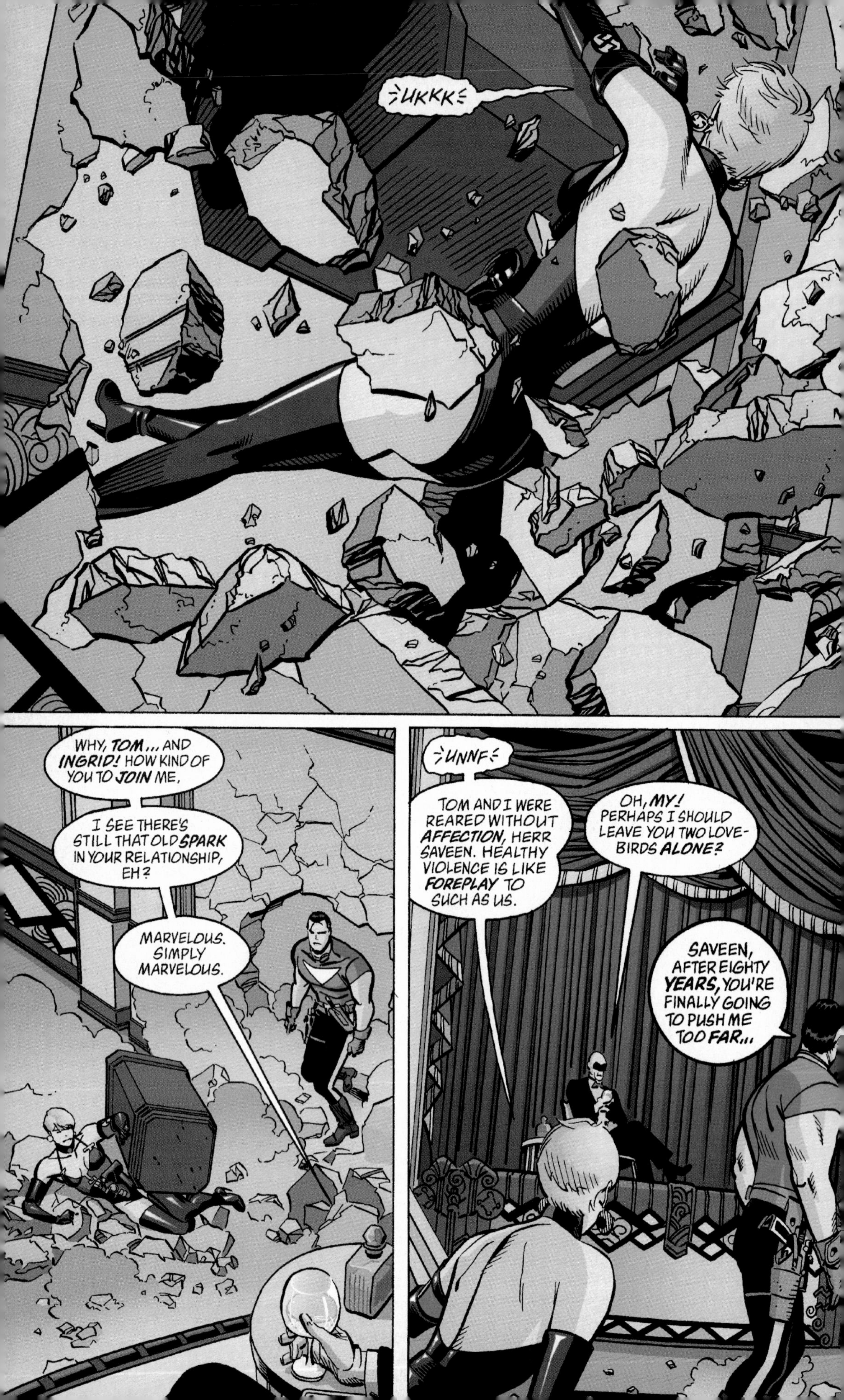
UKKK
WHY, TOM... AND INGRID! HOW KIND OF YOU TO JOIN ME.
I SEE THERE'S STILL THAT OLD SPARK IN YOUR RELATIONSHIP, EH?
MARVELOUS. SIMPLY MARVELOUS.
UNNF
TOM AND I WERE REARED WITHOUT AFFECTION, HERR SAVEEN. HEALTHY VIOLENCE IS LIKE FOREPLAY TO SUCH AS US.
OH, MY! PERHAPS I SHOULD LEAVE YOU TWO LOVE-BIRDS ALONE?
SAVEEN, AFTER EIGHTY YEARS, YOU'RE FINALLY GOING TO PUSH ME TOO FAR...

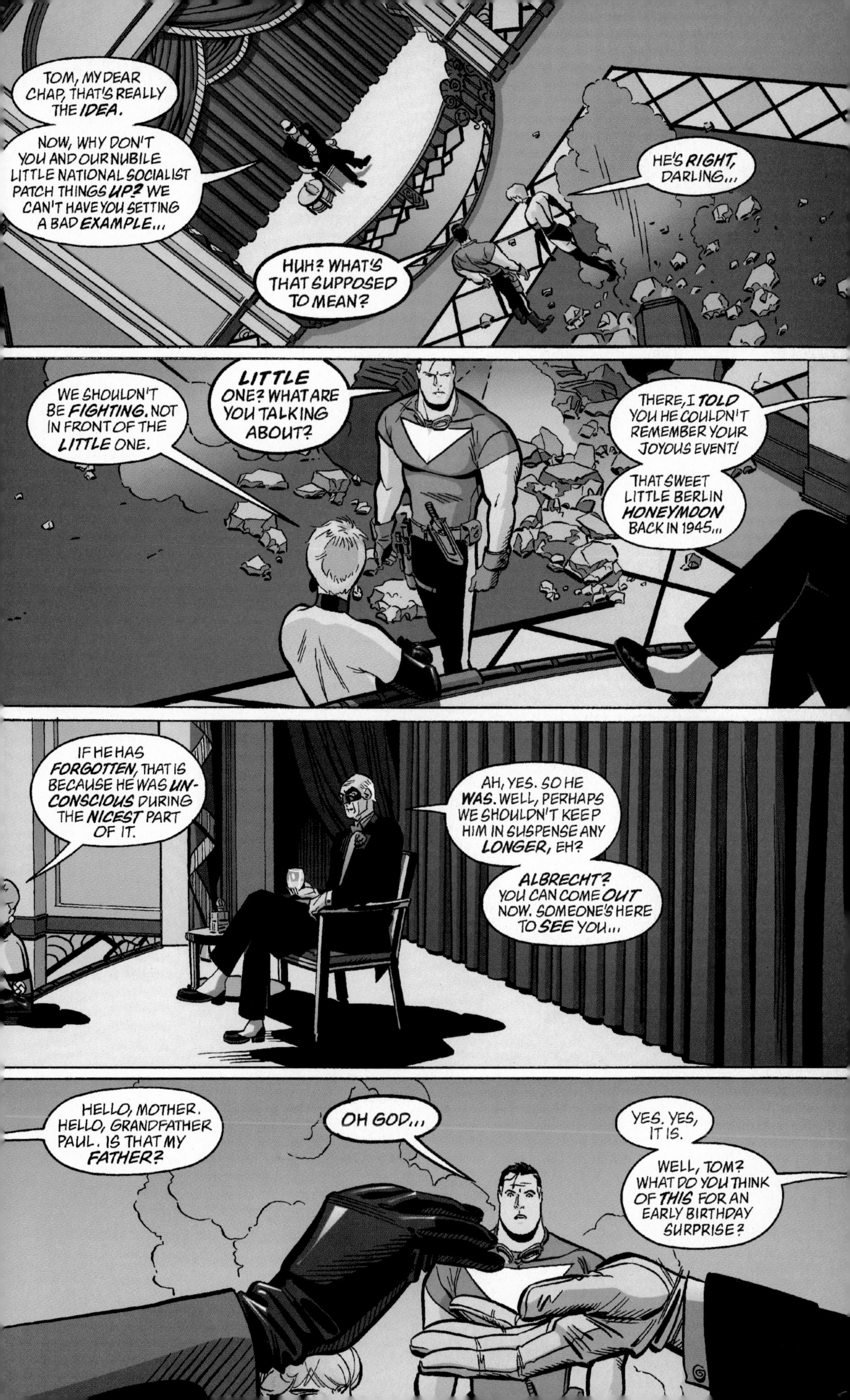
TOM, MY DEAR CHAP, THAT'S REALLY THE IDEA.
NOW, WHY DON'T YOU AND OUR NUBILE LITTLE NATIONAL SOCIALIST PATCH THINGS UP? WE CAN'T HAVE YOU SETTING A BAD EXAMPLE...
HE'S RIGHT, DARLING...
HUH? WHAT'S THAT SUPPOSED TO MEAN?
WE SHOULDN'T BE FIGHTING. NOT IN FRONT OF THE LITTLE ONE.
LITTLE ONE? WHAT ARE YOU TALKING ABOUT?
THERE, I TOLD YOU HE COULDN'T REMEMBER YOUR JOYOUS EVENT!
THAT SWEET LITTLE BERLIN HONEYMOON BACK IN 1945...
IF HE HAS FORGOTTEN, THAT IS BECAUSE HE WAS UN-CONSCIOUS DURING THE NICEST PART OF IT.
AH, YES. SO HE WAS. WELL, PERHAPS WE SHOULDN'T KEEP HIM IN SUSPENSE ANY LONGER, EH?
ALBRECHT? YOU CAN COME OUT NOW. SOMEONE'S HERE TO SEE YOU...
HELLO, MOTHER. HELLO, GRANDFATHER PAUL. IS THAT MY FATHER?
OH GOD...
YES. YES, IT IS.
WELL, TOM? WHAT DO YOU THINK OF THIS FOR AN EARLY BIRTHDAY SURPRISE?

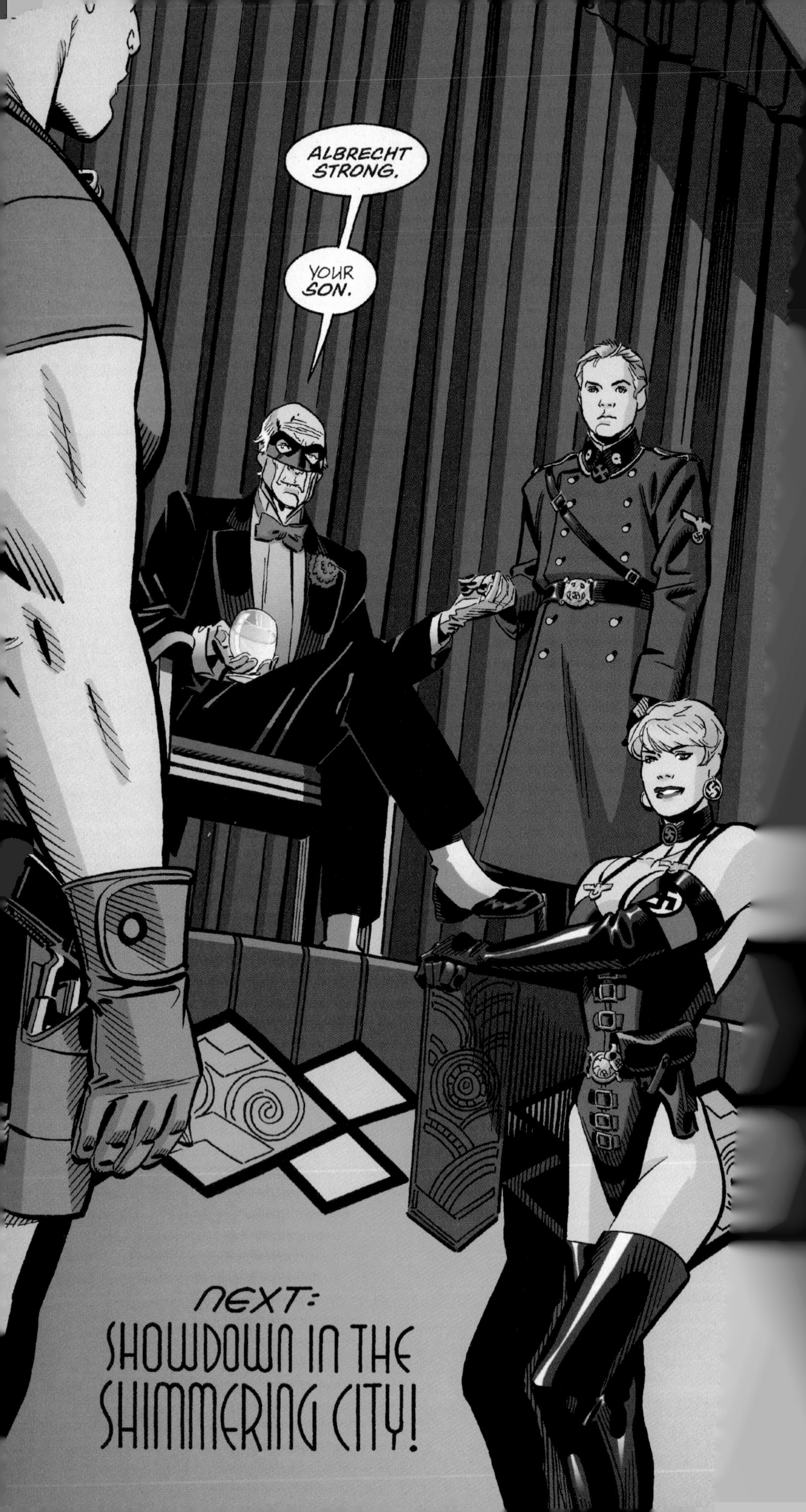
ALBRECHT STRONG.
YOUR SON.
NEXT:
SHOWDOWN IN THE SHIMMERING CITY!

CHAPTER SEVEN

**In which TOM considers the Future,
his Enemies glory in the Past, and
DHALUA tackles the Present.**

**Cover art:
Gary Frank &
Cam Smith**

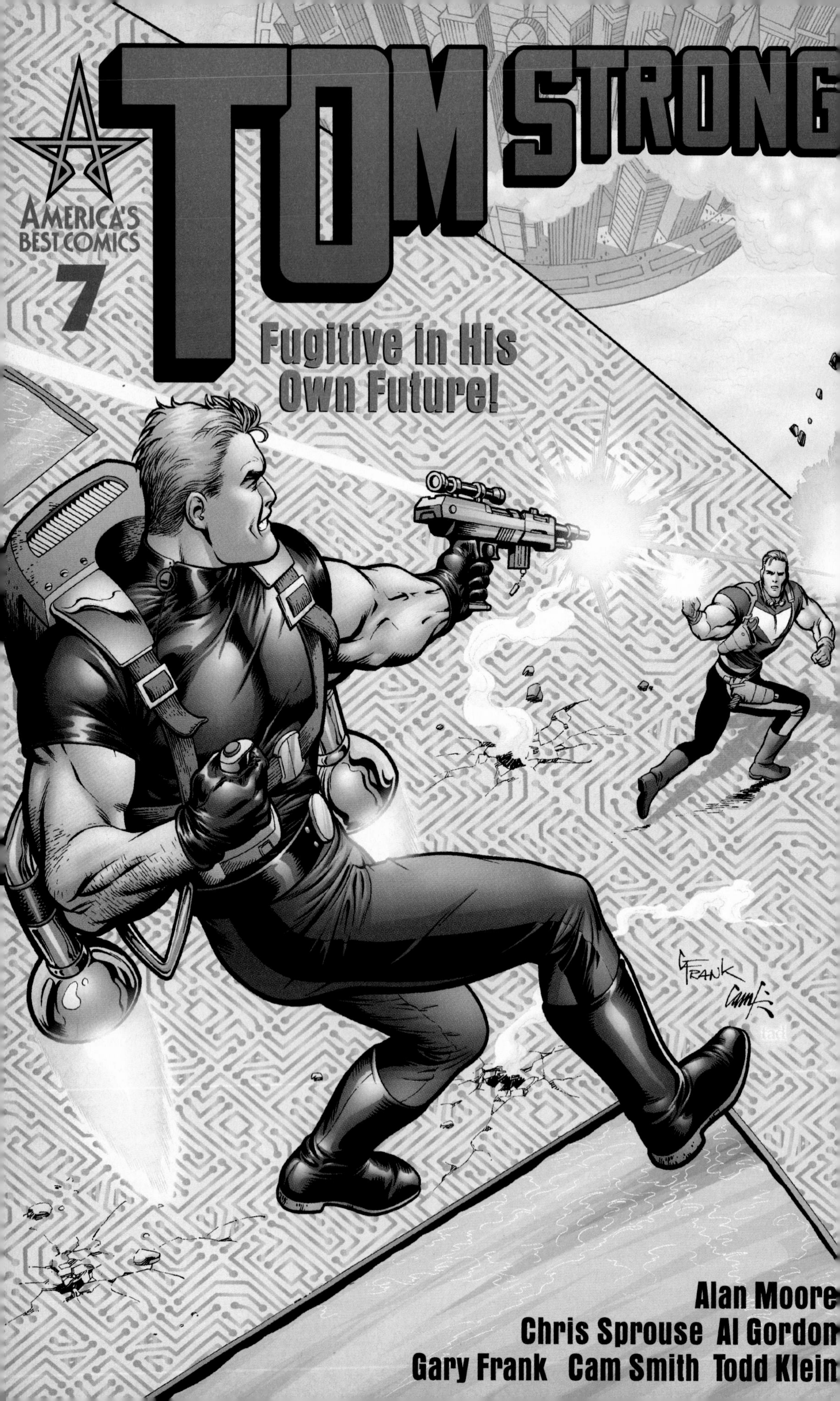
AMERICA'S BEST COMICS
7
TOM STRONG
Fugitive in His Own Future!
G FRANK
Alan Moore
Chris Sprouse Al Gordon
Gary Frank Cam Smith Todd Klein

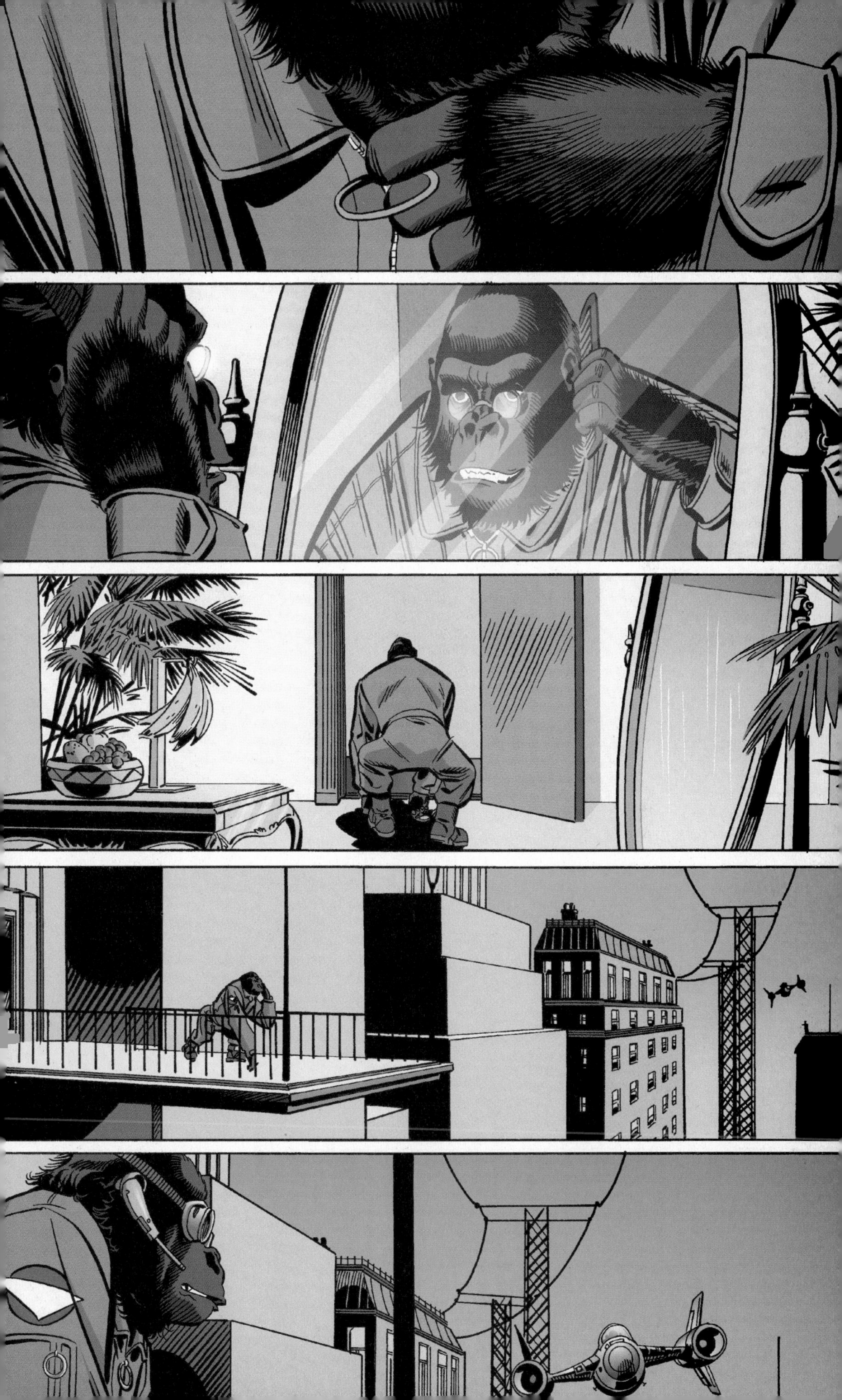

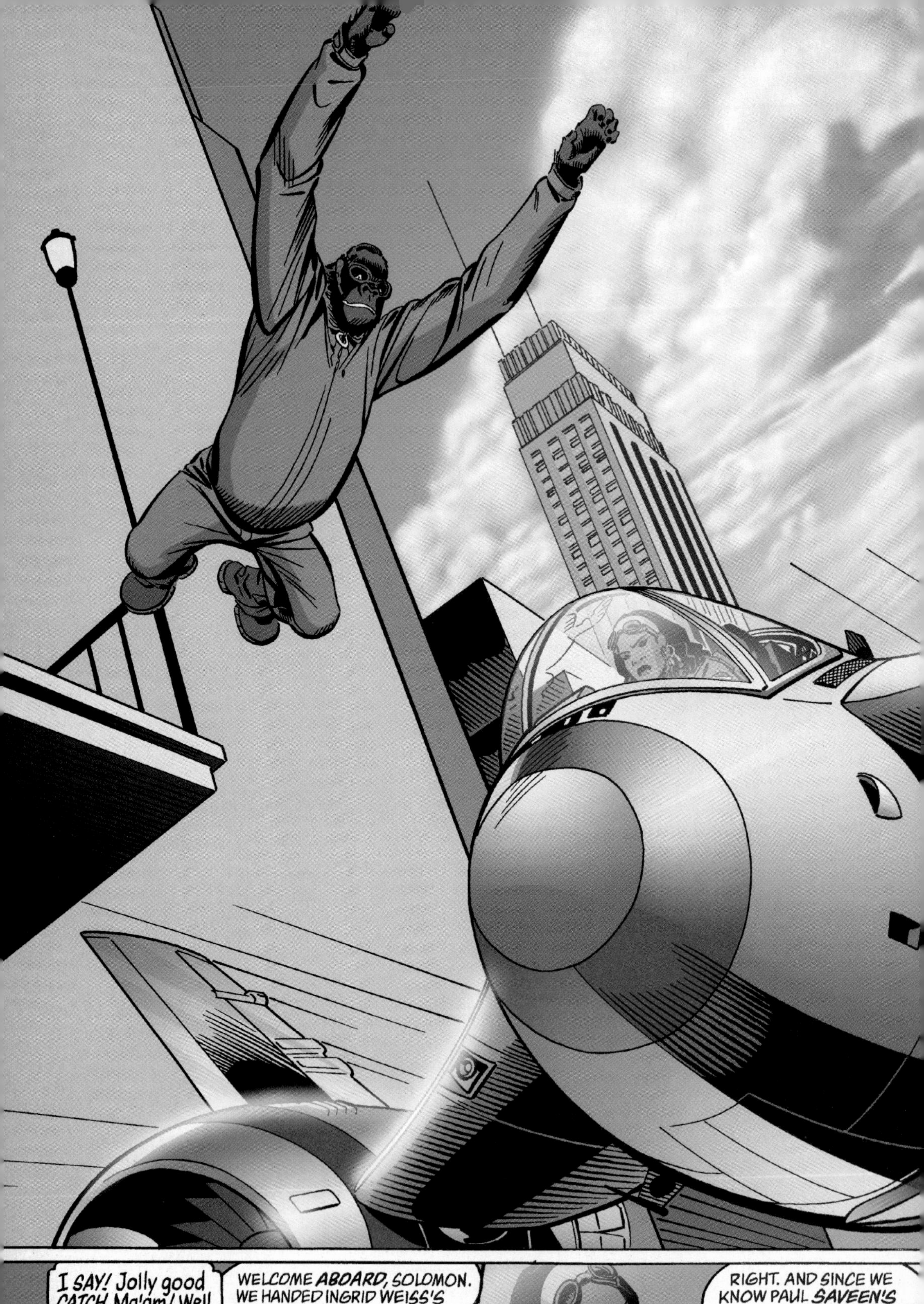

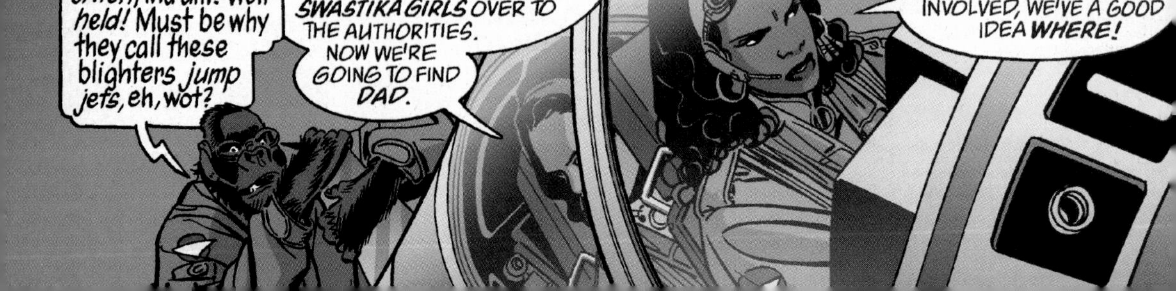
I SAY! Jolly good CATCH, Ma'am! Well held! Must be why they call these blighters jump jets, eh, wot?
WELCOME ABOARD, SOLOMON. WE HANDED INGRID WEISS'S SWASTIKA GIRLS OVER TO THE AUTHORITIES. NOW WE'RE GOING TO FIND DAD.
RIGHT. AND SINCE WE KNOW PAUL SAVEEN'S INVOLVED, WE'VE A GOOD IDEA WHERE!

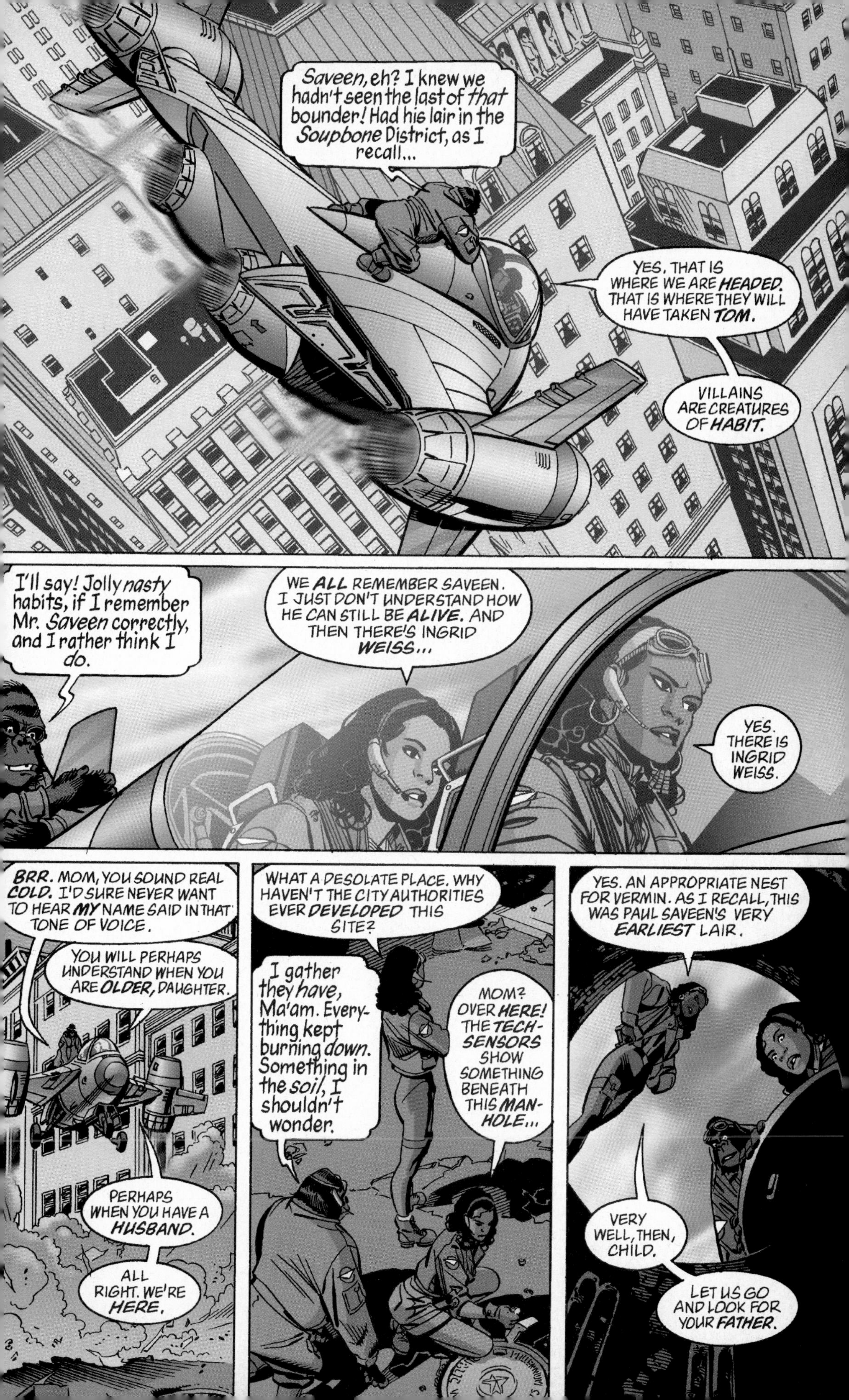
Saveen, eh? I knew we hadn't seen the last of *that* bounder! Had his lair in the *Soupbone* District, as I recall...
YES, THAT IS WHERE WE ARE **HEADED**. THAT IS WHERE THEY WILL HAVE TAKEN **TOM**.
VILLAINS ARE CREATURES OF **HABIT**.
I'll say! Jolly *nasty* habits, if I remember Mr. *Saveen* correctly, and I rather think I do.
WE **ALL** REMEMBER SAVEEN. I JUST DON'T UNDERSTAND HOW HE CAN STILL BE **ALIVE**. AND THEN THERE'S INGRID **WEISS**...
YES. THERE IS INGRID WEISS.
BRR. MOM, YOU SOUND REAL **COLD**. I'D SURE NEVER WANT TO HEAR **MY** NAME SAID IN THAT TONE OF VOICE.
YOU WILL PERHAPS UNDERSTAND WHEN YOU ARE **OLDER**, DAUGHTER.
PERHAPS WHEN YOU HAVE A **HUSBAND**.
ALL RIGHT. WE'RE **HERE**.
WHAT A DESOLATE PLACE. WHY HAVEN'T THE CITY AUTHORITIES EVER **DEVELOPED** THIS SITE?
I gather they *have*, Ma'am. Everything kept burning *down*. Something in the *soil*, I shouldn't wonder.
MOM? OVER **HERE**! THE **TECH-SENSORS** SHOW SOMETHING BENEATH THIS **MAN-HOLE**...
YES. AN APPROPRIATE NEST FOR VERMIN. AS I RECALL, THIS WAS PAUL SAVEEN'S VERY **EARLIEST** LAIR.
VERY WELL, THEN, CHILD.
LET US GO AND LOOK FOR YOUR **FATHER**.

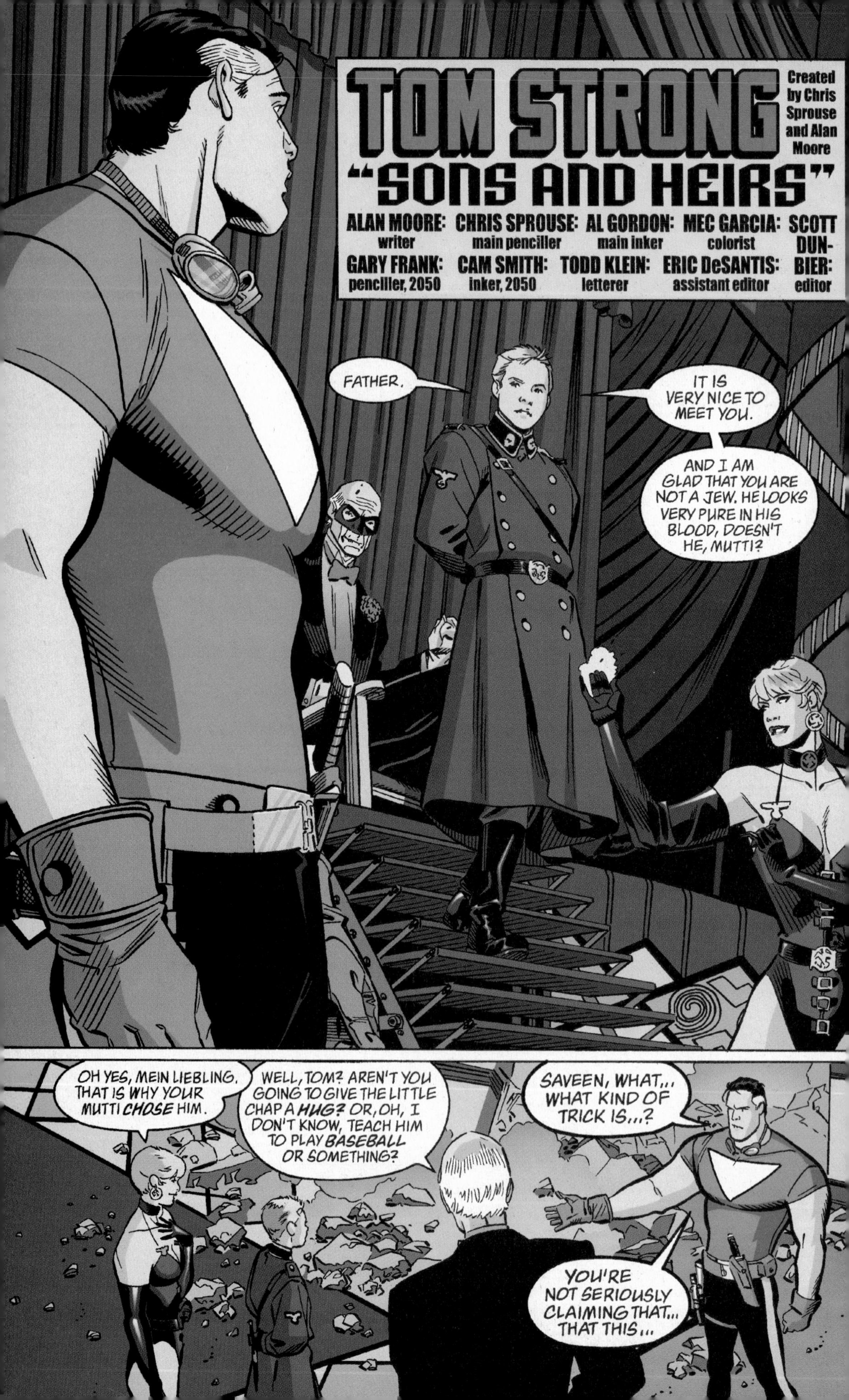
TOM STRONG
Created by Chris Sprouse and Alan Moore
"SONS AND HEIRS"
ALAN MOORE: writer
CHRIS SPROUSE: main penciller
AL GORDON: main inker
MEC GARCIA: colorist
SCOTT DUNBIER: editor
GARY FRANK: penciller, 2050
CAM SMITH: inker, 2050
TODD KLEIN: letterer
ERIC DeSANTIS: assistant editor
FATHER.
IT IS VERY NICE TO MEET YOU.
AND I AM GLAD THAT YOU ARE NOT A JEW. HE LOOKS VERY PURE IN HIS BLOOD, DOESN'T HE, MUTTI?
OH YES, MEIN LIEBLING. THAT IS WHY YOUR MUTTI CHOSE HIM.
WELL, TOM? AREN'T YOU GOING TO GIVE THE LITTLE CHAP A HUG? OR, OH, I DON'T KNOW, TEACH HIM TO PLAY BASEBALL OR SOMETHING?
SAVEEN, WHAT... WHAT KIND OF TRICK IS...?
YOU'RE NOT SERIOUSLY CLAIMING THAT... THAT THIS...

...IS YOUR *SON?* TOM, YOU DON'T NEED TO ASK, DO YOU? LOOK AT HIS *FACE.* ALBRECHT'S *YOURS,* TOM.

YOUR OWN FLESH AND *BLOOD.*

BUT... HOW...?

THAT *BUNKER* IN *BERLIN,* TOM.

I HAD *HOURS* BEFORE YOU WOKE UP ON THAT *TABLE.*

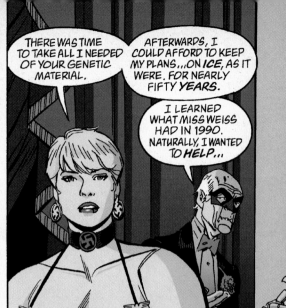

THERE WAS TIME TO TAKE ALL I NEEDED OF YOUR GENETIC MATERIAL.

AFTERWARDS, I COULD AFFORD TO KEEP MY PLANS...ON *ICE,* AS IT WERE. FOR NEARLY FIFTY *YEARS.*

I LEARNED WHAT MISS WEISS HAD IN 1990. NATURALLY, I WANTED TO *HELP...*

YES. GRANDFATHER PAUL HAS BEEN VERY *KIND* TO MUTTI AND I.

BEFORE I WAS *BORN,* HE SENT *MONEY.* THEN, WHEN I WAS *FIVE,* HE FIRST CAME TO *VISIT* US.

DEAR GOD. WEISS...SAVEEN... WHAT YOU'VE DONE HERE IS *MONSTROUS.*

ALBRECHT...

ALBRECHT, LISTEN. I...I CAN IMAGINE HOW YOUR MOTHER HAS *RAISED* YOU. THE THINGS SHE'S BROUGHT YOU UP TO *BELIEVE.*

YOU MUST UNDERSTAND...SHE DID ALL THOSE THINGS BECAUSE SHE WANTED TO HURT *ME.* SHE'S USED YOU AS A *WEAPON.*

NOW, IT SEEMS THAT WITHOUT MY *KNOWLEDGE* OR *CONSENT,* I'M YOUR *FATHER.*

I WANT YOU TO KNOW THAT THERE'S A BETTER WAY TO *THINK.* A BETTER WAY TO *LIVE.* PERHAPS YOU'LL LET ME *SHOW* IT TO YOU.

WHAT DO YOU SAY?

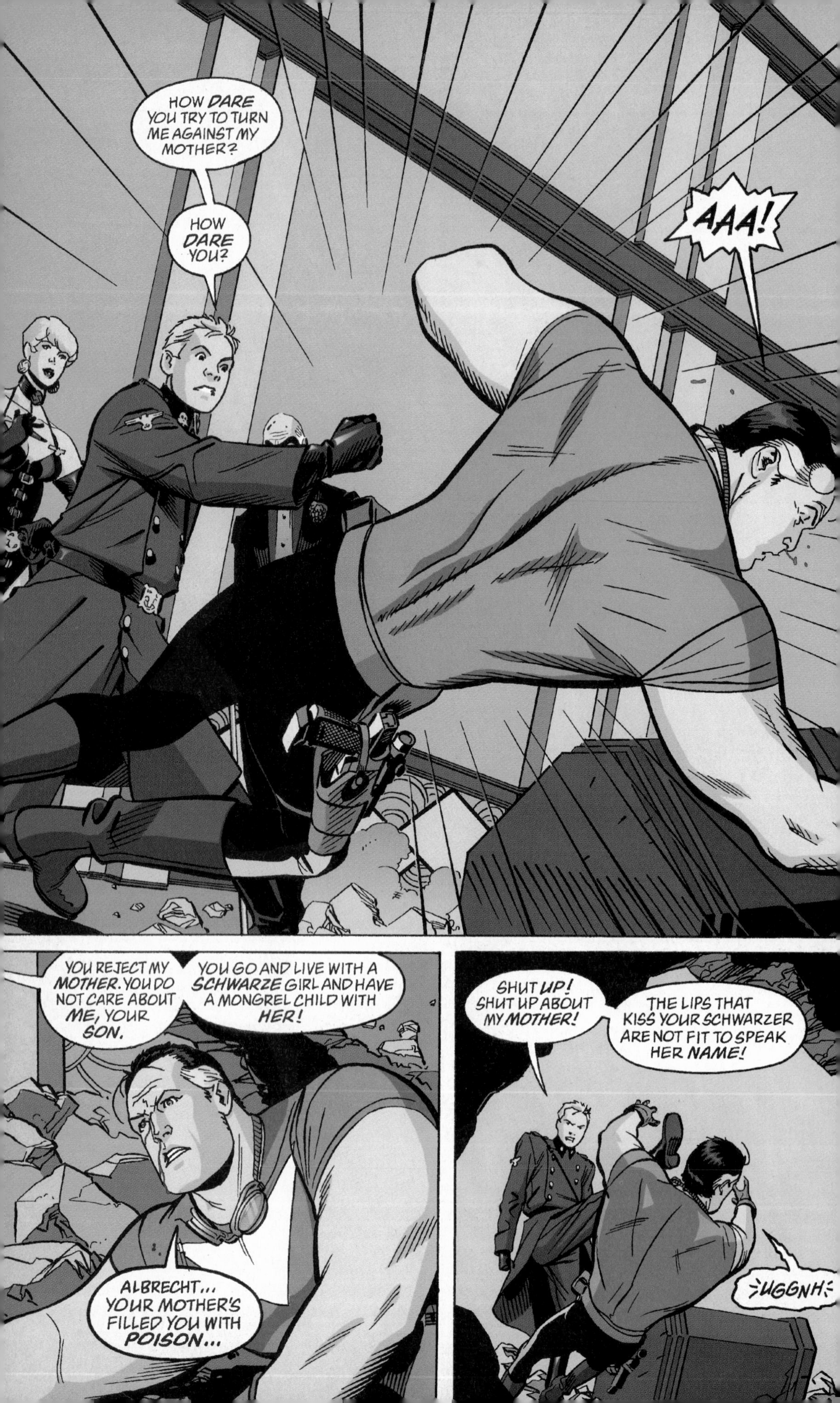

HOW DARE YOU TRY TO TURN ME AGAINST MY MOTHER?
HOW DARE YOU?
AAA!
YOU REJECT MY MOTHER. YOU DO NOT CARE ABOUT ME, YOUR SON.
YOU GO AND LIVE WITH A SCHWARZE GIRL AND HAVE A MONGREL CHILD WITH HER!
ALBRECHT... YOUR MOTHER'S FILLED YOU WITH POISON...
SHUT UP! SHUT UP ABOUT MY MOTHER!
THE LIPS THAT KISS YOUR SCHWARZER ARE NOT FIT TO SPEAK HER NAME!
UGGNH

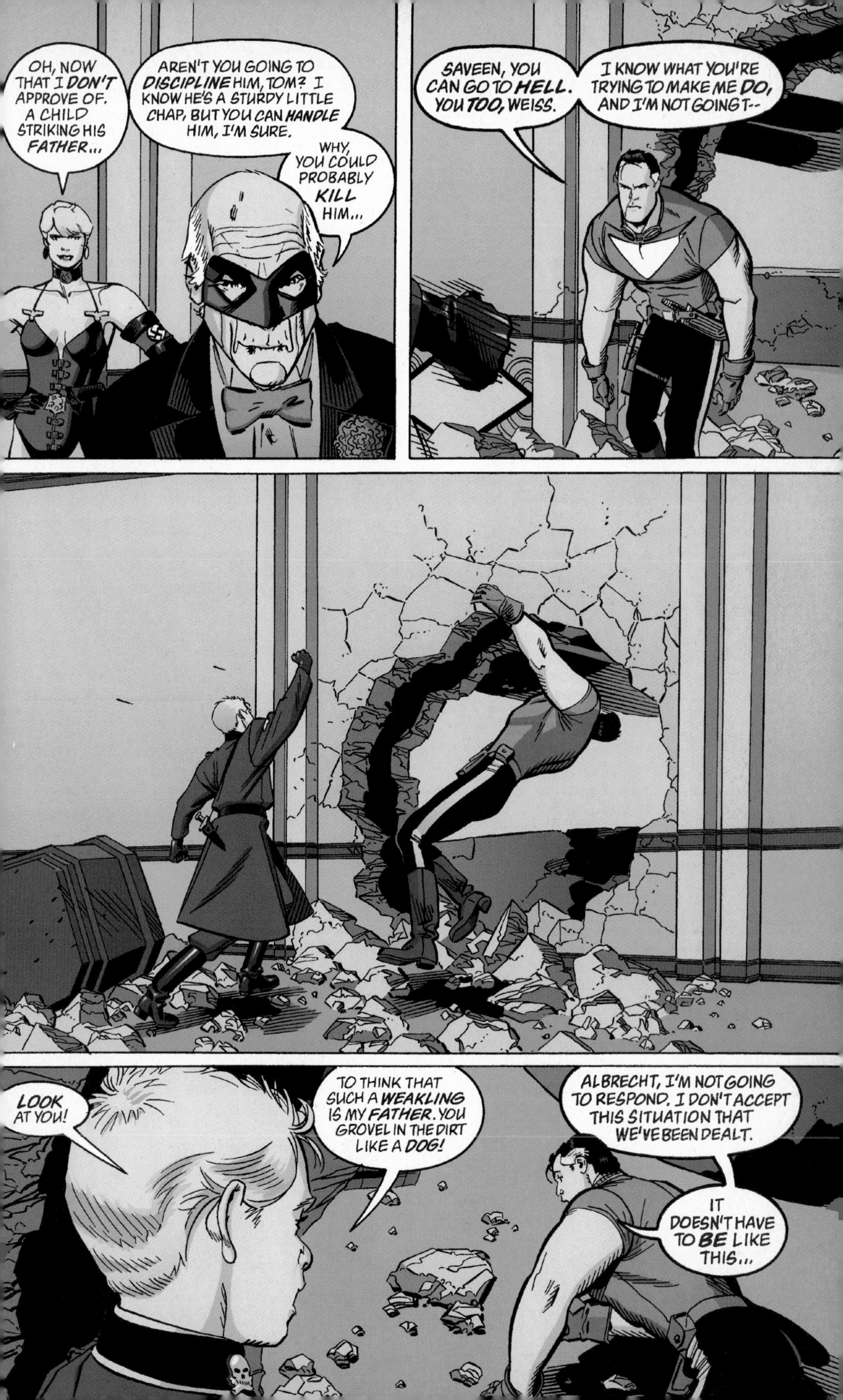
OH, NOW THAT I DON'T APPROVE OF. A CHILD STRIKING HIS FATHER...
AREN'T YOU GOING TO DISCIPLINE HIM, TOM? I KNOW HE'S A STURDY LITTLE CHAP, BUT YOU CAN HANDLE HIM, I'M SURE.
WHY, YOU COULD PROBABLY KILL HIM...
SAVEEN, YOU CAN GO TO HELL. YOU TOO, WEISS.
I KNOW WHAT YOU'RE TRYING TO MAKE ME DO, AND I'M NOT GOING T--
LOOK AT YOU!
TO THINK THAT SUCH A WEAKLING IS MY FATHER. YOU GROVEL IN THE DIRT LIKE A DOG!
ALBRECHT, I'M NOT GOING TO RESPOND. I DON'T ACCEPT THIS SITUATION THAT WE'VE BEEN DEALT.
IT DOESN'T HAVE TO BE LIKE THIS...

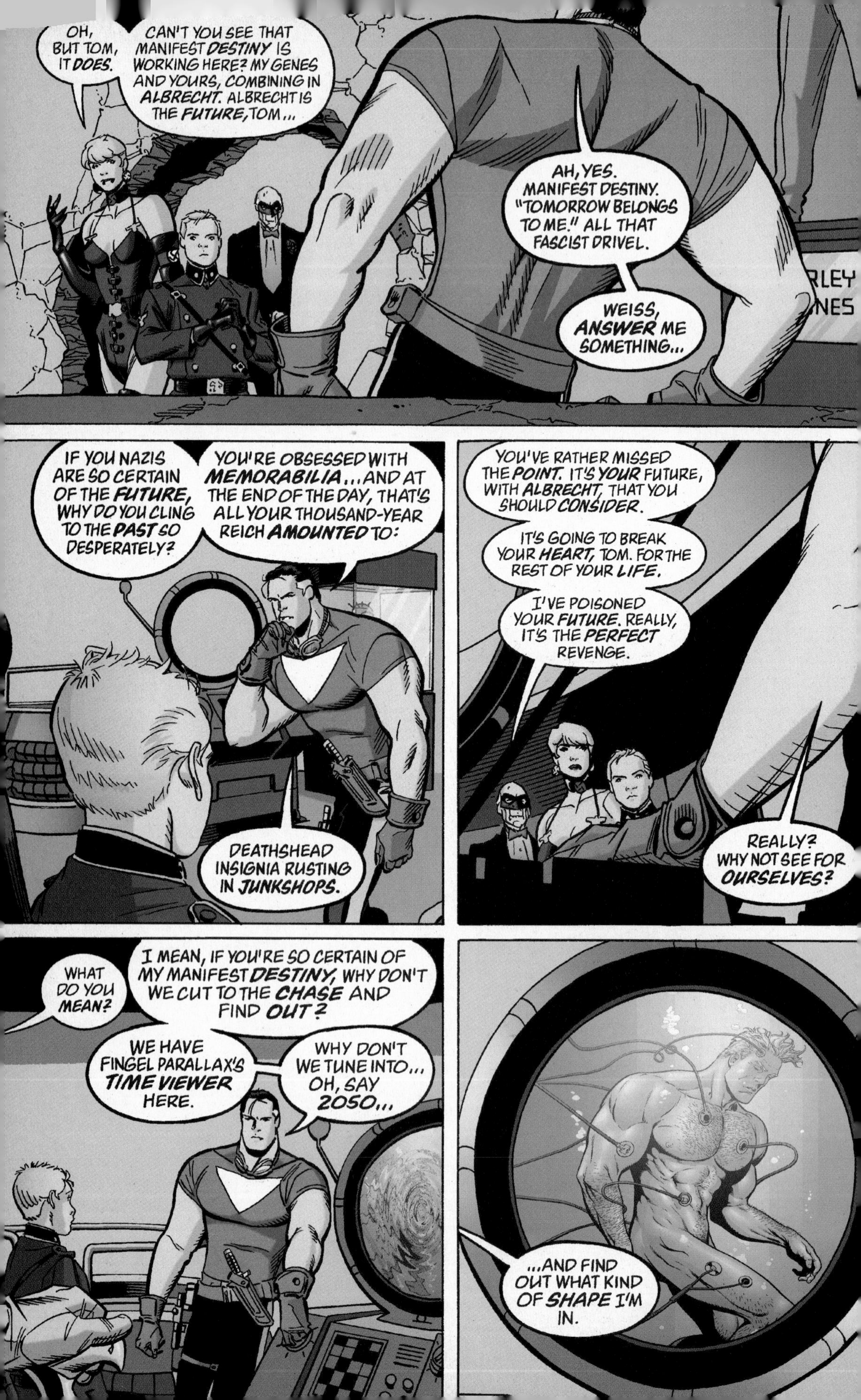

OH, BUT TOM, IT DOES.
CAN'T YOU SEE THAT MANIFEST DESTINY IS WORKING HERE? MY GENES AND YOURS, COMBINING IN ALBRECHT. ALBRECHT IS THE FUTURE, TOM...
AH, YES. MANIFEST DESTINY. "TOMORROW BELONGS TO ME." ALL THAT FASCIST DRIVEL.
WEISS, ANSWER ME SOMETHING...
IF YOU NAZIS ARE SO CERTAIN OF THE FUTURE, WHY DO YOU CLING TO THE PAST SO DESPERATELY?
YOU'RE OBSESSED WITH MEMORABILIA... AND AT THE END OF THE DAY, THAT'S ALL YOUR THOUSAND-YEAR REICH AMOUNTED TO:
DEATHSHEAD INSIGNIA RUSTING IN JUNKSHOPS.
YOU'VE RATHER MISSED THE POINT. IT'S YOUR FUTURE, WITH ALBRECHT, THAT YOU SHOULD CONSIDER.
IT'S GOING TO BREAK YOUR HEART, TOM. FOR THE REST OF YOUR LIFE.
I'VE POISONED YOUR FUTURE. REALLY, IT'S THE PERFECT REVENGE.
REALLY? WHY NOT SEE FOR OURSELVES?
WHAT DO YOU MEAN?
I MEAN, IF YOU'RE SO CERTAIN OF MY MANIFEST DESTINY, WHY DON'T WE CUT TO THE CHASE AND FIND OUT?
WE HAVE FINGEL PARALLAX'S TIME VIEWER HERE.
WHY DON'T WE TUNE INTO... OH, SAY 2050...
...AND FIND OUT WHAT KIND OF SHAPE I'M IN.

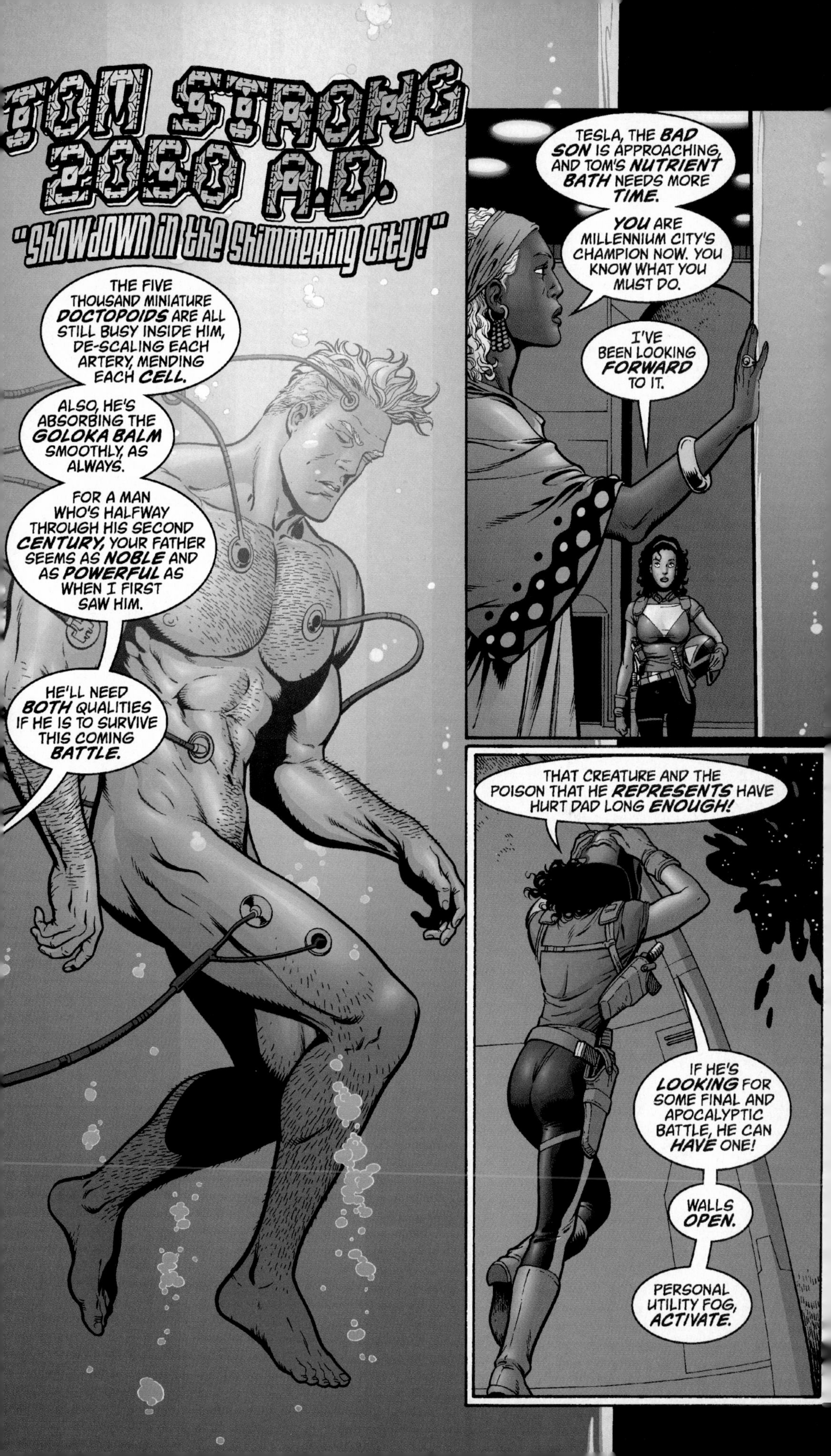
TOM STRONG 2080 A.D.
"SHOWDOWN IN THE SHIMMERING CITY!"
THE FIVE THOUSAND MINIATURE DOCTOPOIDS ARE ALL STILL BUSY INSIDE HIM, DE-SCALING EACH ARTERY, MENDING EACH CELL.
ALSO, HE'S ABSORBING THE GOLOKA BALM SMOOTHLY, AS ALWAYS.
FOR A MAN WHO'S HALFWAY THROUGH HIS SECOND CENTURY, YOUR FATHER SEEMS AS NOBLE AND AS POWERFUL AS WHEN I FIRST SAW HIM.
HE'LL NEED BOTH QUALITIES IF HE IS TO SURVIVE THIS COMING BATTLE.
TESLA, THE BAD SON IS APPROACHING, AND TOM'S NUTRIENT BATH NEEDS MORE TIME.
YOU ARE MILLENNIUM CITY'S CHAMPION NOW. YOU KNOW WHAT YOU MUST DO.
I'VE BEEN LOOKING FORWARD TO IT.
THAT CREATURE AND THE POISON THAT HE REPRESENTS HAVE HURT DAD LONG ENOUGH!
IF HE'S LOOKING FOR SOME FINAL AND APOCALYPTIC BATTLE, HE CAN HAVE ONE!
WALLS OPEN.
PERSONAL UTILITY FOG, ACTIVATE.

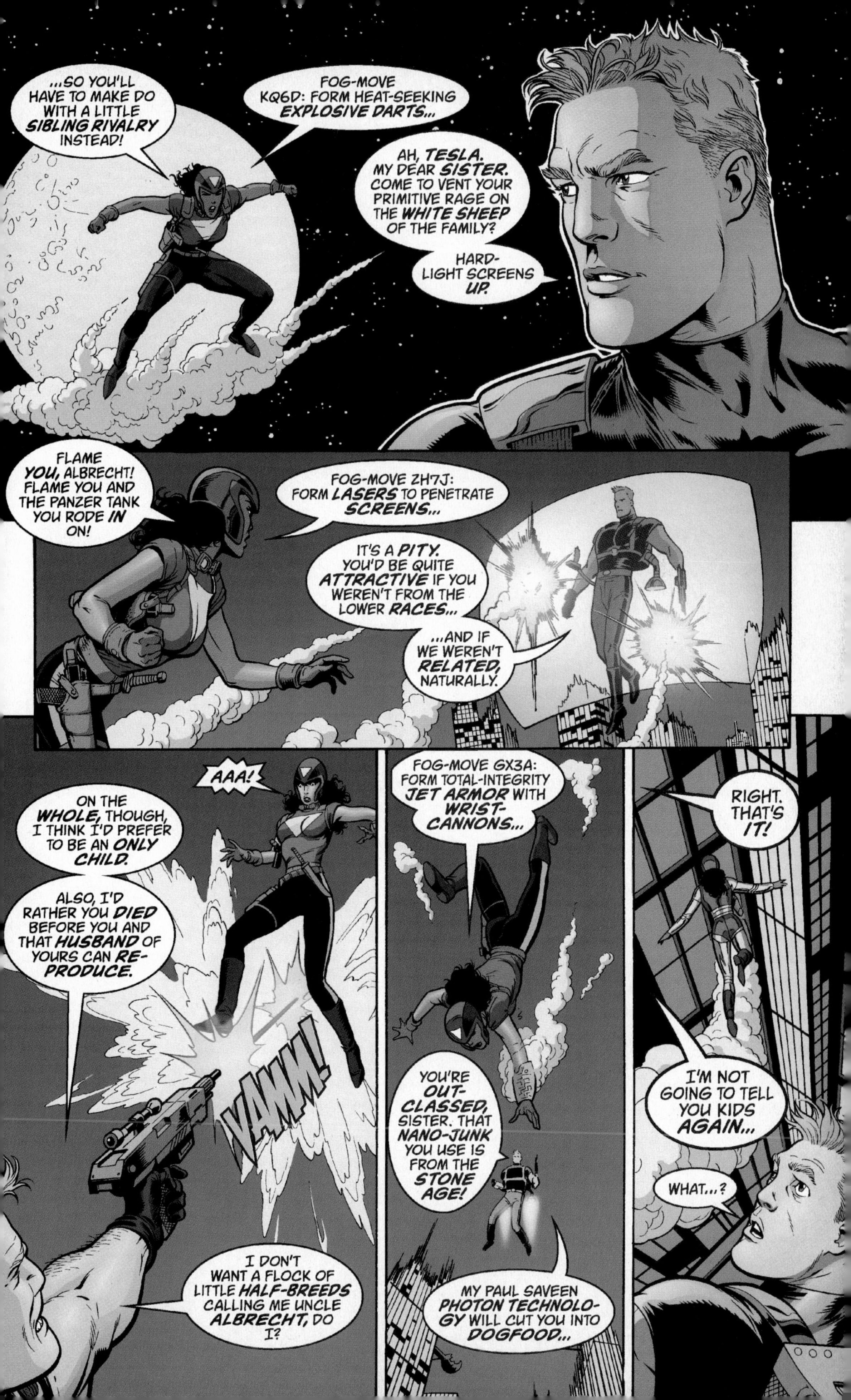

...SO YOU'LL HAVE TO MAKE DO WITH A LITTLE SIBLING RIVALRY INSTEAD!
FOG-MOVE KQ6D: FORM HEAT-SEEKING EXPLOSIVE DARTS...
AH, TESLA. MY DEAR SISTER. COME TO VENT YOUR PRIMITIVE RAGE ON THE WHITE SHEEP OF THE FAMILY?
HARD-LIGHT SCREENS UP.
FLAME YOU, ALBRECHT! FLAME YOU AND THE PANZER TANK YOU RODE IN ON!
FOG-MOVE ZH7J: FORM LASERS TO PENETRATE SCREENS...
IT'S A PITY. YOU'D BE QUITE ATTRACTIVE IF YOU WEREN'T FROM THE LOWER RACES...
...AND IF WE WEREN'T RELATED, NATURALLY.
AAA!
ON THE WHOLE, THOUGH, I THINK I'D PREFER TO BE AN ONLY CHILD.
ALSO, I'D RATHER YOU DIED BEFORE YOU AND THAT HUSBAND OF YOURS CAN RE-PRODUCE.
VAMM!
I DON'T WANT A FLOCK OF LITTLE HALF-BREEDS CALLING ME UNCLE ALBRECHT, DO I?
FOG-MOVE GX3A: FORM TOTAL-INTEGRITY JET ARMOR WITH WRIST-CANNONS...
YOU'RE OUT-CLASSED, SISTER. THAT NANO-JUNK YOU USE IS FROM THE STONE AGE!
MY PAUL SAVEEN PHOTON TECHNOLO-GY WILL CUT YOU INTO DOGFOOD...
RIGHT. THAT'S IT!
I'M NOT GOING TO TELL YOU KIDS AGAIN...
WHAT...?

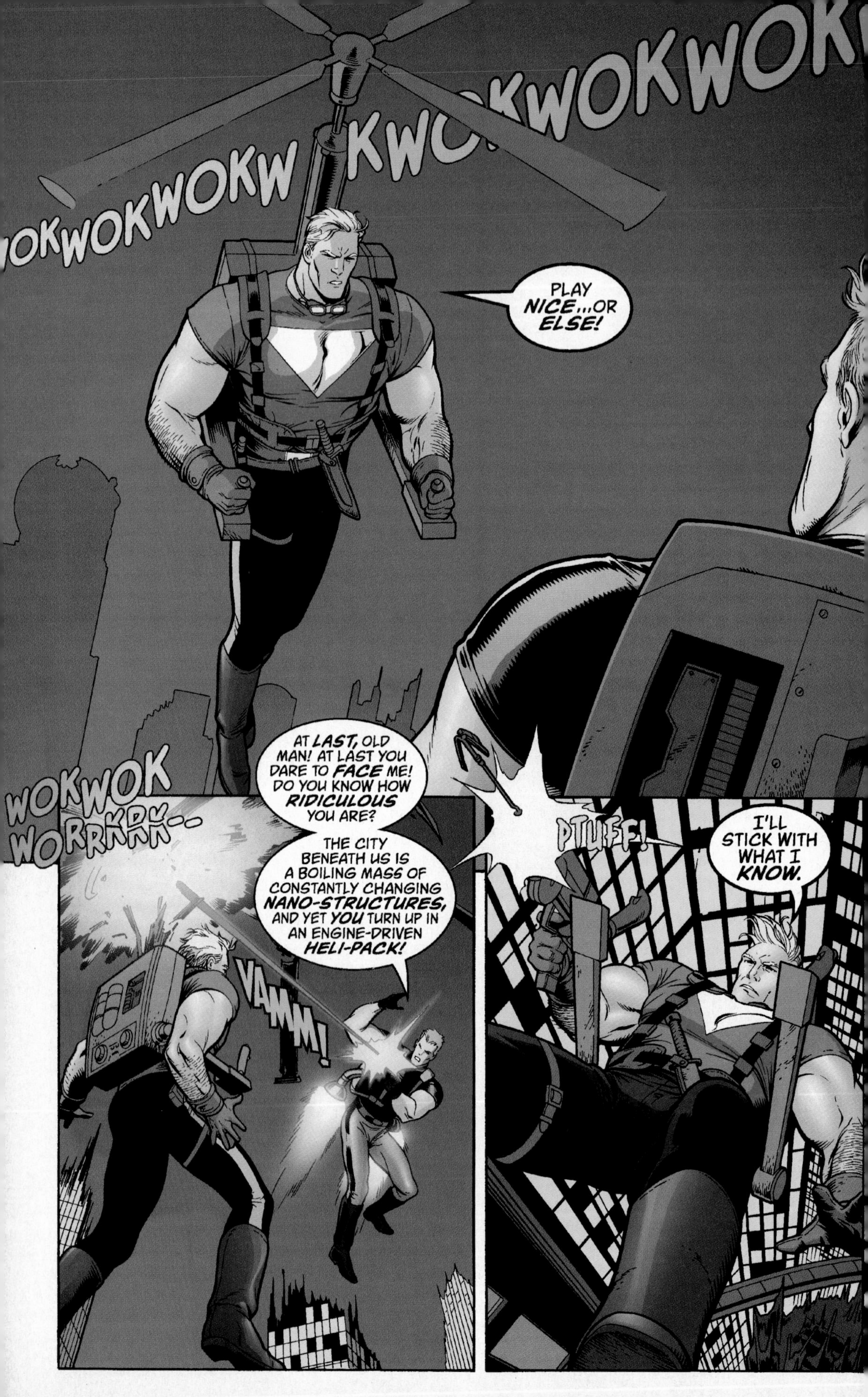

WOKWOKWOKWOKW KWOKWOKWOKWOK
PLAY NICE...OR ELSE!
WOKWOK WORRRKKKK--
AT LAST, OLD MAN! AT LAST YOU DARE TO FACE ME! DO YOU KNOW HOW RIDICULOUS YOU ARE?
THE CITY BENEATH US IS A BOILING MASS OF CONSTANTLY CHANGING NANO-STRUCTURES, AND YET YOU TURN UP IN AN ENGINE-DRIVEN HELI-PACK!
VAMM!
PTUFF!
I'LL STICK WITH WHAT I KNOW.

AAA! YOU SENILE *IDIOT!* YOUR WEIGHT WILL TAKE US *BOTH* DOWN!

DON'T WORRY, DAD!

I'LL TAKE HIM OUT BE-FORE HE CAN *RESPOND!*

TEZ, *NO! I'M* HANDLING THIS! STAY OUT OF HIS *RANGE,* OR HE'LL...

THERE! YOU *SEE,* SIS? YOU SHOULD ALWAYS LISTEN TO *DAD...*

...EVEN IF HE *IS* A RIDICULOUS *FOSSIL,* STILL CLINGING TO THE CHILDISH OP-TIMISM OF THE LAST *CEN-TURY!*

:GHUUGH:

YAMM

IT BREAKS MY HEART TO *SAY* THIS, ALBRECHT...

...BUT YOU GEN-UINELY ARE A DESPICABLE LITTLE BASTARD.

THE LAST CENTURY WAS A TORRENT OF *WAR* AND *IGNORANCE...* AND IT'S *YOUR* KIND THAT BELONGS THERE, NOT *MINE!*

RRAGH! LET *GO!* YOU'RE *CRASHING* US...

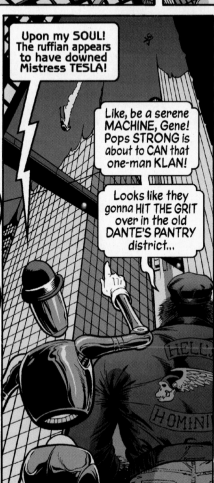

Upon my SOUL! The ruffian appears to have downed Mistress TESLA!

Like, be a serene MACHINE, Gene! Pops STRONG is about to CAN that one-man KLAN!

Looks like they gonna HIT THE GRIT over in the old DANTE'S PANTRY district...

:UFFF:

NNNGH... TH-THIS IS WHERE YOU'RE GOING TO *DIE,* FATHER.

AMONGST SORRY, CRUMBLING *RUINS* THAT ARE LIKE *YOU* AND EVERYTHING YOU *STAND* FOR!

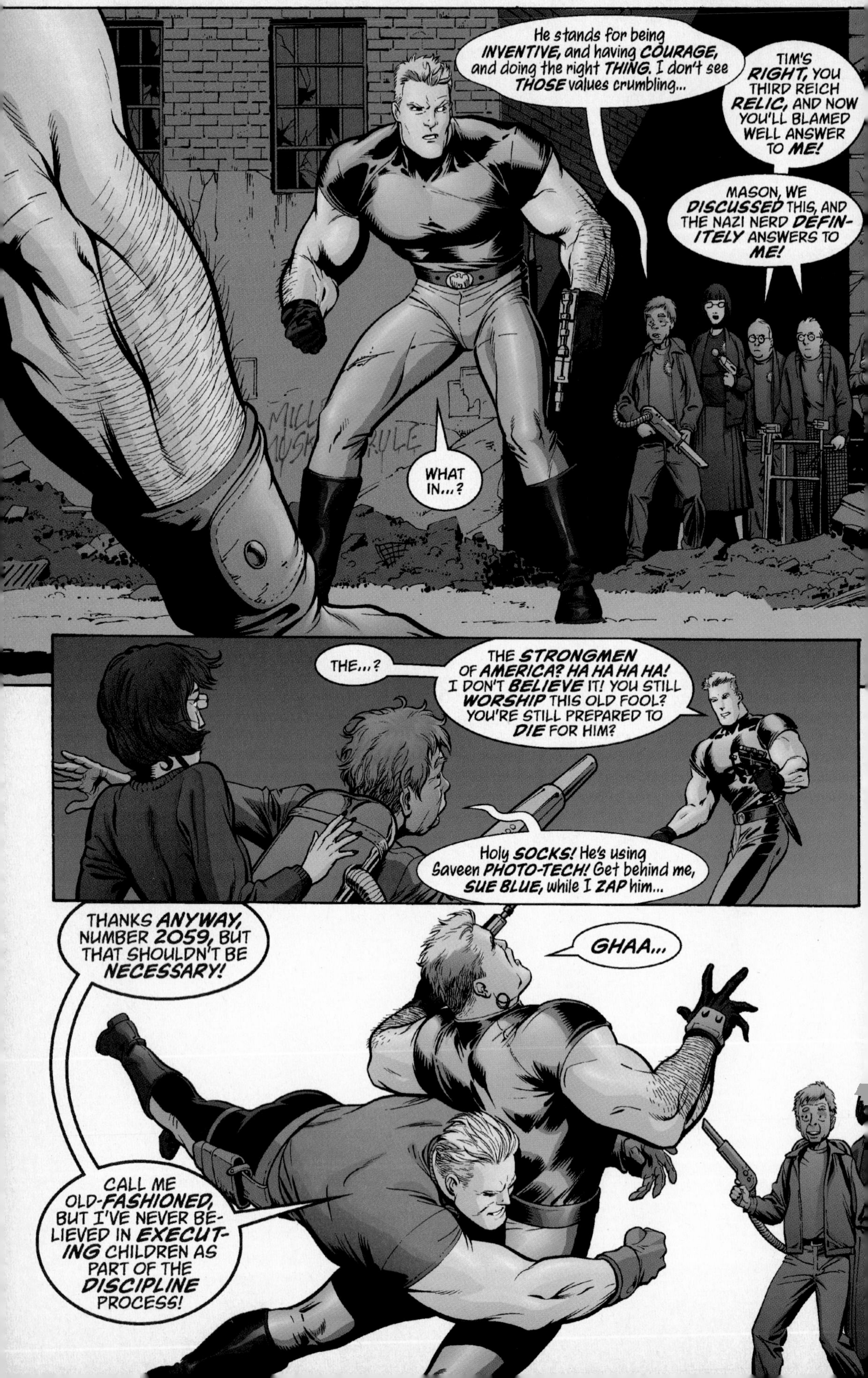

He stands for being INVENTIVE, and having COURAGE, and doing the right THING. I don't see THOSE values crumbling...
TIM'S RIGHT, YOU THIRD REICH RELIC, AND NOW YOU'LL BLAMED WELL ANSWER TO ME!
MASON, WE DISCUSSED THIS, AND THE NAZI NERD DEFIN-ITELY ANSWERS TO ME!
WHAT IN...?
THE...?
THE STRONGMEN OF AMERICA? HA HA HA HA! I DON'T BELIEVE IT! YOU STILL WORSHIP THIS OLD FOOL? YOU'RE STILL PREPARED TO DIE FOR HIM?
Holy SOCKS! He's using Saveen PHOTO-TECH! Get behind me, SUE BLUE, while I ZAP him...
THANKS ANYWAY, NUMBER 2059, BUT THAT SHOULDN'T BE NECESSARY!
GHAA...
CALL ME OLD-FASHIONED, BUT I'VE NEVER BE-LIEVED IN EXECUT-ING CHILDREN AS PART OF THE DISCIPLINE PROCESS!

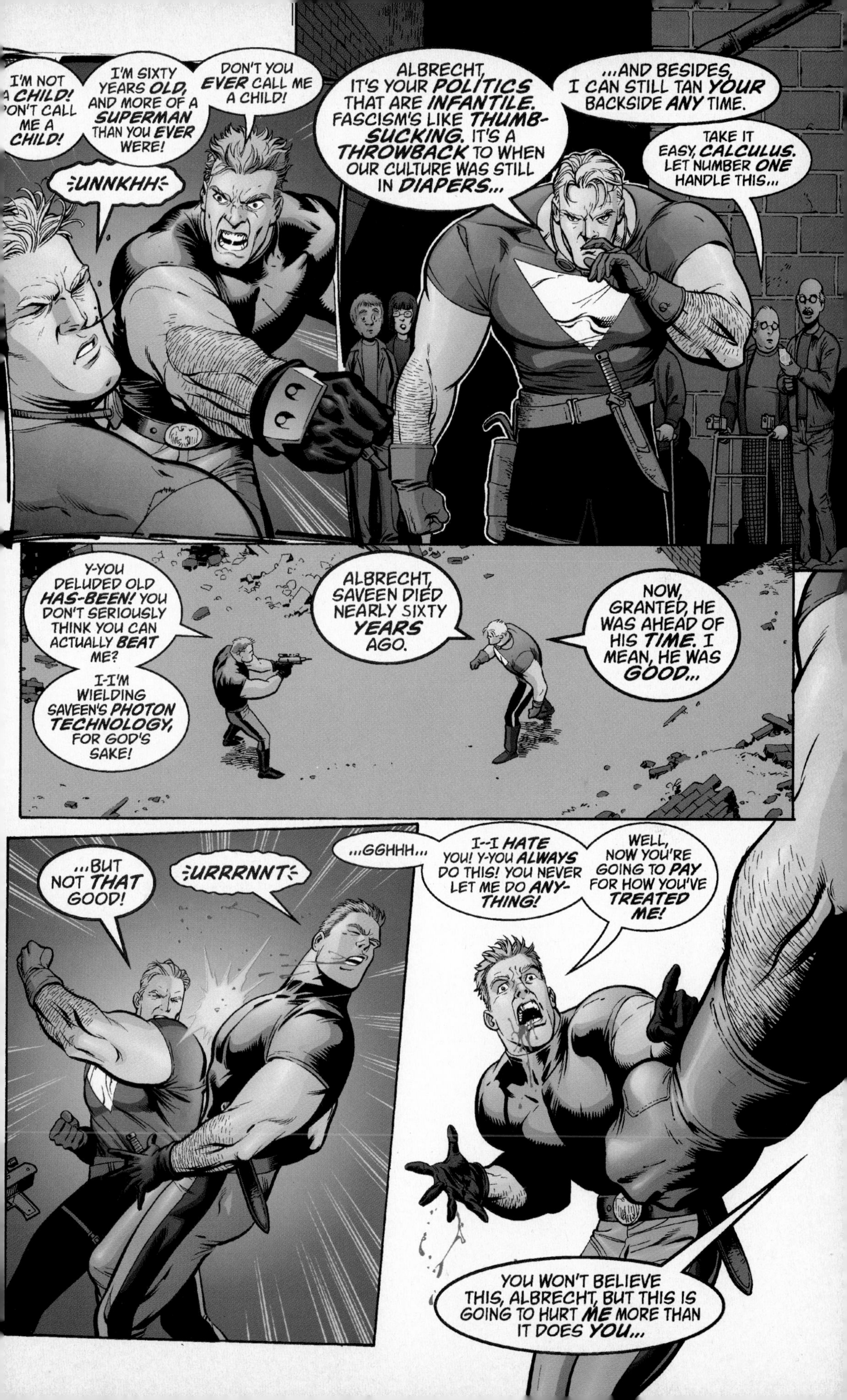
I'M NOT A CHILD! DON'T CALL ME A CHILD!
I'M SIXTY YEARS OLD, AND MORE OF A SUPERMAN THAN YOU EVER WERE!
DON'T YOU EVER CALL ME A CHILD!
UNNKHH
ALBRECHT, IT'S YOUR POLITICS THAT ARE INFANTILE. FASCISM'S LIKE THUMB-SUCKING. IT'S A THROWBACK TO WHEN OUR CULTURE WAS STILL IN DIAPERS...
...AND BESIDES, I CAN STILL TAN YOUR BACKSIDE ANY TIME.
TAKE IT EASY, CALCULUS. LET NUMBER ONE HANDLE THIS...
Y-YOU DELUDED OLD HAS-BEEN! YOU DON'T SERIOUSLY THINK YOU CAN ACTUALLY BEAT ME?
I-I'M WIELDING SAVEEN'S PHOTON TECHNOLOGY, FOR GOD'S SAKE!
ALBRECHT, SAVEEN DIED NEARLY SIXTY YEARS AGO.
NOW, GRANTED, HE WAS AHEAD OF HIS TIME. I MEAN, HE WAS GOOD...
...BUT NOT THAT GOOD!
URRRNNT
...GGHHH...
I--I HATE YOU! Y-YOU ALWAYS DO THIS! YOU NEVER LET ME DO ANY-THING!
WELL, NOW YOU'RE GOING TO PAY FOR HOW YOU'VE TREATED ME!
YOU WON'T BELIEVE THIS, ALBRECHT, BUT THIS IS GOING TO HURT ME MORE THAN IT DOES YOU...

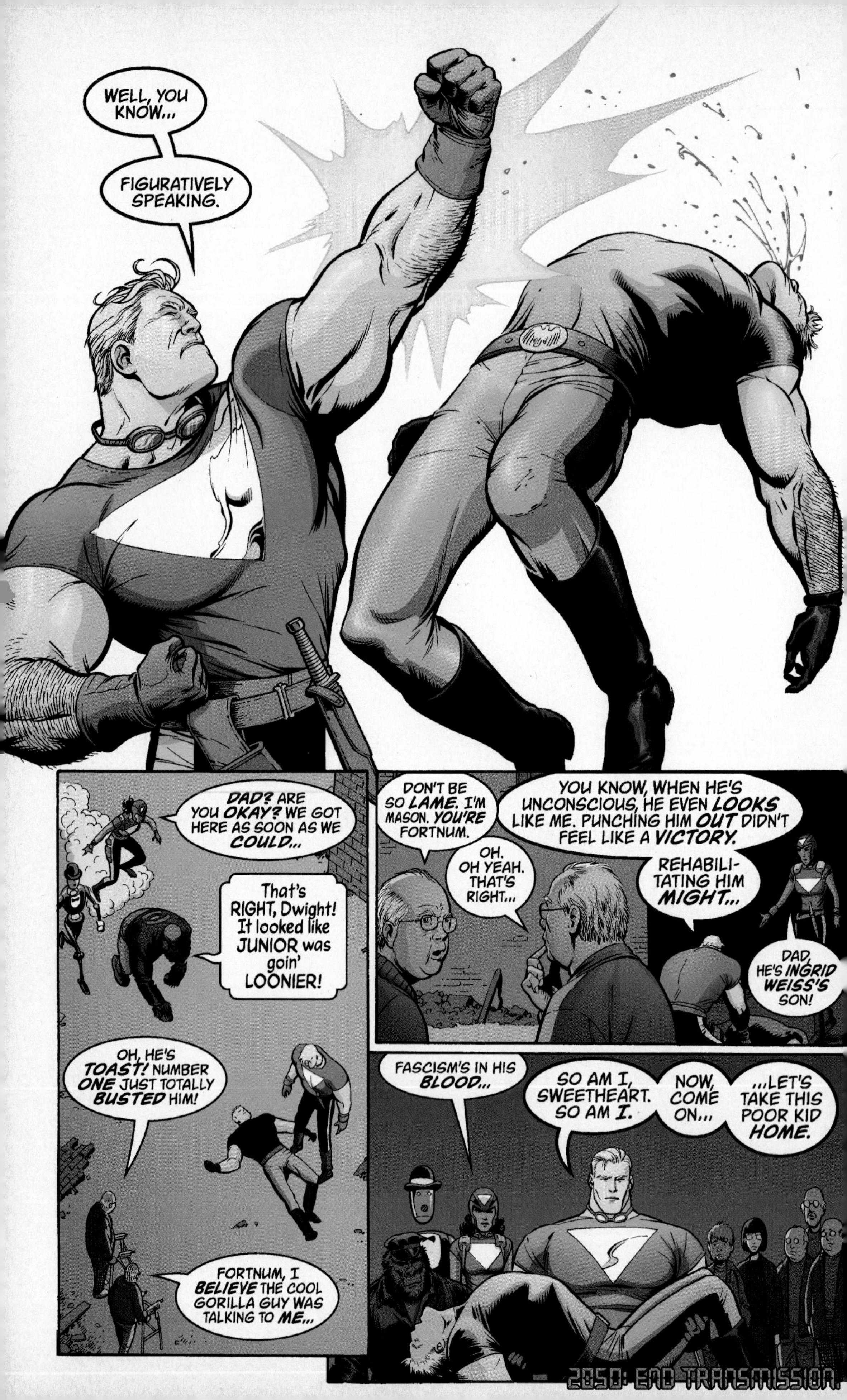
WELL, YOU KNOW...
FIGURATIVELY SPEAKING.
DAD? ARE YOU OKAY? WE GOT HERE AS SOON AS WE COULD...
That's RIGHT, Dwight! It looked like JUNIOR was goin' LOONIER!
OH, HE'S TOAST! NUMBER ONE JUST TOTALLY BUSTED HIM!
FORTNUM, I BELIEVE THE COOL GORILLA GUY WAS TALKING TO ME...
DON'T BE SO LAME. I'M MASON. YOU'RE FORTNUM.
OH. OH YEAH. THAT'S RIGHT...
YOU KNOW, WHEN HE'S UNCONSCIOUS, HE EVEN LOOKS LIKE ME. PUNCHING HIM OUT DIDN'T FEEL LIKE A VICTORY.
REHABILI-TATING HIM MIGHT...
DAD, HE'S INGRID WEISS'S SON!
FASCISM'S IN HIS BLOOD...
SO AM I, SWEETHEART. SO AM I.
NOW, COME ON...
...LET'S TAKE THIS POOR KID HOME.
2050: END TRANSMISSION.

NO! I WILL NOT **STAND** FOR IT!

I WILL NOT BE **PITIED** BY YOU!

THIS FUTURE IS A **LIE!** IT WILL NEVER **HAPPEN!**

TRUE, IT MAY NOT. THAT'S THE **NATURE** OF THE FUTURE. LOOK ON IT AS AN **AL-TERNATIVE.**

ALL THE **SAME,** IT SAID SOME INTERESTING THINGS ABOUT THE **PAST,** DON'T YOU THINK?

WH-WHAT ARE YOU SAYING?

I'M SAYING THAT THE FUTURE OF 2050 SEEMS TO THINK THAT SAVEEN HAS BEEN DEAD FOR NEARLY SIXTY YEARS.

THAT WOULD MAKE THE DATE OF DEATH... LET'S SEE. SOMEWHERE AROUND 1992? CORRECT ME IF I'M **WRONG,** SAVEEN.

I MEAN, YOU NEVER **DID** EXPLAIN THE FAKED DEATH IN AFRICA; THE SKELETON IDENTIFIED BY DENTAL RECORDS...

EARTHQUAKE BOOTS

UHH...

HERR **SAVEEN?** WH-WHAT DOES HE **MEAN?**

NOTHING. IGNORE HIM.

TOM, MY DEAR CHAP, **THAT** BODY WAS A **CLONE.** OTHERWISE I COULDN'T **BE** HERE, COULD I?

GOOD **POINT.** I'LL BE **GETTING** TO THAT IN A MOMENT.

SO, SAVEEN, THIS **CLONE;** IT SOUNDS **INGENIOUS,** EVEN FOR **YOU.** HOW DID YOU CLONE EVERY CHIPPED **TOOTH?** EVERY EXACT **FILLING?**

I..., UH...

LOOK, YOU CAN'T EXPECT ME TO REMEMBER EVERY **DETAIL...**

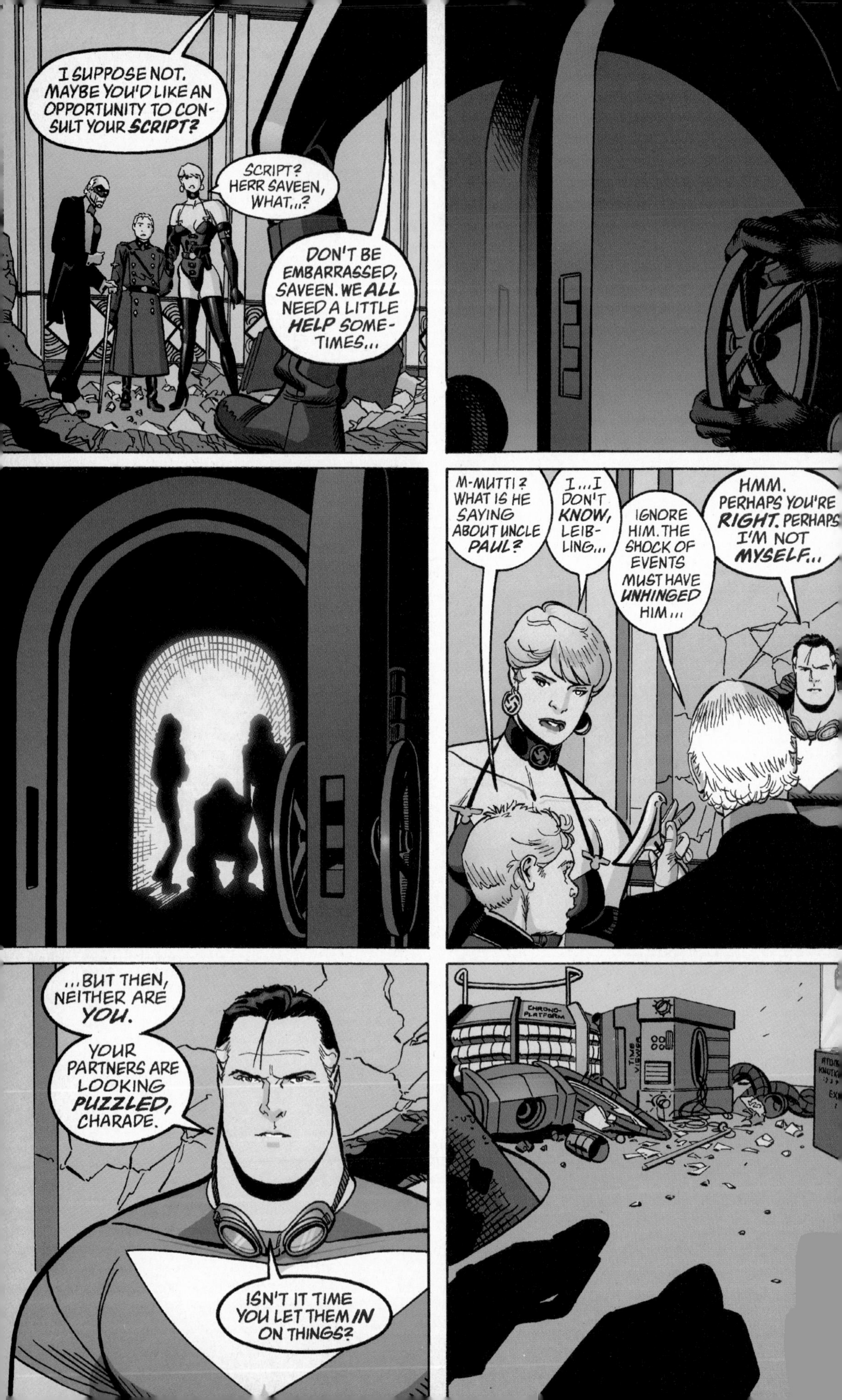
I SUPPOSE NOT. MAYBE YOU'D LIKE AN OPPORTUNITY TO CONSULT YOUR **SCRIPT?**
SCRIPT? HERR SAVEEN, WHAT...?
DON'T BE EMBARRASSED, SAVEEN. WE **ALL** NEED A LITTLE **HELP** SOMETIMES...
M-MUTTI? WHAT IS HE SAYING ABOUT UNCLE **PAUL?**
I...I DON'T **KNOW,** LEIBLING...
IGNORE HIM. THE SHOCK OF EVENTS MUST HAVE **UNHINGED** HIM...
HMM. PERHAPS YOU'RE **RIGHT.** PERHAPS I'M NOT **MYSELF...**
...BUT THEN, NEITHER ARE **YOU.**
YOUR PARTNERS ARE LOOKING **PUZZLED,** CHARADE.
ISN'T IT TIME YOU LET THEM **IN** ON THINGS?
CHRONO-PLATFORM
TIME VIEWER

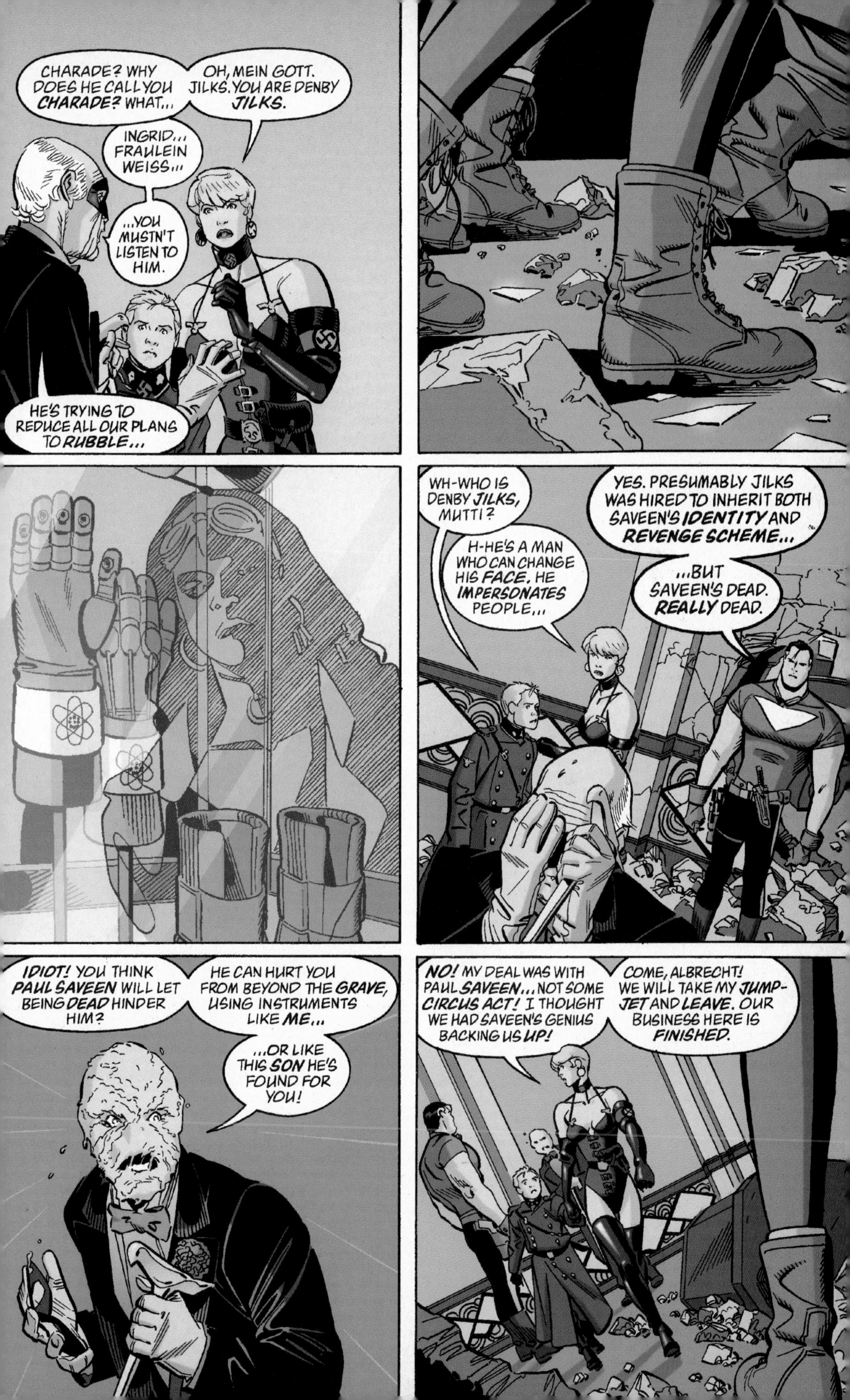
CHARADE? WHY DOES HE CALL YOU CHARADE? WHAT...
OH, MEIN GOTT. JILKS. YOU ARE DENBY JILKS.
INGRID... FRAULEIN WEISS...
...YOU MUSTN'T LISTEN TO HIM.
HE'S TRYING TO REDUCE ALL OUR PLANS TO RUBBLE...
WH-WHO IS DENBY JILKS, MUTTI?
H-HE'S A MAN WHO CAN CHANGE HIS FACE. HE IMPERSONATES PEOPLE...
YES. PRESUMABLY JILKS WAS HIRED TO INHERIT BOTH SAVEEN'S IDENTITY AND REVENGE SCHEME...
...BUT SAVEEN'S DEAD. REALLY DEAD.
IDIOT! YOU THINK PAUL SAVEEN WILL LET BEING DEAD HINDER HIM?
HE CAN HURT YOU FROM BEYOND THE GRAVE, USING INSTRUMENTS LIKE ME...
...OR LIKE THIS SON HE'S FOUND FOR YOU!
NO! MY DEAL WAS WITH PAUL SAVEEN... NOT SOME CIRCUS ACT! I THOUGHT WE HAD SAVEEN'S GENIUS BACKING US UP!
COME, ALBRECHT! WE WILL TAKE MY JUMP-JET AND LEAVE. OUR BUSINESS HERE IS FINISHED.

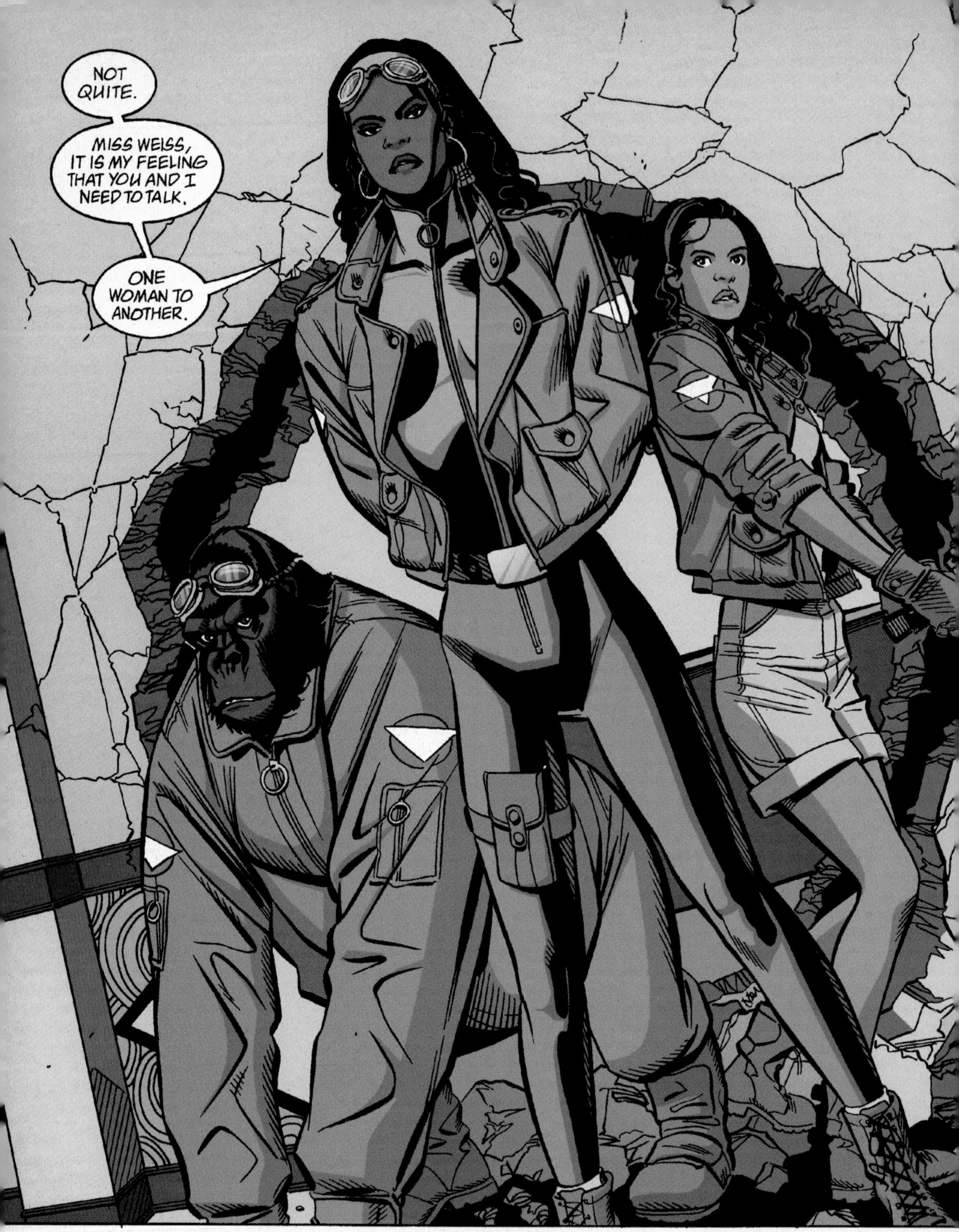
NOT QUITE.
MISS WEISS, IT IS MY FEELING THAT YOU AND I NEED TO TALK.
ONE WOMAN TO ANOTHER.

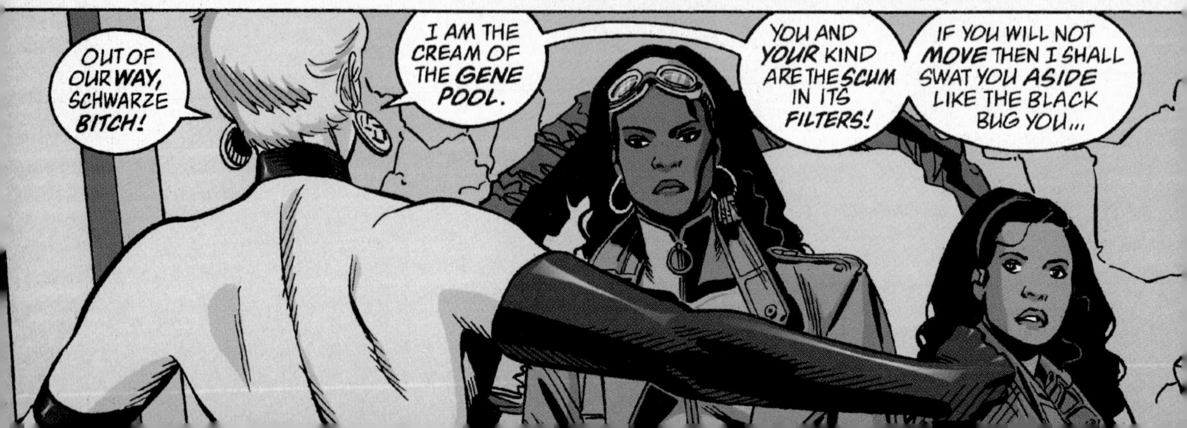
OUT OF OUR WAY, SCHWARZE BITCH!
I AM THE CREAM OF THE GENE POOL.
YOU AND YOUR KIND ARE THE SCUM IN ITS FILTERS!
IF YOU WILL NOT MOVE THEN I SHALL SWAT YOU ASIDE LIKE THE BLACK BUG YOU...

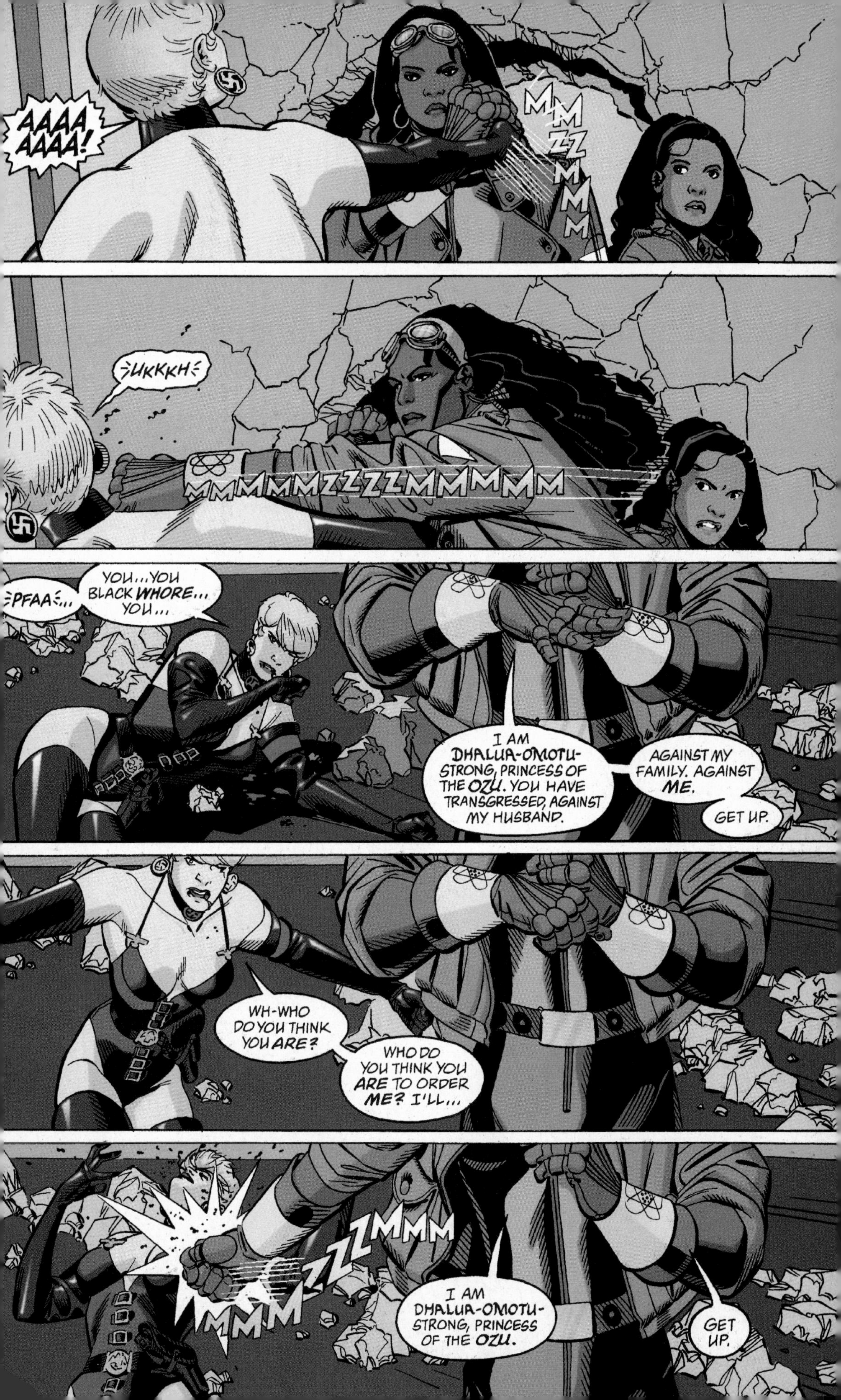
AAAA AAAA!
MMMZZMMMM
UKKKH
MMMMMZZZZMMMMMM
PFAA...
YOU...YOU BLACK WHORE... YOU...
I AM DHALUA-OMOTU-STRONG, PRINCESS OF THE OZU. YOU HAVE TRANSGRESSED, AGAINST MY HUSBAND.
AGAINST MY FAMILY. AGAINST ME.
GET UP.
WH-WHO DO YOU THINK YOU ARE?
WHO DO YOU THINK YOU ARE TO ORDER ME? I'LL...
MMMZZZMMM
I AM DHALUA-OMOTU-STRONG, PRINCESS OF THE OZU.
GET UP.

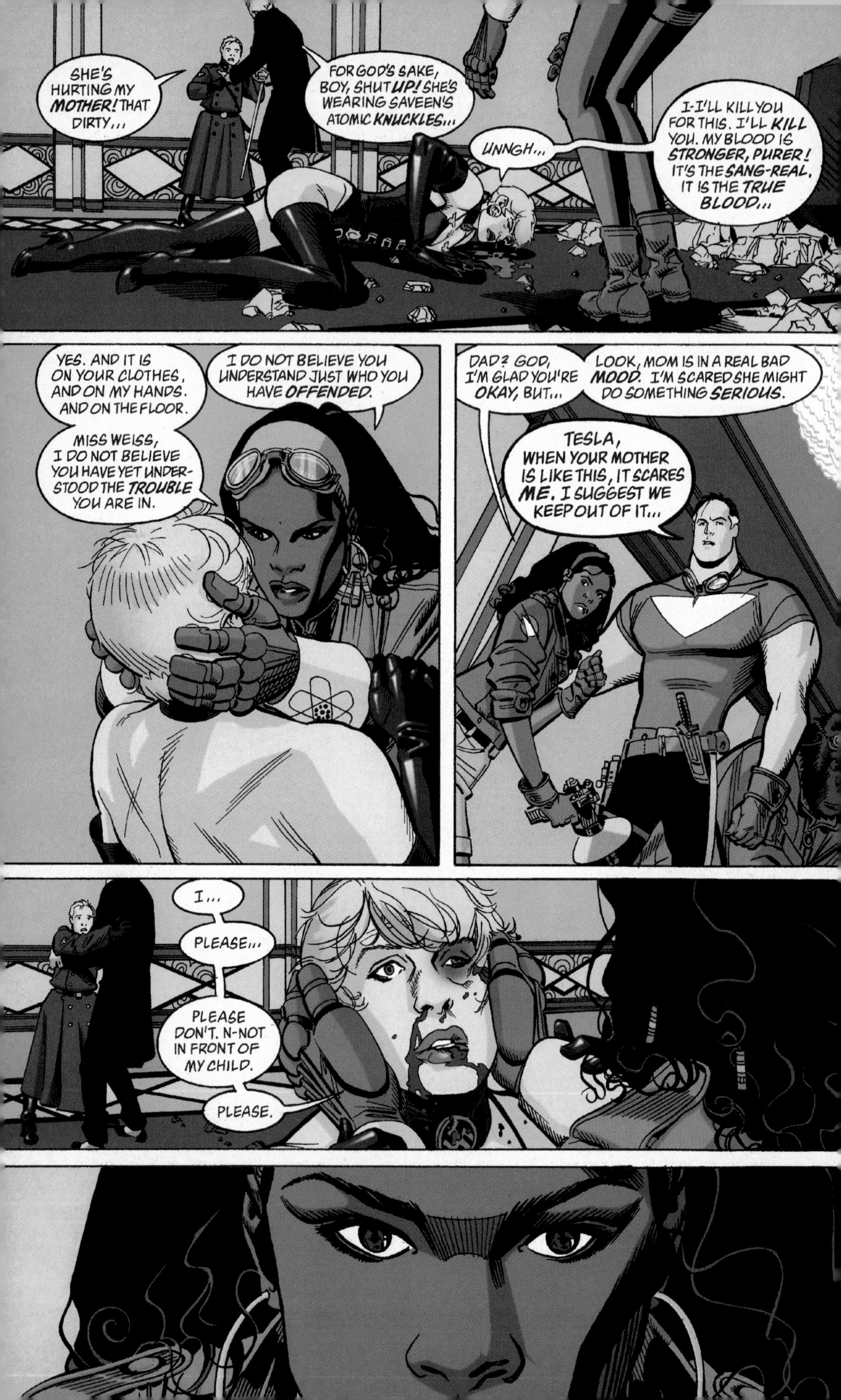
SHE'S HURTING MY MOTHER! THAT DIRTY...
FOR GOD'S SAKE, BOY, SHUT UP! SHE'S WEARING SAVEEN'S ATOMIC KNUCKLES...
UNNGH...
I-I'LL KILL YOU FOR THIS. I'LL KILL YOU. MY BLOOD IS STRONGER, PURER! IT'S THE SANG-REAL. IT IS THE TRUE BLOOD...
YES. AND IT IS ON YOUR CLOTHES, AND ON MY HANDS. AND ON THE FLOOR.
I DO NOT BELIEVE YOU UNDERSTAND JUST WHO YOU HAVE OFFENDED.
MISS WEISS, I DO NOT BELIEVE YOU HAVE YET UNDER-STOOD THE TROUBLE YOU ARE IN.
DAD? GOD, I'M GLAD YOU'RE OKAY, BUT...
LOOK, MOM IS IN A REAL BAD MOOD. I'M SCARED SHE MIGHT DO SOMETHING SERIOUS.
TESLA, WHEN YOUR MOTHER IS LIKE THIS, IT SCARES ME. I SUGGEST WE KEEP OUT OF IT...
I...
PLEASE...
PLEASE DON'T. N-NOT IN FRONT OF MY CHILD.
PLEASE.

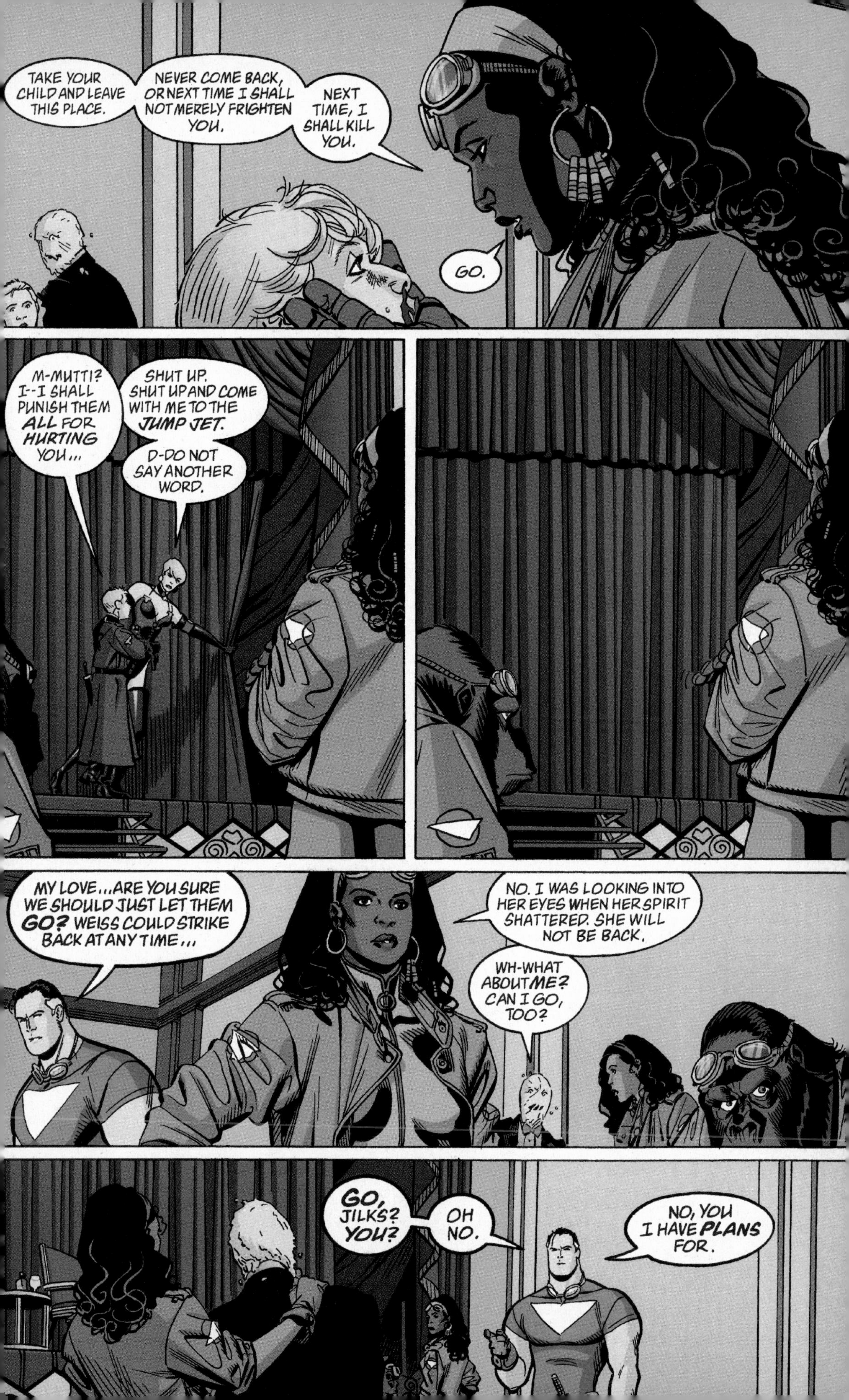
TAKE YOUR CHILD AND LEAVE THIS PLACE.
NEVER COME BACK, OR NEXT TIME I SHALL NOT MERELY FRIGHTEN YOU.
NEXT TIME, I SHALL KILL YOU.
GO.
M-MUTTI? I--I SHALL PUNISH THEM ALL FOR HURTING YOU...
SHUT UP. SHUT UP AND COME WITH ME TO THE JUMP JET.
D-DO NOT SAY ANOTHER WORD.
MY LOVE...ARE YOU SURE WE SHOULD JUST LET THEM GO? WEISS COULD STRIKE BACK AT ANY TIME...
NO. I WAS LOOKING INTO HER EYES WHEN HER SPIRIT SHATTERED. SHE WILL NOT BE BACK.
WH-WHAT ABOUT ME? CAN I GO, TOO?
GO, JILKS? YOU?
OH NO.
NO, YOU I HAVE PLANS FOR.

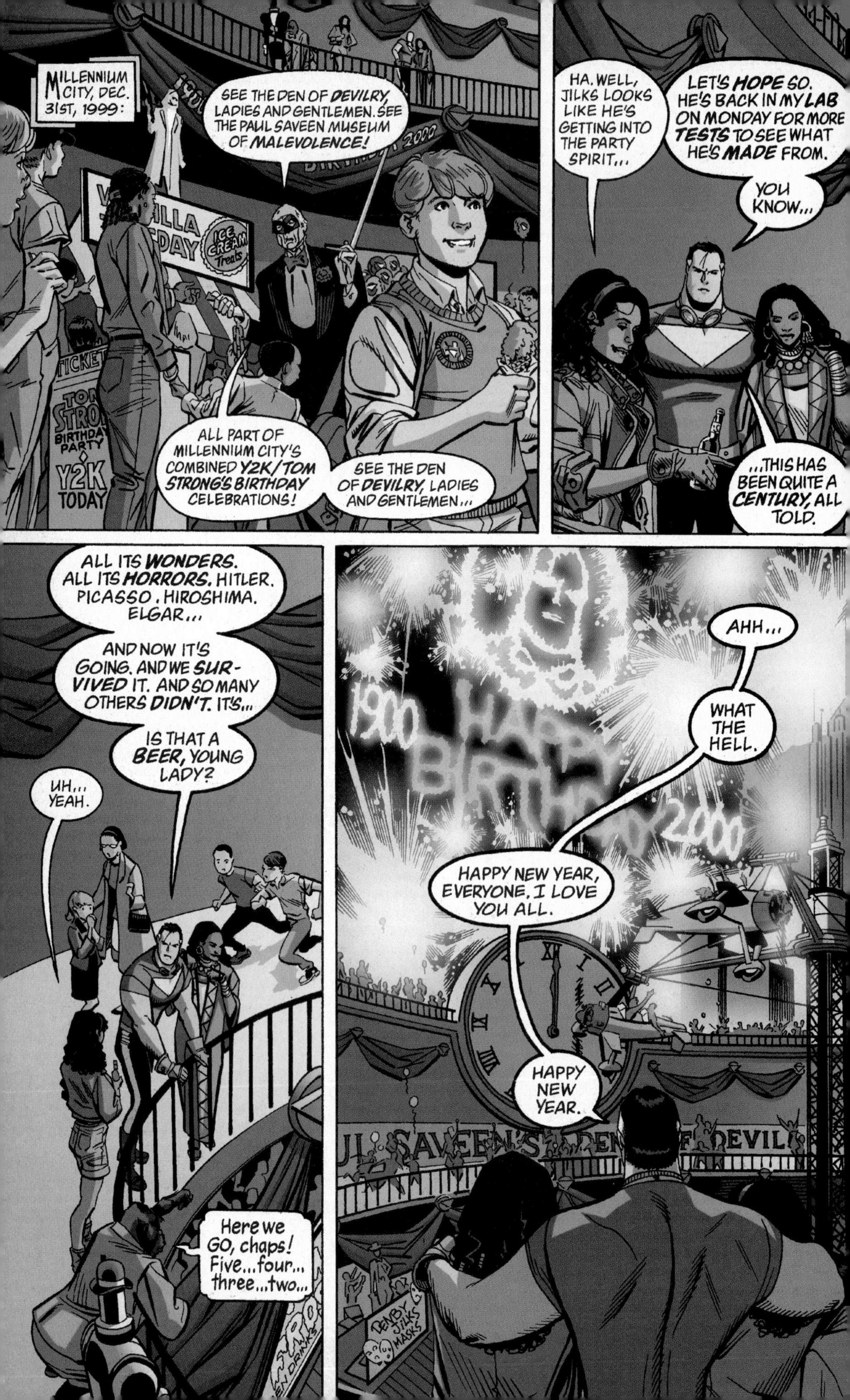
MILLENNIUM CITY, DEC. 31ST, 1999:
SEE THE DEN OF DEVILRY, LADIES AND GENTLEMEN. SEE THE PAUL SAVEEN MUSEUM OF MALEVOLENCE!
ICE CREAM Treats
ALL PART OF MILLENNIUM CITY'S COMBINED Y2K/TOM STRONG'S BIRTHDAY CELEBRATIONS!
SEE THE DEN OF DEVILRY, LADIES AND GENTLEMEN...
HA. WELL, JILKS LOOKS LIKE HE'S GETTING INTO THE PARTY SPIRIT...
LET'S HOPE SO. HE'S BACK IN MY LAB ON MONDAY FOR MORE TESTS TO SEE WHAT HE'S MADE FROM.
YOU KNOW...
...THIS HAS BEEN QUITE A CENTURY, ALL TOLD.
ALL ITS WONDERS. ALL ITS HORRORS. HITLER. PICASSO. HIROSHIMA. ELGAR...
AND NOW IT'S GOING. AND WE SURVIVED IT. AND SO MANY OTHERS DIDN'T. IT'S...
IS THAT A BEER, YOUNG LADY?
UH... YEAH.
Here we GO, chaps! Five...four... three...two...
AHH...
WHAT THE HELL.
HAPPY NEW YEAR, EVERYONE. I LOVE YOU ALL.
HAPPY NEW YEAR.
DERBY JILKS MASKS

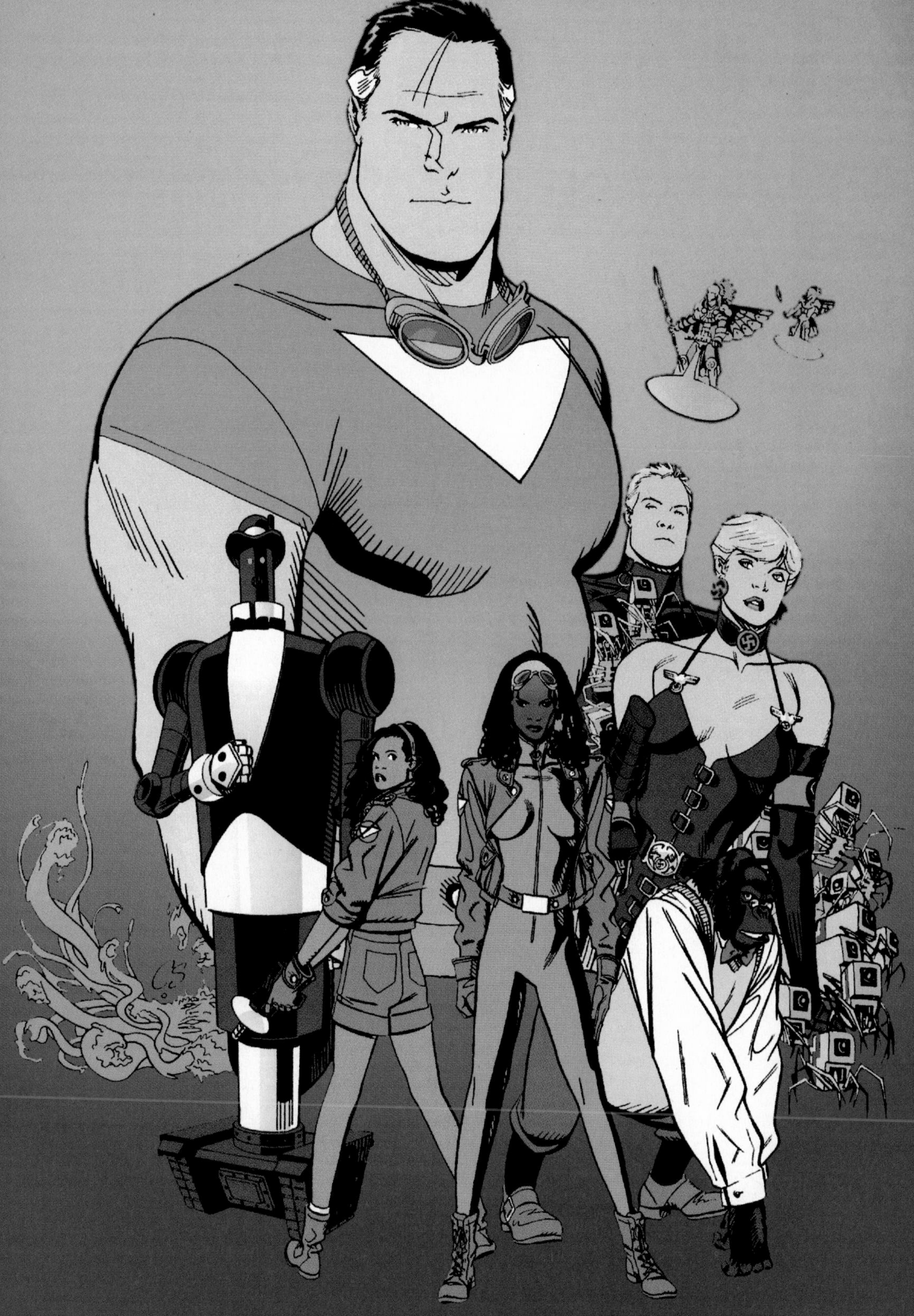

TOM STRONG GALLERY

Designs by CHRIS SPROUSE based on concepts by ALAN MOORE

Before beginning to draw the finished pages of TOM STRONG, Chris develops the characters and costumes in a series of design/model drawings, such as those included here and on the following pages.

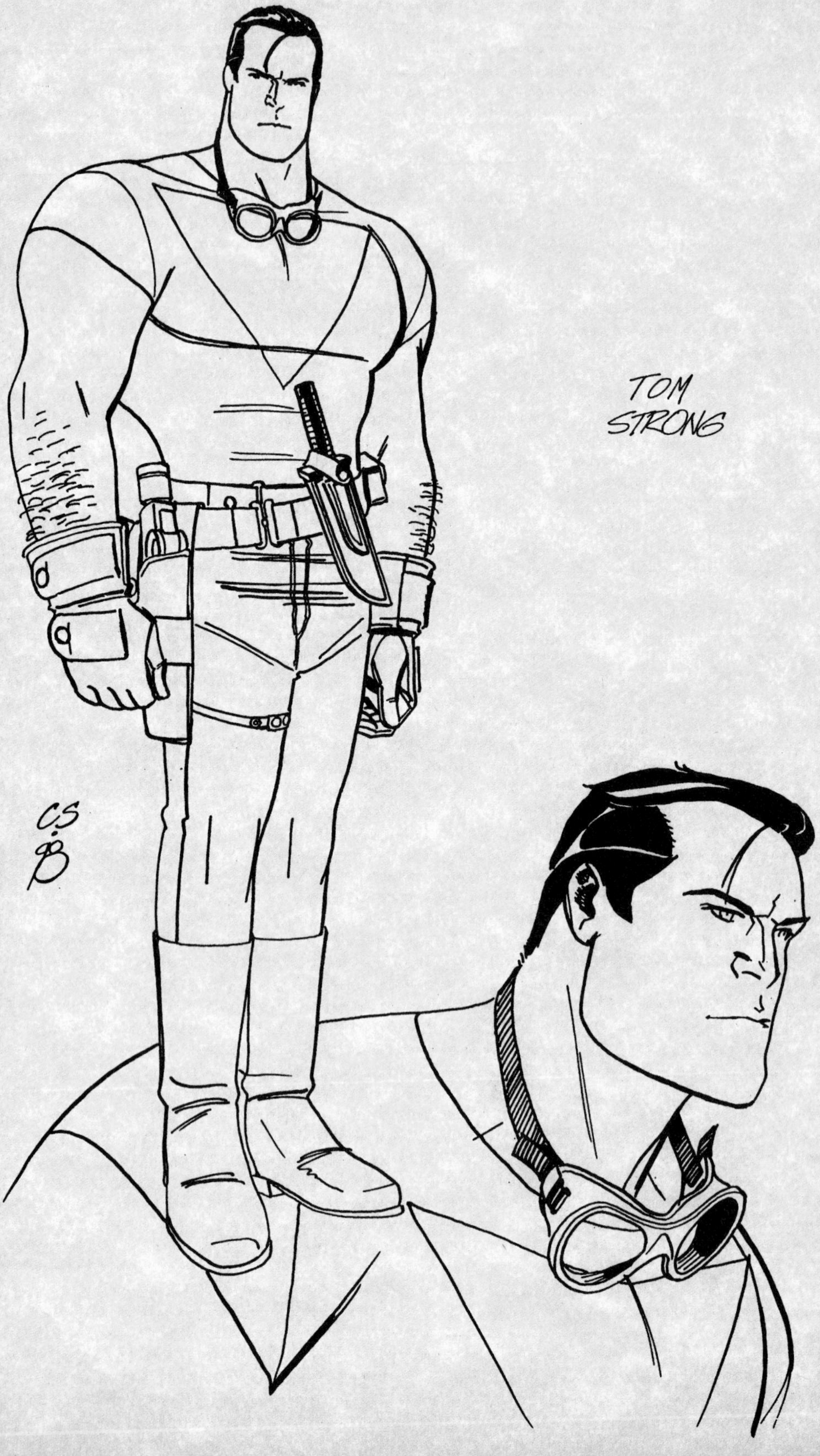
TOM
STRONG
C.S
98

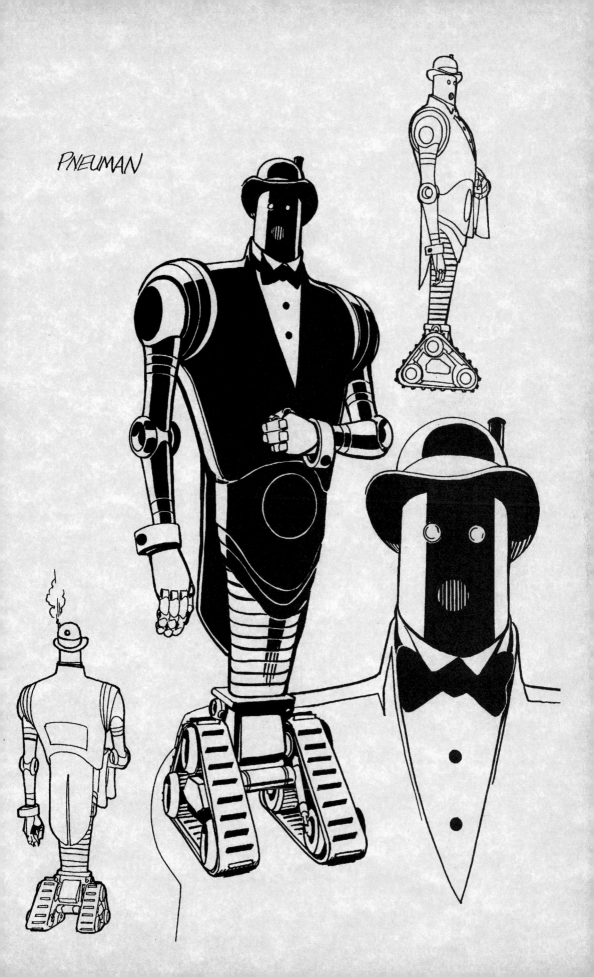

PNEUMAN

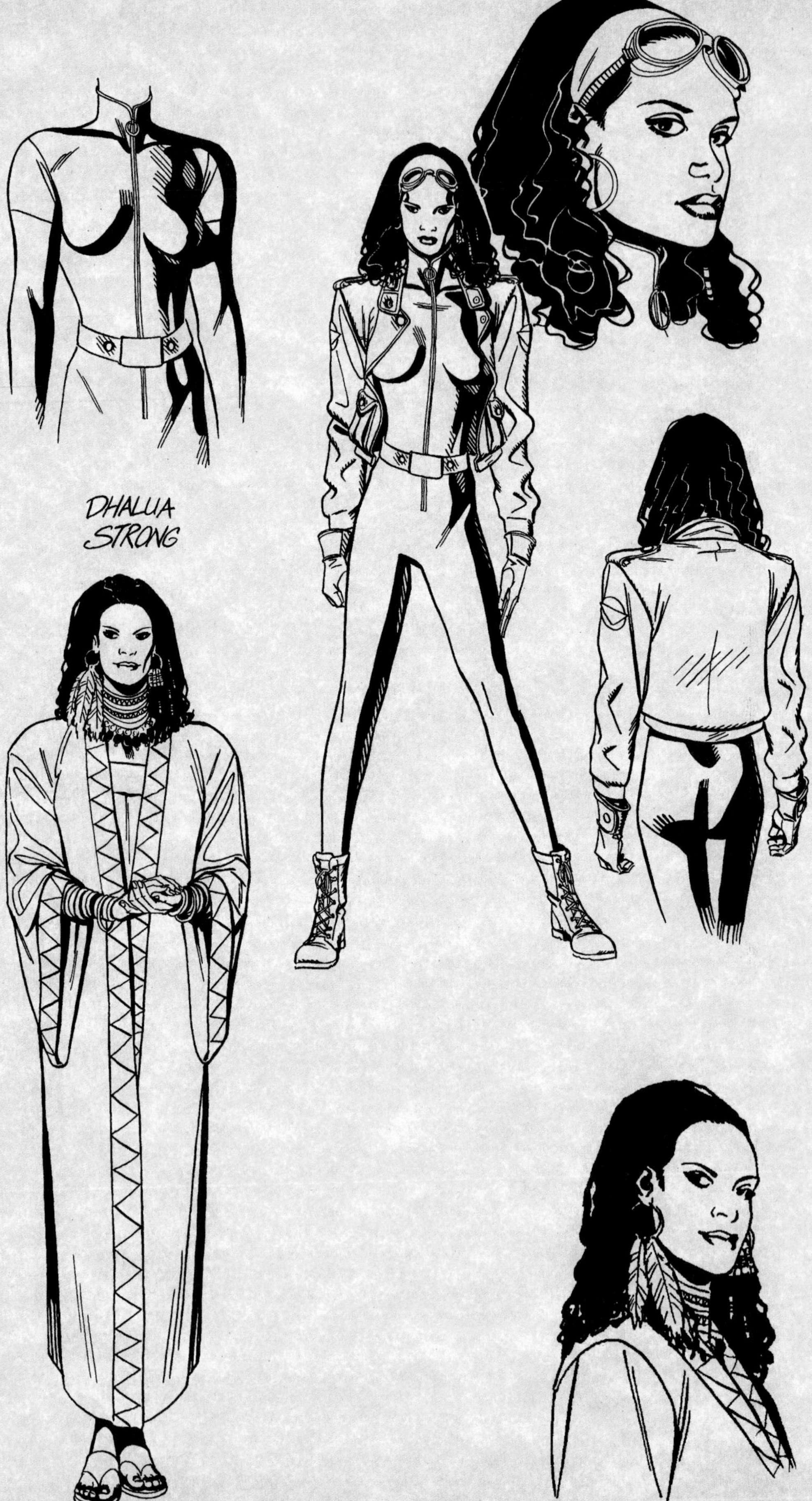
DHALUA
STRONG

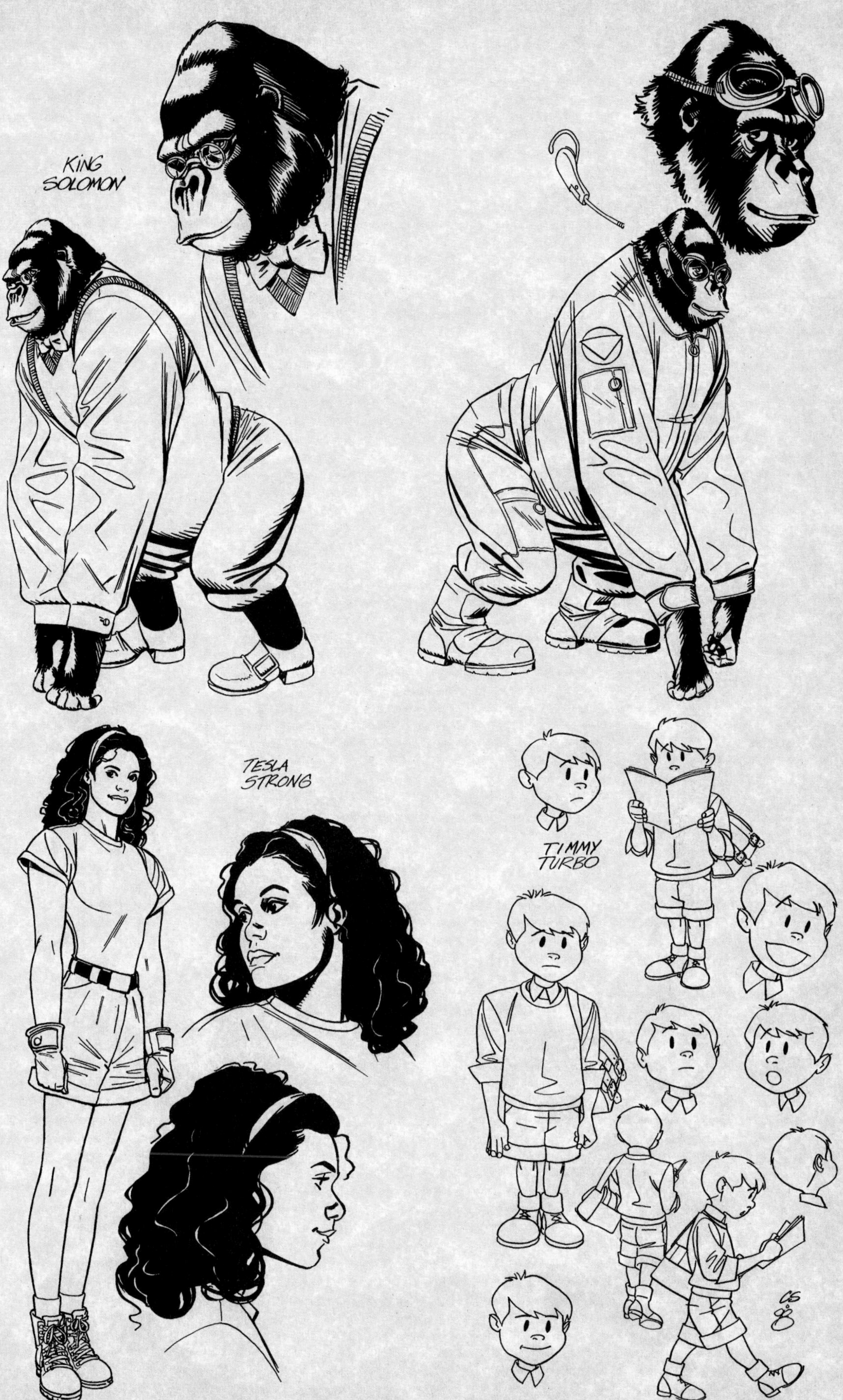

KING SOLOMON
TESLA STRONG
TIMMY TURBO

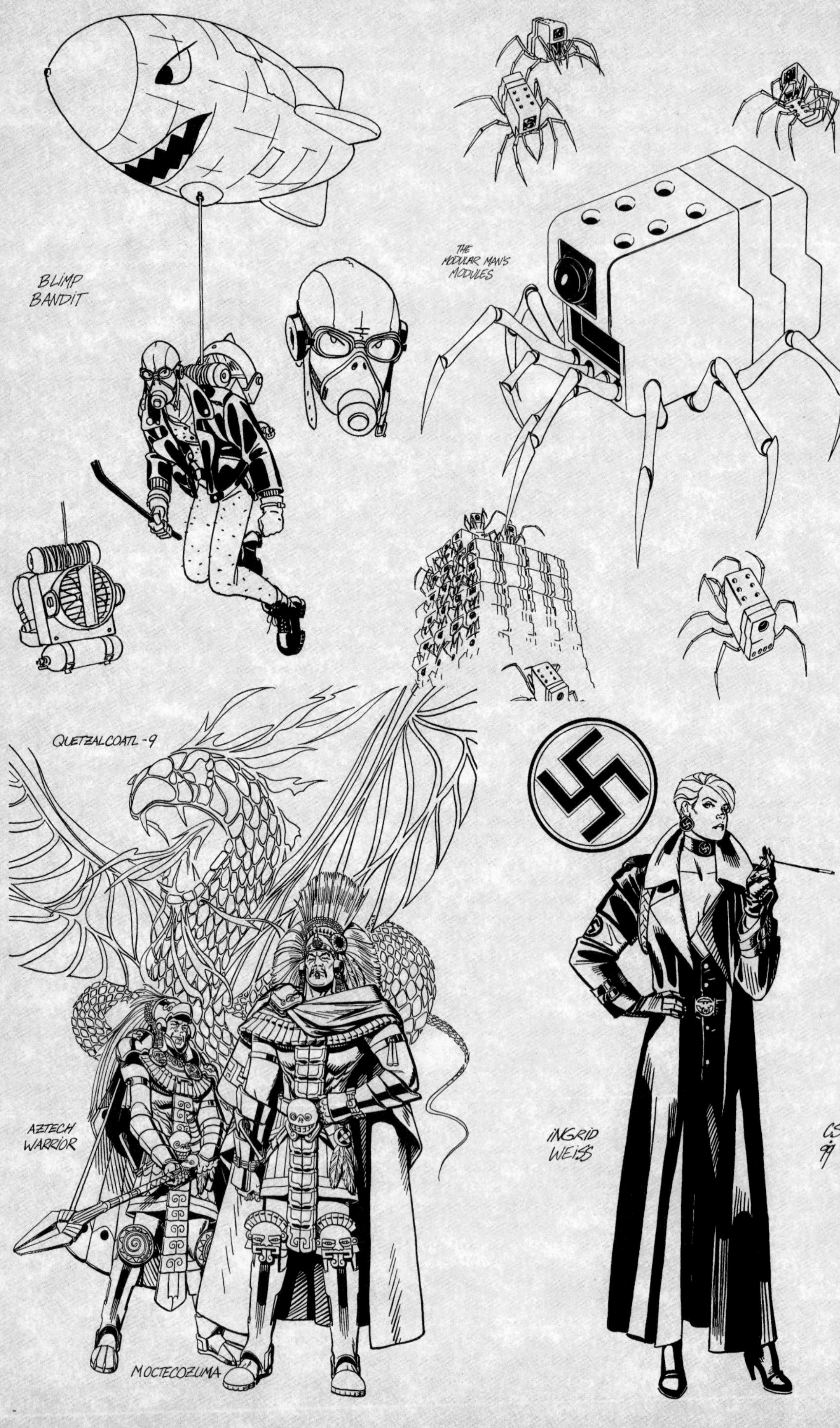
BLIMP BANDIT
THE MODULAR MAN'S MODULES
QUETZALCOATL-9
AZTECH WARRIOR
MOCTECOZUMA
INGRID WEISS
CS. 99

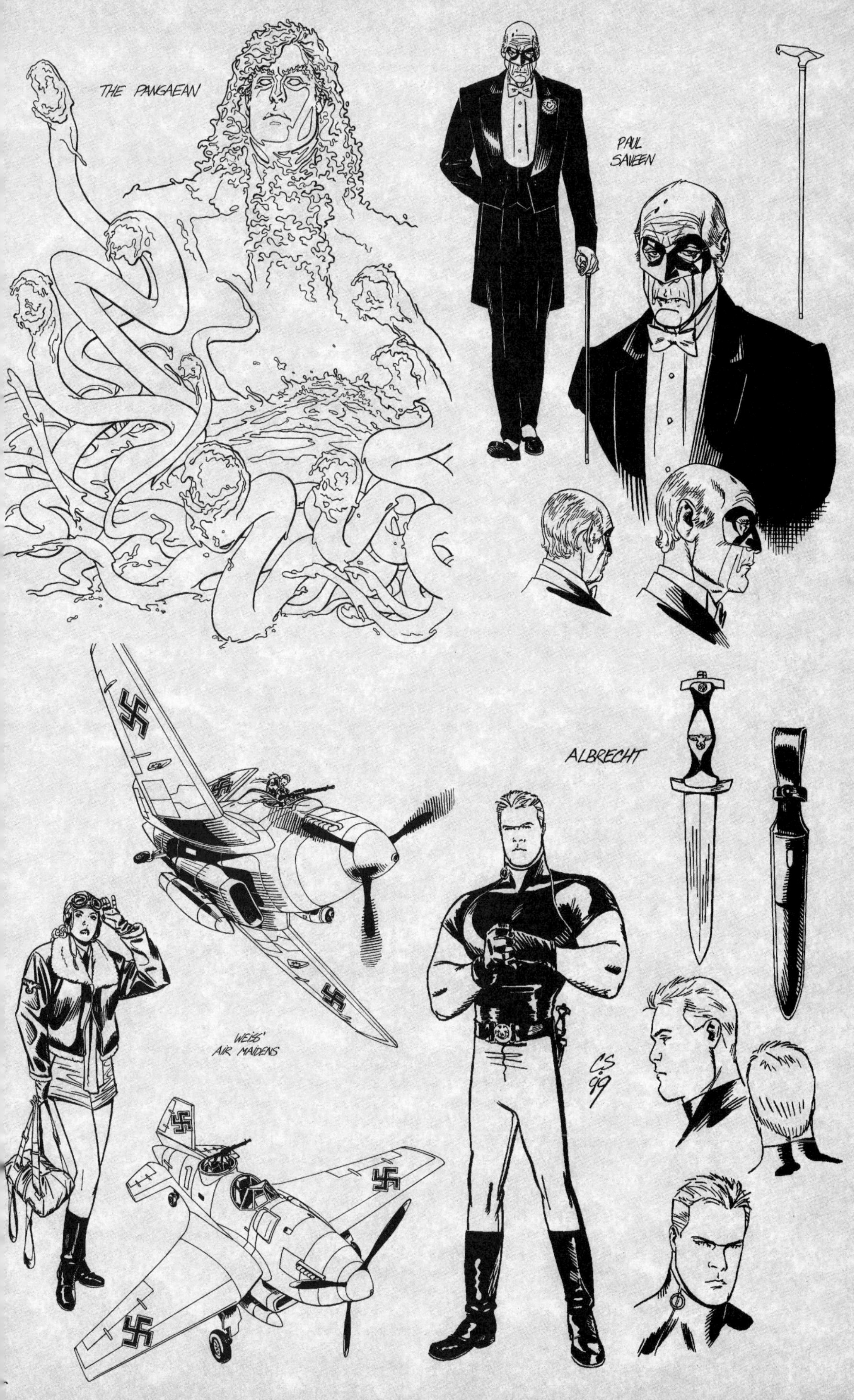
THE PANGAEAN
PAUL SAVEEN
ALBRECHT
WEISS' AIR MAIDENS
CS 99

Here are three more unpublished pieces by Chris for your enjoyment, including a variant on the Strongmen of America button art.

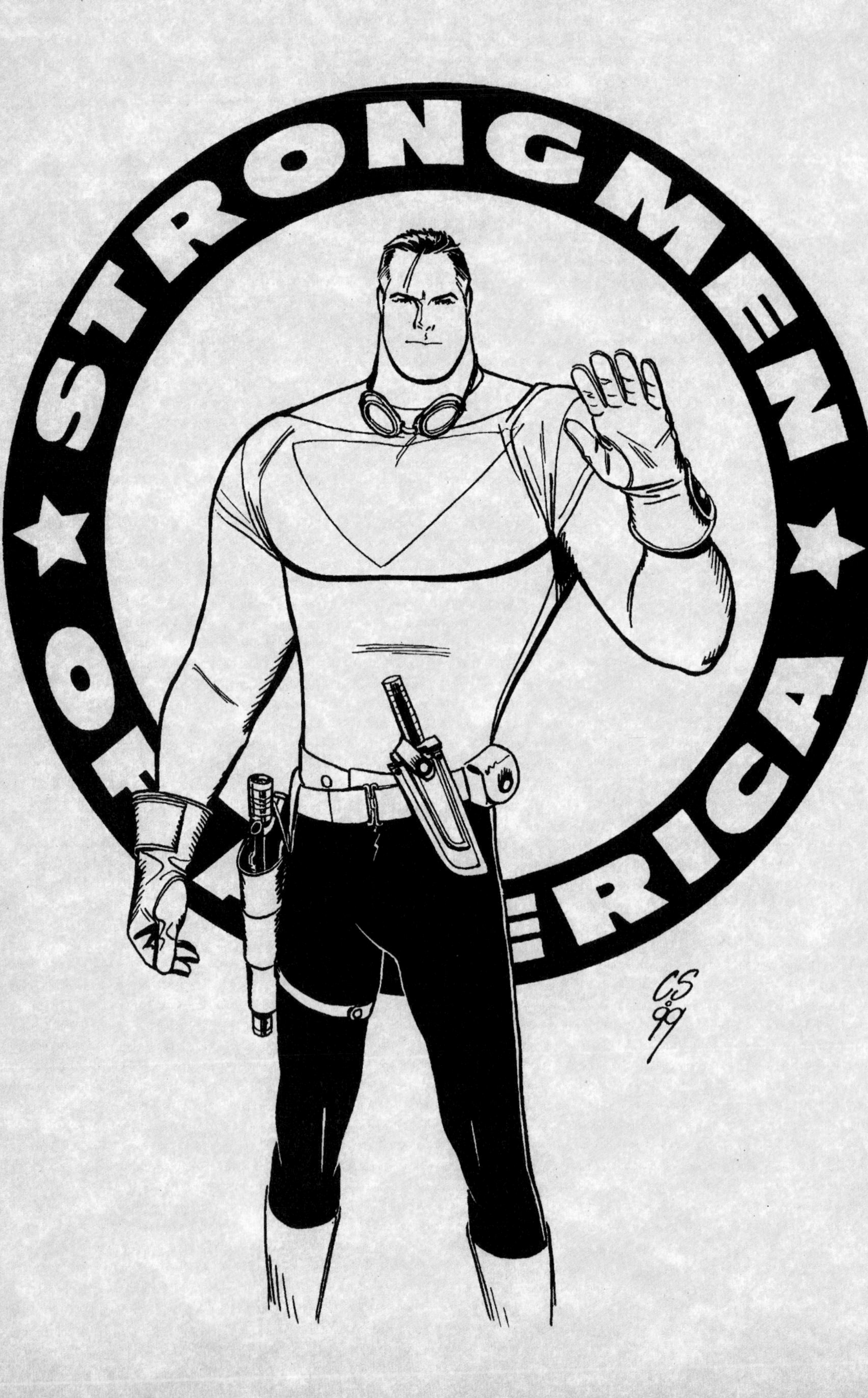
STRONGMEN

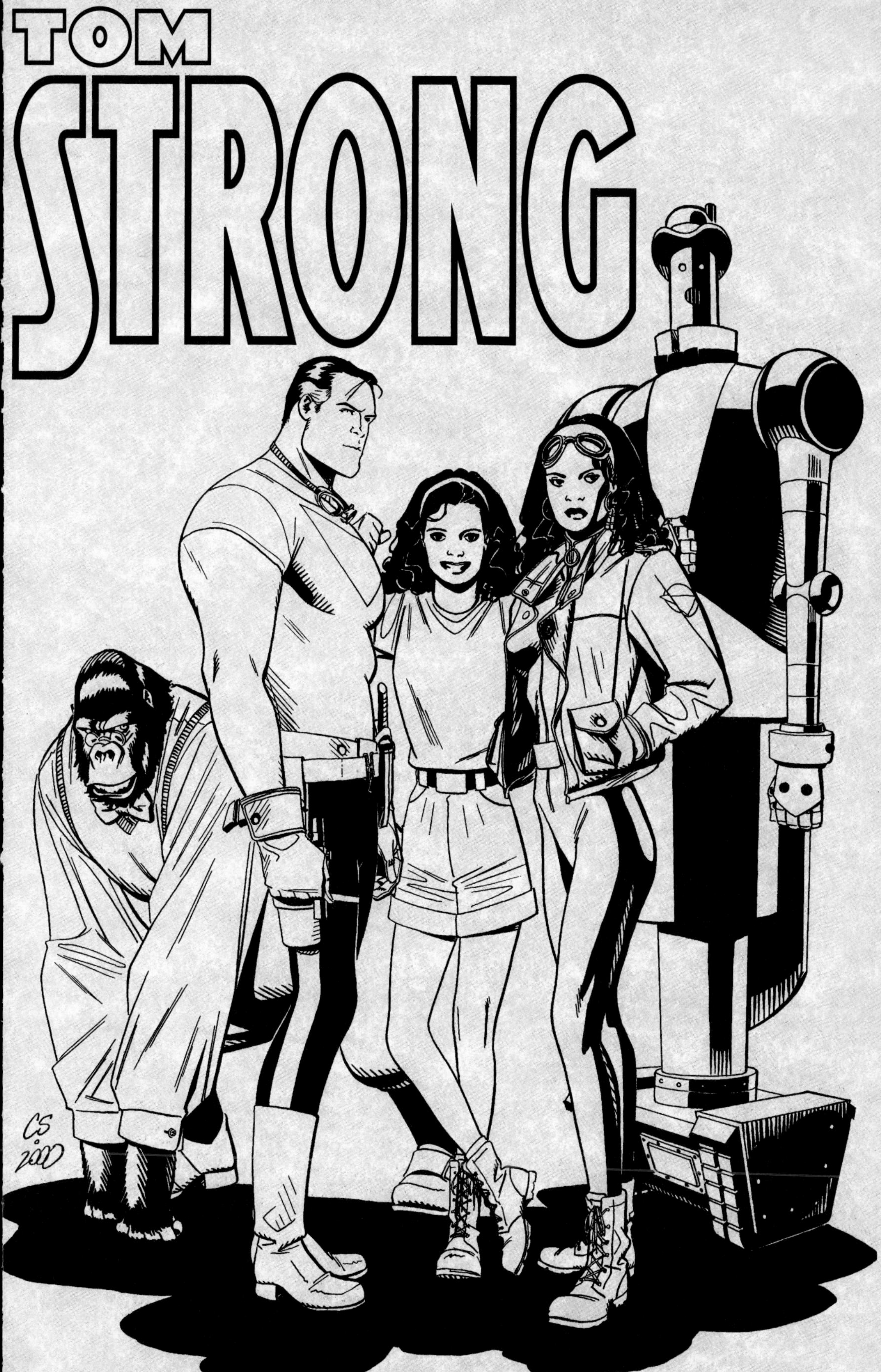
TOM
STRONG
CS 2000

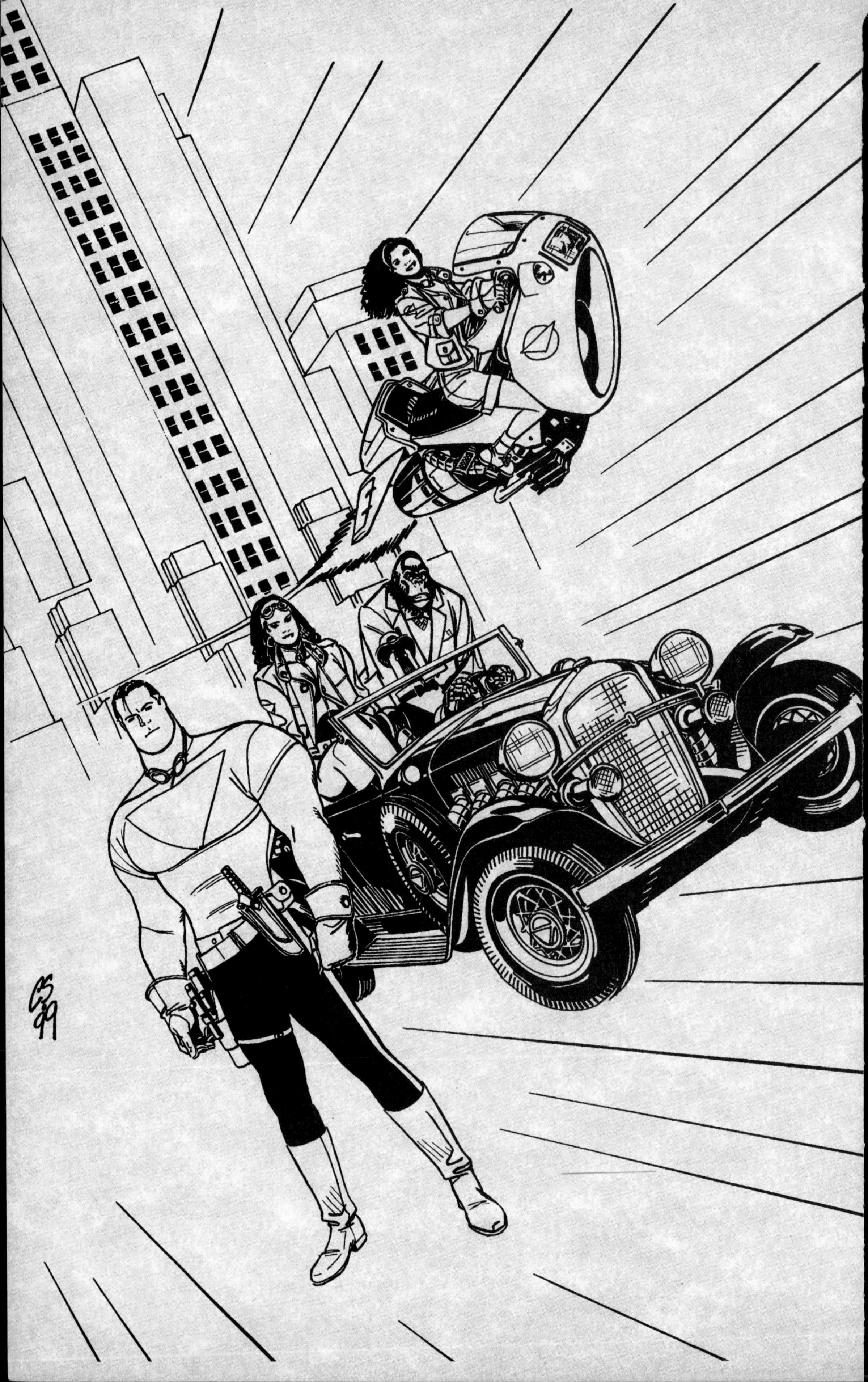

DEDICATIONS

To Leah, Amber, and Melinda;
To all my family, all my friends.

ALAN MOORE is perhaps the most acclaimed writer in the graphic story medium, having garnered many awards for such works as WATCHMEN, FROM HELL, MIRACLEMAN, SWAMP THING and SUPREME, among others, along with the many fine artists he has collaborated with on those works. He is currently master-minding the entire America's Best Comics line, writing PROMETHEA, TOP 10 and TOMORROW STORIES in addition to TOM STRONG, with more in the planning stages. He resides in central England.

Thanks to Alan for giving me the chance to do this; to Mike, Gary, Robert and Hiroshi for their friendship and support; and especially to Patty for being there through it all.

CHRIS SPROUSE, the penciller and co-creator of TOM STRONG, began working in comics in 1989, gathering approval for his work on such books as LEGIONNAIRES. He previously worked with Alan Moore on SUPREME. Chris currently lives in Ohio.

Tom Strong is about a lot of things. If you were to judge from his name, you'd assume it's about strength...though, I think, not the physical kind.
To my mom and my brother, who taught me about strength.

ALAN GORDON, teamed as inker with Chris on TOM STRONG, is a veteran of the comics business, having worked on many projects. His favorites include WILDSTAR and JUSTICE LEAGUE. He began partnering with Chris on LEGION OF SUPER-HEROES, and joined Alan and Chris on SUPREME.
Al lives in California.

AMERICA'S BEST COMICS COLLECTED EDITION

THE LEAGUE OF EXTRAORDINARY GENTLEMEN VOLUME 1
Alan Moore, Kevin O'Neill

PROMETHEA BOOK 1, BOOK 2, BOOK 3
Alan Moore, J. H. Williams III & Mick Gray

TOM STRONG BOOK 1, BOOK 2
Alan Moore, Chris Sprouse, Alan Gordon

TOMORROW STORIES BOOK 1
Alan Moore, Kevin Nowlan, Rick Veitch, Jim Baikie, Melinda Gebbie, Hilary Barta

TOP 10 BOOK 1, BOOK 2
Alan Moore, Gene Ha & Zander Cannon